QUERY:

**Getting Information from Data
with the Wolfram Language**

QUERY:

Getting Information from Data with the Wolfram Language

SETH J. CHANDLER

Wolfram Media

*This book is dedicated to my father, Horace W. Chandler,
who staked me to my first copy of Mathematica in 1993
and who made it to see that generosity culminate here.*

Query: Getting Information from Data with the Wolfram Language

Copyright © 2023 by Seth J. Chandler

Wolfram Media, Inc.
wolfram-media.com
ISBN 978-1-57955-085-1 (paperback)
ISBN 978-1-57955-086-8 (ebook)

Library of Congress Cataloging-in-Publication Data

Names: Chandler, Seth J., author.
Title: Query : getting information from data with the Wolfram language /
    Seth J. Chandler.
Description: Champaign : Wolfram Media, [2023] | Includes index.
Identifiers: LCCN 2023020532 (print) | LCCN 2023020533 (ebook) | ISBN
    9781579550851 (paperback ; acid-free paper) | ISBN 9781579550868 (ebook)

Subjects: LCSH: Wolfram language (Computer program language) | Mathematica
    (Computer file) | Query languages (Computer science)
Classification: LCC QA76.73.W65 C43 2023 (print) | LCC QA76.73.W65
    (ebook) | DDC 005.13/3—dc23/eng/20230602
LC record available at https://lccn.loc.gov/2023020532
LC ebook record available at https://lccn.loc.gov/2023020533

Typeset with Wolfram Notebooks: wolfram.com/notebooks

Printed by Friesens, Manitoba, Canada. ∞ Acid-free paper. First edition. First printing.

Table of Contents

1 | Introduction

Purpose

Our modern world abounds in both data and computational power. Too often, however, that data is not in a form where that computational power can provide insight about its meaning or importance to a particular audience. This book shows how the Wolfram Language can serve as a bridge between the world of data and the world of information. Whether your data is embedded in a spreadsheet, complex Wolfram Language expression, or some large CSV or JSON file, you can use this book to help you liberate it and then transform it into information for purposes of statistical analysis, machine learning, or just advanced counting. The methods shown here are powerful and more general than SQL, often more terse than Python, and often quite rapid in execution. Moreover, with the Wolfram Engine now available free of charge and accessible from alternative clients such as Jupyter Notebooks, opportunity has grown in recent times to use the Wolfram Language as a major tool in data preparation and data analysis. In short, after reading this book, you should be able to approach data with confidence, transforming it as you see fit into information.

Audience

This book is intended for intermediate users of the Wolfram Language. It's not right for those completely unfamiliar with the Wolfram Language. You should understand, for example, that working with the Wolfram Language is kind of like working with the internet: it's a client-server architecture. There's a server somewhere—it could be on your machine, a machine in your local network, a cluster, or the Wolfram Cloud. The server runs a Wolfram Language kernel (or kernels) or Wolfram Engine that does all the nitty-gritty computations, such as computing the parameters of a logistic regression, training a neural network, creating geographic primitives, undertaking "map reduce" operations on a dataset, or, indeed, doing virtually any computation you can imagine, including those it might offload via external functions and other techniques to computers running Python, R, JavaScript, or many other languages.

The client is generally on your own machine. It is most likely the Wolfram Language front end, but it could be the Wolfram Cloud interface, a Jupyter Notebook, or a terminal session running wolframscript. It could even be the computational engine of another language such as Python or Java, which in turn could be running on your local machine or via some network.

To use this book, you should also have a basic understanding of functional programming and pattern matching, particularly as implemented in the Wolfram Language. If you don't know how to define a function or use a couple of functional constructs such as Map or Select, or if you don't know how to determine whether an expression matches a basic pattern, you need to start with a more basic text. Some I recommend include Stephen Wolfram's *An Elementary Introduction to the Wolfram Language*; Cliff Hastings, Kelvin Mischo, and Michael Morrison's *Hands-on Start to Wolfram Mathematica and Programming in the Wolfram Language*; or even the older but still outstanding work by Paul Wellin, *Programming with Mathematica*. In short, if all you've ever done with the Wolfram Language is calculus homework (for which it is indeed very useful), you probably need to preface your study of this book with some more general texts on the language.

Here's a quick test to see if this book is right for you. If you can accurately predict the output of these expressions in your head, you're ready.

```
In[·]:= Function [ x, x² ] [ 5 ]
```

```
In[·]:= Map [ Sqrt, { 1, 4, 9 } ]
```

```
In[·]:= { 3, 4 } /. x_ /; EvenQ [ x ] :> 2 x
```

I believe this book is also appropriate for more advanced users of the Wolfram Language. True, you might understand what the code below does, but I'd like to think there are still tips and concepts that will prove useful. From what I can gather on various forums such as StackExchange or Wolfram Community, there is still much that remains unclear about functions like Query and Dataset. These are emphasized in this book, and I hope will further their usage overall.

Here's an example of the type of use I intend for Query:

```
In[·]:= Query [ Select [ #sex === "female" & ] /* ( DeleteMissing [ #, 1 ] & ) /*
           ( <| "mean age" → Mean [ #1 ], "median age" → Median [ #1 ] |> & ),
           ( #age & ) ] [ ExampleData [ { "Dataset", "Titanic" } ] ]
```

mean age	28.6959
median age	27

Out[·]=

Also, don't think you need to know a lot of advanced mathematics to enjoy this book. Although I show how to transform data so that it is ready for statistical analysis, machine learning, or other techniques that might not be learned until college or thereafter, and although I sometimes show more advanced computations, those computations are not the main point of the book. I've worked hard to make sure you don't really need to understand them, and I've done so because the point of this book is to make you fluent in the transformation of data so that it is in the optimal form for whatever sort of computer analysis you want to undertake. This means I emphasize operations like filtering data, grouping data, putting data in a form that maps inputs to outputs, dealing with missing values, cleaning data, and combining bits of data that have elements in common. And while you might initially think all of that's a simple matter—hardly the sort of advanced differential equation solving or probability theory or complexity theory for which the sophistication of the Wolfram Language may be rightly heralded—I promise these sorts of nuts and bolts will often prove a worthy challenge in the Wolfram Language, though I believe often less of one than in competing platforms.

This book also embraces a relatively newer style of Wolfram Language programming that emphasizes use of composed operators. It does so because that's the form that the Query function—a centerpiece of this book—desires, so even those intermediate users familiar with Wolfram Language programming with only limited interest in data analysis may find this book helpful.

Let me also provide you what in the world of entertainment would be called a "trailer." No, there won't be literal explosions, and the particular issues depicted here may not fascinate you, but if you recognize them as the kind of information you would like to be able to extract in your own research, this book should enhance and accelerate your work. At least you stand a good chance of avoiding the head scratching, mistakes, dreaded pink error boxes, and, yes, I admit it, the very occasional kernel crash that has accompanied my own efforts in this field over the years and that has motivated me to produce this book.

> Take data from the Wolfram Data Repository and determine the biggest team payrolls in Major League Soccer (MLS):

$$\{\{LA, \boxed{\text{Year: 2010}}\} \to \$9.09386 \times 10^7, \{NY, \boxed{\text{Year: 2010}}\} \to \$5.56666 \times 10^7,$$

$$\{TOR, \boxed{\text{Year: 2015}}\} \to \$2.21365 \times 10^7, \{TOR, \boxed{\text{Year: 2016}}\} \to \$2.17985 \times 10^7,$$

$$\{NYCFC, \boxed{\text{Year: 2016}}\} \to \$2.11278 \times 10^7, \{LA, \boxed{\text{Year: 2015}}\} \to \$2.09176 \times 10^7,$$

$$\{LA, \boxed{\text{Year: 2016}}\} \to \$1.81057 \times 10^7, \{NYCFC, \boxed{\text{Year: 2015}}\} \to \$1.74143 \times 10^7,$$

$$\{NY, \boxed{\text{Year: 2012}}\} \to \$1.67281 \times 10^7, \{TOR, \boxed{\text{Year: 2014}}\} \to \$1.67126 \times 10^7\}$$

> Take data from the Wolfram Data Repository and generate a time series of MLS base team compensation:

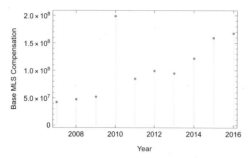

> Show the order of operations of a Query to be performed on a multilevel data structure:

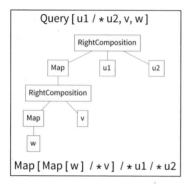

> Take data from the Wolfram Data Repository and show with user-controlled formats the mean age of Titanic passengers broken down by cabin class and gender:

1st	female	37 yr
	male	41 yr
2nd	male	31 yr
	female	28 yr
3rd	male	26 yr
	female	22 yr

	male	female
1st	41 yr	37 yr
2nd	31 yr	28 yr
3rd	26 yr	22 yr

Mean ages of Titanic passengers

> Take data from the Wolfram Data Repository and map the largest American Indian reservations within a given region of the United States:

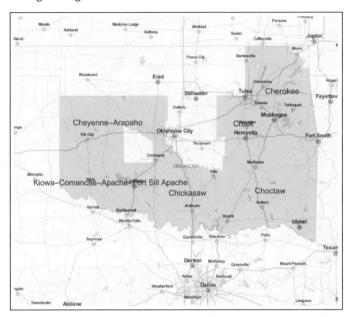

> Take data in a Google Sheets spreadsheet and produce a timeline of the United States Supreme Court case of Marbury v. Madison:

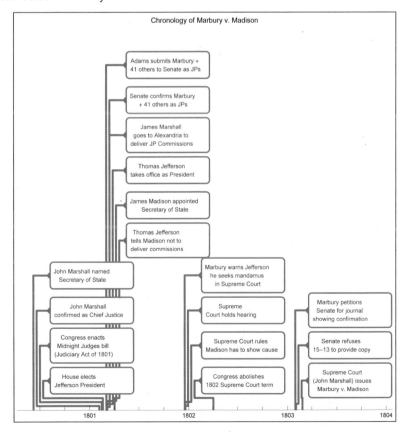

How to Read This Book

This book is designed to be read either in an online format or on paper. If you are online, you should be able to actually run the code by following along in your own notebook. You will, however, need internet access to do so. That's because much of the data used in the book lies in the Wolfram Data Repository (wolfr.am/WDR). Moreover, some of the functions used in this book are not built into the Wolfram Language but have been placed (after vetting by Wolfram Research) in the Wolfram Function Repository (wolfr.am/WFR). Recognizing that fast internet is not always available, however, I've tried to avoid datasets that place high demands on service. Moreover, you may only need internet access intermittently. You can store most of the data on your own system or just read the text during moments when internet resources are unavailable. Access the chapters of this book in notebook format at wolfr.am/chandler-query.

Chapter Roadmap

This book is organized as a progression. Although you can start anywhere you want, later chapters assume you have understood the prior material. Let me provide a roadmap here, a kind of annotated table of contents. The book has a basic component that will be available in hard copy and electronically. It comprises Chapters 2–8. It deals with what I might call the traditional Wolfram Language, in which the entirety of the computation tends to be conducted within the Wolfram kernel. If you've seen functions such as **Association** or **Query** or **Dataset**, that's the kind of material that's addressed in these seven chapters of the book. The second part of the book will be released in periodic installments following publication of this book. It will be available electronically only and will address features of the Wolfram Language developed to some maturity with its most recent versions. This material will extend the techniques shown in this book to now access and manipulate data contained in the Wolfram Knowledgebase and the more general **Entity** framework. It will include how one can access data contained in relational databases hosted on your own machine or some distant server. I will also include a chapter on how to use the large language model interface to perform some of the tasks shown in this book. Don't worry. Those capabilities don't (yet) obsolete the skills shown in the main part of this book, but they are a great supplement.

Each chapter comes with a problem set (with answers at the end of the book) that are intended to assess and then to develop your understanding of the material. Each chapter also comes with technical notes that address material that may prove of interest but whose presentation in the main text would either disrupt the flow or are thought unlikely to excite as many readers as material in the main text.

Chapter 2: Data Structures and Functions

I start with some intermediate-level Wolfram Language programming. Here I rapidly survey some true fundamentals of the Wolfram Language: everything is an expression, expressions have parts and levels, and functions exist apart from the data on which they operate. Because the Wolfram Language flourished well before the introduction of associations and datasets that should today prevail, and because there's often still good reason to use earlier data structures either on their own or in combination with Association-based structures, I also address data structures intermediate-level Wolfram Language users are likely to have encountered before, most notably lists and arrays, or lists of lists.

This chapter pays particular attention to functional programming and to the use and composition of operator forms, functions that tend to take one argument and serve as little units of computation. I do so because functional programming often lies at the heart of efficient, idiomatic Wolfram Language programming and because composition of operators (a kind of function) is critical to effective use of the Query function, which lies at the heart of this book. I also stress functions that restructure lists or arrays, such as GatherBy and Transpose.

The chapter ends, as do several subsequent chapters, with a walkthrough of various "real-world" problems. In this chapter, the problems are taken from data involving salaries in Major League Soccer (MLS), the primary association of men's club soccer (football) in the United States. The idea is to show how these computations can be performed (often well) using early Wolfram Language constructs and then in later chapters to show how use of progressively more powerful tools, like Association and Query, enable these computations to be done either more swiftly or in a way whose intent is more transparent.

Chapter 3: Association

The next chapter introduces Association, which joined the Wolfram Language in Version 10 in 2014. No longer is the user forced to remember the column number or row number in which some data is kept and use memorized integers to reference components of the data. Instead, the user can now give rows and columns memorable names. Moreover, along with Association comes various powerful functions useful in creating them, such as GroupBy and Counts, or in manipulating them, such as Merge and JoinAcross. This chapter again uses functional programming and compositions to extend the techniques used in the preceding chapter to cover associations and certain data structures containing them, such as lists. I use data from MLS in order to illustrate the concepts as well as data from the doomed ship Titanic.

Also, there's one feature of associations I don't try to squeeze into this chapter: the use of Association as something similar to a function. That feature is so important and powerful, I defer its consideration to the next chapter, which focuses on just one Wolfram Language function, Query.

Chapter 4: Query

Query is central to modern approaches to data analysis in the Wolfram Language. Although it initially seems mysterious to many, once mastered, it's an incredibly powerful functional programming tool. I will admit to a bit of schadenfreude watching Stephen Wolfram himself attempt in a live programming exercise to extract from a hierarchical data structure the mean mass of the moons of Mars. Moreover, it's a tool that can be used not only on newer data structures, such as Association (and the cousin found in the next chapter, Dataset), but can and should be used on traditional data structures such as lists of lists. The chapter shows how Query creates a pipeline of operators (themselves often composed of operators) intended to work on different levels of a Wolfram Language expression. Drawing on the discussion of operator pipelines in the preceding chapters, it spends considerable time providing a conceptual and practical understanding of the sometimes challenging issue of the order of operations in Query-generated pipelines. I show how use of Normal when applied to a Query can both show the order of operations and provide numerous examples that facilitate understanding of basic Query principles.

I know all of this can be challenging. That's why I make some effort using the wonderful TreeForm function to provide visualizations that I believe help explain it. I also show—and this was the matter deliberately not addressed in the preceding chapter—how one can make it appear that an Association is a function through the implicit construction of a Query.

The latter part of the Query chapter tries to make it all concrete. I essentially redo the analysis of MLS and the Titanic, this time using the Query construct. I hope you'll be excited to see that with the mastery of Query, data analysis that proved challenging in the preceding chapter is now somewhat easier. I also hope you are gratified, as I am, to see that the code is more concise. Programming errors are roughly proportionate to program size.

Chapter 5: Dataset

One of the ideas of this book is that an awful lot can be done without Dataset. You can just use conventional Wolfram Language data structures, such as nested mixtures of lists and associations. And I also like to show that with the Query function and operator pipelines, one can transform data in this form in powerful ways. In this chapter, however, I want to show the advantages gained by wrapping these data structures with Dataset.

Dataset is a command whose utility is greatest when using the Wolfram Language front end or the Wolfram Cloud as the client. In these settings, wrapping Dataset around Wolfram Language expressions powerfully extends the ability to visualize and manipulate data. The presentation is dynamic: various mouse clicks let the user burrow deep into data, with the option to paste results into cells below. It's sort of a hierarchical spreadsheet of a type not available in many other programming environments. I've found it immensely valuable and suspect you will too.

Even when the client doesn't have these dynamic capabilities, however, Dataset is important because it can provide a picture of the data, a static tabular form. And, as I will show, in more recent versions of the Wolfram Language, datasets can be formatted in custom ways to make them particularly attractive. I spend considerable time in the chapter explaining how that formatting can be done precisely, also briefly examining a very complex topic: the internal structure of Dataset objects. This information is useful to ensure that the presentation of derived data, such as that produced through grouping and filtering operations, is exactly the way you want it. Even if you don't want visualization, Dataset can be important because it provides a structure that can optimize various queries.

Chapter 6: Basic Recipes

Some people are understandably impatient. They don't want to know—at least quite yet—the intricacies of how and why. They don't want to know the theory of the Maillard reaction; they just want to know how to cook a nicely browned hamburger. Right now. So, if you want to know, for example, how to add columns to a Dataset based on pre-existing data, add row headers to a Dataset, convert row headers into columns, or learn the "Double Transpose Trick," the many recipes in this chapter are for you. Even if you prefer learning things in a more theoretical way, the examples provided here should provide insight into the ideas behind Association, Query, and the other aspects of the Wolfram Language emphasized in this part of the book.

Chapter 7: Advanced Recipes

Getting data in the right form isn't always easy, and while it may be easier in the Wolfram Language than in competing programming languages for some tasks, the distance between the form of the original data and the desired form means that there will inevitably be complications. Moreover, having poked over the years through more than my share of data scattered over the internet, I can assure you that a lot of data is a structural mess or just contains errors. In this chapter, I survey the types of complex problems I have come across most frequently when using the sort of programming techniques fostered in this book and in confronting the sorts of problems shown in this book.

I try to stick with the Titanic example insofar as possible to leverage understanding of that dataset and its transformation, but in this chapter, I also consider data found in the Wolfram Data Repository on Indian reservations or more hierarchical data, such as that on planetary moons. Problems addressed include creating attractive datasets with data grouped in multiple ways, placing data in forms optimal for Wolfram Language machine learning functionality, placing data in forms optimal for Wolfram Language statistical analysis, and placing data in a form for charting or geographic mapping.

Chapter 8: Import and Export

Thus far the book has used data that's already within the Wolfram ecosystem: data generated from within the Wolfram Language, example data built into the Wolfram Language, or data from the Wolfram Data Repository, but you are likely to be working with "wild" data from somewhere on the internet or perhaps generated by you using some other computer language, such as Python, R, C, or Google Sheets, or even data generated by a device. Moreover, you may need to share your data with persons who need or prefer to transform it further using a system other than the Wolfram Language, such as Excel, Tableau, or Julia. This chapter teaches you how to "domesticate" wild data and how to export data in typical forms, such as CSV, XLSX, JSON, and ZIP.

This chapter on import and export ends the hard copy version of the book, the material that every user needs to understand in order to transform data into information using the Wolfram Language.

Version

This book was written in Version 13 of the Wolfram Language. It was also developed on a Mac running the Big Sur version of OS/X. Almost all of it will run on Version 11.3 and beyond and all of it should run on Windows or Linux. It should also work letting the Wolfram Cloud serve as the kernel or letting the free Wolfram Engine serve as the main computational back end, and I've committed to making sure that the code is updated through at least the next major release of the Wolfram Language, so this book and your reliance on it should have some longevity.

Front End

This book was written and produced using Wolfram Notebooks and Mathematica, and the code and notebooks are fully available for free download on the book's site at wolfr.am/chandler-query. Right now, however, the Wolfram Language is opening up, and it is quite possible to drive the Wolfram Engine from within other programming environments, most notably Jupyter, an open-source front end that bears a strong resemblance to the Wolfram Language front end and that interfaces with many languages, notably Julia, Python, and R, and now the Wolfram Language. The primary difference you will notice using that environment is that Jupyter will not produce a dynamic object that the Wolfram Language front end would render if the object were a dataset or an entity store or a few other data structures used in this book. Instead, Jupyter will often render the result in input form, showing the internals of that object. Still, all of the code used in this book was tested by me using Jupyter, including calls to the Wolfram Data Repository, the Wolfram Function Repository, Wolfram|Alpha, and the Wolfram Knowledgebase, which worked well from within Jupyter.

Repositories

The Wolfram Data Repository

This book makes use of lots of data. Some of it is data, such as information on the passengers on board the Titanic, that is already present in ExampleData that comes with the Wolfram Language. Other data, such as that on salaries in Major League Soccer, comes from the Wolfram Data Repository, which is also available to virtually anyone (even non-users of the Wolfram Language). Some of that data has actually been put there by others, and some has been put there by me, partly for my own scholarly use and partly in anticipation of this book.

Although I provide the data in forms particularly adapted to the Wolfram Language, such as lists of lists or lists of associations or datasets, I also try to provide the data in more raw formats.

Here's how you get the data. The first time you run this code, it may take a while depending on your internet connection. You should get a ResourceObject that will format dynamically within the Wolfram Language front end. While I've deliberately avoided massive datasets—I want to teach the concepts, not tax your CPU or hard drive—I've also avoided purely toy datasets that don't have the complexity needed to demonstrate needed concepts. Once you've downloaded the data though, all should run smoothly.

Acquire the ResourceObject from the Wolfram Data Repository:

In[ ]:= **ro = ResourceObject ["Sample Data for Query Book"]**

Out[ ]:= ResourceObject[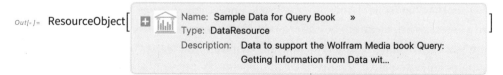]

The Wolfram Function Repository

I also make significant use of the Wolfram Function Repository in this book. This repository contains a variety of functions that are not presently part of the official Wolfram Language, even in experimental form, but nonetheless contains functions produced by users of the Wolfram Language that have been vetted by Wolfram Research staff, are documented and debugged, and cohere well with the remainder of the Wolfram Language. Often the repository functions on which I rely here are operator forms of existing functions or compositions of several functions that make the presentation of code more clear. You'll know a function is from the repository by its special formatting: generally a gray "summary box" that looks something like this: [◦] Terse + .

Conventions

I use a number of conventions in this book. The first is that when I discuss concepts that are cognates of Wolfram Language functions, I capitalize the word in question. Thus, I say something like, "I then Select the data after having done a GroupBy." I even capitalize words I use that are just different grammatical forms of the actual function. I say, "After KeyTaking on the rows of the data," even though KeyTaking is not a function (KeyTake is). I also sometimes abuse grammar by using as verbs functions whose names are not verbs. On occasion I say, "I Terse the results," meaning I shorten the results using the Terse ResourceFunction. The idea is to get you used to the relationship between common ways of speaking about data analysis and the Wolfram Language constructs.

A second convention relates to use of the terms Wolfram Language, Mathematica, and kernel. In general, I try to use the term Wolfram Language to describe the language in which the code is written. When I specifically want to make reference to how the kernel handles expressions in the Wolfram Language, however, I'll use the term kernel explicitly.

Exercises

All (or almost all) of the chapters in this book have exercises. I've inserted them not because I regard this as a textbook but because they should help the reader assess whether they have understood the material. The exercises range in difficulty. The early exercises are meant to be easier and a little more straightforward. The later exercises are challenges, however, and will require some mastery. Moreover, since the chapters are cumulative, the exercises in the later chapters of the book are often more challenging than those presented earlier on. I've tried to sprinkle the exercises with hints, however, to avoid excessive floundering. Answers to the exercises are found in a separate part of the book.

Technical Notes

Many of the chapters (except this one) end with a Technical Notes section. These provide additional material that, while important in my view, is either more advanced or less important than that presented in the main text. They are not intended as a substitution for the elaborate official documentation provided with the Wolfram Language.

A Little about Me

I'm admittedly an odd duck: the law professor who loves the Wolfram Language. From that moment in early 1993 when, after a week of floundering, I grokked the underscore in f[x_] := x + 1 with the Wolfram Language (then known as Mathematica) through the moment in 2014 when I figured out what the heck Query was doing and even to today as I see the Wolfram Engine and various repositories open computation to new users, I've found it a marvelous and pervasive way to think about ideas. It makes practical a lifelong fascination with the ways in which math and computation help clarify the human world.

And so I've used the Wolfram Language almost every week of my life since that time, seeing the product grow to have a programmatic notebook front end and the ability to import and export data from a variety of formats; interface with Python, R, Java, and other LLVM languages; handle regular expressions; generate interactive displays with controls (Manipulate); process social networks; handle statistical analysis in a brilliant way; and tackle machine learning with a level of automation that other software systems are only now beginning to facilitate. It's grown from when I could use it only on a NeXT cluster of computers (named after characters on the Simpsons) located in a distant campus building, to one where I could use it on my own desktop (lovingly enhanced with an 8087 math coprocessor), to one where I can use it pretty seamlessly on multiple machines, some expensive and some not, or in the cloud, or even using the Jupyter open-source and free front end.

The Wolfram Language has let me handle projects that I would otherwise find impossible. I'm not so great at abstract math, but between persistence, a developed fluency in what amounts to a foreign language, and the ability to benefit from the interactive dialogue of Mathematica, it's let me tackle some fairly sophisticated matters across a variety of domains. I've used it intensively in projects ranging from the examination of legal doctrines and government programs in insurance law, to actuarial examinations of pension plans, to the network structure of Supreme Court cases, to fun stuff like figuring out what would happen in a baseball game if no one ever swung the bat. And yes, while I've flirted with a variety of other systems over the years, R and Julia having been two affairs, I find myself always coming back to the Wolfram Language. It just lets you get your work done.

On the way, I've authored over one hundred interactive Demonstrations on topics ranging from insurance regulation, legal theory, political science, microeconomics, pure computer science (Turing snakes), and even Shakespeare (good writer). Some of my work even made it (anonymously, alas) on to the television show *Numb3rs*. I've even managed to make the Wolfram Language a central feature of a course (Analytic Methods for Lawyers) taught to an unusual audience, American law students, but it turns out that immersion in a terse yet expressive language ends up creating students, generally with no background in computer science, who have some clue what goes on when I do automated machine learning over a dataset or explain centrality measures on precedent networks. I have over 50 YouTube videos addressing various topics in the Wolfram Language (wolfr.am/analytic-methods).

I think of this book as an opportunity to give back. I've learned a lot about the Wolfram Language over the years and, more recently, how to use it to effectively analyze data using features such as Association, Query, and Dataset. This book is an opportunity to share and explain matters in my own words and in my own way. I hope you enjoy reading it as much as I have enjoyed its production.

Houston & Red Feather Lakes, 2023

More to Explore

For the complete list of my interactive works, look at my Wolfram Demonstrations (wolfr.am/ChandlerDemonstrations)

Check out Stephen Wolfram's livestreams to learn special tips and the history of many functions (livestreams.stephenwolfram.com)

2 | Data Structures and Functions

Mathematica and the Wolfram Language existed for 23 years and made it through nine major releases before the release of **Association**, **Dataset**, **Query**, and many of the constructs discussed in this book. A lot of very productive computing got done during that time, so before going into the capabilities created since the introduction of these constructs with Version 10 in July 2014, it is worth spending a little time on data structures that existed prior thereto. This chapter is not intended as a comprehensive review on the Wolfram Language. There are many fine works on that subject. It is intended, however, to make clear what is possible without the use of the newer tools. Indeed, computation today can often still best be done—or at least most rapidly—without the overhead these constructs introduce.

This chapter uses a data resource from the Wolfram Data Repository (wolfr.am/WDR). To access the data, evaluate the following code.

Acquire the **ResourceObject** from the Wolfram Data Repository:

In[ ]:= **ro = ResourceObject ["Sample Data for Query Book"]**

Out[ ]:= ResourceObject[⊞ 𝚷𝚷 Name: Sample Data for Query Book »
Type: DataResource
Description: Data to support the Wolfram Media book Query:
Getting Information from Data wit...]

The Mathematica Expression

In some computer languages, everything is an "object." It's a unifying paradigm that simplifies programming. In the Wolfram Language, there's a different unifying paradigm: everything is an **Expression**. Among other virtues, the ubiquity of expressions means that knowledge gained in working with one area of the Wolfram Language generalizes over essentially every other area. Therefore, although it is definitely an investment to learn the Wolfram Language (and perhaps to unlearn programming paradigms prevalent in other languages), doing so pays extraordinary dividends in doing programming across domains.

An expression can be atomic, meaning it is deliberately made difficult to break apart. Examples of atomic expressions are numbers (including integers, reals, rational numbers, and complex numbers), strings, symbols, and certain compound objects, such as a Graph. This atomicity does not mean these expressions cannot be manipulated by the user; it just means one has to use some special capabilities to do so. Functions frequently employed in the Wolfram Language, such as Part or Map, won't accomplish anything on atoms. The rational number $\frac{2}{3}$ is atomic, for example, but one can extract the numerator using the Numerator function.

To tell if the Wolfram Language considers an expression to be atomic, use AtomQ:

In[•]:= `{AtomQ[3], AtomQ[4.2], AtomQ[2 / 3], AtomQ[Σ], AtomQ[3 + 4 I],`
`    AtomQ["hello world"], AtomQ[f], AtomQ[Graph[{1 → 2}]],`
`    AtomQ[` France (country) ✓ `], AtomQ[Cos[2]]}`

Out[•]= `{True, True, True, True, True, True, True, True, False, False}`

Check Whether Various Expressions Are Atoms

Even atomic expressions have something called a head. You can think of the head as being something a little bit like the "type" or "class" of a value in an object-oriented language, but the variety of "types" is much greater in the built-in Wolfram Language than it is in out-of-the-box versions of typical object-oriented languages such as Python, Java, or C++.

Here are the heads of the previous expressions:

In[•]:= `{Head[3], Head[4.2], Head[2 / 3], Head[Σ], Head[3 + 4 I],`
`    Head["hello world"], Head[f], Head[Graph[{1 → 2}]],`
`    Head[` France (country) ✓ `], Head[Cos[2]]}`

Out[•]= `{Integer, Real, Rational, Symbol, Complex, String, Symbol, Graph, Entity, Cos}`

Heads of Common Expressions

Lots of Wolfram Language expressions are not atomic. They not only have a Head, but they also have various elements that can themselves be atoms or compound expressions. One often writes the expression in a way that emphasizes the head. It comes first. The remaining elements—which are sometimes called parts or arguments (or even operands)—are separated by commas. Often one refers to an expression written with all the heads set forth explicitly as being in FullForm. If many but not all of the heads are set forth explicitly and no use is made of advanced two-dimensional typesetting, the expression is often referred to as being in InputForm.

Here are some examples; the semicolon at the end of the input suppresses the output:

In[•]:= $\{f[6], h[3,4], Sin[3], g[8, h[x, y, 9]], \{\{f[x] \rightarrow 4 + e^x c_1\}\}\};$

As explained more fully in some of the basic references on the subject, such as Section 33 of Stephen Wolfram's *An Elementary Introduction to the Wolfram Language*, there is also syntactic sugar to simplify inputs and avoid explicitly writing out the Head. The Wolfram Language front end also sometimes uses syntactic sugar in representing outputs. The most common example is the List data container. Although one can certainly write it as List [3, 4], the more common way is to surround the arguments in curly braces like this: {3, 4}. Notice that by default the Wolfram Language front end represents Lists using this syntactic sugar.

Expressions with a List Head get placed in curly braces by default:

In[•]:= **List [3, 4]**

Out[•]= {3, 4}

The Wolfram Language typically represents many of its operators using syntactic sugar. The following input shows some of the many occasions in which the Wolfram Language front end takes expressions input using FullForm but renders them in a more pleasing standard form (called StandardForm).

StandardForm representation of expressions:

In[•]:= **{ Plus [a, b] , Plus [Times [Power [5, Rational [−1, 2]] , x] ,**
Power [y, 2] , Power [z, −1]] , Blank [j] }

Out[•]= $\left\{ a + b, \dfrac{x}{\sqrt{5}} + y^2 + \dfrac{1}{z}, \_j \right\}$

The Part Function

Part is the basic function for probing the structure of a Wolfram Language expression. It relies on the idea of creating an indexing between the recognizable components of the expression and an integer (or list of integers). Thus, in the expression h [3, 4], the Head h is the zeroth part, the integer 3 is the first part, and the integer 4 is the second part. Here's how I can ask for just the second part of the expression.

Get a numbered Part of an expression:

In[•]:= **Part [h [3, 4] , 2]**

Out[•]= 4

And here I ask for the third part of the second part of g [8, h [x, y, 9]]. By the way, I'm going to use this example expression a lot in the chapter, but, rather than assigning it to a symbol (or variable) and asking you to keep looking at this page to remember what it means, I ask you to kind of memorize and recognize it.

Get **Part** of an expression beyond the first level:

In[ ]:= **Part [g [8, h [x, y, 9]], 2, 3]**

Out[ ]= 9

The first argument to **Part** is the structure to be probed. The second argument is like a set of directions to navigate to that structure's desired component.

To see what is going on in the example code and to understand the structure of Wolfram Language expressions in general, it is often useful to use a visualization function known as **TreeForm**.

Visualize the **TreeForm** of the expression **g [8, h [x, y, 9]]** :

In[ ]:= **TreeForm [g [8, h [x, y, 9]]]**

Out[ ]//TreeForm=

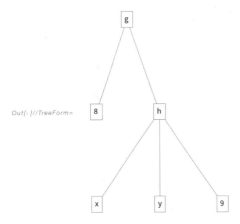

You can see now that the symbol g has two descendants, 8 and h [x, y, 9] and that the symbol h has three descendants, x, y, and 9, so by saying Part [g [8, h [x, y, z]], 2, 3], one is essentially giving directions to a tree-descent algorithm. First, take the second argument and then take the third argument of what you find. That yields 9.

One can also use **Part** to get multiple parts of an expression. Here I first retrieve the second part of the expression, then the first part, and then the second part again. The results of the retrieval are separated by commas and the **Head** of the entire expression is preserved.

Retrieve multiple parts of an expression:

In[ ]:= **Part [g [8, h [x, y, 9]], { 2, 1, 2 }]**

Out[ ]= g [h [x, y, 9], 8, h [x, y, 9]]

Thus far, I have used positive integers to designate the **Part**. But one can also designate parts using negative integers, which count backwards from the end of the expression.

Here I ask for the second from the last part:

In[ ]:= **Part [g [8 , h [x , y , 9]] , −2]**

Out[ ]= 8

Or I could ask for the third from the last part of the last part.

Use negative part numbers:

In[ ]:= **Part [g [8 , h [x , y , 9]] , −1 , −3]**

Out[ ]= X

Also, if I want the head of an expression, I use part 0. Indeed, so far as I can figure out, Head is really just a short way of asking for part 0. Here are two examples.

Use part 0 to get the heads:

In[ ]:= **{ Part [g [8 , h [x , y , 9]] , 0] , Part [g [8 , h [x , y , 9]] , 2 , 0] }**

Out[ ]= { g , h }

There is syntactic sugar that many people use when trying to determine the Parts of Wolfram Language expressions: the double square bracket. One provides the expression and then follows that with the part number (or sequence of numbers) inside a mirrored opening and closing pair of double square brackets. Here is how one might get the second part of an expression.

Use [[...]] notation:

In[ ]:= **g [8 , h [x , y , 9]] ⟦2⟧**

Out[ ]= h [x , y , 9]

Here's how to get the negative third part of the second part.

Combine negative Part specifications with [[...]] notation:

In[ ]:= **g [8 , h [x , y , 9]] ⟦2 , −3⟧**

Out[ ]= X

Here's how to get both the second part and the negative second part.

Retrieve multiple parts with [[...]] notation:

In[ ]:= **g [8 , h [x , y , 9]] ⟦{ 2 , −2 }⟧**

Out[ ]= g [h [x , y , 9] , 8]

Span and All Part Specifications

One other way to specify Parts is with Span. Here I build the characters "a" to "z" and then get out the third character ("c") and every fourth character thereafter, not exceeding the 15th character.

CharacterRange yields all the characters between two elements of a kind:

In[•]:= **CharacterRange ["a", "z"] ⟦Span [3, 15, 4] ⟧**

Out[•]= {c, g, k, o}

There's syntactic sugar for Span, which makes use of double semicolons:

In[•]:= **CharacterRange ["a", "z"] ⟦3 ;; 15 ;; 4⟧**

Out[•]= {c, g, k, o}

If I omit the final value of Span, it is assumed to be 1:

In[•]:= **CharacterRange ["a", "z"] ⟦4 ;; 7⟧**

Out[•]= {d, e, f, g}

If I omit the first or second value, it is taken to mean the lowest or highest possible value given the data on which it is operating:

In[•]:= **{ CharacterRange ["a", "z"] ⟦23 ;;⟧, CharacterRange ["a", "z"] ⟦ ;; 5⟧}**

Out[•]= { {w, x, y, z}, {a, b, c, d, e} }

I can also use All to designate every possible part:

In[•]:= **CharacterRange ["a", "z"] ⟦All⟧**

Out[•]= {a, b, c, d, e, f, g, h, i, j, k, l, m, n, o, p, q, r, s, t, u, v, w, x, y, z}

The Function

Single Functions

Like almost all modern computer languages, the Wolfram Language has the notion of a function. Essentially, a function is a set of instructions specifying how to transform one Wolfram Language expression into another. As of Version 13.3, Mathematica comes with thousands of them, and one can do a tremendous amount with these functions. The point of Wolfram Language programming, however, is often to augment the built-in functions with functions of one's own creation. The Wolfram Language provides a rich vocabulary. You create the sentences or, as I sometimes think of it, the poetry.

The Wolfram Language contains a variety of ways to specify a function. I'm going to start with one that takes an expression and squares it. Here is one way to write it. It's not necessarily the quickest way, but it is the most explicit.

A canonical way of defining a function:

In[•]:= **Function [x , x^2] ;**

The idea is that this variant of Function has two arguments. The first argument is a symbol that is used to designate the data that the function will confront. Here I picked the traditional x, but I could have selected anything that can be parsed as a symbol, such as z, zebra, ϕ, $\beta2$, q, or even Ⱥ. The second argument says how the data is to be transformed using the name for the data specified in the first argument. That transformation can be simple, as it is here, or extremely complex.

Many alternative ways exist to specify a function. Here's one that I like. It uses a kind of infix notation in which the function arrow separates a left-hand side, which is the first argument to the traditional Function specification and a right-hand side, which is the second argument to the traditional Function specification. It's designed to look like the way functions (or "mappings") are sometimes denoted in traditional Western math texts.

Use the infix $\longmapsto$ operator to define a function:

In[•]:= **x $\longmapsto$ x^2;**

Notice that in the code, nothing really happened yet. The function just lies in wait, hoping that data will one day arrive. It is what computer scientists call a "lambda expression."

Here's how one applies a function to data. The standard way is to put the function first and then include the data surrounded in square brackets with different elements of data separated by commas if there is more than one element. Here's an example.

Apply a function to a value:

In[•]:= **Function [x , x^2] [3]**

Out[•]= **9**

Notice also that in the earlier code, I gave the data a local name x. Suppose I previously defined x to be 7. What happens when I write the following?

Function variables are localized:

In[•]:= **x = 7;**
   Function [x , x^2] [3]

Out[•]= **9**

The answer is still 9. It is not 49. This is so because the symbol designated as the first argument to Function is "local." It does not have the same meaning as a symbol with the same name defined more globally in one's Wolfram Language session. Think of it as being like a file name. One might have a file named "memo.docx" sitting in a "Documents" directory and a file named "memo.docx" sitting in one's "Projects" directory. The fact that the two files have the same name does not mean they are the same thing. You can think of Function as creating a kind of temporary "directory" (or, to use a more Wolfram-like term, "scope") in which names have different meanings than they do when used elsewhere.

Of course, one can make use of globally defined variables in functions if one chooses. Here I write a function that adds its argument to the pre-defined global value of x.

Make use of global symbols inside a function with local symbols:

In[ ]:= **Function [z, x + z] [8]**

Out[ ]= 15

When functions have one argument, one can save a little bit of typing by using the @ symbol to denote function application.

The @ syntactic sugar:

In[ ]:= **Function [x, x^2] @ 3**

Out[ ]= 9

Here's how to write a function of more than one argument. Place the names of the locally defined symbols inside curly braces as the first argument and then just write the transformation as the second argument. Here's a Pythagorean function that finds the square root of the sum of the squares of two pieces of data.

A function with two variables:

In[ ]:= **Function [{ x, y }, $\sqrt{x^2 + y^2}$] ;**

Apply a function of two variables to a comma-separated sequence with real data:

In[ ]:= **Function [{ x, y }, $\sqrt{x^2 + y^2}$] [3, 4]**

Out[ ]= 5

The data doesn't have to be numeric. Here I apply the function to symbolic expressions.

Apply a function to symbolic variables:

In[ ]:= **Function [{ x, y }, $\sqrt{x^2 + y^2}$] [a, b]**

Out[ ]= $\sqrt{a^2 + b^2}$

It's not necessary to provide the function with an explicit name for the data. Here's another way of defining a function. It isn't assigned to a symbol and is thus called an "anonymous function." Basically, you designate the arguments through numbered "slots." Here's our first squaring function.

Use the & postfix operator to define a function:

In[•]:= **Slot [1]^2 &;**

This says when you confront a sequence of expressions, take the first of them and square it. The Slot[1] means to take the first expression in the sequence and not, for example, the second or third. The ampersand terminating the expression means that one is defining a function.

And here's our second variant of the Pythagorean function.

Use the & operator with multivariable functions:

In[•]:= $\sqrt{\text{Slot [1]}^2 + \text{Slot [2]}^2}$ **&;**

Also, the little ampersand operator at the end has low precedence, so I generally wrap my "slot functions" defined with ampersands inside parentheses. Sometimes you can get away with not doing it, but I think it's good practice to wrap ampersand-defined functions in parentheses as a matter of course. Here are two examples.

Wrap & functions in parentheses:

In[•]:= **{ (Slot [1]^2 &), ($\sqrt{\text{Slot [1]}^2 + \text{Slot [2]}^2}$ &) };**

If you've looked at Wolfram Language code before, you may be wondering why you haven't seen things that have a Slot head. That's because there's frequently used syntactic sugar, the Slot symbol (#). You can write the previous code as follows.

The # syntactic sugar:

In[•]:= **#1^2 &;**

In[•]:= $\sqrt{\text{#1}^2 + \text{#2}^2}$ **&;**

Indeed, if a function has just one argument, one can omit the number 1 and just use the Slot symbol itself.

Just use # for single-variable functions:

In[•]:= **#^{2} &;**

Function Composition

Suppose I have one function that says to take a number, multiply it by 3, and then add 1 and I have a second function that says to take the hyperbolic tangent of that number. (Don't worry if you don't know what a hyperbolic tangent is; it's just a function over the real numbers that produces values between -1 and 1).

Here's how I could write the functions:

In[∘]:= **f1 = Function [x , 3 x + 1] ;**

In[∘]:= **f2 = Function [x , Tanh [x]] ;**

Now I want to find out what happens when I take the number $\frac{1}{2}$, apply the first function, and then take the result of that application and apply the second function to it. I could write the following. It works just fine.

This is also called function chaining:

In[∘]:= **f2 [f1 [1 / 2]]**

Out[∘]= $\text{Tanh}\left[\dfrac{5}{2}\right]$

However, I could also first ask that the functions be "composed" and then apply the composed function to $\frac{1}{2}$. To do this, I use the Composition function.

A standard function composition applied to a value:

In[∘]:= **Composition [f2, f1] [1 / 2]**

Out[∘]= $\text{Tanh}\left[\dfrac{5}{2}\right]$

Notice that the last function to be applied comes first in the argument sequence. If I want the functions to be applied in the same order as the arguments, I use the RightComposition function.

RightComposition of two functions and application to a value:

In[∘]:= **RightComposition [f1, f2] [1 / 2]**

Out[∘]= $\text{Tanh}\left[\dfrac{5}{2}\right]$

These composition operations are sufficiently common—and I will use them extensively throughout this book—that the Wolfram Language provides syntactic sugar. I first show the conventional (left) Composition syntactic sugar. The parentheses are required.

The @* syntactic sugar for standard Composition:

In[∘]:= **(f2 @* f1) [0.5]**

Out[∘]= 0.986614

It may be a matter of style, but I find that I don't use the conventional Composition that much. What I do use a lot in this book and in my research is RightComposition. Here's the RightComposition sugar that I will be using *all the time* in this book. Separate the functions to be composed with a / *.

The / * syntactic sugar for RightComposition:

In[◦]:= **(f1 / * f2) [1 / 2]**

Out[◦]= $\text{Tanh}\left[\dfrac{5}{2}\right]$

Note that if I want the numeric value, I can just add the N function at the end of the RightComposition pipeline.

Apply a three-function RightComposition to a value:

In[◦]:= **(f1 / * f2 / * N) [1 / 2]**

Out[◦]= 0.986614

The List

Prior to the introduction of Associations in Version 10, and quite arguably even today, the fundamental data structure in the Wolfram Language was the List. Here's the most typical way of writing a List. One puts the elements of the List inside curly braces and separates them with commas.

Use { ... } to bracket a List:

In[◦]:= **{3, 4, 5};**

One can also write it in FullForm in which the Head of the expression is clearly revealed. The Wolfram Language front end typically outputs Lists (even those input in FullForm) using curly braces.

FullForm of a List and its output in StandardForm:

In[◦]:= **List [3, 4, 5]**

Out[◦]= {3, 4, 5}

Lists can contain elements that themselves have different heads. Here I create a heterogeneous List that mixes integers, reals, symbols, and strings.

Lists may be (and often are) heterogeneous:

In[◦]:= **heteroList = { 3, 4.2, f, "hello world" }**

Out[◦]= {3, 4.2, f, hello world }

I can use Part to extract pieces of Lists. Here I create a List that contains Parts of Lists.

Get Parts out of Lists:

In[◦]:= **List [Part [heteroList, 2] , heteroList⟦1⟧, heteroList⟦ { 4, 3 } ⟧]**

Out[◦]= {4.2, 3, { hello world, f} }

Nested Lists

As shown earlier, a List can have a List as an element. Indeed, a typical data structure might be a List of Lists. Here's one in which the inner Lists have different numbers of elements—a "ragged" List.

A ragged List of Lists:

In[∘]:= **{ { 3, 4 }, { 5, 6, 7 }, { 8, 9, 10, 11 } };**

It's very typical to have a List in which each inner List has the same number of elements. Sometimes we call these matrices or arrays. Here's an example. I'll assign the expression to the symbol nestedList.

A List of Lists in which the inner Lists have the same number of elements:

In[∘]:= **nestedList = { { ▨, 5, 0.08, GeoPosition [{ −4, 86 }] , "Thurgood Marshall" },**
        { ▨, 2, 0.83, GeoPosition [{ −43, −113 }] , "Elena Kagan" },
        { ■, 4, 0.07, GeoPosition [{ −22, −40 }] , "Oliver Ellsworth" },
        { ▨, 4, 0.35, GeoPosition [{ 17, 78 }] , "William Rehnquist" },
        { ▨, 9, 0.87, GeoPosition [{ 14, 64 }] , "Oliver Wendell Holmes, Jr." } } ;

The All setting can be used with Part and in other circumstances. Here I extract the second element of All the inner Lists. If one thinks of these Lists of Lists as being like a conventional matrix or array, one can think of these inner Lists as being like a row of data.

Use All as an argument to Part:

In[∘]:= **Part [nestedList, All, 2]**

Out[∘]= **{ 5, 2, 4, 4, 9 }**

There are some attractive ways of formatting these Lists of Lists in which all the inner Lists have the same number of elements. There is the built-in Grid function.

Use Grid to make an attractive matrix:

In[∘]:= **Grid [nestedList]**

▨	5	0.08	GeoPosition [{ −4, 86 }]	Thurgood Marshall
▨	2	0.83	GeoPosition [{ −43, −113 }]	Elena Kagan
■	4	0.07	GeoPosition [{ −22, −40 }]	Oliver Ellsworth
▨	4	0.35	GeoPosition [{ 17, 78 }]	William Rehnquist
▨	9	0.87	GeoPosition [{ 14, 64 }]	Oliver Wendell Holmes, Jr.

Out[∘]=

Grid can be used with Dividers if desired. (I like Dividers.)

Use Grid with Dividers to make the structure of a matrix more clear:

In[•]:= **Grid [nestedList, Dividers → All]**

Out[•]=

	5	0.08	GeoPosition [{ −4, 86 }]	Thurgood Marshall
	2	0.83	GeoPosition [{ −43, −113 }]	Elena Kagan
	4	0.07	GeoPosition [{ −22, −40 }]	Oliver Ellsworth
	4	0.35	GeoPosition [{ 17, 78 }]	William Rehnquist
	9	0.87	GeoPosition [{ 14, 64 }]	Oliver Wendell Holmes, Jr.

There's also TableForm, which can be used with headings. Here I give each of the rows a heading (an integer running from 1 to 5) and each of the columns a heading that attempts to describe the contents of the associated values.

Use TableForm to attach headings to matrices:

In[•]:= **TableForm [nestedList, TableHeadings →**
{ Range [5] , { "A color", "An integer", "A real", "A place", "Justice" } }]

Out[•]//TableForm=

	A color	An integer	A real	A place	Justice
1		5	0.08	GeoPosition [{ −4, 86 }]	Thurgood Marshall
2		2	0.83	GeoPosition [{ −43, −113 }]	Elena Kagan
3		4	0.07	GeoPosition [{ −22, −40 }]	Oliver Ellsworth
4		4	0.35	GeoPosition [{ 17, 78 }]	William Rehnquist
5		9	0.87	GeoPosition [{ 14, 64 }]	Oliver Wendell Holmes, Jr.

There's also a ResourceFunction called DatasetForm that makes the data look like a Wolfram Language dataset, without all of the overhead—often useful overhead—that comes with the real Dataset function.

Use the ResourceFunction DatasetForm to emulate the presentation of a true dataset:

In[•]:= **[•] DatasetForm + [nestedList]**

Out[•]=

	5	0.08	4.0°S 86.0°E	Thurgood Marshall
	2	0.83	43.0°S 113.0°W	Elena Kagan
	4	0.07	22.0°S 40.0°W	Oliver Ellsworth
	4	0.35	17.0°N 78.0°E	William Rehnquist
	9	0.87	14.0°N 64.0°E	Oliver Wendell Holmes, Jr.

Levels

Wolfram Language expression parts have levels. In the expression g [8, h [x, y, 9]] , 8 and h [x, y, 9] lie at the first level because they are arguments to the function g, which lies at the top of the expression. One can find this out by using the Level function. The second argument, here an integer wrapped in a List, represents a request for *only* those parts of the expression lying at a level corresponding to the integer. This second argument is called a "level specification."

Get the parts of an expression at level 1 (the "top level"):

In[◦]:= **Level[g[8, h[x, y, 9]], {1}]**

Out[◦]= {8, h[7, y, 9]}

But x, y, and 9 are arguments in the expression h[x, y, 9], which lies at the first level. So x, y, and 9 lie at the second level.

Get the parts of an expression at level 2:

In[◦]:= **Level[g[8, h[x, y, 9]], {2}]**

Out[◦]= {7, y, 9}

If one does not wrap the level specification in a List, Level produces all expressions lying from level 1 to the level indicated by the integer.

Get the parts of an expression at all levels up through 2:

In[◦]:= **Level[g[8, h[x, y, 9]], 2]**

Out[◦]= {8, 7, y, 9, h[7, y, 9]}

To get the whole expression back, use level specification {0}.

Level 0 gets the whole expression:

In[◦]:= **Level[g[8, h[x, y, 9]], {0}]**

Out[◦]= {g[8, h[7, y, 9]]}

Position: Part and Level

The Position function lets one find the Part numbers of an expression that match some pattern; by looking at the number of elements in a Part number, one can also determine the Level at which the matching expression lies. Here I find the Part numbers of the expression {4, 5, 6}. I do so by asking for matches for _ (Blank), which matches any single expression. I need to include the Heads → False option unless I want to see the Part {0} included; Heads are generally "part 0" of an expression.

Use Position to get the Part indices of an expression that match a pattern:

In[◦]:= **Position[{4, 5, 6}, _, Heads → False]**

Out[◦]= {{1}, {2}, {3}, {}}

Here I find all the Part numbers of the expression that are integers. I don't need the Heads → False option because the Head of List is not an Integer and therefore does not match.

Get the Part indices of an expression that have an Integer Head:

In[ ]:= **Position [g [8, h [q, 8, y, 9]] , _Integer]**

Out[ ]= { {1}, {2, 2}, {2, 4} }

I can also tell Position to look only at a particular Level of the expression. Here I ask it to first find integers at level 1 of g [8, h [q, 8, y, 9]] and then to find all parts of the same expression at level 1 (but to ignore Heads).

Restrict Position to look only at a certain Level:

In[ ]:= **Position [g [8, h [q, 8, y, 9]] , _Integer, {1}]**

Out[ ]= { {1} }

In[ ]:= **Position [g [8, h [q, 8, y, 9]] , _, {1}, Heads → False]**

Out[ ]= { {1}, {2} }

Because Position wraps the found positions in a List and because the Extract function wants part numbers wrapped in a List, the two functions complement each other: the output from Position (or output in the form returned by Position) can be used as the input to Extract.

Find the subexpressions in one expression that have the same position as the integers in another expression:

In[ ]:= **Extract [r [3, s [p, 1, y, 7]] , Position [g [8, h [q, 8, y, 9]] , _Integer]]**

Out[ ]= {3, 1, 7}

Functional Programming Constructs

Map

One of the paradigmatic features of Wolfram Language programming is its strong support for "functional programming," in which functions frequently accept (indeed, demand) that some of their arguments also be functions. Perhaps this is best seen with an immediate example. I'll use what is surely the Wolfram Language's most common functional programming construct, the Map function.

Here I Map the function f over the expression g [1, 4, 9] :

In[ ]:= **Map [f, g [1, 4, 9]]**

Out[ ]= g [f [1], f [4], f [9]]

The head of the expression remains unchanged; it is still g, but each of the first-level parts of g now has the function f applied to it. Here's a practical use for it.

Vectorize computations with **Map**:

In[•]:= **Map [Sqrt, g [1, 4, 9]]**

Out[•]= **g [1, 2, 3]**

TreeForm provides another way to show what is happening. Basically, the Map here causes the function f to insert itself between the Head g and each of the first-level parts of g.

Visualize how **Map** works:

In[•]:= **{ TreeForm [g [1, 4, 9]], TreeForm [Map [f, g [1, 4, 9]]] } / / Framed**

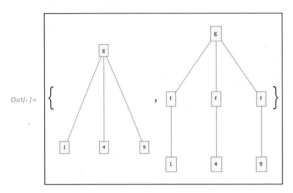

Out[•]=

Here is the f function Mapped over an expression I've been recycling in this chapter.

Map over complicated expressions:

In[•]:= **Map [f, g [8, h [q, 8, y, 9]]]**

Out[•]= **g [f [8], f [h [q, 8, y, 9]]]**

Again, I will show the original expression and the expression after Map is applied in TreeForm just to clarify what is going on.

Visualize **Map** working on multilevel expressions:

In[•]:= **{ TreeForm [g [8, h [x, y, 9]]], TreeForm [Map [f, g [8, h [q, 8 y, 9]]]] } / / Framed**

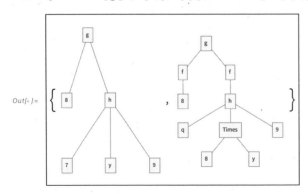

Out[•]=

There's also a three-argument form of Map in which the third argument is a level specification. Here I ask that the function f be applied only to those parts of the expression that lie at level 2.

Use a level specification with Map:

In[•]:= **Map [f, g [8, h [x, y, 9]], {2}]**

Out[•]= g [8, h [f [7], f [y], f [9]]]

TreeForm shows where the insertion takes place.

Visualize Map working at deeper levels:

In[•]:= **{ TreeForm [g [8, h [x, y, 9]]],**
       TreeForm [Map [f, g [8, h [q, 8, y, 9]], {2}]] } / / Framed

Out[•]=
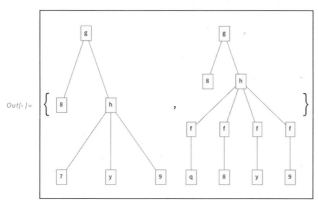

Here's a common use of Map. One has some sort of array of data and one wants to do the same thing to every element in the array. Here I ask for the Head of every expression at the first level, then the second level, and then the third level of nestedList.

Map applied at different levels of the same expression:

In[•]:= **nestedList = { { { ▢ , 5, 0.08, GeoPosition [{ −4, 86 }], "Thurgood Marshall" },**
       { ▢ , 2, 0.83, GeoPosition [{ −43, −113 }], "Elena Kagan" },
       { ▣ , 4, 0.07, GeoPosition [{ −22, −40 }], "Oliver Ellsworth" },
       { ▢ , 4, 0.35, GeoPosition [{ 17, 78 }], "William Rehnquist" },
       { ▣ , 9, 0.87, GeoPosition [{ 14, 64 }], "Oliver Wendell Holmes, Jr." } } ;

In[•]:= **Map [Head, nestedList]**

Out[•]= { List, List, List, List, List }

In[•]:= **Map [Head, nestedList, {2}]**

Out[•]= { { RGBColor, Integer, Real, GeoPosition, String },
     { RGBColor, Integer, Real, GeoPosition, String },
     { RGBColor, Integer, Real, GeoPosition, String },
     { RGBColor, Integer, Real, GeoPosition, String },
     { RGBColor, Integer, Real, GeoPosition, String } }

In[•]:=   **Map [Head, nestedList, { 3 }]**

Out[•]=   { { RGBColor [Real, Real, Real] , 5, 0.08, GeoPosition [List] , Thurgood Marshall } ,
   { RGBColor [Real, Real, Real] , 2, 0.83, GeoPosition [List] , Elena Kagan } ,
   { RGBColor [Real, Real, Real] , 4, 0.07, GeoPosition [List] , Oliver Ellsworth } ,
   { RGBColor [Real, Real, Real] , 4, 0.35, GeoPosition [List] , William Rehnquist } ,
   { RGBColor [Real, Real, Real] , 9, 0.87, GeoPosition [List] , Oliver Wendell Holmes, Jr. } }

There's also what is called an "operator form" of Map. Here one uses the function to be applied as the single argument to Map. One then applies this operator to data. Here's a simple example.

Map has an operator form:

In[•]:=   **Map [Sqrt] [{ 1, 4, 9 }]**

Out[•]=   { 1, 2, 3 }

One can't directly use this operator form of Map when one wants a function to apply beyond the first level of the expression. One can either use the MapLevel ResourceFunction or, without it, one has to do something a little awkward. Here I Map the Map [Head] function over nestedList, which is the same thing as operating at level 2. I use a doubly nested operator form to Map at level 3.

A "sneaky" way to use Map at deeper levels with operator forms:

In[•]:=   **Map [Map [Head]] [nestedList]**

Out[•]=   { { RGBColor, Integer, Real, GeoPosition, String } ,
   { RGBColor, Integer, Real, GeoPosition, String } ,
   { RGBColor, Integer, Real, GeoPosition, String } ,
   { RGBColor, Integer, Real, GeoPosition, String } ,
   { RGBColor, Integer, Real, GeoPosition, String } }

In[•]:=   **Map [Map [Map [Head]]] [nestedList]**

Out[•]=   { { RGBColor [Real, Real, Real] , 5, 0.08, GeoPosition [List] , Thurgood Marshall } ,
   { RGBColor [Real, Real, Real] , 2, 0.83, GeoPosition [List] , Elena Kagan } ,
   { RGBColor [Real, Real, Real] , 4, 0.07, GeoPosition [List] , Oliver Ellsworth } ,
   { RGBColor [Real, Real, Real] , 4, 0.35, GeoPosition [List] , William Rehnquist } ,
   { RGBColor [Real, Real, Real] , 9, 0.87, GeoPosition [List] , Oliver Wendell Holmes, Jr. } }

Here's how you can use the MapLevel ResourceFunction to use an operator form of Map at deeper levels.

The MapLevel ResourceFunction:

In[•]:= ⟦•⟧ **MapLevel** + **[Head, { 3 }] [nestedList]**

Out[•]= { { RGBColor [Real, Real, Real] , 5, 0.08, GeoPosition [List] , Thurgood Marshall },
{ RGBColor [Real, Real, Real] , 2, 0.83, GeoPosition [List] , Elena Kagan },
{ RGBColor [Real, Real, Real] , 4, 0.07, GeoPosition [List] , Oliver Ellsworth },
{ RGBColor [Real, Real, Real] , 4, 0.35, GeoPosition [List] , William Rehnquist },
{ RGBColor [Real, Real, Real] , 9, 0.87, GeoPosition [List] , Oliver Wendell Holmes, Jr. } }

One can use composed functions inside Map. Here I Map the composition in which I first apply f1 (Function [x + 3 x + 1]) and then apply f2 (Function [x, Tanh [x]]) over some values.

Composed functions work well with Map:

In[•]:= **Map [f1 / ∗ f2, { 1 / 2, 3, 0 }]**

Out[•]= $\left\{ \text{Tanh}\left[\dfrac{5}{2}\right], \text{Tanh} [10], \text{Tanh} [1] \right\}$

If I want numeric values, I just add the built-in N function to the end of the pipeline:

In[•]:= **Map [f1 / ∗ f2 / ∗ N, { 1 / 2, 3, 0 }]**

Out[•]= { 0.986614, 1., 0.761594 }

Finally, one should be aware of frequently used syntactic sugar for mapping at the first level: the / @ notation. Here's a shorter way of Mapping z over the expression { 1, 2, 3 }. One can't use the / @ infix notation if one wants to Map at deeper levels of an expression.

The / @ syntactic sugar for Map:

In[•]:= **z / @ { 1, 2, 3 }**

Out[•]= { z [1] , z [2] , z [3] }

Map's Cousins

MapThread

Map has a large number of cousin functions. Let's start with MapThread. One can use the function when one has two or more similar Lists that all have the same number of elements. Consider, for example, the data structures in the following List. They have the same Head (List), and they each have three elements.

A data structure that is a List of Lists:

In[•]:= **List [List [1, 2, 3] , List [4, 5, 6]]**

Out[•]= { { 1, 2, 3 }, { 4, 5, 6 } }

Here's what happens if we MapThread the function f over this structure.

A canonical use of MapThread:

In[ ]:= **MapThread [f, List [List [1, 2, 3] , List [4, 5, 6]]]**

Out[ ]= { f [1, 4] , f [2, 5] , f [3, 6] }

The same operation but using syntactic sugar to represent the Lists:

In[ ]:= **MapThread [f, { { 1, 2, 3 }, { 4, 5, 6 } }]**

Out[ ]= { f [1, 4] , f [2, 5] , f [3, 6] }

The first argument of the first List pairs with the first argument of the second List and the function f is applied to it, the second argument of the first List pairs with the second argument of the second List and the function f is applied to it, and the third argument of the first List pairs with the third argument of the second List and the function f is applied to it.

In data analysis, you're going to find that MapThread is very useful in trying to build a new column out of two or more existing columns. Consider, for example, data in which one column has the heights of various rectangles and another has the widths. Here's what one might do to compute the areas of the rectangles and make them a new column.

Use MapThread to create a new column using multiple existing columns in matrix-like data:

In[ ]:= **MapThread [{ #1, #2, Times [#1, #2] } &, { { 3, 7, 2 }, { 4, 5, 9 } }]**

Out[ ]= { { 3, 4, 12 }, { 7, 5, 35 }, { 2, 9, 18 } }

MapIndexed

With MapThread we saw how one can take two expressions and apply a function to corresponding parts of each expression. Sometimes, however, the second expression to which the function is applied can be readily inferred from the first expression. The MapIndexed function provides a way of generating that second expression without having to actually write it down. It's for a special case but an extremely common one. The second expression MapIndexed implicitly generates is the position numbers of each Part of the first expression. The position numbers are wrapped in List. So MapIndexed [f, {a, b}] creates {f [a, {1}], f [a, {2}]} not {f [a, 1], f [a, 2]}.

Let's get concrete. Suppose, for example, that the first chunk of data was a two-dimensional matrix and the second chunk of data one wanted was simply the index of each row. If one lived in a world without MapIndexed, one could write the following code. Remember that Prepend [{ a, b, c }, d] yields {d, a, b, c}. The Position function gets the part numbers of the first argument matching the pattern in the second argument but looks only at the level specified in the third argument.

A view of what goes on inside MapThread; Echo is used to print out the positions of nestedList that match _ at the first level:

```
In[ ]:=  Module [ { positionsAtLevel },
            positionsAtLevel = Position [ nestedList, _, { 1 }, Heads → False ];
            Echo [ positionsAtLevel ];
            MapThread [ Prepend [ #1, #2 〚1〛 ] &, { nestedList, positionsAtLevel } ]
          ]
```

>> { {1}, {2}, {3}, {4}, {5} }

Out[ ]= { {1, ▢, 5, 0.08, GeoPosition [{ −4, 86 }], Thurgood Marshall },
          {2, ▢, 2, 0.83, GeoPosition [{ −43, −113 }], Elena Kagan },
          {3, ■, 4, 0.07, GeoPosition [{ −22, −40 }], Oliver Ellsworth },
          {4, ▢, 4, 0.35, GeoPosition [{ 17, 78 }], William Rehnquist },
          {5, ▤, 9, 0.87, GeoPosition [{ 14, 64 }], Oliver Wendell Holmes, Jr. } }

The built-in MapIndexed function provides a different and generally shorter method of achieving this output. Let's first see it in action.

A canonical use of MapIndexed:

```
In[ ]:=  MapIndexed [ Prepend [ #1, #2 〚1〛 ] &, nestedList, { 1 } ]
```

Out[ ]= { {1, ▢, 5, 0.08, GeoPosition [{ −4, 86 }], Thurgood Marshall },
          {2, ▢, 2, 0.83, GeoPosition [{ −43, −113 }], Elena Kagan },
          {3, ■, 4, 0.07, GeoPosition [{ −22, −40 }], Oliver Ellsworth },
          {4, ▢, 4, 0.35, GeoPosition [{ 17, 78 }], William Rehnquist },
          {5, ▤, 9, 0.87, GeoPosition [{ 14, 64 }], Oliver Wendell Holmes, Jr. } }

The {1} in the third argument basically instructs the Wolfram Language kernel to construct the Part numbers of nestedList (excluding heads) that lie at the first level. As shown next, if the third argument is omitted, the level specification defaults to {1}.

MapIndexed without a third argument uses {1} as the default level specification:

```
In[ ]:=  MapIndexed [ Prepend [ #1, #2 〚1〛 ] &, nestedList ]
```

Out[ ]= { {1, ▢, 5, 0.08, GeoPosition [{ −4, 86 }], Thurgood Marshall },
          {2, ▢, 2, 0.83, GeoPosition [{ −43, −113 }], Elena Kagan },
          {3, ■, 4, 0.07, GeoPosition [{ −22, −40 }], Oliver Ellsworth },
          {4, ▢, 4, 0.35, GeoPosition [{ 17, 78 }], William Rehnquist },
          {5, ▤, 9, 0.87, GeoPosition [{ 14, 64 }], Oliver Wendell Holmes, Jr. } }

One can use MapIndexed with different level specifications.

MapIndexed in which one matches Parts at only the second level:

```
In[ ]:=  MapIndexed [ h, { { a, b, c }, { d, e, f, g } }, { 2 } ]
```

Out[ ]= { {h [a, {1, 1}], h [b, {1, 2}], h [c, {1, 3}] },
          {h [d, {2, 1}], h [e, {2, 2}], h [f, {2, 3}], h [g, {2, 4}] } }

MapIndexed generalizes to many operations and can save a lot of typing—and prevent the mistakes that accompany such efforts.

MapAt

Sometimes, one just wants to apply a function to selected positions in data. Suppose, for example, that I wanted to apply the Reverse function just to the second and fourth rows of nestedList. Here's how I could do it. I wrap the result in Grid so it is easier to see.

MapAt lets one apply functions at only certain positions:

In[ ]:= **Grid [MapAt [Reverse, nestedList, { {2}, {4} }], Dividers → All]**

Out[ ]=

	5	0.08	GeoPosition [{−4, 86}]	Thurgood Marshall
Elena Kagan	GeoPosition [{−43, −113}]	0.83	2	
	4	0.07	GeoPosition [{−22, −40}]	Oliver Ellsworth
William Rehnquist	GeoPosition [{17, 78}]	0.35	4	
	9	0.87	GeoPosition [{14, 64}]	Oliver Wendell Holmes, Jr.

Notice that I had to encapsulate the position information in Lists. Although this may seem to be a nuisance, it permits code like this to be unambiguous. If I weren't required to stick the position information in Lists, the Wolfram Language would not know if, in the following code, I intended to try to apply Framed to both the second and first rows of the data or whether I intended to apply it only to the first column of the second row.

Position specifications in MapAt can be very detailed:

In[ ]:= **Grid [MapAt [Framed, nestedList, { {2, 1} }], Dividers → All]**

Out[ ]=

	5	0.08	GeoPosition [{−4, 86}]	Thurgood Marshall
	2	0.83	GeoPosition [{−43, −113}]	Elena Kagan
	4	0.07	GeoPosition [{−22, −40}]	Oliver Ellsworth
	4	0.35	GeoPosition [{17, 78}]	William Rehnquist
	9	0.87	GeoPosition [{14, 64}]	Oliver Wendell Holmes, Jr.

I can use more complex position specifications in MapAt.

Apply the Framed function to the fifth position of elements in All rows:

In[•]:=   **Grid [MapAt [Framed, nestedList, { { All, 5 } }] , Dividers → All]**

Out[•]=

	5	0.08	GeoPosition [{ −4, 86 }]	Thurgood Marshall
	2	0.83	GeoPosition [{ −43, −113 }]	Elena Kagan
	4	0.07	GeoPosition [{ −22, −40 }]	Oliver Ellsworth
	4	0.35	GeoPosition [{ 17, 78 }]	William Rehnquist
	9	0.87	GeoPosition [{ 14, 64 }]	Oliver Wendell Holmes, Jr.

Apply

The Map function causes the function to insert itself into the expression tree. It basically adds—at least temporarily—a new level to the expression, although sometimes this new level disappears after the inserted function evaluates its arguments. Often, that's exactly what one wants, but sometimes instead of adding a level, one wants to replace heads of the expression at some level of the expression. Apply is the Wolfram Language function to do this. There's a standard example that shows how it works.

A canonical example of Apply:

In[•]:=   **Apply [Plus, List [2, 2]]**

Out[•]=   **4**

In the example, the Plus Head has replaced the List Head, but while List [2, 3] cannot be evaluated further, the Wolfram Language knows that Plus [2, 2] is 4.

I can also show what Apply does using TreeForm. Notice how the f Head replaces the List Head in the expression.

Visualize how Apply works with TreeForm; notice the use of the operator form of Map and postfix notation:

In[•]:=   **{ { 2, 2 }, Apply [f, { 2, 2 }] } / / Map [TreeForm] / ∗ Framed**

Out[•]=
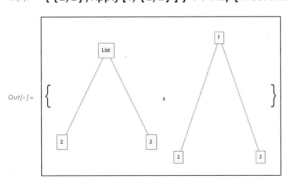

By default, Apply works at level 0 of the expression, right on the top-level Head. As with Map, one can ask Apply to work at different levels. Here I take the more complicated expression and Apply f at level 1. I'll show the results using TreeForm.

Use Apply at deeper levels:

In[ ]:= **{ TreeForm [g [8, h [x, y, 9]]],**
       TreeForm [Apply [f, g [8, h [x, y, 9]], { 1 }]] } // Framed

Out[ ]=
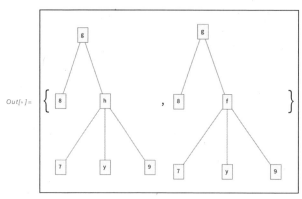

As of Version 13.1, there is also MapApply, which works at level 1 of the expression.

MapApply is equivalent to Apply at level 1:

In[ ]:= **VerificationTest [MapApply [f, { { a }, { b } }], Apply [f, { { a }, { b } }, { 1 }]] [**
      { "ExpectedOutput", "VerificationTest" }]

Out[ ]= **<| ExpectedOutput → { f [a], f [b] },**
      VerificationTest → VerificationTest [f @@@ { { a }, { b } }, { f [a], f [b] }, { },
          TestID → None, SameTest → SameQ, TimeConstraint → ∞, MemoryConstraint → ∞] |>

Just as there is an operator form for Map built into the Wolfram Language and a ResourceFunction that permits use of the operator form at deeper levels, so too with Apply.

Use an operator form of Apply:

In[ ]:= **Apply [Plus] [{ 2, 3 }]**

Out[ ]= 5

Use the ApplyLevel ResourceFunction to apply the function at a deeper level of the expression:

In[ ]:= **[≡] ApplyLevel ⊕ [Plus, { 1 }] [{ { 2, 3 }, { 4, 5 } }]**

Out[ ]= **{ 5, 9 }**

There are two forms of syntactic sugar for Apply. The double "at" in f @@ x means to Apply f to x at level 0. The triple "at" in f @@@ x means to Apply f to x at level 1.

Thread

This book uses the Thread command a lot. It's a little bit like MapThread. Here's an example.

A canonical example of Thread:

In[*]:= **Thread[f[{a, b, c}, {d, e, f}]]**

Out[*]= {f[a, d], f[b, e], f[c, f]}

As with MapThread, each element in each of the inner structures (like {a, b, c} or {d, e, f}) pairs up with an element of the other inner structures in the same position within that structure.

There's also a very handy special case of Thread. Remember that MapThread only works if the inner data structures have the same length. Thus, this fails to do anything.

MapThread generally fails if the second argument is a List with differing structures:

In[*]:= **MapThread[f, {{a, b, c}, d}]**

> (⋯) MapThread : Object d at position {2, 2} in MapThread [f, {{a, b, c }, d}] has only 0 of required 1 dimensions.

Out[*]= MapThread[f, {{a, b, c}, d}]

However, Thread takes any atomic value and assumes it is essentially the same thing as an array of the same length as the other structures on which Thread is operating and whose values are all equal to that one atomic value.

Thread can work where some of the elements of the second argument are atoms:

In[*]:= **Thread[f[{a, b, c}, d]]**

Out[*]= {f[a, d], f[b, d], f[c, d]}

By the way, if there's only one inner data structure, Thread works a lot like Map.

Map disguised as Thread:

In[*]:= **Thread[f[{a, b, c}]]**

Out[*]= {f[a], f[b], f[c]}

Indeed, if one gives a Function a Listable attribute, it automatically threads over Lists without having to write Thread explicitly. Here is one way of making a Function Listable: just include that word as a third argument to Function. (You can't use this method if you use the ampersand notation or if you use the function arrow (↦) notation to create the function; it only works if you write out Function literally.)

Make a function Listable:

In[ ]:= **q = Function [{ x , y } , x − y , Listable]**

Out[ ]= Function [{ x, y } , x − y, Listable]

Now **q** will Thread over the arguments. I don't have to write Thread.

Listable functions thread without the need for **Thread**:

In[ ]:= **q [{ 6 , 7 , 8 } , { 1 , 0 , 13 }]**

Out[ ]= { 5, 7, −5 }

In[ ]:= **q [{ 6 , 7 , 8 } , 5]**

Out[ ]= { 1, 2, 3 }

Common Operations on Lists

The Wolfram Language has a large number of operations that work on Lists (and other data containers that we have not yet examined). Many of these operations make use of functions as arguments. I present a few here that are most commonly used in this book.

Length

The Length function computes how many elements are in the top level of an expression.

Use **Length** to count elements:

In[ ]:= **Map [Length] [{ { 4 , 5 , 6 } , g [3 , 4 , 5 , 6 , 7] , g [8 , h [q , 8 , y , 9]] }]**

Out[ ]= { 3, 5, 2 }

SortBy

One can use SortBy to sort a List (or another data structure) according to the value of some function applied to each element of the List. Here I use SortBy to sort a bunch of strings according to the number of characters they contain.

Sort strings by their number of characters:

In[ ]:= **SortBy [{ "zebra", "yak", "wombat", "stegosaurus" } , StringLength]**

Out[ ]= { yak, zebra, wombat, stegosaurus }

Here I sort a List of Lists according to the value of its last element.

Sort Lists of numbers by their Last value:

In[ ]:= **SortBy [{ {3, 1}, {4, 6}, {5, 2}, {11, 3, 4} }, Last]**

Out[ ]= { {3, 1}, {5, 2}, {11, 3, 4}, {4, 6} }

There's a cousin function, ReverseSortBy, which does exactly what you think it does.

ReverseSortBy is SortBy and then Reverse:

In[ ]:= **ReverseSortBy [{"zebra", "yak", "wombat", "stegosaurus"}, StringLength]**

Out[ ]= {stegosaurus, wombat, zebra, yak}

Both of these functions have frequently used operator forms.

Operator forms of SortBy and ReverseSortBy:

In[ ]:= **{ SortBy [StringLength] [{"zebra", "yak", "wombat", "stegosaurus"}],**
ReverseSortBy [StringLength] [{"zebra", "yak", "wombat", "stegosaurus"}] }

Out[ ]= { {yak, zebra, wombat, stegosaurus}, {stegosaurus, wombat, zebra, yak} }

GatherBy

Another common operation is to collect elements of the data in different Lists depending on specific aspects of the data. Here's an example that uses many features of the Wolfram Language described in this chapter. I write a function northernHemisphereQ that yields True if the Latitude of its fourth element is greater than the Latitude of the equator. I then use northernHemisphereQ to group the rows in nestedList.

A function to figure out if a location is north of the equator:

In[ ]:= **northernHemisphereQ = row ⟼ Latitude [row ⟦4⟧] > Quantity [0, "AngularDegrees"]**

Out[ ]= Function[row, Latitude [row ⟦4⟧] > 0°]

Use GatherBy to encapsulate data in Lists depending on the value of a function applied to that data:

In[ ]:= **gathered = GatherBy [nestedList, northernHemisphereQ]**

Out[ ]= { { { ▢, 5, 0.08, GeoPosition [{ −4, 86}], Thurgood Marshall},
{▢, 2, 0.83, GeoPosition [{ −43, −113}], Elena Kagan},
{■, 4, 0.07, GeoPosition [{ −22, −40}], Oliver Ellsworth} },
{ {▢, 4, 0.35, GeoPosition [{ 17, 78}], William Rehnquist},
{▢, 9, 0.87, GeoPosition [{ 14, 64}], Oliver Wendell Holmes, Jr.} } }

The symbol gathered now holds a List of Lists of Lists. If I now look at the first part of gathered (a List of Lists), I see all the points are in the Southern Hemisphere.

Look at the first part of gathered:

In[ ]:= **gathered[[1]]**

Out[ ]=   { { ▢, 5, 0.08, GeoPosition [{ −4, 86 }] , Thurgood Marshall },
   { ▢, 2, 0.83, GeoPosition [{ −43, −113 }] , Elena Kagan },
   { ■, 4, 0.07, GeoPosition [{ −22, −40 }] , Oliver Ellsworth } }

The second part of gathered has points in only the Northern Hemisphere.

Look at the second part of gathered:

In[ ]:= **gathered[[2]]**

Out[ ]=   { { ▢, 4, 0.35, GeoPosition [{ 17, 78 }] , William Rehnquist },
   { ▢, 9, 0.87, GeoPosition [{ 14, 64 }] , Oliver Wendell Holmes, Jr. } }

One can GatherBy recursively. Here I first break down the data by whether the last value in the row is in the Northern Hemisphere. Then I break it down by whether the second number in the row is even. What we now see is a List of Lists of Lists of Lists!

Use GatherBy with a List of functions to recursively break down data:

In[ ]:= **evenQ2 = Function [row, EvenQ [row[[2]]]]**

Out[ ]=   Function [row, EvenQ [row[[2]]]]

In[ ]:= **GatherBy [nestedList, { northernHemisphereQ, evenQ2 }]**

Out[ ]=   { { { { ▢, 5, 0.08, GeoPosition [{ −4, 86 }] , Thurgood Marshall } },
   { { ▢, 2, 0.83, GeoPosition [{ −43, −113 }] , Elena Kagan },
      { ■, 4, 0.07, GeoPosition [{ −22, −40 }] , Oliver Ellsworth } } },
   { { { ▢, 4, 0.35, GeoPosition [{ 17, 78 }] , William Rehnquist } },
      { { ▢, 9, 0.87, GeoPosition [{ 14, 64 }] , Oliver Wendell Holmes, Jr. } } } }

Notice that this is different than a GatherBy in which I compute the List { northernHemisphereQ [#] , EvenQ [#] } & for each row. In this latter case, I separate the data into categories based on the value of a List whose first value determines whether the row's fourth element represents a location in the Northern Hemisphere and whose second value determines whether the row's second element is even. There are thus four possibilities.

Use a function that generates a List to do more complex breakdowns of data:

In[ ]:= **GatherBy [nestedList, { northernHemisphereQ [#] , evenQ2 [#] } &]**

Out[ ]=   { { { ▢, 5, 0.08, GeoPosition [{ −4, 86 }] , Thurgood Marshall } },
   { { ▢, 2, 0.83, GeoPosition [{ −43, −113 }] , Elena Kagan },
      { ■, 4, 0.07, GeoPosition [{ −22, −40 }] , Oliver Ellsworth } },
   { { ▢, 4, 0.35, GeoPosition [{ 17, 78 }] , William Rehnquist } },
   { { ▢, 9, 0.87, GeoPosition [{ 14, 64 }] , Oliver Wendell Holmes, Jr. } } }

There are two matters to keep in mind with respect to GatherBy. First, as of Version 13, there's no operator form of GatherBy. Second, GatherBy has a powerful cousin, GroupBy, that you will meet in a subsequent chapter after I have introduced Association.

Select

Often, one wants to just filter data: some one wants to keep and some one wants to discard. There are several functions to accomplish this in the Wolfram Language. Here I will present the Select function. It's another functional construct. One writes the data to be filtered as the first argument and a function that yields a True or False (Boolean) value as the second argument. Here I select just those rows in nestedList that are in the Northern Hemisphere.

A canonical example of Select to filter data:

In[•]:= **Select [nestedList, northernHemisphereQ]**

Out[•]= { { ▨, 4, 0.35, GeoPosition [{ 17, 78 }] , William Rehnquist },
      { ▨, 9, 0.87, GeoPosition [{ 14, 64 }] , Oliver Wendell Holmes, Jr. } }

There's an operator form of Select that takes the selection function as its only argument.

Select has an operator form:

In[•]:= **Select [northernHemisphereQ] [nestedList]**

Out[•]= { { ▨, 4, 0.35, GeoPosition [{ 17, 78 }] , William Rehnquist },
      { ▨, 9, 0.87, GeoPosition [{ 14, 64 }] , Oliver Wendell Holmes, Jr. } }

Transpose

All of the functions in this section can be used on Lists of Lists or even more deeply nested constructs. There is one function, however, that I find particularly salient in data analysis, Transpose. The idea is to take a List of Lists data structure in which each inner List has the same number of elements (the nestedList I've been using here is an example) and then "flip" the data so that the rows become columns and the columns become rows.

Use Transpose to flip rows and columns of matrix-like data:

In[•]:= **Transpose [nestedList]**

Out[•]= { { ▨, ▨, ▨, ▨, ▨ }, { 5, 2, 4, 4, 9 }, { 0.08, 0.83, 0.07, 0.35, 0.87 },
      { GeoPosition [{ −4, 86 }] , GeoPosition [{ −43, −113 }] , GeoPosition [{ −22, −40 }] ,
      GeoPosition [{ 17, 78 }] , GeoPosition [{ 14, 64 }] }, { Thurgood Marshall,
      Elena Kagan, Oliver Ellsworth, William Rehnquist, Oliver Wendell Holmes, Jr. } }

Now instead of the first column being a bunch of colors, the first row is a List of colors, and instead of the fifth column being a bunch of United States Supreme Court justices, now the fifth row is a List of those justices.

Transposing is useful for many reasons, but exploitation of implicit Listability is the one on which I want to focus here. Code often runs faster if, instead of Mapping a function over some List of values element by element, one instead calls a Listable function once, then executes it on a List of values. This is particularly important where the function in question has to make calls to internet resources, such as the Wolfram Cloud, or where it would otherwise take time to load. Here's an example in which I generate 20 random dates and represent them as strings. I postfix the ResourceFunction Terse after the assignment to spare us needless detail (and save paper). Terse is essentially an operator form of Short. The number and structure of elided elements when using functions like Short and ResourceFunctions like Terse and AugmentedTerse will depend on the operating system and details of the Wolfram Language front end you are using. Do not be troubled if your output when using these functions varies slightly from what is shown in the book.

After using SeedRandom, use RandomDate to create 20 dates from 1999 and convert them to strings using DateString:

```
In[•]:= (randomDates = (SeedRandom[20221230];
            Map[DateString[#, {"Year", "/", "Month", "/", "Day"}] &,
               RandomDate[DateObject[{1999}, "Year"], 20]])) // [•] Terse + [3]
```

```
Out[•]//Short=  {1999/10/24, 1999/07/03, 1999/11/25, 1999/01/25,
                 ≪12≫, 1999/07/24, 1999/04/16, 1999/12/29, 1999/03/17}
```

Now I ask the Wolfram Language interpreter, which through Version 13 makes use of Wolfram servers to do its work, to convert each of these dates to a DateObject on which computation can be easily done. I apply EchoTiming to get information on how long it takes; I use the // postfix "afterthought" operator to do so.

Mapping Interpreter over data can take a long time in Version 13.2:

```
In[•]:= Map[Interpreter["Date"], randomDates] // EchoTiming
```

⏱ 7.47826

Now I take advantage of the implicit Listability of Interpreter and instead call the function once, applying it to the entire List of dates.

Exploit Listability to speed up Interpreter and other functions:

In[•]:= **Interpreter ["Date"] [randomDates] // EchoTiming**

🕐 1.07579

Out[•]= { Sun 24 Oct 1999 , Sat 3 Jul 1999 , Thu 25 Nov 1999 , Mon 25 Jan 1999 , Thu 9 Sep 1999 ,

Mon 3 May 1999 , Tue 21 Sep 1999 , Thu 25 Feb 1999 , Mon 12 Jul 1999 , Mon 3 May 1999 ,

Fri 17 Dec 1999 , Sat 6 Feb 1999 , Wed 10 Mar 1999 , Tue 7 Dec 1999 , Sat 18 Sep 1999 ,

Thu 3 Jun 1999 , Sat 24 Jul 1999 , Fri 16 Apr 1999 , Wed 29 Dec 1999 , Wed 17 Mar 1999 }

Even with a short list, using the non-threaded version takes much longer.

Now notice that with Transpose, I can take separated elements of a nested List and collect them into a cohesive List to take advantage of implicit listability and then use Transpose again to restore the original structure of the data. Suppose, for example, I want to get the Entity corresponding to each of the persons in the last element of the rows of nestedList. I could do this using MapAt with a Part specification of {All, 5}, which says to take all the rows and apply Interpreter to each of the fifth Parts.

Running Interpreter on the values in a column of data is relatively slow:

In[•]:= **MapAt [Interpreter ["Person"] , nestedList, { { All, 5 } }] // EchoTiming**

🕐 2.41613

Out[•]= {{ ▢, 5, 0.08, GeoPosition [{ −4, 86 }], Thurgood Marshall },

{ ▢, 2, 0.83, GeoPosition [{ −43, −113 }], Elena Kagan },

{ ▪, 4, 0.07, GeoPosition [{ −22, −40 }], Oliver Ellsworth },

{ ▢, 4, 0.35, GeoPosition [{ 17, 78 }], William Rehnquist },

{ ▪, 9, 0.87, GeoPosition [{ 14, 64 }], Oliver Wendell Holmes, Jr. }}}

Or I could try this alternative version in which I first Transpose the data and then use MapAt with a Part specification of 5, telling Mathematica to find the fifth Part (now a List of justices) and make a single call to Interpreter that gets Entity specifications for all of the elements in the List.

Running Interpreter in a listable way over a row in a transposed matrix is faster:

In[•]:= **Transpose [MapAt [Interpreter ["Person"] , Transpose [nestedList] , { {5} }]] // EchoTiming**

⏱ 0.007426

Out[•]= {{ ▢, 5, 0.08, GeoPosition [{ −4, 86}] , [Thurgood Marshall] },

　　{ ▢, 2, 0.83, GeoPosition [{ −43, −113}] , [Elena Kagan] },

　　{ ▪, 4, 0.07, GeoPosition [{ −22, −40}] , [Oliver Ellsworth] },

　　{ ▢, 4, 0.35, GeoPosition [{ 17, 78}] , [William Rehnquist] },

　　{ ▪, 9, 0.87, GeoPosition [{ 14, 64}] , [Oliver Wendell Holmes, Jr.] }}

As you can see, the second method works a lot faster. By the way, you will notice I Transposed the data, performed an operation on what became a row of that Transposed data, and then Transposed the results back to the original orientation. I will do this a lot in this book. I call this technique the "Double Transpose Trick." Real mathematicians, I am advised, sometimes call a similar technique "conjugation."

A Sample Problem Using "Old-School" Wolfram Language Methods

Data Retrieval

Let's analyze some sports data using these old-school functions. I start by retrieving a ResourceObject created for this book containing salary information from 2007–2017 for soccer (a.k.a. football) players in Major League Soccer (MLS) in the United States.

Acquire the ResourceObject from the Wolfram Data Repository:

In[•]:= **ro = ResourceObject ["Sample Data for Query Book"]**

Out[•]= ResourceObject [➕ 🏛 Name: Sample Data for Query Book »
　　　　　　　　　　　　　　　　Type: DataResource
　　　　　　　　　　　　Description: Data to support the Wolfram Media book Query:
　　　　　　　　　　　　　　　　　Getting Information from Data wit...]

The symbol ro now refers to a ResourceObject containing various forms of data. The "MLS List of Lists" element of that ResourceObject contains a matrix with 5553 rows and seven columns. I can assign that element to the symbol mls. By postfixing the AugmentedTerse ResourceFunction after the assignment, I show the output as a List of Lists (a matrix) but also show the structure of data.

Retrieve data on soccer salaries and use the AugmentedTerse ResourceFunction to provide information on the structure of the data:

In[ ]:= (mls = ResourceData [ro, "MLS List of Lists"]) / / [■] AugmentedTerse + [10]

Out[ ]= {{{CHI, Armas, Chris, M, $225 000.00 , $225 000.00 , Year: 2007 },

{CHI, Banner, Michael, M, $12 900.00 , $12 900.00 , Year: 2007 },

{CHI, Barrett, Chad, F, $41 212.50 , $48 712.50 , Year: 2007 },

{CHI, Blanco, Cuauhtemoc, F, $2.49232 × 10^6 , $2.66678 × 10^6 , Year: 2007 },

≪5546≫, {VAN, Williams, Sheanon, D, $175 000.00 , $184 000.00 , Year: 2017 },

{Missing [ ], Babouli, Mo, F, $54 075.00 , $54 075.00 , Year: 2017 }, {Missing [ ],

Ramajo, David Mateos, D, $420 000.00 , $453 333.33 , Year: 2017 }}, {5553, 7}}

Data Exploration

Here's a sample of the first five rows. I'll put it in a Grid with dividers to make it easier to see. The first column is the club for which the person played, the second and third columns are the last and first names of the player, the fourth column contains an abbreviation for the position (or positions) of the player, the fifth column contains a base salary, the sixth column contains any guaranteed compensation (defined as base plus annualized bonuses), and the seventh column contains the year to which the data is applicable.

Show the first five rows of the data:

In[ ]:= **Grid [mls⟦Range [5] ⟧, Dividers → All]**

Out[ ]=

CHI	Armas	Chris	M	$225 000.00	$225 000.00	Year: 2007
CHI	Banner	Michael	M	$12 900.00	$12 900.00	Year: 2007
CHI	Barrett	Chad	F	$41 212.50	$48 712.50	Year: 2007
CHI	Blanco	Cuauhtemoc	F	$2.49232 × 10^6	$2.66678 × 10^6	Year: 2007
CHI	Brown	C.J.	D	$106 391.00	$106 391.00	Year: 2007

Let's look to see if there are any missing values in the data. To do this, we'll use Position. I have to look at level 2, because all the rows have at least some data.

Use Position to find Missing values in the data:

In[ ]:= **Position [mls, _Missing, { 2 }]**

Out[ ]= { {560, 5}, {560, 6}, {1818, 3}, {2113, 3}, {2357, 3}, {2549, 1}, {2641, 1},
{2670, 3}, {2684, 1}, {2812, 1}, {2929, 3}, {3025, 1}, {3244, 3}, {3303, 1},
{3397, 3}, {3429, 1}, {3500, 3}, {3505, 3}, {3577, 1}, {3820, 3}, {3939, 1},
{4043, 1}, {4064, 3}, {4067, 3}, {4106, 1}, {4205, 3}, {4294, 4}, {4334, 1},
{4723, 3}, {4750, 3}, {4932, 1}, {4933, 1}, {4934, 1}, {4935, 1}, {4936, 1},
{4937, 1}, {4984, 3}, {5203, 3}, {5339, 3}, {5367, 3}, {5552, 1}, {5553, 1} }

We can get the columns in which the data is missing by mapping Last over these positions.

Use % to capture the last output; Map Last to get the second element of each List:

In[ ]:= **Map [Last, %]**

Out[ ]= {5, 6, 3, 3, 3, 1, 1, 3, 1, 1, 3, 1, 3, 1, 3, 1, 3, 3,
1, 3, 1, 1, 3, 3, 1, 3, 4, 1, 3, 3, 1, 1, 1, 1, 1, 1, 3, 3, 3, 3, 1, 1}

If we now look at the columns in which the Missings occur, it turns out that some of them are in 3, which is the first name of the player. This is not due to a failing of the dataset originators but due to the fact that many Brazilian players choose to play under a single name such "Pele" or "Kaka" rather than the conventional first name–last name system. I want to preserve those often important players in our analysis. On the other hand, some of the columns for which I have missing data involve club name (column 1) or salary (column 5) or guaranteed compensation (column 6). If that information is missing, I do want to exclude the rows from my analysis.

Here's how I can use Select to filter out the rows that contain crucial missing data.

Combine Or, Not, and MissingQ to create a function that lets Select preserve those rows in which the needed information is present:

In[ ]:= **(mls2 = Select [mls, Not [Or [MissingQ [# [[1]]] ,**
MissingQ [# [[5]]] , MissingQ [# [[6]]]]] &]) / / Dimensions

Out[ ]= { 5532, 7 }

The result, assigned to variable mls2, has fewer rows than the original data because some of the rows "contaminated" with Missings have been deleted.

Data Transformations

Sorting

Let's first do something simple: who have been the highest paid players in MLS?

Use ReverseSortBy and a function to find the highest paid players:

In[ ]:= **Grid [Take [ReverseSortBy [mls2, # ⟦6⟧ &] , 10] , Dividers → All]**

Out[ ]=

ORL	Kaka	Missing [ ]	M	$6.66 × 10^6$	$7.1675 × 10^6$	Year: 2017
ORL	Kaka	Missing [ ]	M	$6.66 × 10^6$	$7.1675 × 10^6$	Year: 2016
ORL	Kaka	Missing [ ]	M	$6.66 × 10^6$	$7.1675 × 10^6$	Year: 2015
ORL	Kaka	Missing [ ]	M	$6.66 × 10^6$	$7.1675 × 10^6$	Year: 2014
TOR	Giovinco	Sebastian	M	$5.6 × 10^6$	$7.11556 × 10^6$	Year: 2015
TOR	Giovinco	Sebastian	F	$5.6 × 10^6$	$7.11556 × 10^6$	Year: 2017
TOR	Giovinco	Sebastian	F	$5.6 × 10^6$	$7.11556 × 10^6$	Year: 2016
SEA	Dempsey	Clint	F	$4.913 × 10^6$	$6.69519 × 10^6$	Year: 2014
LA	Beckham	David	M	$5.5 × 10^6$	$6.5 × 10^6$	Year: 2011
LA	Beckham	David	M	$5.5 × 10^6$	$6.5 × 10^6$	Year: 2010

It turns out that Brazil's Kaka, Italy's Sebastian Giovinco, England's David Beckham and America's Clint Dempsey top the list.

Plotting

Let's create a scatter plot of the base salary versus the guaranteed compensation. I can do this using the Part function and then wrapping the results in ListPlot. Notice the use of All in the Part specification, which gets me all rows of the data. The {6, 7} gets me the fifth (base salary) and sixth (guaranteed compensation) column of each row. I've iconized the ListPlot options as they are inessential to what I am trying to show here.

Get two columns from the data and make a scatter plot with ListPlot:

In[ ]:= **ListPlot [mls2⟦All, { 5, 6 } ⟧, ⋯ ✦]**

Out[ ]=

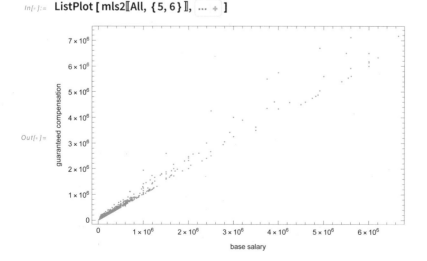

Sorting with Selection

It seems as if, for many players, the base compensation is the same as the guaranteed amount, but for others, the guaranteed amount is higher. I'd like to know the identity of players for whom the ratio between guaranteed amount and base amount is greatest. Here I use ReverseSortBy and Part to accomplish the job.

Combine ReverseSortBy and Part operators:

In[•]:= **Grid [Part [ReverseSortBy [mls2, ♯〚6〛 / ♯〚5〛 &] , Range [10]] , Dividers → All]**

Out[•]=

CHV	Courtois	Laurent	M	$60 000.00	$206 000.00	Year: 2011
TFC	Wynne	Marvell	D	$47 500.00	$150 000.00	Year: 2008
TFC	Wynne	Marvell	D	$47 500.00	$150 000.00	Year: 2007
TFC	White	O'Brian	F	$36 000.00	$113 000.00	Year: 2009
POR	Nagbe	Darlington	M / F	$65 000.00	$201 000.00	Year: 2011
POR	Okugo	Amobi	D–M	$65 004.00	$187 941.50	Year: 2017
TFC	Wynne	Marvell	D	$57 000.00	$159 500.00	Year: 2009
PHI	Stahl	Toni	M	$40 000.00	$110 300.00	Year: 2010
CLB	Duka	Dilaver	M	$80 000.00	$213 000.00	Year: 2010
TFC	Edu	Maurice	M	$50 000.00	$132 500.00	Year: 2007

By the way, where the desired Parts of an expression are adjacent to each other, I can use the Take function rather than Part.

Use Take when the Parts you want are adjacent:

In[•]:= **Take [ReverseSortBy [mls2, ♯〚6〛 / ♯〚5〛 &] , 10] === Part [ReverseSortBy [mls2, ♯〚6〛 / ♯〚5〛 &] , Range [10]]**

Out[•]= True

Gathering and Aggregating

Let's also see how total league payroll has varied over time. First, I gather the data together by year, which is in column seven. The result is a number of matrices, one for each year of the data, and each one of which has seven columns, just like the original matrix.

Use GatherBy to break up the data by year:

In[•]:= **Map [Dimensions, mlsByYear = GatherBy [mls2, ♯〚7〛 &]]**

Out[•]= { {371, 7}, {410, 7}, {388, 7}, {411, 7}, {525, 7}, {552, 7}, {573, 7}, {569, 7}, {570, 7}, {549, 7}, {614, 7} }

Now I get compensation and year information for each person in each year. The result is a List of matrices that have the same number of rows as the corresponding matrices in the input data but in which there are only two columns.

Grab the year and guaranteed compensation information for each year:

In[ ]:= **Map [Dimensions, mlsYearCompensation = mlsByYear⟦All, All, { 7, 6 } ⟧]**

Out[ ]= { {371, 2}, {410, 2}, {388, 2}, {411, 2}, {525, 2},
{552, 2}, {573, 2}, {569, 2}, {570, 2}, {549, 2}, {614, 2} }

Let's focus on one of these matrices.

Look at the first five rows of the first matrix:

In[ ]:= **mlsYearCompensation⟦1, Range [5] ⟧**

Out[ ]= {{ Year: 2007 , $225 000.00 }, { Year: 2007 , $12 900.00 }, { Year: 2007 , $48 712.50 },
{ Year: 2007 , $2.66678 × 10^6 }, { Year: 2007 , $106 391.00 }}

What I see is the year information is the same. This result is expected; the first matrix was created by gathering all the data from the first-confronted year together, so to create a relationship between year and total compensation, I just need the first column of the first row to get the year for the entire matrix. And I need the Total of the second column of each matrix to get the total compensation for that year. I use the Map function to do this for all the matrices.

I first define the function to be used to create the data structure.

Write a function to take a two-column matrix and get the top-left element and the Total of all the second-column elements:

In[ ]:= **yearTotal = matrix ⟼ { matrix⟦1, 1⟧, Total [matrix ⟦All, 2⟧] } ;**

Now use the operator form of Map to evaluate yearTotalCompensation over all the years:

In[ ]:= **mlsYearTotalCompensation = Map [yearTotal] [mlsYearCompensation]**

Out[ ]= {{ Year: 2007 , $4.22237 × 10^7 },
{ Year: 2008 , $4.72925 × 10^7 }, { Year: 2009 , $5.18781 × 10^7 },
{ Year: 2010 , $7.1305 × 10^7 }, { Year: 2011 , $8.50795 × 10^7 },
{ Year: 2012 , $9.91309 × 10^7 }, { Year: 2013 , $9.48496 × 10^7 },
{ Year: 2014 , $1.29335 × 10^8 }, { Year: 2015 , $1.67018 × 10^8 },
{ Year: 2016 , $1.75127 × 10^8 }, { Year: 2017 , $2.00394 × 10^8 }}

Now if I just wrap a DateListPlot around the result, I get an attractive graphic. Again, I iconize out the details.

Make a **DateListPlot** of total guaranteed compensation paid by year in MLS:

In[•]:= **DateListPlot [mlsYearTotalCompensation, ··· +]**

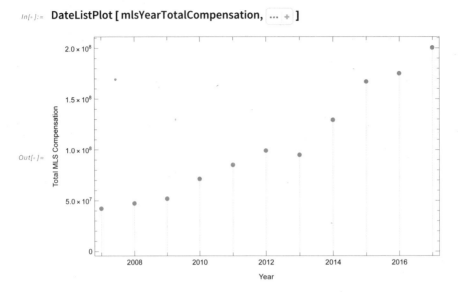

I'd also like to see if the same pattern holds for base salary, but now I'd like to put all the code together and do it in one step. Indeed, I'd like to do it using operator forms.

Let's graph using a DateListPlot:

In[•]:= **((⧣ ⟦All, All, { 7, 5 } ⟧ &) /* Map [yearTotal] /* (DateListPlot [⧣, ··· +] &)) [**
mlsByYear]

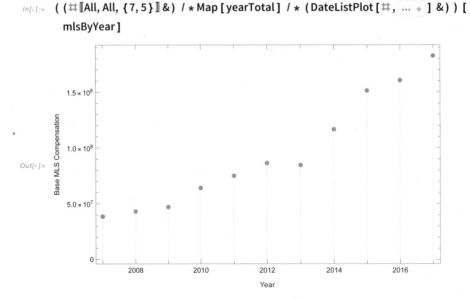

The pattern is indeed very similar.

From Gathering to Aggregating to Sorting

I wonder what teams had the highest payroll. Let's GatherBy team and year then total up the guaranteed compensation. I'll proceed in multiple steps though this could be written as a one-liner.

First, let's break down the number of players by year and by team. There ends up being 213 combinations.

Break down the MLS data by a combination of team and year:

In[•]:= **Dimensions [mlsByTeamYear = GatherBy [mls2, {#〚1〛, #〚7〛} &]]**

Out[•]= {213}

Let's get the Dimensions of each of these and see if, as I predict, they are all *n* rows by seven columns. To do this, I compute the Dimensions of each matrix and then Map a MatchQ operator over the results. The MatchQ operator in this example yields True if the expression it confronts is a List whose first element is some positive integer and whose last element is the number 7. I then Apply the And function to the resulting List of Boolean values to see if all the values are True.

Find out if the groups resulting from GatherBy have the same number of columns:

In[•]:= **Apply [And,**
     Map [MatchQ [{ _Integer ? Positive, 7 }] , Map [Dimensions, mlsByTeamYear]]]

Out[•]= True

Indeed, everything is an $n \times 7$ matrix of data. This finding suggests that if we took the sixth part of each row in each of these matrices and then totaled up the values, we'd get the desired result. Here's the sixth item in each row in each of the gathered rows.

Use a sequence of arguments to Part to retrieve data that has been subjected to GatherBy:

In[•]:= **(compensationsByTeamYear = Part [mlsByTeamYear, All, All, 6]) / / [•] Terse + [2]**

Out[•]//Short= {{ \$225 000.00 , \$12 900.00 , \$48 712.50 , \$2.66678 × 10^6 , \$106 391.00 ,

  \$58 008.00 , \$50 500.00 , \$151 500.00 , \$44 100.00 , \$12 900.00 , \$120 750.00 ,

  \$17 700.00 , \$187 500.00 , \$126 500.00 , \$136 000.00 , \$12 900.00 , \$17 700.00 ,

  \$12 900.00 , \$69 300.00 , \$32 340.00 , \$30 000.00 , \$42 500.00 , \$74 700.00 ,

  \$12 900.00 , \$50 800.00 , \$78 000.00 , \$36 625.00 , \$267 500.00 , \$12 900.00 },

  ≪211≫, { \$85 000.00 , \$253 500.00 , \$70 475.00 , \$65 000.00 , \$140 000.00 ,

  \$202 000.00 , \$183 833.33 , \$71 885.00 , \$73 800.00 , \$66 849.00 ,

  \$180 000.00 , \$131 250.00 , \$175 000.00 , \$885 500.00 , \$67 500.00 ,

  \$65 000.00 , \$120 000.00 , \$1.8 × 10^6 , \$65 004.00 , \$378 933.33 , \$99 600.00 ,

  \$533 700.04 , \$65 004.00 , \$65 004.00 , \$54 075.00 , \$670 000.00 , \$308 333.33 ,

  \$377 000.00 , \$194 000.00 , \$80 000.00 , \$368 125.00 , \$184 000.00 }}

Now I just Map the Total function over this:

In[·]:= (totalCompensationsByTeamYear = Map [Total, compensationsByTeamYear]) / / Short

Out[·]//Short= $\{$ 4.7163×10^6 , 1.78965×10^6 , 2.10823×10^6 , 2.2813×10^6 , 3.07276×10^6 ,

2.27639×10^6 , 2.43415×10^6 , 2.63755×10^6 , 9.32205×10^6 , 1.94585×10^6 ,

4.92809×10^6 , $83\,100.00$, 1.97425×10^6 , 2.65399×10^6 , 9.17767×10^6 ,

2.2153×10^6 , 2.45709×10^6 , 2.50338×10^6 , 3.36759×10^6 , $127\,200.00$,

2.55105×10^6 , 2.72648×10^6 , $\ll 169 \gg$, 1.29523×10^7 , 6.74754×10^6 ,

8.04062×10^6 , 6.82576×10^6 , 5.27245×10^6 , 5.09122×10^6 , 6.58835×10^6 ,

1.21829×10^7 , $118\,008.00$, 5.32286×10^6 , 5.29461×10^6 , 5.80012×10^6 ,

1.79304×10^7 , 6.89519×10^6 , 1.32192×10^7 , 7.11701×10^6 , 1.08241×10^7 ,

7.41936×10^6 , 1.03062×10^7 , 6.95929×10^6 , 2.23998×10^7 , 8.07937×10^6 $\}$

In some sense, I'm done, but the results aren't very meaningful because I don't know what team and years these values correspond to. Here's how I get that. I realize that the first and seventh part of each of the gathered rows has to be the same for each row: that's how the gathered rows were created, so if I look at just the first row of each grouping and take the first and seventh parts, I get the needed information.

Use Part to get the team and year associated with each payroll value:

In[·]:= (teamYears = Part [mlsByTeamYear, All, 1, {1, 7}]) / / Short

Out[·]//Short= $\{\{$CHI, Year: 2007 $\}$, $\ll 211 \gg$, $\{$VAN, ... 2017 $\}\}$

By using Thread, I can get the relationship I need. I'll ReverseSort the results based on total compensation so that the team with the biggest payroll comes first, and I'm done. Toronto, which had the highly compensated Sebastian Giovinco, Michael Bradley, and Jozy Altidore during the period 2015–2017, tops the list.

Use Thread and ReverseSortBy to put team-year data together with the total compensation such that the big payroll teams come up first:

In[·]:= **Take [ReverseSortBy [**
Thread [Rule [teamYears, totalCompensationsByTeamYear]] , Last] , 10]

Out[·]= $\{\{$TOR, Year: 2017 $\} \rightarrow$ 2.23998×10^7 , $\{$TOR, Year: 2015 $\} \rightarrow$ 2.21365×10^7 ,

$\{$TOR, Year: 2016 $\} \rightarrow$ 2.17985×10^7 , $\{$LA, Year: 2015 $\} \rightarrow$ 2.12676×10^7 ,

$\{$NYCFC, Year: 2016 $\} \rightarrow$ 2.11278×10^7 , $\{$LA, Year: 2016 $\} \rightarrow$ 1.81057×10^7 ,

$\{$NYCFC, Year: 2017 $\} \rightarrow$ 1.79304×10^7 , $\{$NYCFC, Year: 2015 $\} \rightarrow$ 1.74143×10^7 ,

$\{$NY, Year: 2012 $\} \rightarrow$ 1.67281×10^7 , $\{$TOR, Year: 2014 $\} \rightarrow$ 1.67126×10^7 $\}$

An Operator Approach to the Same Computations

Let's try these two latter computations again using operators. First, I'll recreate the graphic showing the total compensation time series. I start by writing a function that takes data and gathers elements together that share the same seventh element. The gathered rows are wrapped in a List.

Create an operator form for a specific application of GatherBy:

In[◦]:= **league1 = data ⟼ GatherBy [data , # ⟦7⟧ &] ;**

Here's how it works:

In[◦]:= **Map [Dimensions, league1 [mls2]]**

Out[◦]= { {371, 7}, {410, 7}, {388, 7}, {411, 7}, {525, 7},
　　　　{552, 7}, {573, 7}, {569, 7}, {570, 7}, {549, 7}, {614, 7} }

Next, I create an operator that extracts the seventh and sixth parts of every row (second All) of every matrix (first All) that it confronts.

Create an operator form to get certain parts of data:

In[◦]:= **league2 = data ⟼ data⟦All, All, {7, 6}⟧;**

I'll RightCompose that operator with league1. Now I get matrices of varying lengths but that each have just two columns.

Apply a RightComposition of two functions to the MLS data:

In[◦]:= **Map [Dimensions, (league1 /* league2) [mls2]]**

Out[◦]= { {371, 2}, {410, 2}, {388, 2}, {411, 2}, {525, 2},
　　　　{552, 2}, {573, 2}, {569, 2}, {570, 2}, {549, 2}, {614, 2} }

Now I'll create an operator that takes a list of matrices, and for each one, generates a pair of values in a List. The first element of the output list is the first column of the first row of the matrix. The second element is the total of all elements in the second column. Note that I use the operator form of Map to do this.

Create an operator that turns a matrix into a List:

In[◦]:= **league3 = Map [matrix ⟼ { matrix ⟦1, 1⟧, Total [matrix ⟦All, 2⟧] }] ;**

Again, I add the new operator to our RightComposition pipeline.

Make a three-function pipeline using RightComposition and apply it to the MLS data:

In[•]:= (league1 /* league2 /* league3) [mls2]

Out[•]= {{ | Year: 2007 |, 4.22237×10^7 },

{ | Year: 2008 |, 4.72925×10^7 }, { | Year: 2009 |, 5.18781×10^7 },

{ | Year: 2010 |, 7.1305×10^7 }, { | Year: 2011 |, 8.50795×10^7 },

{ | Year: 2012 |, 9.91309×10^7 }, { | Year: 2013 |, 9.48496×10^7 },

{ | Year: 2014 |, 1.29335×10^8 }, { | Year: 2015 |, 1.67018×10^8 },

{ | Year: 2016 |, 1.75127×10^8 }, { | Year: 2017 |, 2.00394×10^8 }}}

Finally, I add to the pipeline an operator I won't bother naming that makes a DateListPlot. I've iconized some of the inessential options of the DateListPlot function.

Add an operator form of DateListPlot to the pipeline to show compensation trends:

In[•]:= (league1 /* league2 /* league3 /* (DateListPlot [#, ... ⊕] &)) [mls2]

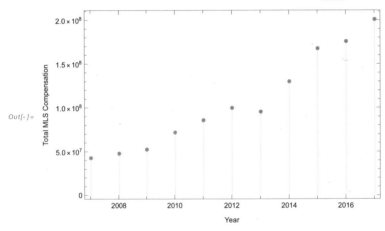

Now I recreate the ranking of teams and years with total compensation using operators. The first operator this time is one that takes data and gathers it according to its first and then seventh parts.

Create another special operator form of GatherBy:

In[•]:= team1 = GatherBy [#, { #⟦1⟧, #⟦7⟧ } &] &;

If I apply it, I get that List of 213 matrices:

In[•]:= Dimensions [(team1) [mls2]]

Out[•]= {213}

The second operator creates a pair of values as a List. The first element is the first (team) and seventh (year) elements of the first row of the data. The second element is the sixth (guaranteed compensation) element of each row of each grouping within the data.

Write an operator that takes a List of matrices and produces a List:

In[•]:= **team2 = ({ Part [#, All, 1, {1, 7}], Part [#, All, All, 6] } &) ;**

I now create a RightComposition of team1 and team2 and apply it to the data. The first element of the created List has the dimensions of 213 rows by two columns (the team and the year). The second element contains salary data for all the players on the team that year.

RightComposition of team1 and team2; use the AugmentedTerse ResourceFunction to compress the output and show its dimensionality:

In[•]:= **Map [[•] AugmentedTerse + [1], (team1 / * team2) [mls2]]**

Out[•]= $\{\{\{$CHI, Year: 2007 $\}, \{$CHV, Year: 2007 $\}, \ll210\gg, \{$VAN, Year: 2017 $\}\}, \{213, 2\}\}$,

$\{\{\{ \$225\,000.00 , \$12\,900.00 , \$48\,712.50 , \$2.66678 \times 10^6 , \$106\,391.00 , \$58\,008.00 ,$

$\$50\,500.00 , \$151\,500.00 , \$44\,100.00 , \$12\,900.00 , \$120\,750.00 , \$17\,700.00 ,$

$\$187\,500.00 , \$126\,500.00 , \$136\,000.00 , \$12\,900.00 , \$17\,700.00 ,$

$\$12\,900.00 , \$69\,300.00 , \$32\,340.00 , \$30\,000.00 , \$42\,500.00 , \$74\,700.00 ,$

$\$12\,900.00 , \$50\,800.00 , \$78\,000.00 , \$36\,625.00 , \$267\,500.00 , \$12\,900.00 \}$,

$\ll211\gg, \{ \$85\,000.00 , \$253\,500.00 , \$70\,475.00 , \$65\,000.00 , \$140\,000.00 ,$

$\$202\,000.00 , \$183\,833.33 , \$71\,885.00 , \$73\,800.00 , \$66\,849.00 ,$

$\$180\,000.00 , \$131\,250.00 , \$175\,000.00 , \$885\,500.00 , \$67\,500.00 ,$

$\$65\,000.00 , \$120\,000.00 , \$1.8 \times 10^6 , \$65\,004.00 , \$378\,933.33 , \$99\,600.00 ,$

$\$533\,700.04 , \$65\,004.00 , \$65\,004.00 , \$54\,075.00 , \$670\,000.00 , \$308\,333.33 ,$

$\$377\,000.00 , \$194\,000.00 , \$80\,000.00 , \$368\,125.00 , \$184\,000.00 \}\}, \{213\}\}\}$

The third operator does nothing to the first part of its data but computes the Total of the second part. I can use MapAt to perform this task. The Part specification says to take the second element of the List and to Total all elements of it.

Use MapAt to apply a function only to all parts of the second part of an expression:

In[•]:= **team3 = MapAt [Total, { 2, All }] ;**

I now create a RightComposition of team1, team2, and team3. The result is a List in which the first element is again the List of team-years and the second element is the total salaries for that team-year.

RightComposition of team1, team2, and team3; use the AugmentedTerse ResourceFunction to compress the output and show its dimensionality:

In[·]:= **Map [[▪] AugmentedTerse + [1] , (team1 / ∗ team2 / ∗ team3) [mls2]]**

Out[·]= $\{\{\{\text{CHI},\ \boxed{\text{Year: 2007}}\},\{\text{CHV},\ \boxed{\text{Year: 2007}}\},\ll210\gg,\{\text{VAN},\ \boxed{\text{Year: 2017}}\}\},\{213,2\}\},$

$\{\{\$4.7163\times10^6\ ,\ \$1.78965\times10^6\ ,\ \$2.10823\times10^6\ ,\ \$2.2813\times10^6\ ,\ \$3.07276\times10^6\ ,$

$\$2.27639\times10^6\ ,\ \$2.43415\times10^6\ ,\ \$2.63755\times10^6\ ,\ \$9.32205\times10^6\ ,\ \$1.94585\times10^6\ ,$

$\$4.92809\times10^6\ ,\ \$83\,100.00\ ,\ \$1.97425\times10^6\ ,\ \$2.65399\times10^6\ ,\ \$9.17767\times10^6\ ,$

$\$2.2153\times10^6\ ,\ \$2.45709\times10^6\ ,\ \$2.50338\times10^6\ ,\ \$3.36759\times10^6\ ,\ \$127\,200.00\ ,$

$\$2.55105\times10^6\ ,\ \$2.72648\times10^6\ ,\ \$2.55306\times10^6\ ,\ \$2.51595\times10^6\ ,\ \$4.80817\times10^6\ ,$

$\$2.41838\times10^6\ ,\ \$2.48785\times10^6\ ,\ \$4.88167\times10^6\ ,\ \$2.37268\times10^6\ ,\ \$129\,000.00\ ,$

$\$2.778\times10^6\ ,\ \$2.20004\times10^6\ ,\ \$3.27887\times10^6\ ,\ \$3.40721\times10^6\ ,\ \$2.1162\times10^6\ ,$

$\$3.54934\times10^6\ ,\ \$2.24655\times10^6\ ,\ \$2.61414\times10^6\ ,\ \$4.15217\times10^6\ ,$

$\$2.69583\times10^6\ ,\ \$2.43012\times10^6\ ,\ll132\gg,\ \$5.20566\times10^6\ ,\ \$5.67416\times10^6\ ,$

$\$6.75245\times10^6\ ,\ \$1.81057\times10^7\ ,\ \$6.74101\times10^6\ ,\ \$5.98084\times10^6\ ,$

$\$2.11278\times10^7\ ,\ \$5.82985\times10^6\ ,\ \$1.15544\times10^7\ ,\ \$5.67432\times10^6\ ,\ \$62\,500.00\ ,$

$\$6.83354\times10^6\ ,\ \$5.9569\times10^6\ ,\ \$1.07288\times10^7\ ,\ \$6.4094\times10^6\ ,\ \$2.17985\times10^7\ ;$

$\$6.5656\times10^6\ ,\ \$9.00776\times10^6\ ,\ \$1.29523\times10^7\ ,\ \$6.74754\times10^6\ ,\ \$8.04062\times10^6\ ,$

$\$6.82576\times10^6\ ,\ \$5.27245\times10^6\ ,\ \$5.09122\times10^6\ ,\ \$6.58835\times10^6\ ,\ \$1.21829\times10^7\ ,$

$\$118\,008.00\ ,\ \$5.32286\times10^6\ ,\ \$5.29461\times10^6\ ,\ \$5.80012\times10^6\ ,\ \$1.79304\times10^7\ ,$

$\$6.89519\times10^6\ ,\ \$1.32192\times10^7\ ,\ \$7.11701\times10^6\ ,\ \$1.08241\times10^7\ ,\ \$7.41936\times10^6\ ,$

$\$1.03062\times10^7\ ,\ \$6.95929\times10^6\ ,\ \$2.23998\times10^7\ ,\ \$8.07937\times10^6\ \},\{213\}\}\}$

Our fourth operator Threads the first element of a List over the second element of a List using Rule.

Use Thread to create an operator form:

In[·]:= **team4 = Thread [Rule [♯ [[1]], ♯ [[2]]]] &;**

Our fifth operator performs ReverseSortBy using the Last element and then takes the first 10 values.

Create an operator that takes the 10 rows of data with the highest Last values:

In[·]:= **team5 = data ⟼ Take [ReverseSortBy [data , Last] , 10] ;**

And I make a big RightComposition and get exactly the result I want.

Create a five-operator pipeline and get the teams with the highest payrolls:

In[ ]:= (team1 /* team2 /* team3 /* team4 /* team5) [mls2]

Out[ ]= $\Big\{\Big\{$TOR, $\boxed{\text{Year: 2017}}\Big\} \to$ \$2.23998 × 10^7 , $\Big\{$TOR, $\boxed{\text{Year: 2015}}\Big\} \to$ \$2.21365 × 10^7 ,

$\Big\{$TOR, $\boxed{\text{Year: 2016}}\Big\} \to$ \$2.17985 × 10^7 , $\Big\{$LA, $\boxed{\text{Year: 2015}}\Big\} \to$ \$2.12676 × 10^7 ,

$\Big\{$NYCFC, $\boxed{\text{Year: 2016}}\Big\} \to$ \$2.11278 × 10^7 , $\Big\{$LA, $\boxed{\text{Year: 2016}}\Big\} \to$ \$1.81057 × 10^7 ,

$\Big\{$NYCFC, $\boxed{\text{Year: 2017}}\Big\} \to$ \$1.79304 × 10^7 , $\Big\{$NYCFC, $\boxed{\text{Year: 2015}}\Big\} \to$ \$1.74143 × 10^7 ,

$\Big\{$NY, $\boxed{\text{Year: 2012}}\Big\} \to$ \$1.67281 × 10^7 , $\Big\{$TOR, $\boxed{\text{Year: 2014}}\Big\} \to$ \$1.67126 × 10$^7\Big\}$

Alternatively, I could give the RightComposition a name and apply it.

Name a RightComposition of functions:

In[ ]:= **biggestPayrolls = (team1 /* team2 /* team3 /* team4 /* team5)**

Out[ ]= GatherBy [#1, {#1〚1〛, #1〚7〛} &] /* ({#1〚All, 1, {1, 7} 〛, #1〚All, All, 6〛} &) /*
MapAt [Total, {2, All}] /* (Thread [#1〚1〛 → #1〚2〛] &) /*
Function [data, Take [ReverseSortBy [data, Last], 10]]

Apply a named RightComposition to the data:

In[ ]:= **biggestPayrolls [mls2]**

Out[ ]= $\Big\{\Big\{$TOR, $\boxed{\text{Year: 2017}}\Big\} \to$ \$2.23998 × 10^7 , $\Big\{$TOR, $\boxed{\text{Year: 2015}}\Big\} \to$ \$2.21365 × 10^7 ,

$\Big\{$TOR, $\boxed{\text{Year: 2016}}\Big\} \to$ \$2.17985 × 10^7 , $\Big\{$LA, $\boxed{\text{Year: 2015}}\Big\} \to$ \$2.12676 × 10^7 ,

$\Big\{$NYCFC, $\boxed{\text{Year: 2016}}\Big\} \to$ \$2.11278 × 10^7 , $\Big\{$LA, $\boxed{\text{Year: 2016}}\Big\} \to$ \$1.81057 × 10^7 ,

$\Big\{$NYCFC, $\boxed{\text{Year: 2017}}\Big\} \to$ \$1.79304 × 10^7 , $\Big\{$NYCFC, $\boxed{\text{Year: 2015}}\Big\} \to$ \$1.74143 × 10^7 ,

$\Big\{$NY, $\boxed{\text{Year: 2012}}\Big\} \to$ \$1.67281 × 10^7 , $\Big\{$TOR, $\boxed{\text{Year: 2014}}\Big\} \to$ \$1.67126 × 10$^7\Big\}$

Conclusion

There's obviously a lot more I could do with our data, but this isn't a study of Major League Soccer and it isn't the end of our study of data analysis. In fact, as I will show in a later chapter, it will prove considerably easier to do these sorts of computations once we have features such as **Association**, **Dataset**, and **Query** available. In the meantime, though, I hope you have appreciated the power of even the old-school Wolfram Language in dealing with data and, critically, an operator-focused style of programming.

Exercises

2.1 Here is a list of expressions: $\{-46, 7, p[4], p[3, 4], p[2, q[5, 6]], 4+7\,i, \frac{9}{10}\}$. Which of them can you successfully use **Part** on and which generate an error message?

2.2 Write a function that takes a **List**, such as $\{3, 5\}$, and computes the absolute value of the difference between the two numbers. Here the right answer would be 2. Hint 1: The function for computing absolute value is **Abs**. Hint 2: Your function should use **Part**.

2.3 Use **Total** and **Map** to compute the sum of the absolute value of the differences between the following pairs of numbers $\{\{3, 5\}, \{8, 9\}, \{6, 6\}, \{-2, 11\}\}$. You should get 16.

2.4 The Manhattan distance between two points is the sum of the absolute value of the differences in the x coordinates and y coordinates. So, if one point is at $\{2, 9\}$ and the other point is at $\{5, 1\}$, the absolute value of the differences are 3 and 8 and the Manhattan distance is 11. Find me the Manhattan distance between the points given below. Hint: You should probably use **Thread** or **Transpose**. (There is a built-in **ManhattanDistance** function; it would be clever to use it, but you would lose the educational benefits of the exercise.)

```
point1 = {4, 12};
point2 = {3, 5};
```

These next exercises ask you to use the MLS data. I'd suggest you evaluate the code that creates the mls2 variable and use it.

2.5 Augment the matrix of information contained in **mls2** by inserting a first column that numbers the players from 1 to 4899.

2.6 Find the base salary of the last player in the **mls2** data.

2.7 Find the median base salary of all the players in the **mls2** data.

2.8 Find the **Mean** difference between the guaranteed compensation and base salary for all players in the mls2 data. Then do the same computation but **Select** only players whose last names are not equal to Beckham. The **Unequal** operator in the Wolfram Language is !=.

2.9 Here's some code that would let you find rows of the MLS dataset that are from 2009:

Select [# [[7]] == Year: 2009 &] [mls2] . Find me the player on the Houston Dynamo team with the highest guaranteed compensation in 2009. Hint: Your answer output should be $\{$Ricardo, Clark$\}$.

2.10 What team-year combination had the highest number of players with base salaries over \$250,000? Hint: To write \$250,000 use Quantity [250000, "USDollars"] .

Tech Notes

- I used TreeForm to show the structure of a Wolfram Language expression. Another alternative is to use FullForm, which is kind of how the kernel thinks about an expression. In FullForm, no syntactic sugar is used and the structure of the expression is made explicit. Here I compare how one might represent the solution to a quadratic equation in InputForm (the way a user might type it), in FullForm (the way the kernel thinks about it), and in TreeForm (an easier-to-read variant of FullForm).

In[·]:= {InputForm[Solve[a z² + b z + c == 0, z]], FullForm[Solve[a z² + b z + c == 0, z]],
      TreeForm[Solve[a z² + b z + c == 0, z], ImageSize → 400]} // Framed

Out[·]=

- At several points in this chapter (and this book), I use glyphs like ↦ that may seem impossible to type on a keyboard. There are several ways of typing these glyphs. The first is to use the escape code representation for the glyph. For example, typing ⎡esc⎤ fn ⎡esc⎤ produces the function arrow. A second method is to use the \[method. If I type \[and then immediately follow it with the characters Function], I get the function arrow.

- At several points in this chapter (and this book), I make use of ResourceFunctions. These are functions stored in the Wolfram Function Repository (wolfr.am/WFR) that, while not part of the official Wolfram Language, have been sufficiently vetted and documented to be deemed worthy of public use. To retrieve a known ResourceFunction, you just encapsulate a string representation of the function's name in the ResourceFunction header.

In[·]:= **ResourceFunction["SameAsQ"]**

Out[·]= [■] SameAsQ ✦

- If you have internet access at the time you evaluate this, a search will be done of various locations and an icon representing the function will be returned. To use the function in the Wolfram Language front end, you can either use a mouse to cut the iconized representation of the function and paste it where it needs to be used or you can eschew the mouse and just type ResourceFunction ["SameAsQ"] , so you could write either of the following. You could also select the input ResourceFunction ["SameAsQ"] and use the **Evaluate in Place** menu command to get an attractive iconized representation of the function.

In[•]:=   { ⬡ SameAsQ + [4] [2 + 2] , ResourceFunction ["SameAsQ"] [4] [2 + 2] }

Out[•]=   { True, True }

- There is now an operator form for **Part**, although one has to access the Wolfram Function Repository to get it easily. It is ResourceFunction ["Slice"] . Here are examples of the way the function works.

In[•]:=   { ⬡ Slice + [3] [{ "a", "b", "c", "d" }] , ⬡ Slice + [2, 1] [g [8, h [x, y, 9]]] ,
       ⬡ Slice + [All, 2] [{ { ▪, 5, 0.08, GeoPosition [{ −4, 86 }] , "Thurgood Marshall" } ,
            { ▪, 2, 0.83, GeoPosition [{ −43, −113 }] , "Elena Kagan" } ,
            { ▪, 4, 0.07, GeoPosition [{ −22, −40 }] , "Oliver Ellsworth" } ,
            { ▪, 4, 0.35, GeoPosition [{17, 78}] , "William Rehnquist" } ,
            { ▪, 9, 0.87, GeoPosition [{14, 64}] , "Oliver Wendell Holmes, Jr." } }] }

Out[•]=   { c, x, {5, 2, 4, 4, 9} }

- With Version 13, there are convenient ways to create Lists whose elements are homogeneous in their types. Here, for example, I represent the second column of **nestedList** as a **NumericArray** of signed integers with 16 possible binary digits. When speed or data size is at a premium, this ability may prove useful.

In[•]:=   **NumericArray [nestedList⟦All, 2⟧, "SignedInteger16"]**

Out[•]=   NumericArray[⊞ Type: Integer16
                       Dimensions: {5}]

- In the main text, I just showed **MapIndexed** where the **Part** indices reflected what was on level 1 of the expression, but I can also ask for it to use **Part** indices reflecting what is in deeper levels of an expression. Here I ask it to find those Parts at level 2 of the expression and then, for each one, apply the **f** function to a sequence of arguments, the first of which is the original **Part** and the second of which is its position in the original expression.

In[•]:=   **MapIndexed [f, g [8, h [x, y, 9]] , {2}]**

Out[•]=   g [8, h [f [x, {2, 1}] , f [y, {2, 2}] , f [9, {2, 3}]]]

- Most of the time in this book and in Wolfram Language code generally, it is conventional to use prefix notation and write the operator first, f{ [x, y] } , but it is sometimes useful to put the operator last. To use this postfix notation, you use the double slash, { x, y } //f. I find that postfix notation complements well the use of Right Composition, so I could write the following.

In[∘]:= **mls2 / / (team1 / ∗ team2 / ∗ team3 / ∗ team4 / ∗ team5)**

Out[∘]= $\Big\{\Big\{$TOR, $\boxed{\text{Year: 2017}}\Big\} \rightarrow \$2.23998 \times 10^7$, $\Big\{$TOR, $\boxed{\text{Year: 2015}}\Big\} \rightarrow \$2.21365 \times 10^7$,

$\Big\{$TOR, $\boxed{\text{Year: 2016}}\Big\} \rightarrow \$2.17985 \times 10^7$, $\Big\{$LA, $\boxed{\text{Year: 2015}}\Big\} \rightarrow \$2.12676 \times 10^7$,

$\Big\{$NYCFC, $\boxed{\text{Year: 2016}}\Big\} \rightarrow \$2.11278 \times 10^7$, $\Big\{$LA, $\boxed{\text{Year: 2016}}\Big\} \rightarrow \$1.81057 \times 10^7$,

$\Big\{$NYCFC, $\boxed{\text{Year: 2017}}\Big\} \rightarrow \$1.79304 \times 10^7$, $\Big\{$NYCFC, $\boxed{\text{Year: 2015}}\Big\} \rightarrow \$1.74143 \times 10^7$,

$\Big\{$NY, $\boxed{\text{Year: 2012}}\Big\} \rightarrow \$1.67281 \times 10^7$, $\Big\{$TOR, $\boxed{\text{Year: 2014}}\Big\} \rightarrow \$1.67126 \times 10^7\Big\}$

Visually, this looks more like a pipeline: start with mls2 and then feed it team1, then feed it team2, etc. I can't do mls2 / ∗ (team1 / ∗team2 / ∗team3 / ∗team4 / ∗team5) because mls2 is not itself a function.

3 | Association

This chapter uses a data resource from the Wolfram Data Repository (wolfr.am/WDR). To access the data, evaluate the following code.

Acquire the **ResourceObject** from the Wolfram Data Repository:

In[ ]:= **ro = ResourceObject ["Sample Data for Query Book"]**

Out[ ]= ResourceObject[🏛 Name: Sample Data for Query Book »
Type: DataResource
Description: Data to support the Wolfram Media book Query:
Getting Information from Data wit...]

In a traditional Wolfram Language expression, one automatically gets to access components of that expression through the Part function (or its cousins like Take and Drop) and through an automatic indexing between those components and integers (or a list of integers), so to get the second part of { "a", "b" }, I don't have to tell Mathematica anything. It already knows that "a" is Part 1 and "b" is Part 2. Indeed, I couldn't change that even if I wanted to.

This system works quite well, but it has at least one shortcoming. It requires a good deal of human memory. If I have, for example, a matrix of employee data in which each row contains seven elements, I might have to remember that the salary information is contained in column five. Now, of course this might not be too burdensome if there were just seven columns in the data. Perhaps I could manage that, but even those with great memories might be challenged where, as is often the case, each row of data contains one hundred or one thousand values.

Association is the Wolfram Language construction created as of Version 10 to solve this problem (and do more as well). It lets one create a correspondence between the values in a List-like data structure and names that are called keys. Association is similar (though not identical) to containers from other computer languages, such as Consed pairs, Dicts, Dictionary, Hashes, Keylists, Maps, HashMaps, Associative Arrays, and Key-Value pairs (or stores).

A Home-Brewed Indexed Data Structure

Before turning to the real Association, it's worth considering how one might brew it oneself. What I would likely need to do is set up some sort of correspondence between the integers and some descriptive account of the columns. Thus, if I revert to the Major League Soccer (MLS) data discussed in a prior chapter, I could write it down in some sort of code book, or, if I felt more programmatically inclined, I might write a set of rules like this.

Create rules that enumerate column names:

In[ ]:= **soccerColumnIndex = { "team" → 1, "lastName" → 2, "firstName" → 3,**
     "position" → 4, "baseSalary" → 5, "guaranteedSalary" → 6, "year" → 7}

Out[ ]= { team → 1, lastName → 2, firstName → 3,
     position → 4, baseSalary → 5, guaranteedSalary → 6, year → 7 }

Then, when I want to extract information on a player's salary, I might do something like this.

Use substitution rules to convert column names into integers:

In[ ]:= **Part [{ "HOU", "Ching", "Brian", "F", $220 000.00 , $220 000.00 , Year: 2007 },**
     "baseSalary" /. soccerColumnIndex]

Out[ ]= $220 000.00

However, having to do this every time I want to access data is rather cumbersome. Moreover, for better or worse, the indexing information becomes decoupled from the data.

The Association

These issues, and others, give rise to Association, in which the user basically gets to tightly couple their own desired names (the "keys") to the values in the expression. An Association is written as a sequence or List of Rules in which the left-hand sides represent the "keys" (kind of like Part numbers), and the right-hand sides represent the "values." Each Rule in the sequence is often known as a key-value pair. The Head of the expression is Association.

For something like the MLS data, one would write the following. I'm going to reuse this example, so I assign it to the variable chingAssociation.

An Association uses Rules wrapped with the Head Association:

In[ ]:= **chingAssociation = Association ["team" → "HOU", "lastName" → "Ching",**
"firstName" → "Brian", "position" → "F", "baseSalary" → $220 000 ,
"guaranteedSalary" → $220 000 , "year" → Year: 2007 **] ;**

I could equivalently have created a List of Rules rather than a sequence. The Wolfram Language would basically unwrap the List and create a sequence.

Another way to do it:

In[ ]:= **Association [{ "team" → "HOU", "lastName" → "Ching",**
"firstName" → "Brian", "position" → "F", "baseSalary" → $220 000 ,
"guaranteedSalary" → $220 000 , "year" → Year: 2007 **}] === chingAssociation**

Out[ ]= True

Using Part with Association

I can continue to remember that, for example, base salary is the fifth key-value pair in the chingAssociation data structure, so I can still use Part with integer arguments.

The key-value pairs in an Association have numbers that can be used for extraction:

In[ ]:= **Part [chingAssociation, 5]**

Out[ ]= $220 000

But now I don't have to remember that base salary is in the fifth position or set up an explicit index like soccerColumnIndex. Instead, I can directly use the Part function.

The key-value pairs in an Association can be referenced by the name of the key wrapped in Key:

In[ ]:= **Part [chingAssociation, Key ["baseSalary"]]**

Out[ ]= $220 000

Or I can use double-square-bracket notation ([[...]]).

Double square brackets are syntactic sugar for Part:

In[ ]:= **chingAssociation⟦Key ["baseSalary"] ⟧**

Out[ ]= $220 000

If the key is a string, I don't have to wrap the key in Key. The Wolfram Language figures it out for me. Thus, both of these work. This syntactic sugar is one reason that people very frequently use strings as keys in their Associations.

The Key wrapper can be omitted if the Key is a string:

In[ ]:= **{Part[chingAssociation, "baseSalary"], chingAssociation⟦"baseSalary"⟧}**

Out[ ]= **{ $220 000 , $220 000 }**

There is more syntactic sugar for Associations that many people like. It's similar to the idea of using { ... } to enclose Lists rather than writing List and then enclosing the arguments in [...]. For Associations, one uses ‹| ... |› to enclose the arguments.

Using ‹| ... |› to wrap a List or Sequence of Rules creates an Association:

In[ ]:= **‹| "team" → "HOU", "lastName" → "Ching", "firstName" → "Brian", "position" → "F",**
"baseSalary" → $220 000 , "guaranteedSalary" → $220 000 , "year" → | Year: 2007 | |› ;

Even if I change the order of these key-value pairs within the Association, the command works the same. Here I move the base salary key-value pair to the beginning, but the Part function doesn't care. It works.

Results are invariant to key-value pair order within the Association when one uses a key (rather than an integer) for access:

In[ ]:= **chingAssociation2 = Association ["baseSalary" → $220 000 ,**
"team" → "HOU", "lastName" → "Ching", "firstName" → "Brian",
"position" → "F", "guaranteedSalary" → $220 000 , "year" → | Year: 2007 |] ;

In[ ]:= **chingAssociation2⟦"baseSalary"⟧**

Out[ ]= **$220 000**

I can extract multiple parts the same as with traditional expressions.

Multiple key-value pairs can be accessed with a single Part function:

In[ ]:= **chingAssociation2⟦ { "baseSalary", "position" } ⟧**

Out[ ]= **‹| baseSalary → $220 000 , position → F |›**

The output is an Association, so I can continue to reference components using the keys.

Part preserves the Association Head:

In[ ]:= **chingAssociation2⟦ { "baseSalary", "position" } ⟧⟦"position"⟧**

Out[ ]= **F**

Indeed, using the Keys is a more robust way of retrieving information from an Association. If, for example, I think that the base salary information is contained in column 5, I will get the right answer if I use that on chingAssociation, but I will get the wrong answer if I use it on chingAssociation2, so where one is uncertain about the order of key-value pairs within an Association, using integer representations for Part is a very bad idea.

The Keys function yields the keys of an Association:

In[◦]:=   **{ Part [chingAssociation, 5] , Part [chingAssociation2, 5] }**

Out[◦]:= $\left\{ \$220\,000 , F \right\}$

Keys gets the keys of an Association:

In[◦]:=   **Keys [chingAssociation]**

Out[◦]:=   { team, lastName, firstName, position, baseSalary, guaranteedSalary, year }

The Values function yields the values of an Association.

Values gets the values of an Association:

In[◦]:=   **Values [chingAssociation]**

Out[◦]:= $\left\{ \text{HOU, Ching, Brian, F,}\ \$220\,000, \ \$220\,000, \boxed{\text{Year: } 2007} \right\}$

The Normal function yields the key-value pairs as rules stripped of the Association Head.

Normal converts Association into a List of Rules:

In[◦]:=   **Normal [chingAssociation]**

Out[◦]:= $\Big\{$ team → HOU, lastName → Ching, firstName → Brian, position → F,

  baseSalary → $\$220\,000$, guaranteedSalary → $\$220\,000$, year → $\boxed{\text{Year: } 2007}$ $\Big\}$

These expressions, of course, can be further manipulated. Here I sort the keys by their number of characters.

SortBy works on the values of an Association:

In[◦]:=   **SortBy [Keys [chingAssociation] , StringLength]**

Out[◦]:=   { team, year, lastName, position, firstName, baseSalary, guaranteedSalary }

With KeySortBy, one can also sort based on the keys. Here I sort the key-value pairs based on the number of bytes consumed by the key. In a succeeding chapter, I'll show that KeySort can be surprisingly useful when dealing with Datasets.

Use KeySortBy to sort key-value pairs based on the key:

In[◦]:=   **KeySortBy [chingAssociation, ByteCount]**

Out[◦]:= $\Big\langle \Big|$ team → HOU, year → $\boxed{\text{Year: } 2007}$, baseSalary → $\$220\,000$, firstName → Brian,

  lastName → Ching, position → F, guaranteedSalary → $\$220\,000$ $\Big| \Big\rangle$

In theory, I can use most Wolfram Language expressions for either a Key or a Value in the Association. And neither the Keys nor Values within an Association have to be of the same type. Thus, this is a nutty but perfectly valid Association.

One can use almost any Wolfram Language expression as a key:

In[•]:= **nutty = ⟨| 8 → 1, { 1, 2, 3, 4, 5, 6 } → 23, 4.5` → True,**

    2 → `Mon 1 Jan 1900 00:33:39 GMT–5.` **, "stringkey" → 8, False → π, "a" → 6, "b" → "gee" |⟩**

Out[•]= ⟨| 8 → 1, { 1, 2, 3, 4, 5, 6 } → 23, 4.5 → True,

    2 → `Mon 1 Jan 1900 00:33:39 GMT–5` , stringkey → 8, False → π, a → 6, b → gee |⟩

I can extract components as before.

Wrapping Key around exotic keys often permits extraction with Part:

In[•]:= **{ nutty⟦Key [4.5] ⟧, nutty⟦Key [8] ⟧, nutty⟦Key [Range [6]] ⟧, nutty⟦Key [False] ⟧}**

Out[•]= { True, 1, 23, π }

I would ordinarily recommend avoiding this degree of creativity. There are other crucial capabilities of Associations that face challenges unless the Key is a non-negative integer or a string.

Functions on Associations

A function can have an Association as an argument. Thus, one can clearly do the following.

Functions can work on Associations:

In[•]:= **{ Length [chingAssociation] , Reverse [chingAssociation] }**

Out[•]= {7, ⟨| year → `Year: 2007` , guaranteedSalary → $220 000 , baseSalary → $220 000 ,

    position → F, firstName → Brian, lastName → Ching, team → HOU |⟩}

One can also have a function that works on the values of an Association. To do so, the best way is to use a variant of the Slot function. Here's a function that gets the difference between the guaranteed salary and the base salary. I'm going to write it out very explicitly. In a few moments, I'll show syntactic sugar that simplifies the input.

Use Slot to make functions that work on particular values within an Association, not the entire Association:

In[•]:= **bonus = Function [Slot ["guaranteedSalary"] – Slot ["baseSalary"]] ;**

I can now apply the bonus function to the chingAssociation:

In[•]:= **bonus [chingAssociation]**

Out[•]= $0

What you see is that instead of having numbers as Slot arguments, there are strings that correspond to keys in the Association, and you also see that the function operates on the values in the Association. Most functions do not operate on the keys (in the same way that most Wolfram Language functions do not operate on the Part indices of a traditional expression). Also, notice that one does *not* surround the string with the function Key. The Wolfram Language already assumes that the stuff inside Slot is a Key.

Here's the first piece of syntactic sugar for functions that work on Associations. Just as one can write Slot[3] as ♯3, one can write Slot["*something*"] as ♯ "*something*" or ♯ *something*. Here's an example.

The ♯ can be used to denote a Slot function:

In[•]:= **♯"position" & [chingAssociation]**

Out[•]= F

One can write complex functions using this ♯ syntax:

In[•]:= **{ StringJoin [♯"firstName", " ", ♯"lastName"] , ♯"guaranteedSalary" } & [chingAssociation]**

Out[•]= { Brian Ching, $220 000 }

Indeed, if the string argument to Slot could have been a Wolfram Language symbol, then there's a nice piece of syntactic sugar that can be applied: get rid of the quotation marks.

If the key name could have been a symbol, quotation marks aren't needed with ♯:

In[•]:= **{ StringJoin [♯firstName, " ", ♯lastName] , ♯guaranteedSalary } & [chingAssociation]**

Out[•]= { Brian Ching, $220 000 }

This is enough of an advantage that I generally try to convert keys that have an annoying space in them that prevents them from being used as a symbol into their camel case variant, for example, "base salary" would become "baseSalary". Note, though, that if one is using Slot explicitly instead of ♯, one must keep the quotation marks.

The following code fails because quotation marks were not used:

In[•]:= **bonusFail = Function [Slot [guaranteedSalary] − Slot [baseSalary]] ;**

⋯ Function : Slot [guaranteedSalary] (in Slot [guaranteedSalary] − Slot [baseSalary] &) should contain a
non −negative integer or string.

Associations inside Other Expressions

One can nest Associations inside other Wolfram Language expressions. Here is a List of Associations. It's a description of some of the people on board an (imaginary) dinghy on the doomed Titanic.

Describe the passengers on an imaginary dinghy launched from the Titanic:

In[ ]:= **dinghy = ResourceData [ro, "Dinghy List of Associations"]**

Out[ ]= { <| class → 3rd, age → 16, sex → female, survived → True |>,
  <| class → 1st, age → 65, sex → male, survived → False |>,
  <| class → 3rd, age → 2, sex → female, survived → False |>,
  <| class → 3rd, age → Missing [ ] , sex → female, survived → True |>,
  <| class → 3rd, age → 18, sex → female, survived → False |> }

I can display this nicely, by the way, via ResourceFunction ["DatasetForm"] :

In[ ]:= [▪] **DatasetForm** + **[dinghy]**

Out[ ]=

class	age	sex	survived
3rd	16	female	True
1st	65	male	False
3rd	2	female	False
3rd	—	female	True
3rd	18	female	False

One can use Part on this structure. Here are some examples. Notice that because the Keys are strings, I don't have to wrap the string with Key. Also notice that All means every possible part at the specified level.

Part works on structures of Associations:

In[ ]:= **{ Part [dinghy, 3] , Part [dinghy, All, Key ["sex"]] ,**
  Part [dinghy, 2, Key ["survived"]] , dinghy⟦5, "class"⟧ }

Out[ ]= { <| class → 3rd, age → 2, sex → female, survived → False |>,
  { female, male, female, female, female } , False, 3rd }

Or one can have an Association of Associations. Indeed, one frequently does.

Here's an example of an Association of Associations:

In[∘]:= **dinghyk = ResourceData [ro, "Dinghy Association of Associations"]**

Out[∘]= ‹| Anna → ‹| class → 3rd, age → 16, sex → female, survived → True |›,
Bob → ‹| class → 1st, age → 65, sex → male, survived → False |›,
Clarisse → ‹| class → 3rd, age → 2, sex → female, survived → False |›,
Diane → ‹| class → 3rd, sex → female, survived → True |›,
Emily → ‹| class → 3rd, age → 18, sex → female, survived → False |› |›

Wolfram Language expressions most definitely include Associations of Associations.

Again, I can use DatasetForm to assist with visualization:

In[∘]:= [∘] **DatasetForm** + **[dinghyk]**

	class	age	sex	survived
Anna	3rd	16	female	True
Bob	1st	65	male	False
Clarisse	3rd	2	female	False
Diane	3rd	—	female	True
Emily	3rd	18	female	False

Out[∘]=

Now I can use Part to extract Bob's age or Clarisse's survival or all the data on Diane or all the values for sex.

Part sequences get specific values out of a structure of Associations:

In[∘]:= **{ Part [dinghyk, "Bob", "age"] , dinghyk〚"Clarisse", "survived"〛,
Part [dinghyk, "Diane"] , Part [dinghyk, All, "sex"] }**

Out[∘]= { 65, False, ‹| class → 3rd, sex → female, survived → True |›,
‹| Anna → female, Bob → male, Clarisse → female, Diane → female, Emily → female |› }

Notice that when I do this and call for more than one piece of information, the Part function returns an Association. When I want just one piece of information, however, the Association disappears and we just get the value.

Of course, Associations can also be nested inside things other than Lists. This is a perfectly usable Wolfram Language expression.

Another nested Association:

In[•]:= **g [7, chingAssociation]**

Out[•]= g[7, ⟨| team → HOU, lastName → Ching, firstName → Brian, position → F,

baseSalary → $220 000 , guaranteedSalary → $220 000 , year → ⟨Year: **2007** ⟩ |⟩]

I can still use **Part** to extract information:

In[•]:= **Part [g [7, chingAssociation] , 2, Key ["firstName"]]**

Out[•]= Brian

Although **Part** does not have a pre-built operator form, the Wolfram Function Repository (wolfr.am/WFR) contains **Slice**, which works as one. Observe.

Slice works as a Part operator form:

In[•]:= ⟨•⟩ **Slice** + **["firstName"] [chingAssociation]**

Out[•]= Brian

In[•]:= ⟨•⟩ **Slice** + **[{ "firstName", "lastName", "position" }] [chingAssociation]**

Out[•]= ⟨| firstName → Brian, lastName → Ching, position → F |⟩

I will make good use of this added capability, and we will see that the **Query** function actually uses the progenitor of **Slice** quite extensively in doing its work.

Position on Association

By using **Position**, one can see all of the specifications to **Part** one might use to access components of an **Association**. Here I show all of the Parts in **dinghy**, which, you will recall, is a List of Associations. You can see that the rows of the data have an integer as their first index and a **Key** as their second index.

Position used with Associations extracts the name of Keys each wrapped in Key:

In[•]:= **Position [dinghy, _, { 1, 2 }, Heads → False]**

Out[•]= { {1, Key [class] }, {1, Key [age] }, {1, Key [sex] }, {1, Key [survived] }, {1},
{2, Key [class] }, {2, Key [age] }, {2, Key [sex] }, {2, Key [survived] }, {2},
{3, Key [class] }, {3, Key [age] }, {3, Key [sex] }, {3, Key [survived] }, {3},
{4, Key [class] }, {4, Key [age] }, {4, Key [sex] }, {4, Key [survived] }, {4},
{5, Key [class] }, {5, Key [age] }, {5, Key [sex] }, {5, Key [survived] }, {5} }

When the data is an **Association** of Associations, the Parts are a List of Keys. The rows themselves contain just one element: the key for the row. The individual items like "male" or "65" contain two elements, one key for the row and one key for the column.

Part specifications for nested Associations are Lists of Keys:

In[·]:= **Position [dinghyk, _, {1, 2}, Heads → False]**

Out[·]= { { Key [Anna] , Key [class] }, { Key [Anna] , Key [age] }, { Key [Anna] , Key [sex] },
{ Key [Anna] , Key [survived] }, { Key [Anna] }, { Key [Bob] , Key [class] },
{ Key [Bob] , Key [age] }, { Key [Bob] , Key [sex] }, { Key [Bob] , Key [survived] },
{ Key [Bob] }, { Key [Clarisse] , Key [class] }, { Key [Clarisse] , Key [age] },
{ Key [Clarisse] , Key [sex] }, { Key [Clarisse] , Key [survived] }, { Key [Clarisse] },
{ Key [Diane] , Key [class] }, { Key [Diane] , Key [sex] }, { Key [Diane] , Key [survived] },
{ Key [Diane] }, { Key [Emily] , Key [class] }, { Key [Emily] , Key [age] },
{ Key [Emily] , Key [sex] }, { Key [Emily] , Key [survived] }, { Key [Emily] } }

KeyTake and KeyDrop

There are two functions used all the time in referencing components of an Association: KeyTake and KeyDrop. They are similar to Take and Drop, which operate on normal expressions such as those existing before the Wolfram Language had Associations. KeyTake uses the Association as its first argument and then either a single key (with *no* Key wrapper) as its second argument or a list of keys as its second argument. KeyTake and KeyDrop, when successful, always return Associations, and this is true even when one requests just one item from the Association.

KeyTake extracts single or multiple key-value pairs:

In[·]:= **{ KeyTake [chingAssociation, "baseSalary"] ,**
 KeyTake [chingAssociation, { "baseSalary", "team" }] }

Out[·]= $\left\{ \langle\,|\, \text{baseSalary} \to \$220\,000 \,|\rangle, \langle\,|\, \text{baseSalary} \to \$220\,000 \,, \text{team} \to \text{HOU} \,|\rangle \right\}$

KeyTake has an operator form that uses the key designation as its argument:

In[·]:= **KeyTake [{ "baseSalary", "team" }] [chingAssociation]**

Out[·]= $\langle\,|\, \text{baseSalary} \to \$220\,000 \,, \text{team} \to \text{HOU} \,|\rangle$

Three other points. First, again, do not wrap the strings in Key.

Don't wrap keys in Key when using KeyTake:

In[·]:= **KeyTake [chingAssociation, Key ["baseSalary"]]**

Out[·]= $\langle\,|\, |\rangle$

Second, KeyTake works on the Normal form of Associations but does not work on non-Associations.

KeyTake doesn't work on bare Lists:

```
In[•]:=  { KeyTake [ Normal [ chingAssociation ] , "firstName" ] ,
          KeyTake [ Values [ chingAssociation ] , "firstName" ] ,
          KeyTake [ Values [ chingAssociation ] , 3 ] }
```

> ⋯ KeyTake : The argument {HOU, Ching, Brian, F, $220000 , $220000 , DateObject [{2007}, Year,
>
>   Gregorian, −5.]} is not a valid Association or a list of rules.

> ⋯ KeyTake : The argument {HOU, Ching, Brian, F, $220000 , $220000 , DateObject [{2007}, Year,
>
>   Gregorian, −5.]} is not a valid Association or a list of rules.

```
Out[•]=  { <| firstName → Brian |> ,

          KeyTake[ {HOU, Ching, Brian, F, $220000 , $220000 , Year: 2007 }, firstName ] ,

          KeyTake[ {HOU, Ching, Brian, F, $220000 , $220000 , Year: 2007 }, 3 ] }
```

Third, if KeyTake can't find the Key, it returns an Association without the requested key-value pair. That's the intended behavior. It does *not* return an error message. Here's an example of how KeyTake behaves in this circumstance. I use the operator form of KeyTake, but the result would be the same if I used the conventional two-argument form.

If a key is not present, KeyTake does not give an error:

```
In[•]:=  { KeyTake [ "goals" ] [ chingAssociation ] ,
          KeyTake [ { "goals", "year" } ] [ chingAssociation ] }
```

```
Out[•]=  { <| |> , <| year → Year: 2007 |> }
```

The Lookup function discussed in a moment is what you want if you want more specific control over missing keys.

KeyDrop is KeyTake's negative cousin. It has the same syntax as KeyTake and does exactly what you think it does. It has a similar operator form.

KeyDrop drops key-value pairs based on the key:

```
In[•]:=  { KeyDrop [ chingAssociation, { "baseSalary", "firstName" } ] ,
          KeyDrop [ { "baseSalary", "firstName" } ] [ chingAssociation ] }
```

```
Out[•]=  { <| team → HOU, lastName → Ching, position → F, guaranteedSalary → $220000 ,

          year → Year: 2007 |> , <| team → HOU, lastName → Ching,

          position → F, guaranteedSalary → $220000 , year → Year: 2007 |> }
```

Lookup

Lookup is somewhat like KeyTake / * Values but addresses the missing key problem differently. Here's an example where it basically works the same as KeyTake / * Values.

Lookup extracts just the values based on the key, not the key-value pair:

In[•]:= { (KeyTake [{ "baseSalary", "team" }] / * Values) [chingAssociation],
        Lookup [chingAssociation, { "baseSalary", "team" }] }

Out[•]= {{ $220 000 , HOU}, { $220 000 , HOU}}

It has an operator form, just like KeyTake.

Lookup has an operator form:

In[•]:= Lookup [{ "baseSalary", "team" }] [chingAssociation]

Out[•]= { $220 000 , HOU}

Here's an example where the behavior is different. I ask for a key that isn't present in the data; it doesn't say anything about how many goals Brian Ching might have scored.

Lookup produces Missings by default if it can't find the key:

In[•]:= { (KeyTake [{ "goals", "year" }] / * Values) [chingAssociation],
        Lookup [{ "goals", "year" }] [chingAssociation] }

Out[•]= {{ Year: 2007 }, {Missing [KeyAbsent, goals], Year: 2007 }}

Notice that instead of just omitting the unfound goals information from the output, Lookup yields a Missing expression and provides information that it can't find a goals key.

The provision of a Missing is the default behavior for Lookup, and it's the only behavior I can get if I want to use the built-in operator form, but by adding a third argument, I can get more control over what to do when Lookup seeks a key that is not present.

One can change Lookup's output when it doesn't find a key:

In[•]:= Lookup [chingAssociation, { "goals", "year" },
        Style ["Hey, I can't find any information", { Red, 24 }]]

Out[•]= {Hey, I can't find any information, Year: 2007 }

Slice

The ResourceFunction Slice is an extremely useful chimera of Part, the KeyTake operator, and the Lookup operator. Here, it looks just like KeyTake. For single key requests, it returns just the Value. For multiple key requests, it returns an Association. It can also work with Integer specifications for Parts.

Slice is kind of like KeyTake in that it returns key-value pairs:

In[⋅]:=   `{ [▪] Slice ✛ ["baseSalary"] [chingAssociation],`
`        [▪] Slice ✛ [{"baseSalary", "team"}] [chingAssociation],`
`        [▪] Slice ✛ [{2, -1}] [chingAssociation] }`

Out[⋅]=   { $220 000 , ⟨| baseSalary → $220 000 , team → HOU |⟩,

⟨| lastName → Ching, year → Year: 2007 |⟩ }

When one gives Slice an argument that contains missing Keys, it neither omits the key-value pair altogether nor omits the missing key. Instead, it gives a key-value pair in which the Key is the (missing) Key requested and the Value is a Missing expression. Very useful!

Slice doesn't omit key-value pairs for missing keys. It keeps the pair but sets the value to Missing; indeed, this is one of the reasons why the function was created:

In[⋅]:=   `[▪] Slice ✛ [{"baseSalary", "goals"}] [chingAssociation]`

Out[⋅]=   ⟨| baseSalary → $220 000 , goals → Missing[KeyAbsent, goals] |⟩

Slice, like Part, can also work on Associations contained in deeper structures.

Slice works on nested structures with Associations:

In[⋅]:=   `[▪] Slice ✛ [All, "sex"] [dinghy]`

Out[⋅]=   {female, male, female, female, female}

In[⋅]:=   `[▪] Slice ✛ ["Anna", "sex"] [dinghyk]`

Out[⋅]=   female

In[⋅]:=   `[▪] Slice ✛ [All, "age"] [dinghyk]`

Out[⋅]=   ⟨| Anna → 16, Bob → 65, Clarisse → 2, Diane → Missing[KeyAbsent, age], Emily → 18 |⟩

Slice, to its credit, works on Associations and non-Associations alike.

Building Associations

The Wolfram Language contains numerous ways to build an Association. Typing out Rules going from keys to values is one way of building an Association, but the Wolfram Language contains many other methods of construction.

AssociationThread

One frequently used method of construction is the built-in AssociationThread function. One can think of it as being the RightComposition of (1) a function that Threads Rule over its first and second arguments and (2) the Association function.

A reconstruction of AssociationThread using Thread:

```
In[•]:=  fakeAssociationThread =
            Function [ { keys, values } , Thread [ Rule [ keys, values ] ] ] / * Association;
          fakeAssociationThread [ { "a", "b", "c" } , { 5, 9, "hello" } ]
```

```
Out[•]=  <| a → 5, b → 9, c → hello |>
```

AssociationThread lets me skip all that and just write it this way.

AssociationThread is easy to use:

```
In[•]:=  AssociationThread [ { "a", "b", "c" } , { 5, 9, "hello" } ]
```

```
Out[•]=  <| a → 5, b → 9, c → hello |>
```

AssociationMap

AssociationMap is used when one wants to compute the values in an Association based on a List of keys.

AssociationMap builds Associations from potential keys:

```
In[•]:=  AssociationMap [ StringLength, { "yak", "zebra", "armadillo" } ]
```

```
Out[•]=  <| yak → 3, zebra → 5, armadillo → 9 |>
```

AssociationMap has an operator form:

```
In[•]:=  AssociationMap [ StringLength ] [ { "yak", "zebra", "armadillo" } ]
```

```
Out[•]=  <| yak → 3, zebra → 5, armadillo → 9 |>
```

Counts

Perhaps the Counts function doesn't really belong here since it isn't a typical way of building an Association, but (1) because it's so useful and (2) because it's very helpful to use it in the following code, I insert it into the seamless web of Wolfram Language programming right here. Basically, Counts forms an Association in which the keys are the items it encounters and the values are the number of times it encounters them. The order of the key-value pairs depends on the order of data in the underlying data structure being probed.

Here I show that the space followed by the letter "o" are the two most common characters in a line of dialog from *Hamlet*.

Counts builds an Association in which the expressions found are the keys and the frequency with which they are found are the values:

In[ ]:= **ReverseSort@Counts [StringPartition ["To be or not to be", 1]]**

Out[ ]= <| → 5, o → 4, t → 2, e → 2, b → 2, n → 1, r → 1, T → 1|>

Merge

Right now, the data in dinghy is stored in what can be described as a row-wise fashion. Each row has its own key-value pair. If the keys in a list of Associations tended to be quite similar, however, one might compress this information, as other computer languages do, by storing it in what could be called a column-wise fashion. The function with which to do this is Merge.

I now Merge dinghy, using the abstract function f as the second argument. Notice that the values for each column are all now Listed together as the value (with the function f applied) to a single common key.

Merge turns multiple Associations into a single Association:

In[ ]:= **Merge [dinghy,f]**

Out[ ]= <| class → f [{ 3rd, 1st, 3rd, 3rd, 3rd }], age → f [{ 16, 65, 2, Missing [ ], 18 }],
        sex → f [{ female, male, female, female, female }],
        survived → f [{ True, False, False, True, False }] |>

Merge has an operator form in which the merging function is the sole argument:

In[ ]:= **Merge [f] [dinghy]**

Out[ ]= <| class → f [{ 3rd, 1st, 3rd, 3rd, 3rd }], age → f [{ 16, 65, 2, Missing [ ], 18 }],
        sex → f [{ female, male, female, female, female }],
        survived → f [{ True, False, False, True, False }] |>

If the second argument to Merge is Identity, I get back just a list of values. This result occurs because Identity basically says to do nothing to its argument:

In[ ]:= **Merge [dinghy,Identity]**

Out[ ]= <| class → { 3rd, 1st, 3rd, 3rd, 3rd }, age → { 16, 65, 2, Missing [ ], 18 },
        sex → { female, male, female, female, female },
        survived → { True, False, False, True, False } |>

Here are some other examples of things one can do with Merge: just get the first value one confronts, Compress the information, find the Commonest value and then get only the first element of the resulting List, and get Counts of the Values. I use AssociationMap to show which output goes with which argument to Merge.

The argument to the Merge operator determines how the values found with the same key are combined:

In[ ]:= **AssociationMap [function ⟼ Merge [function] [dinghy],**
  { First, Compress, (Commonest / ∗ First), Counts }]

Out[ ]= ⟨| First → ⟨| class → 3rd, age → 16, sex → female, survived → True |⟩, Compress →
    ⟨| class → 1:eJxTTMoPSmNlYGAoZgESPpnFJcHMQIZxUQqYNkTjI9EAPtoKrQ==, age →
      1:eJxTTMoPSmNlYGAoZgESPpnFJZkCQEamI4hgAhJpDCBJdiDhm1lcnJmXnikEZAM`·.
        AC+IJhg==, sex →
      1:eJxTTMoPSmNlYGAoZgESPpnFJcFsQEZaam5iTmowSAzMQBLDygQAMdQQxQ==,
    survived →
      1:eJxTTMoPSmNlYGAoZgESPpnFJWBGSFFpajFI2C0xpxiZhSkJAN6TDxo= |⟩,
    Commonest / ∗ First → ⟨| class → 3rd, age → 16, sex → female, survived → False |⟩,
    Counts → ⟨| class → ⟨| 3rd → 4, 1st → 1 |⟩,
      age → ⟨| 16 → 1, 65 → 1, 2 → 1, Missing [ ] → 1, 18 → 1 |⟩,
      sex → ⟨| female → 4, male → 1 |⟩, survived → ⟨| True → 2, False → 3 |⟩ |⟩ |⟩

Here is a common usage of Merge in data analysis. We all know that there were second-class passengers on the Titanic, but if I perform a Counts of the classes in our dinghy, I find that there is no key-value pair that explicitly tells me the number of dinghy passengers from second class.

Merge can be used to modify the results from Counts:

In[ ]:= **Counts [Part [dinghy, All, "class"]]**

Out[ ]= ⟨| 3rd → 4, 1st → 1 |⟩

In[ ]:= **Merge [{ Counts [Part [dinghy, All, "class"]], ⟨| "2nd" → 0 |⟩ }, First]**

Out[ ]= ⟨| 3rd → 4, 1st → 1, 2nd → 0 |⟩

Here's how to create an Association that looks more like
⟨| "3rd" → 4, "1st" → 1, "2nd" → 0 |⟩.

Use AssociationThread to construct an Association that sets forth what to write when no instances of a particular key are found:

In[ ]:= **default=AssociationThread [{ "1st", "2nd", "3rd" }, 0]**

Out[ ]= ⟨| 1st → 0, 2nd → 0, 3rd → 0 |⟩

Now I use the operator form of Merge with First as its argument to merge the Counts result with the Association now stored in the default symbol. This technique will be used frequently throughout this book, particularly in several computational adventures. Perhaps at some point the Wolfram Function Repository or the Wolfram Language will incorporate a vehicle for getting this kind of output more directly.

Merge [First] combines with Counts to produce an output with default count values for missing items in the underlying data:

In[•]:= **Merge [First] [{ Counts [Part [dinghy, All, "class"]] , default }]**

Out[•]= ‹| 3rd → 4, 1st → 1, 2nd → 0 |›

JoinAcross

Suppose I have additional information that describes the cabins on the Titanic by listing their class, their square footage, whether they include a window, and the decks on which they were located. (The actual values are imaginary, but that should not matter here.)

An imaginary data structure of cabins on the Titanic:

In[•]:= **titanicCabins = ResourceData [ro, "Titanic Cabins List of Associations"]**

Out[•]= { ‹| class → 1st, squarefeet → 300, window → True, decklocations → {1, 2} |›,
‹| class → 2nd, squarefeet → 200, window → True, decklocations → {3, 4} |›,
‹| class → 3rd, squarefeet → 100, window → False, decklocations → {4, 5, 6} |›,
‹| class → crew, squarefeet → 80, window → False, decklocations → {6, 7} |› }

I now want a single list of Associations in which I have for each passenger not just their age, gender, survival, and cabin class, but the actual characteristics of their cabin. The function to do this is JoinAcross. It's like the SQL function Join. The first two arguments are the lists of the Associations to be joined. The third argument determines the basis for the joinder, i.e. a key the two lists of Associations have in common. I show the results using DatasetForm to make them clearer.

JoinAcross combines two structures of Associations:

In[•]:= ([▪] DatasetForm ✦) [JoinAcross [dinghy, titanicCabins, "class"]]

Out[•]=

class	age	sex	survived	squarefeet	window	decklocations
1st	65	male	False	300	True	{1, 2}
3rd	16	female	True	100	False	{4, 5, 6}
3rd	2	female	False	100	False	{4, 5, 6}
3rd	—	female	True	100	False	{4, 5, 6}
3rd	18	female	False	100	False	{4, 5, 6}

JoinAcross is sometimes confused with Merge. Think Merge if you have a single list of Associations and want an Association between the union of keys in the constituent Associations and some structure of values. Think JoinAcross if you have two lists of Associations and want to combine them into a single list of Associations. An element from the first list is combined with an element from the second list based on their having identical values of specified sets of keys.

Sometimes the name of the column in one list of Associations (or other data) will differ from the name of the column in another list of Associations (or other data), but the columns have the same meaning. Suppose, for example, the name of the first column in titanicCabins was "cabinclass" rather than "class" but the meaning of the column was the same as the "class" column in dinghy. Later, I'll show efficient mechanisms for changing the keys in an Association or List of Associations, but for right now, I'll get the data from the repository for this book.

The same data structure as titanicCabins but using "cabinclass" instead of "class" as a key:

In[•]:= **titanicCabins2 = ResourceData [ro, "Titanic Cabins 2 List of Associations"]**

Out[•]= { <| cabinclass → 1st, squarefeet → 300, window → True, decklocations → {1, 2} |>,
      <| cabinclass → 2nd, squarefeet → 200, window → True, decklocations → {3, 4} |>,
      <| cabinclass → 3rd, squarefeet → 100, window → False, decklocations → {4, 5, 6} |>,
      <| cabinclass → crew, squarefeet → 80, window → False, decklocations → {6, 7} |> }

Let's join the two lists of Associations. I show the results using DatasetForm.

Use a Rule for the join specification when joining two columns with the same meaning but different names:

In[•]:= [≡] **DatasetForm** + [**JoinAcross [dinghy, titanicCabins2, "class" → "cabinclass"]**]

class	age	sex	survived	cabinclass	squarefeet	window	decklocations
1st	65	male	False	1st	300	True	{1, 2}
3rd	16	female	True	3rd	100	False	{4, 5, 6}
3rd	2	female	False	3rd	100	False	{4, 5, 6}
3rd	—	female	True	3rd	100	False	{4, 5, 6}
3rd	18	female	False	3rd	100	False	{4, 5, 6}

Out[•]=

Notice how there are now two duplicate columns, one named "class" and the other named "cabinclass" in which the values match up. There are several methods to eliminate the duplication. The first is simply to delete one of the offending columns.

Map KeyDrop over the joined data to eliminate a duplicative column:

In[ ]:=   [▪] **DatasetForm** + **[Map [KeyDrop ["class"]] [**
       JoinAcross [dinghy, titanicCabins2, "class" → "cabinclass"]]]

Out[ ]=

age	sex	survived	cabinclass	squarefeet	window	decklocations
65	male	False	1st	300	True	{1, 2}
16	female	True	3rd	100	False	{4, 5, 6}
2	female	False	3rd	100	False	{4, 5, 6}
—	female	True	3rd	100	False	{4, 5, 6}
18	female	False	3rd	100	False	{4, 5, 6}

A second method would be to change the name of the column in one of the datasets so that it precisely matched that of the corresponding column in the other dataset. One can then use a simple form of JoinAcross, specifying the now common key name as the joining column.

Map the KeyReplace function over the dinghy data so that the key "class" is turned into "cabinclass". Then use JoinAcross with the common "cabinclass" key to join the two related pieces of data together:

In[ ]:=   [▪] **DatasetForm** + **[**
       JoinAcross [Map [[▪] KeyReplace + ["class" → "cabinclass"]] [dinghy] ,
          titanicCabins2, "cabinclass"]]

Out[ ]=

cabinclass	age	sex	survived	squarefeet	window	decklocations
1st	65	male	False	300	True	{1, 2}
3rd	16	female	True	100	False	{4, 5, 6}
3rd	2	female	False	100	False	{4, 5, 6}
3rd	—	female	True	100	False	{4, 5, 6}
3rd	18	female	False	100	False	{4, 5, 6}

Functional Programming Constructs Used on Associations

Most of the functional programming constructs examined in a prior chapter for use on non-Association data work in a highly analogous fashion on Associations.

Map

Various Map constructs that can work over non-atomic Wolfram Language expressions that are not Associations can also work on Associations. Suppose, for example, that one wished to take the CRC32 hash of every value in chingAssociation. (You don't need to worry about exactly what this is; just assume it somehow turns expressions into strings.)

The keys are preserved and the values are hashed:

In[ ]:= **CRC32 = Hash [♯ , "CRC32", "HexString"] &**

Out[ ]= Hash [♯1, CRC32, HexString] &

Map works on the values of Associations:

In[ ]:= **Map [CRC32, chingAssociation]**

Out[ ]= ⟨| team → ed28f3db, lastName → 484d4815, firstName → b4cd7235, position → 4dbd0b28, baseSalary → a2b68986, guaranteedSalary → a2b68986, year → 282b30d5 |⟩

Or use the operator form of Map. The result is the same; Hash is deterministic:

In[ ]:= **Map [CRC32] [chingAssociation]**

Out[ ]= ⟨| team → ed28f3db, lastName → 484d4815, firstName → b4cd7235, position → 4dbd0b28, baseSalary → a2b68986, guaranteedSalary → a2b68986, year → 282b30d5 |⟩

MapAt

Suppose one wanted to only hash the values that have the keys "baseSalary" and "team". (Notice that if one wants to use multiple keys, one needs to wrap the keys in Lists.) MapAt can be used. The function is applied only to those values associated with the listed keys. The other values (associated with the keys "lastName", "firstName", "position", "guaranteedSalary", and "year") are left alone.

MapAt works on Associations with key specifications:

In[ ]:= **MapAt [CRC32, chingAssociation, { { "baseSalary" }, { "team" } }]**

Out[ ]= ⟨| team → ed28f3db, lastName → Ching, firstName → Brian, position → F, baseSalary → a2b68986, guaranteedSalary → $220 000 , year → [Year: 2007] |⟩

The operator form of MapAt works analogously too.

MapAt has an operator form:

In[ ]:= **MapAt [CRC32, { { "baseSalary" }, { "team" } }] [chingAssociation]**

Out[ ]= ⟨| team → ed28f3db, lastName → Ching, firstName → Brian, position → F, baseSalary → a2b68986, guaranteedSalary → $220 000 , year → [Year: 2007] |⟩

One can also use MapAt at different levels. Suppose I want to perform a number of operations in place on the columns of the dataset. I might, for example, want to use the CRC32 function on the class and survived columns of the passengers in dinghy but want to leave the other columns alone.

MapAt takes a list of keys to operate on deep parts of structures using Associations:

In[∘]:= **MapAt [CRC32, { {All, "class"}, {All, "survived"} }] [dinghy]**

Out[∘]=   { <| class → 8eba3cee, age → 16, sex → female, survived → 5acf213a |>,
         <| class → 8992c9a5, age → 65, sex → male, survived → 7e6f7d72 |>,
         <| class → 8eba3cee, age → 2, sex → female, survived → 7e6f7d72 |>,
         <| class → 8eba3cee, age → Missing [ ], sex → female, survived → 5acf213a |>,
         <| class → 8eba3cee, age → 18, sex → female, survived → 7e6f7d72 |> }

Or I can do yet more complex things, like applying the function only to the class column of the first two rows and the survived column of the last three rows.

Key or part specifications for MapAt can be complicated:

In[∘]:= **MapAt [CRC32, { { {1, 2}, "class"}, { {−3, −2, −1}, "survived"} }] [dinghy]**

Out[∘]=   { <| class → 8eba3cee, age → 16, sex → female, survived → True |>,
         <| class → 8992c9a5, age → 65, sex → male, survived → False |>,
         <| class → 3rd, age → 2, sex → female, survived → 7e6f7d72 |>,
         <| class → 3rd, age → Missing [ ], sex → female, survived → 5acf213a |>,
         <| class → 3rd, age → 18, sex → female, survived → 7e6f7d72 |> }

I can also compose uses of MapAt (and other functions). Here I create a composition of (1) the MapAt operator with CRC32 as its function and the "class" and "sex" columns as its targets and (2) the MapAt operator with Framed as its function and the "age" and "survived" columns as its targets. I then apply that composition to dinghy. Notice that this composition permits me to perform different operations on different columns of data, just as I might in real life.

MapAt can be used in compositions:

In[∘]:= **(MapAt [CRC32, { {All, "class"}, {All, "sex"} }] / ∗MapAt [Framed, { {All, "age"},**
         {All, "survived"} }]) [dinghy]

Out[∘]= { ⟨| class → 8eba3cee, age → ⟦16⟧ , sex → 4a748a6c, survived → ⟦True⟧ |⟩,

       ⟨| class → 8992c9a5, age → ⟦65⟧ , sex → 558de0a9, survived → ⟦False⟧ |⟩,

       ⟨| class → 8eba3cee, age → ⟦2⟧ , sex → 4a748a6c, survived → ⟦False⟧ |⟩,

       ⟨| class → 8eba3cee, age → ⟦Missing [ ]⟧ , sex → 4a748a6c, survived → ⟦True⟧ |⟩,

       ⟨| class → 8eba3cee, age → ⟦18⟧ , sex → 4a748a6c, survived → ⟦False⟧ |⟩ }

MapIndexed

MapIndexed also behaves with Associations in a way that should seem familiar. The first argument to the mapped function is the value associated with the key; the second is the key itself wrapped in a list.

Use MapIndexed with an abstract function f:

In[ ]:= **MapIndexed [f, chingAssociation]**

Out[ ]= ⟨| team → f [HOU, { Key [team] }], lastName → f [Ching, { Key [lastName] }],
firstName → f [Brian, { Key [firstName] }], position → f [F, { Key [position] }],
baseSalary → f[$220 000 , { Key [baseSalary] }],
guaranteedSalary → f[$220 000 , { Key [guaranteedSalary] }],
year → f[Year: 2007 , { Key [year] }]|⟩

MapIndexed takes functions whose first argument will be the value of a key-value pair and whose second argument will be the key (wrapped in Key).

There is an operator form when one wants to map the function at the first level of the data structure:

In[ ]:= **MapIndexed [f] [chingAssociation]**

Out[ ]= ⟨| team → f [HOU, { Key [team] }], lastName → f [Ching, { Key [lastName] }],
firstName → f [Brian, { Key [firstName] }], position → f [F, { Key [position] }],
baseSalary → f[$220 000 , { Key [baseSalary] }],
guaranteedSalary → f[$220 000 , { Key [guaranteedSalary] }],
year → f[Year: 2007 , { Key [year] }]|⟩

There's a related function, KeyValueMap, that works similarly to MapIndexed. I will explain it later in this chapter.

MapThread

One can also use MapThread on Associations, although, truth be told, I have seldom had occasion to do so. In part, this is because the Merge function works very similarly to MapThread. The difference is that in Merge, the function works on a List of values whereas with MapThread, the function works on a sequence.

Here is a comparison between MapThread and Merge:

In[ ]:= **MapThread [f, dinghy]**

Out[ ]= ⟨| class → f [3rd, 1st, 3rd, 3rd, 3rd], age → f [16, 65, 2, Missing [ ], 18],
sex → f [female, male, female, female, female],
survived → f [True, False, False, True, False] |⟩

In[•]:= **Merge [dinghy, f]**

Out[•]= <| class → f [{ 3rd, 1st, 3rd, 3rd, 3rd }] , age → f [{ 16, 65, 2, Missing [ ] , 18 }] ,
sex → f [{ female, male, female, female, female }] ,
survived → f [{ True, False, False, True, False }] |>

Indeed, I can emulate Merge pretty well by just changing the function a bit. I now show this using an operator form of MapThread with f [{ ⊞ }] & as the function and compare the results with Merge using f as the function.

Using MapThread to emulate Merge:

In[•]:= **MapThread [f [{ ⊞ }] &] [dinghy] === Merge [f] [dinghy]**

Out[•]= True

There are some differences between Merge and MapThread, however. MapThread requires that the keys in each Association be the same and in the same order; Merge has no such requirement.

Apply and Transpose

This will be a simple paragraph. Apply and Transpose aren't presently intended to work on Associations, so don't use them. There is, however, a ResourceFunction AssociationTranspose that can help. As stated in its documentation, it mimics the way Transpose rearranges an array to reorganize the levels in an Association.

Use AssociationTranspose to make inner keys become the outer keys and the outer keys become the inner keys:

In[•]:= **[▪] AssociationTranspose** + **[<| 1 → <| a → x |> , 2 → <| a → y |> |>]**

Out[•]= <| a → <| 1 → x, 2 → y |> |>

I'll show in a later chapter, though, that Transpose works wonders on Datasets.

KeyMap

So far, all the variants of Map considered have operated only on the values of the Association, but sometimes one needs to work on the keys. The main function to do this is KeyMap.

Here's one that joins the string "passenger" to all the keys for one row of dinghy:

In[•]:= **KeyMap [StringJoin ["passenger", ♯] &, dinghy⟦1⟧]**

Out[•]= <| passengerclass → 3rd, passengerage → 16,
passengersex → female, passengersurvived → True |>

There's an operator form in which the operator is the function to be applied:

In[•]:= **KeyMap [StringJoin ["passenger", #] &] [dinghy⟦1⟧]**

Out[•]= ‹| passengerclass → 3rd, passengerage → 16,
passengersex → female, passengersurvived → True |›

If I want to apply a function to the keys in a structure of Associations, I have to combine **KeyMap** with one of the **Map** variants.

Here I change the keys for all the rows of dinghy:

In[•]:= **Map [KeyMap [StringJoin ["passenger", #] &]] [dinghy]**

Out[•]= { ‹| passengerclass → 3rd, passengerage → 16,
passengersex → female, passengersurvived → True |›,
‹| passengerclass → 1st, passengerage → 65, passengersex → male,
passengersurvived → False |›, ‹| passengerclass → 3rd, passengerage → 2,
passengersex → female, passengersurvived → False |›,
‹| passengerclass → 3rd, passengerage → Missing [ ] , passengersex → female,
passengersurvived → True |›, ‹| passengerclass → 3rd, passengerage → 18,
passengersex → female, passengersurvived → False |› }

KeyValueMap

Sometimes I need to compute results for each key-value pair in an Association based on both the key and the value. The function to do this is **KeyValueMap**. It looks a lot like **KeyMap** except one writes a function of two arguments: the first argument is the key and the second argument is the value.

The function used for mapping in **KeyValueMap** requires two arguments. The first argument is the key and the second argument is the value:

In[•]:= **KeyValueMap [f, chingAssociation]**

Out[•]= {f [team, HOU] , f [lastName, Ching] , f [firstName, Brian] , f [position, F] ,
f [baseSalary, $220 000] , f [guaranteedSalary, $220 000] , f [year, ⟨Year: 2007⟩]}

Here's a fanciful example that may help with understanding: the output is a list of framed columns, the top element of which is the key and the bottom element of which is the value.

Using Framed and Column isn't necessary but helps provide a more parse-able framework:

In[•]:= **KeyValueMap [{ k , v } ⟼ Framed [Column [{ k , v }]] , chingAssociation]**

Out[•]=

Both KeyValueMap and MapIndexed permit functions that work on both keys and values in an Association of key-value pairs, but their outputs are different. MapIndexed produces an Association in which the keys are the same as the original keys but in which the values are a function of (1) the value and (2) the key wrapped in Key. KeyValueMap produces a List in which the elements are a function of (1) the key (not wrapped in Key) and (2) the value.

KeyValueMap and MapIndexed produce different outputs:

In[•]:= **With [{ assoc = ⟨| "a" → 2, "b" → 3, something → 4 |⟩ },
        { MapIndexed [f] [assoc] , KeyValueMap [f] [assoc] }]**

Out[•]= **{ ⟨| a → f [2, { Key [a] }] , b → f [3, { Key [b] }] ,
        something → f [4, { Key [something] }] |⟩ , { f [a, 2] , f [b, 3] , f [something, 4] } }**

The KeyReplace Resource Function

Often, one doesn't like some of the Keys in an Association. Perhaps, for example, some of the Keys have spaces in them that one wants to get rid of to make it easier to use Slot functions. The ResourceFunction KeyReplace works well in these settings. Here I change the name of the "sex" key to "gender" and the name of the "class" key to "cabin".

KeyReplace replaces keys:

In[•]:= **[▪] KeyReplace + [{ "sex" → "gender", "class" → "cabin" }] [dinghy〚1〛]**

Out[•]= **⟨| cabin → 3rd, age → 16, gender → female, survived → True |⟩**

I can combine KeyReplace with Map to do this for a structure of Associations.

Map and KeyReplace can work together:

In[•]:= **Map [▣ KeyReplace ⊹ [{ "sex" → "gender", "class" → "cabin" }]] [dinghy]**

Out[•]= { <| cabin → 3rd, age → 16, gender → female, survived → True |>,
        <| cabin → 1st, age → 65, gender → male, survived → False |>,
        <| cabin → 3rd, age → 2, gender → female, survived → False |>,
        <| cabin → 3rd, age → Missing [ ] , gender → female, survived → True |>,
        <| cabin → 3rd, age → 18, gender → female, survived → False |> }

Select

One can use Select on Associations. Select applies its filtering function to the values. Here, I use NumericQ with Select on those values in a row of dinghy to find key-value pairs for which the value is numeric.

Select applied to a single Association looks at values but produces Associations of key-value pairs:

In[•]:= **Select [NumericQ] [dinghy〚1〛]**

Out[•]= <| age → 16 |>

One can also use Select on Associations as a whole. Here I use the Slot function ♯ age ≤ 18 & to find children on the dinghy.

With the right Slot function, Select applied to structures of Associations can work on particular values:

In[•]:= **Select [♯age ≤ 18 &] [dinghy]**

Out[•]= { <| class → 3rd, age → 16, sex → female, survived → True |>,
        <| class → 3rd, age → 2, sex → female, survived → False |>,
        <| class → 3rd, age → 18, sex → female, survived → False |> }

GatherBy

One can use GatherBy on lists of Associations. Here I gather the passengers on our dinghy together depending on their sex. The first argument is the data to be gathered. The second argument is the function used to determine categories. Here I use the Slot function ♯ sex &. I end up with two lists. In each list, the value for the "sex" key is the same.

GatherBy turns structures of Associations into lists of such structures:

In[ ]:= **GatherBy [dinghy, ⌗sex &]**

Out[ ]= { { <| class → 3rd, age → 16, sex → female, survived → True |>,
   <| class → 3rd, age → 2, sex → female, survived → False |>,
   <| class → 3rd, age → Missing [ ] , sex → female, survived → True |>,
   <| class → 3rd, age → 18, sex → female, survived → False |> },
   { <| class → 1st, age → 65, sex → male, survived → False |> } }

GroupBy

GroupBy is a more powerful variant of GatherBy that outputs an Association instead of a List of Lists. It works well on both old-school data and structures involving Associations. Here I grab a RandomSample of 20 rows from the MLS data that was used extensively in a previous chapter. I make use of ResourceFunction ["Terse"] to shorten the output. Terse is an operator form of Short that shortens the output display to some default length or, if one specifies an integer as an argument, to approximately that number of lines.

A small sample of the MLS data:

In[ ]:= **mls = ResourceData [ro, "MLS List of Lists"] ;**
SeedRandom [61 119] ;
(mlsSample = RandomSample [mls, 20]) / / [▪] Terse ₊ [5]

Out[ ]//Short= {{COL, Ceus, Steward, GK, $60 000.00 , $70 333.33 , Year: 2013 },

   {CLB, Mendoza, Andres, F, $500 000.00 , $595 000.00 , Year: 2011 },

   ≪16≫, {RSL, Forko, Willis, D, $30 000.00 , $30 000.00 , Year: 2007 },

   {LA, Valentin, Julian, D, $36 000.00 , $36 000.00 , Year: 2009 }}

I now use an operator form of GroupBy. I specify First (⌗[[1]] &) as the function by which to group the rows of data. The idea is to create an Association in which (1) the possible categories for First applied to the data are the keys and (2) the rows of data with a value of First corresponding to that category are the values. It may be easier to see it in action than to describe it. I just show the first few rows of the result.

GroupBy takes structures and produces Associations in which the keys are based on functions of items within the structure:

In[◦]:= **GroupBy [mlsSample, First] / /** [◦] **Terse** ◦ **[8]**

Out[◦]//Short= ⟨| COL → {{COL, Ceus, Steward, GK, $60 000.00 , $70 333.33 , Year: 2013 }},

CLB → {{CLB, Mendoza, Andres, F, $500 000.00 , $595 000.00 , Year: 2011 },

{CLB, Riggs, Alex, GK, $32 600.04 , $32 600.04 , Year: 2011 }}, ≪8≫,

PHI → {{PHI, Gonzalez, Juan Diego, D, $180 000.00 , $184 462.50 , Year: 2010 }},

LA → {{LA, Valentin, Julian, D, $36 000.00 , $36 000.00 , Year: 2009 }}|⟩

One can also often use an operator form of the GroupBy function in which the grouping operations are the argument to GroupBy. One then applies this operator to the expression one wants to group.

An operator form of GroupBy:

In[◦]:= **GroupBy [First] [mlsSample] / /** [◦] **Terse** ◦ **[8]**

Out[◦]//Short= ⟨| COL → {{COL, Ceus, Steward, GK, $60 000.00 , $70 333.33 , Year: 2013 }},

CLB → {{CLB, Mendoza, Andres, F, $500 000.00 , $595 000.00 , Year: 2011 },

{CLB, Riggs, Alex, GK, $32 600.04 , $32 600.04 , Year: 2011 }}, ≪8≫,

PHI → {{PHI, Gonzalez, Juan Diego, D, $180 000.00 , $184 462.50 , Year: 2010 }},

LA → {{LA, Valentin, Julian, D, $36 000.00 , $36 000.00 , Year: 2009 }}|⟩

There are more advanced forms of GroupBy that I use extensively in this book. One can have, for example, a more complex operator for GroupBy. Here I group according to the value of the first part of each row and then obtain only the fifth part of each row. Notice, by the way, that the ampersand functions are wrapped in parentheses to make explicit the order of operations.

GroupBy can do more than just group; it can operate on the grouped items:

In[◦]:= **GroupBy [mlsSample, First → (⌗ ⟦5⟧ &)]**

Out[◦]= ⟨| COL → { $60 000.00 }, CLB → { $500 000.00 , $32 600.04 },

RSL → { $160 000.00 , $125 000.00 , $35 125.00 , $40 000.00 , $240 000.00 , $30 000.00 },

Pool → { $40 000.00 }, CHV → { $70 000.00 , $125 000.00 }, POR → { $60 000.00 },

NE → { $33 000.00 }, HOU → { $220 000.00 }, DAL → { $250 000.00 , $50 004.00 },

SEA → { $165 000.00 }, PHI → { $180 000.00 }, LA → { $36 000.00 }|⟩

Again, one can accomplish the same grouping using an operator form of GroupBy:

In[ ]:= **GroupBy [First → (#⟦5⟧ &)] [mlsSample]**

Out[ ]= ⟨| COL → { $60 000.00 }, CLB → { $500 000.00 , $32 600.04 },

RSL → { $160 000.00 , $125 000.00 , $35 125.00 , $40 000.00 , $240 000.00 , $30 000.00 },

Pool → { $40 000.00 }, CHV → { $70 000.00 , $125 000.00 }, POR → { $60 000.00 },

NE → { $33 000.00 }, HOU → { $220 000.00 }, DAL → { $250 000.00 , $50 004.00 },

SEA → { $165 000.00 }, PHI → { $180 000.00 }, LA → { $36 000.00 } |⟩

There's a variant of GroupBy that is akin to the MapReduce concept used widely in modern programming. This variant can't be done with built-in operator forms. Instead, it takes the following structure. Here I group by the first part (team), get just the fifth part (base salary), and then compute the maximum value of each of the resulting Lists of base salaries.

GroupBy can be made to work similarly to MapReduce in other languages:

In[ ]:= **GroupBy [mlsSample, First → (#⟦5⟧ &) , Max]**

Out[ ]= ⟨| COL → $60 000.00 , CLB → $500 000.00 , RSL → $240 000.00 , Pool → $40 000.00 ,

CHV → $125 000.00 , POR → $60 000.00 , NE → $33 000.00 , HOU → $220 000.00 ,

DAL → $250 000.00 , SEA → $165 000.00 , PHI → $180 000.00 , LA → $36 000.00 |⟩

And there's now a ResourceFunction called MapReduceOperator that lets one mimic map reduction using an operator form:

In[ ]:= [◦] **MapReduceOperator** ⊹ **[First → (#⟦5⟧ &) , Max] [mlsSample]**

Out[ ]= ⟨| COL → $60 000.00 , CLB → $500 000.00 , RSL → $240 000.00 , Pool → $40 000.00 ,

CHV → $125 000.00 , POR → $60 000.00 , NE → $33 000.00 , HOU → $220 000.00 ,

DAL → $250 000.00 , SEA → $165 000.00 , PHI → $180 000.00 , LA → $36 000.00 |⟩

I just showed how GroupBy works on conventional non-Association data, but it particularly shines when it comes to Associations and data structures involving Associations. Here, for example, I look at the MLS data as an Association.

The MLS data as a list of Associations:

In[•]:= (mlsA = ResourceData [ro, "MLS List of Associations"])

Out[•]=
```
{⟨| Club → CHI, LastName → Armas, FirstName → Chris, Position → M, BaseSalary → $225 000.00 ,

   GuaranteedCompensation → $225 000.00 , Year → Year: 2007 |⟩, ◀ 5551 ▶ ,

   ⟨| Club → Missing [ ], LastName → Ramajo, FirstName → David Mateos, Position → D,

   BaseSalary → $420 000.00 , GuaranteedCompensation → $453 333.33 , Year → Year: 2017 |⟩}
```

Full expression not available   (original memory size: 8.4 MB   )

This output is a little hard to read, so I'll display the first eight players as a Dataset. One can see the remaining players by using the interface provided by Dataset.

Use Dataset with a MaxItems → 8 option to show the first eight players and display them in a tabular form:

In[•]:= **Dataset [mlsA, MaxItems → 8]**

Out[•]=

Club	LastName	FirstName	Position	BaseSalary	GuaranteedCompensation	Year
CHI	Armas	Chris	M	$225 000.00	$225 000.00	2007
CHI	Banner	Michael	M	$12 900.00	$12 900.00	2007
CHI	Barrett	Chad	F	$41 212.50	$48 712.50	2007
CHI	Blanco	Cuauhtemoc	F	$2.49232 × 10^6	$2.66678 × 10^6	2007
CHI	Brown	C.J.	D	$106 391.00	$106 391.00	2007
CHI	Busch	Jon	GK	$58 008.00	$58 008.00	2007
CHI	Carr	Calen	F	$38 000.00	$50 500.00	2007
CHI	Conde	Wilman	D	$144 000.00	$151 500.00	2007

rows 1–8 of **5553**

I now want to run that three-argument GroupBy and compute the maximum base salary by team. I don't need to use inscrutable numbered parts as functions anymore. Now I can use Slot functions with string arguments. Before running GroupBy, I use Select with a function that keeps only rows that are free of Missings in the Club, BaseSalary, and GuaranteedCompensation columns.

Use GroupBy to group by team and find the maximum base salaries for each:

In[•]:= **maxTeamSalary =
GroupBy [Select [Not [Or [MissingQ [#Club] , MissingQ [#BaseSalary] ,
MissingQ [#GuaranteedCompensation]]] &] [
mlsA] , (#Club &) → (#BaseSalary &) , Max]**

Out[•]= $\langle |$ CHI → $\$5.4 \times 10^6$, CHV → $\$1. \times 10^6$, CLB → $\$1.175 \times 10^6$,

COL → $\$2.1 \times 10^6$, DAL → $\$1.864 \times 10^6$, DC → $\$1.5 \times 10^6$, HOU → $\$750\,000.00$,

KC → $\$850\,000.00$, LA → $\$6.2 \times 10^6$, NE → $\$3. \times 10^6$, NY → $\$5.544 \times 10^6$,

Pool → $\$40\,000.00$, RSL → $\$1.75 \times 10^6$, TFC → $\$1.864 \times 10^6$, SJ → $\$988\,000.00$,

SEA → $\$4.913 \times 10^6$, PHI → $\$1.131 \times 10^6$, None → $\$120\,000.00$,

VAN → $\$1.4 \times 10^6$, POR → $\$2.2275 \times 10^6$, TOR → $\$6. \times 10^6$, POOL → $\$62\,500.00$,

MTL → $\$1.66667 \times 10^6$, ORL → $\$6.66 \times 10^6$, NYCFC → $\$6. \times 10^6$, ATL → $\$1.9125 \times 10^6$,

NYRB → $\$1.5 \times 10^6$, LAFC → $\$65\,004.00$, MNUFC → $\$550\,008.00$ $| \rangle$

I can make this output more attractive by sorting the data from high to low and putting the top 10 teams in a Dataset. Orlando City SC had the player with the highest base salary.

Sort the team salary information from highest to lowest, display the resulting relationship in a tabular form using Dataset and display the results in groupings of 10 teams:

In[•]:= **Dataset [ReverseSort [maxTeamSalary] , MaxItems → 10]**

Out[•]=

ORL	$\$6.66 \times 10^6$
LA	$\$6.2 \times 10^6$
NYCFC	$\$6. \times 10^6$
TOR	$\$6. \times 10^6$
NY	$\$5.544 \times 10^6$
CHI	$\$5.4 \times 10^6$
SEA	$\$4.913 \times 10^6$
NE	$\$3. \times 10^6$
POR	$\$2.2275 \times 10^6$
COL	$\$2.1 \times 10^6$

rows 1–10 of 29

Associations as Functions

There's one more thing. Associations aren't just data structures. They also act like functions. Here's a snippet. Notice I am *not* using a Part specification to retrieve the information. At least syntactically, it looks as if the Association is a function and the key is an argument.

There's syntactic sugar that makes it look as if Associations can be functions:

In[•]:= **chingAssociation ["team"]**

Out[•]= HOU

This is a huge deal, but it's so huge, further exposition requires its own chapter.

Putting It Together: More Complex Operations Using Operators and Composition

Let's now put our knowledge to use and actually execute some typical database operations. I'll use the full Titanic dataset as our first testbed. Then I'll come back and reprise the MLS problems shown in the previous chapter, but this time using Lists of Associations as our data structure.

Titanic Examples

A list of passengers on the Titanic represented as a List of Associations with common keys:

In[•]:= **titanic = ResourceData [ro, "Titanic List of Associations"]**

Out[•]=
```
{ <| class → 1st, age → 29, sex → female, survived → True |>,
   <| class → 1st, age → 1, sex → male, survived → True |>,
   <| class → 1st, age → 2, sex → female, survived → False |>,
   ⋯ 1304 ⋯ , <| class → 3rd, age → 27, sex → male, survived → False |>,
   <| class → 3rd, age → 29, sex → male, survived → False |> }
```
Full expression not available   (original memory size: 1 MB   ) ⚙

Example 1

Here I get the gender of everyone over the age of 70:

In[•]:= **Map [♯sex &, Select [titanic, ♯age > 70 &]]**

Out[•]= { male, male, female, male, male, male }

I can rewrite the operation using RightComposition of operator forms; I name the result oldGenders:

In[•]:= **oldGenders = Select [♯age > 70 &] / * Map [♯sex &]**

Out[•]= Select [♯age > 70 &] / * Map [♯sex &]

I can then apply this composition to titanic:

In[•]:= **oldGenders [titanic]**

Out[•]= { male, male, female, male, male, male }

Example 2

Count the number of women passengers in each cabin class:

In[•]:= **Counts [Map [♯class &, Select [titanic, ♯sex === "female" &]]]**

Out[•]= <| 1st → 144, 2nd → 106, 3rd → 216 |>

I could write this in a more operator-oriented form:

In[•]:= **Counts [Map [♯class &] [Select [♯sex === "female" &] [titanic]]]**

Out[•]= <| 1st → 144, 2nd → 106, 3rd → 216 |>

Again, I could write it using operator forms and RightComposition. First select just those Associations in which the sex is female, then get the class of each member, and then perform Counts on the resulting list of classes. I call this set of operations womenCountsByCabin.

Apply our composition to titanic:

In[•]:= **womenCountByCabin = Select [♯sex === "female" &] / * Map [♯class &] / * Counts**

Out[•]= Select [♯sex === female &] / * Map [♯class &] / * Counts

In[•]:= **womenCountByCabin [titanic]**

Out[•]= <| 1st → 144, 2nd → 106, 3rd → 216 |>

Example 3

One can chain these operations together to perform more sophisticated analyses of the data. Here's a set of operations that attempts to obtain the mean age of persons on the Titanic but grouped by the class in which the person had a cabin. I'm going to do it imperfectly at first to set up a point for the next chapter. Notice, though, that I need to map the ♯ age & at level 2 because once I have grouped the data by "class", the "age" information no longer lies at the first level. Basically, GroupBy inserts another level into the data structure.

First show the program in a conventional way and then write it in operator form:

In[•]:= **Map [(Mean / * N) , Map [⧓age &, GroupBy [titanic, ⧓class &] , {2}]]**

Out[•]= <| 1st → 0.00309598 (11 123. + 39. Missing [ ]) , 2nd → 0.00361011 (7704. + 16. Missing [ ]) , 3rd → 0.00141044 (12 449. + 208. Missing [ ]) |>

In[•]:= **(GroupBy [⧓class &] / * Map [Map [⧓age &] / * Mean / * N]) [titanic]**

Out[•]= <| 1st → 0.00309598 (11 123. + 39. Missing [ ]) , 2nd → 0.00361011 (7704. + 16. Missing [ ]) , 3rd → 0.00141044 (12 449. + 208. Missing [ ]) |>

You can see that both of the results are identical and that both have Missings that mess everything up. That's because the "age" column of titanic has Missings. To address this here, I need to filter out missing data from the computation of the mean.

I wrap N around the Mean to get decimal results instead of fractions:

In[•]:= **filteredMean = N [Mean [Select [NumericQ] [⧓]]] &;**

In[•]:= **Map [filteredMean, Map [⧓age &, GroupBy [titanic, ⧓class &] , {2}]]**

Out[•]= <| 1st → 39.1655, 2nd → 29.5172, 3rd → 24.8483 |>

I could equally well write the code this way, making greater use of operator forms:

In[•]:= **Map [filteredMean] [Map [⧓age &, GroupBy [⧓class &] [titanic] , {2}]]**

Out[•]= <| 1st → 39.1655, 2nd → 29.5172, 3rd → 24.8483 |>

I could dispense with the level specification on Map and write the following code:

In[•]:= **Map [filteredMean] [Map [Map [⧓age &] , GroupBy [⧓class &] [titanic]]]**

Out[•]= <| 1st → 39.1655, 2nd → 29.5172, 3rd → 24.8483 |>

I could even write it as follows, using RightComposition and operator forms. First group by class, then for each group of Associations, (1) get the age of each member and then (2) compute the mean of the resulting list of ages.

Notice the nested use of RightComposition. I call this operation meanAgeByCabin:

In[•]:= **meanAgeByCabin = GroupBy [⧓class &] / * Map [Map [⧓age &] / * filteredMean] ;**

I can apply this sequence of composed operations to the entire set of data:

In[•]:= **meanAgeByCabin [titanic]**

Out[•]= <| 1st → 39.1655, 2nd → 29.5172, 3rd → 24.8483 |>

I know this seems cumbersome, but I'll show in the next chapter how the Query command can simplify writing these efforts at information extraction. Indeed, not to give too much away at this point, Query can be thought of as a (brilliant) function-producing function that takes a sequence of other functions and uses the position of those functions in that sequence to produce a pipeline of RightComposed operators.

The pipeline's nesting of Map statements is based on both the nature of the functions and the positions of the functions in the argument sequence.

Example 4

Here I select everyone under age 50, group them by whether they survived or not, and then find the Median age:

```
In[•]:= Map [ Median,
        Map [ ♯age &, GroupBy [ Select [ titanic, ♯age < 50 & ], ♯survived & ], {2} ] ] ]
Out[•]= <| True → 26, False → 27 |>
```

Notice that this could be rewritten making heavy use of operator forms and RightComposition.

I call this sequence of operations medianSurvival:

```
In[•]:= medianSurvival = Select [ ♯age < 50 & ] / *
        GroupBy [ ♯survived & ] / * Map [ Map [ ♯age & ] / * Median ] ;
```

I apply this sequence of compose operations to the titanic data:

```
In[•]:= medianSurvival [ titanic ]
Out[•]= <| True → 26, False → 27 |>
```

Example 5

Suppose I have, as described earlier, additional information stored in a variable named titanicCabins that describes the cabins on the Titanic by listing their class, their square footage, whether they include a window, and the decks on which they were located.

Suppose I now want to compute the mean square footage of cabins on the Titanic but broken down by the sex of its occupying passenger. I do so by creating an operator called passengerCabinJoin. This operator does a JoinAcross on (1) the data it confronts and (2) the "class" and "squarefeet" key-value pairs from titanicCabins. It uses the value associated with the "class" key in each list of Associations to perform the Join.

Create a join operator based on the class in which the passenger was berthed:

```
In[•]:= passengerCabinJoin =
        ( JoinAcross [ ♯1, KeyTake [ { "class", "squarefeet" } ] [ titanicCabins ], "class" ] & ) ;
```

I now apply this operator to our list of Associations titanic. I can group the result by sex, map the ♯ squarefeet & over each association in the resulting groupings and then map Mean over each of the sex groupings.

A RightComposition of operators to find the mean square footage of cabins by gender:

```
In[•]:= ( passengerCabinJoin / * GroupBy [ ♯sex & ] / *
        Map [ Map [ ♯squarefeet & ] / * Mean / * N ] ) [ titanic ]
Out[•]= <| female → 184.549, male → 162.752 |>
```

If I did not want to use JoinAcross, I could do the following. I first build an Association called csf that maps cabin class to square footage. The Map function in the composition that follows creates the key-value pairs. The second function turns the result into an Association.

An Association going from cabin class to square footage:

```
In[•]:=  csf = ( Map [ ♯class → ♯squarefeet &] / * Association ) [ titanicCabins ]

Out[•]=  <| 1st → 300, 2nd → 200, 3rd → 100, crew → 80 |>
```

I now group titanic by sex and, for each resulting group, perform a composed operation. The composition consists of (1) mapping the csf function onto the "class" column of each passenger and (2) computing the mean of the result.

Using an Association as a kind of index to link one structure of Associations to another:

```
In[•]:=  ( GroupBy [ ♯sex &] / * Map [ Map [ csf [ ♯class ] &] / * Mean / * N ] ) [ titanic ]

Out[•]=  <| female → 184.549, male → 162.752 |>
```

MLS Examples

Let's now redo the MLS examples explained in the preceding chapter, but instead of using old-school methods, I'll use the more modern Association form. First, I'll purge the Associations of rows with Missing in either the Club, BaseSalary, or Guaranteed-Compensation column. I can use the Select function to accomplish this goal.

Combine Not and Or with MissingQ to create a function that returns True if the needed data is available:

```
In[•]:=  completeClubBaseGuaranteed = Not [ Or [ MissingQ [ ♯Club ] ,
              MissingQ [ ♯BaseSalary ] , MissingQ [ ♯GuaranteedCompensation ] ] ] &;
```

Use Select to preserve only those rows that have the needed data:

```
In[•]:=  mlsA2 = Select [ completeClubBaseGuaranteed ] [ mlsA ]
```

```
Out[•]=  { <| Club → CHI, LastName → Armas, FirstName → Chris, Position → M,

              BaseSalary → $225 000.00 , GuaranteedCompensation → $225 000.00 , Year → Year: 2007 |> ,

          ⋯ 5530 ⋯ , <| Club → VAN, LastName → Williams, FirstName → Sheanon, Position → D,

              BaseSalary → $175 000.00 , GuaranteedCompensation → $184 000.00 , Year → Year: 2017 |> }

         Full expression not available    (original memory size: 8.3 MB   )                    ⚙
```

I'm left with 5532 rows:

In[ ]:= **Length [mlsA2]**

Out[ ]= 5532

Now that our data is cleansed, let's again find out who have been the 10 highest-paid players in MLS. Notice that I now specify that the sort is to be done according to the result of the ♯ GuaranteedCompensation & applied to each row rather than by having to remember, as I did in the previous chapter, that the base salary information is found in the sixth column of each row.

Use ReverseSort and a Slot function to discover that Kaka and Giovinco are the most highly compensated players:

In[ ]:= **Dataset [ReverseSortBy [mlsA2, ♯GuaranteedCompensation &] , MaxItems → 10]**

Out[ ]=

Club	LastName	FirstName	Position	BaseSalary	GuaranteedCompensation	Year
ORL	Kaka	—	M	6.66×10^6	7.1675×10^6	2017
ORL	Kaka	—	M	6.66×10^6	7.1675×10^6	2016
ORL	Kaka	—	M	6.66×10^6	7.1675×10^6	2015
ORL	Kaka	—	M	6.66×10^6	7.1675×10^6	2014
TOR	Giovinco	Sebastian	M	5.6×10^6	7.11556×10^6	2015
TOR	Giovinco	Sebastian	F	5.6×10^6	7.11556×10^6	2017
TOR	Giovinco	Sebastian	F	5.6×10^6	7.11556×10^6	2016
SEA	Dempsey	Clint	F	4.913×10^6	6.69519×10^6	2014
LA	Beckham	David	M	5.5×10^6	6.5×10^6	2011
LA	Beckham	David	M	5.5×10^6	6.5×10^6	2010

↗ ∧ rows 1–10 of **5532** ∨ ↘

Let's recreate a scatter plot of the base salary versus the guaranteed compensation. Now instead of specifying that I want the fifth and sixth columns, I just name the keys explicitly.

Get two columns from the data using keys and make a scatter plot with ListPlot:

In[ ]:= **ListPlot [mlsA2⟦All, { "BaseSalary", "GuaranteedCompensation" } ⟧, ... +]**

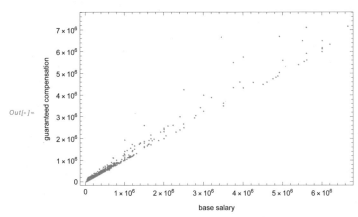

Out[ ]=

Most Highly Compensated Players

It seems as if, for many players, the base compensation is the same as the guaranteed amount, but for others, the guaranteed amount is higher. I'd like to know the identity of players for whom the ratio between guaranteed amount and base amount is greatest. Here I use SortBy and Part to accomplish the job. It looks like some distinct compensation patterns existed in 2010.

Combine Part operators with sorting based on Slot functions:

In[ ]:= **[▪] DatasetForm + [Part [ReverseSortBy [mlsA2,**
#GuaranteedCompensation / #BaseSalary &] , Range [10]]]

Out[ ]=

Club	LastName	FirstName	Position	BaseSalary	GuaranteedCompensation	Year
CHV	Courtois	Laurent	M	$60 000.00	$206 000.00	2011
TFC	Wynne	Marvell	D	$47 500.00	$150 000.00	2008
TFC	Wynne	Marvell	D	$47 500.00	$150 000.00	2007
TFC	White	O'Brian	F	$36 000.00	$113 000.00	2009
POR	Nagbe	Darlington	M/F	$65 000.00	$201 000.00	2011
POR	Okugo	Amobi	D–M	$65 004.00	$187 941.50	2017
TFC	Wynne	Marvell	D	$57 000.00	$159 500.00	2009
PHI	Stahl	Toni	M	$40 000.00	$110 300.00	2010

rows 1–8 of **10**

Payroll over Time

Let's again see how the total league salary has varied over time. You may recall that in the previous chapter, it took an elaborate set of computations. With Associations and GroupBy, it's now one line of code. I group the data according to the Year using a simple Slot function. I then take each row grouped thereby and use a Slot function to extract the GuaranteedCompensation. Then with the third argument, I reduce the list of results by applying the Total function to it.

Use GroupBy to find the total GuaranteedCompensation paid by year in MLS:

In[•]:= **GroupBy [mlsA2, (#Year &) → (#GuaranteedCompensation &) , Total]**

Out[•]= ⟨| Year: **2007** → $4.22237 × 10^7 ,

Year: **2008** → $4.72925 × 10^7 , Year: **2009** → $5.18781 × 10^7 ,

Year: **2010** → $7.1305 × 10^7 , Year: **2011** → $8.50795 × 10^7 ,

Year: **2012** → $9.91309 × 10^7 , Year: **2013** → $9.48496 × 10^7 ,

Year: **2014** → $1.29335 × 10^8 , Year: **2015** → $1.67018 × 10^8 ,

Year: **2016** → $1.75127 × 10^8 , Year: **2017** → $2.00394 × 10^8 |⟩

Although it's a little forced, I can do this with operator forms and produce a graphic. I first construct a function that takes a list of Associations and performs the GroupBy operation described previously. I then pipeline in a DateListPlot operator that has the options iconized away. Notice that I use the // postfix notation here to apply the functions to MLS. Some programmers like this form, and I will confess it has some growing appeal.

The Postfix format is an alternative to the usual bracketed expression, often reducing the complexity of the stacked code:

In[•]:= **mlsA2 / / ((associationList ↦**

GroupBy [associationList , (#Year &) → (#GuaranteedCompensation &) ,
Total]) / ∗ (DateListPlot [#, ... +] &))

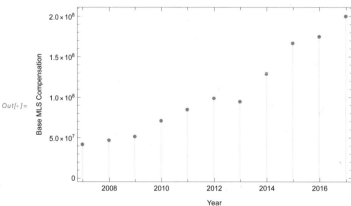

MLS Teams with the Highest Payroll

What took a great deal of code in the preceding chapter is again a one liner!

GroupBy makes it easy to see what clubs had the highest payroll in any particular year:

In[·]:= **Take [ReverseSort [GroupBy [mlsA2,**
({♯Club , ♯Year } &) → (♯GuaranteedCompensation &) , Total]] , 5]

Out[·]= ⟨| {TOR, Year: 2017 } → $2.23998 × 10⁷ ,

{TOR, Year: 2015 } → $2.21365 × 10⁷ , {TOR, Year: 2016 } → $2.17985 × 10⁷ ,

{LA, Year: 2015 } → $2.12676 × 10⁷ , {NYCFC, Year: 2016 } → $2.11278 × 10⁷ |⟩

Exercises

3.1 Get the first three rows of **dinghy**.

3.2 Get the sex and survived columns of **dinghy**.

3.3 Get the age and cellphone number of the third and fourth passengers in **dinghy**. Since the third passenger did not, in fact, have a cellphone, return a **Missing** value for that piece of data. Use operator forms of functions where possible.

3.4 Figure out how to make this.
{ ⟨| "id"→1, "class"→"3rd", "age"→16, "sex"→"female", "survived"→True |⟩, ⟨| "id"→2, "class"→"1st", "age"→65, "sex"→"male", "survived"→False |⟩, ⟨| "id"→3, "class"→"3rd", "age"→2, "sex"→"female", "survived"→False |⟩, ⟨| "id"→4, "class"→"3rd", "age"→Missing [ ], "sex"→"female", "survived"→True |⟩, ⟨| "id"→5, "class"→"3rd", "age"→18, "sex"→"female", "survived"→False |⟩ }

3.5 Now figure out how to make this.
⟨| "Frederica"→⟨| "class"→"3rd", "age"→16, "sex"→"female", "survived"→True |⟩, "George"→ ⟨| "class"→ "1st", "age"→65, "sex"→"male", "survived"→False |⟩, "Harold"→⟨| "class"→"3rd", "age"→2, "sex"→"female" "survived"→False |⟩, "Ida"→⟨| "class"→"3rd", "age"→Missing [ ], "sex"→"female", "survived"→True |⟩, "Jeanette"→⟨| "class"→"3rd", "age"→18, "sex"→"female", "survived"→False |⟩ |⟩

3.6 Compute the median age of the passengers on the Titanic broken down by cabin class. You are going to get error messages if you don't figure out how to deal with data for which the age is missing.

3.7 Find the distribution of guaranteed compensation in 2015 for MLS players based on their listed position. Create a histogram for each position that has at least 25 players. Hint 1: Remember to wrap your years in **DateObject** because that's the way they are denoted in the data. Hint 2: Please remember to put parentheses around your **Slot** functions. Use this **Histogram** function and sample output to guide you.

histo = Histogram [♯ , Automatic, Automatic, PlotRange → { { 0; 1 000 000 } , Automatic }] &;

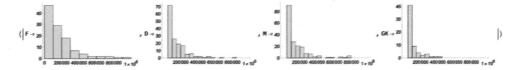

Tech Notes

- Notice that if one uses a **Head** other than **List** to wrap the rules, the Wolfram Language does not strip off the wrapper. **List** is special here.

In[•]:= **Association [f ["class" → "1st", "age" → 29, "sex" → "female", "survived" → True]]**

Out[•]= Association [f [class → 1st, age → 29, sex → female, survived → True]]

- Suppose one has a key that would not, standing alone, be a permissible Wolfram Language symbol. Examples are "plaintiff age" (spaces) or "plaintiff_age" (underscores). If one tries to omit the quotation marks when using these keys in **Slot** functions, one is going to have problems. These two expressions fail.

In[•]:= **{ #plaintiff age& [Association ["plaintiff age" – >29]],**
#plaintiff_age& [Association ["plaintiff_age" – >29]] }

> ⋯ Function : Named Slot plaintiff in   #plaintiff age & cannot be filled from   <|plaintiff age   → 29|>.

> ⋯ Function : Named Slot plaintiff in   #plaintiff _age & cannot be filled from   <|plaintiff _age → 29|>.

Out[•]= { age #plaintiff, _age #plaintiff }

- Use of quotation marks solves the problem.

In[•]:= **{ #"plaintiff age" & [Association ["plaintiff age" → 29]],**
#"plaintiff_age" & [Association ["plaintiff_age" → 29]] }

Out[•]= { 29, 29 }

- Under the hood, a lot of Wolfram Language functions are converted into a variant of the ResourceFunction **Slice** when used with Associations (or Datasets). Examples include **Span**, **Take**, and **Drop**.

- One has to be consistent when specifying parts for **Slice**. Mixing strings and integers as part specifications fails.

In[•]:= [•] **Slice** + **[All, { "age", 4 }] [dinghy]**

Out[•]= { Missing [PartInvalid, { age, 4 }],
Missing [PartInvalid, { age, 4 }], Missing [PartInvalid, { age, 4 }],
Missing [PartInvalid, { age, 4 }], Missing [PartInvalid, { age, 4 }] }

- **Slice** requires its argument to be strings or integers or lists thereof.

In[•]:= **([•] Slice +) [notAString] [**
Association [notAString → 3, notAString2 → 4, "a string" → 5]]

Out[•]= Missing [PartInvalid, notAString]

- But one can fix this by wrapping the symbol in **Key**.

In[•]:= **([•] Slice +) [Key [notAString]] [**
Association [notAString → 3, notAString2 → 4, "a string" → 5]]

Out[•]= 3

- Beware of Associations with integer keys. Compare the results of the following piece of code, which makes use of the "nutty" Association described at the start of the chapter.

In[ ]:= **{ [▣] Slice [+] [8] [nutty] , [▣] Slice [+] [Key @ 8] [nutty] }**

Out[ ]= **{ gee, 1 }**

- Likewise, beware of Associations with Boolean keys (True or False).

In[ ]:= **assocBoolean = Association [True → 8, False → 3]**

Out[ ]= **<| True → 8, False → 3 |>**

- The Part function does not accept Boolean values, nor does the corresponding Slice function. Many errors can occur when the keys are Booleans.

In[ ]:= **{ assocBoolean⟦False⟧, ResourceFunction ["Slice"] [False] [assocBoolean] }**

   (···) Part : The expression False cannot be used as a part specification.

Out[ ]= **{ <| True → 8, False → 3 |> ⟦ False ⟧, Missing [PartInvalid, False] }**

- When it occurs, a fix for this problem is to turn the Boolean keys into strings. This can be done using KeyMap. Here is the result in InputForm so one can see the quotation marks.

In[ ]:= **InputForm [assocBooleanString = KeyMap [ToString, assocBoolean]]**

Out[ ]//InputForm= **< | "True" −> 8, "False" −> 3 | >**

In[ ]:= **{ assocBooleanString⟦"False"⟧,**
   ResourceFunction ["Slice"] ["False"] [assocBooleanString] ,
   #False & [assocBooleanString] }

Out[ ]= **{ 3, 3, 3 }**

- There is the potential to lose information when using Merge. Suppose, for example, that I have a List of Associations that are "ragged," i.e. the set of keys is not identical over the rows.

In[ ]:= **dinghyRagged = DeleteMissing [dinghy, 2, 2]**

Out[ ]= { <| class → 3rd, age → 16, sex → female, survived → True |>,
      <| class → 1st, age → 65, sex → male, survived → False |>,
      <| class → 3rd, age → 2, sex → female, survived → False |>,
      <| class → 3rd, sex → female, survived → True |>,
      <| class → 3rd, age → 18, sex → female, survived → False |> }

Now when I merge, I get Lists of five values for all the keys except age. It's impossible to reverse the merger because I don't know which row omitted the age key.

In[ ]:= **Merge [dinghyRagged, Identity]**

Out[ ]= <| class → { 3rd, 1st, 3rd, 3rd, 3rd }, age → { 16, 65, 2, 18 },
      sex → { female, male, female, female, female },
      survived → { True, False, False, True, False } |>

- There are a growing number of functions with operator forms. This code, which finds many of them, may take a minute or so to run. To get a full list of functions instead of just the number of such functions, try deleting the **Length** wrapper from the code.

In[ ]:= **Length [WolframLanguageData [**

☷**Wolfram Language curryable symbols** (Wolfram Language symbols)]]

Out[ ]= 124

- The Wolfram Language kernel views Associations as "atomic," so some operations, like **Fold**, that work on Lists do not work on Associations. Thus, a **Fold** on the values of **chingAssociation** produces a transformation of the expression.

In[ ]:= **Fold [f, x, Values [chingAssociation]]**

Out[ ]= $f\big[f\big[f\big[f[f[f[f[x,\text{HOU}],\text{Ching}],\text{Brian}],F],\$220\,000\big],\$220\,000\big],$ Year: **2007** $\big]$

- Whereas this use of **Fold** produces an error and just spits back the original expression.

In[ ]:= **Fold [f, x, chingAssociation]**

●●● Fold : Nonatomic expression expected at position 3 in Fold $\Big[$f, x, $\langle\big|$ team $\rightarrow$ HOU, lastName $\rightarrow$ Ching, firstName $\rightarrow$ Brian, position $\rightarrow$ F, baseSalary $\rightarrow$ \$220000 , guaranteedSalary $\rightarrow$ \$220000 , year $\rightarrow$ Year: **2007** $\big|\rangle\Big]$.

Out[ ]= $\text{Fold}\Big[$f, x, $\langle\big|$ team $\rightarrow$ HOU, lastName $\rightarrow$ Ching, firstName $\rightarrow$ Brian, position $\rightarrow$ F, baseSalary $\rightarrow$ \$220 000 , guaranteedSalary $\rightarrow$ \$220 000 , year $\rightarrow$ Year: **2007** $\big|\rangle\Big]$

- Also, when one wants to visualize the **TreeForm** of an **Association**, the **Association** is treated as the single atom that it is.

In[ ]:= **TreeForm [chingAssociation, ImageSize → 600]**

Out[ ]//TreeForm=

- Taking the **Normal** of an **Association** can sometimes help with the visualization of the contents of the **Association**.

In[ ]:= **TreeForm [Normal [chingAssociation] , ImageSize → 600]**

Out[ ]//TreeForm=

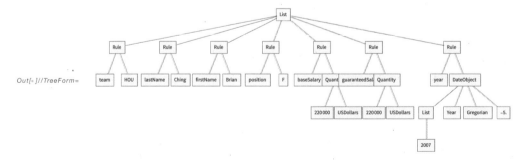

- I can write little functions that go back and forth between a conventional (left) Composition of a sequence of functions and the representation of that Composition using RightComposition. These ancillary functions will sometimes prove useful as I try to decipher what is really going on in some complex composition of functions—such as those, as we will see, that are produced by Query.

In[•]:= **rightCompositionToLeftComposition [RightComposition [f___]] :=**
    Composition @@ (Reverse @ (List @@ f))

In[•]:= **leftCompositionToRightComposition [f___] :=**
    RightComposition @@ (Reverse @ (List @@ f))

- I can test that the functions work as claimed.

In[•]:= **{ SameQ [f / * g / * h, RightComposition [rightCompositionToLeftComposition,**
        leftCompositionToRightComposition] [f / * g / * h] ,
      Composition [leftCompositionToRightComposition,
        rightCompositionToLeftComposition] [f / * g / * h]] ,
      SameQ [f @* g @* h, RightComposition [leftCompositionToRightComposition,
        rightCompositionToLeftComposition] [f @* g @* h] ,
      Composition [rightCompositionToLeftComposition,
        leftCompositionToRightComposition] [f @* g @* h]] }

Out[•]= **{ True, True }**

- There is presently no built-in operator form for the three-argument form of GroupBy that uses a reducer function, but the useful ResourceFunction MapReduceOperator permits inclusion of a reducer function.

In[•]:= **mro =** ⬡ **MapReduceOperator** ⬦ **[(♯sex &) → (♯age &) ,**
    DeleteMissing / * Median / * N, "Parallelize" → True]

Out[•]= **ParallelMap [DeleteMissing / * Median / * N, GroupBy [(♯sex &) → (♯age &)] [♯1]] &**

- I can now apply this operator to dinghy and get the median ages broken down by sex.

In[•]:= **mro [dinghy]**

Out[•]= **<| female → 16., male → 65. |>**

References

L. Shifrin. *Mathematica Programming: An Advanced Introduction*. 2008. www.archive.org/details/ost-computer-science-mathprogrammingintro.

Wolfram Research, Inc., "Function Composition & Operator Forms," *Wolfram Language & System Documentation Center*. (July 27, 2021) reference.wolfram.com/language/guide/FunctionCompositionAndOperatorForms.html. (describing various Wolfram Language functions that implement these concepts)

More to Explore

Guide to Associations in the Wolfram Language (wolfr.am/Associations)

Check out Stephen Wolfram's blog about launching the Wolfram Function Repository (wolfr.am/FunctionRepositoryAnnouncement)

4 | Query

This chapter uses a data resource from the Wolfram Data Repository (wolfr.am/WDR). To access the data, evaluate the following code.

Acquire the ResourceObject from the Wolfram Data Repository:

```
In[·]:=  ro = ResourceObject [ "Sample Data for Query Book" ]
```

Out[·]= ResourceObject[⊞ 🏛 Name: Sample Data for Query Book »
                              Type: DataResource
                        Description: Data to support the Wolfram Media book Query:
                                      Getting Information from Data wit...]

Some of the code in the preceding chapter got pretty obscure. Using different operators at different levels in the same expression can be a challenge. Here is where the Query function often comes to the rescue. In the simplest sense, Query is a functional programming construct like Map, Apply, Select, or CurryApplied. You can think of it as a recipe for creating pipelines of functions. The arguments to Query are generally themselves functions or compositions of functions. Although Query was introduced to the Wolfram Language at about the same time as the Association construct, it is actually quite useful for general programming tasks. This chapter shows how to use Query on a variety of data structures to make your programs more elegant and efficient.

Query Structure

Arguments

The precise pipeline Query creates depends on the position and content of each function or composition in the sequence of arguments presented to it. The first argument generally operates on the entirety of the expression. The second argument generally operates at the first level of the expression. A third argument generally creates code that will operate at the second level of the expression and so on. Each subsequent position of an argument in Query generally operates at the next lower level of the expression to which it will ultimately be applied. The "generally" qualification is present in each of the preceding sentences for good reason, however. The exact order in which Query operates depends on the content of the functions being used. Fortunately, the exceptions are generally logical. And, as I'll show, there's a simple way to determine the order of operations created by Query without having to actually run the Query function on data.

Here's a simple example. Suppose I wanted to Map the function v over each item at level 1 of an expression and then apply the function u to the entire result. Here's how I could do it. I'll use that little expression g[8, h[x, y, 9]] to illustrate the result.

Apply functions at different levels of an expression without Query:

In[∘]:= `u [ Map [ v, g [ 8, h [ x, y, 9 ] ] ] ]`

Out[∘]= `u [ g [ v [ 8 ], v [ h [ x, y, 9 ] ] ] ]`

Here's how I could do it using Query. I make u the first argument to Query because I basically want it to work at the top level (level 0) and make v the second argument because I want it to work on everything at the first level.

Apply functions at different levels with Query:

In[∘]:= `Query [ u, v ] [ g [ 8, h [ x, y, 9 ] ] ]`

Out[∘]= `u [ g [ v [ 8 ], v [ h [ x, y, 9 ] ] ] ]`

Discovering the Order of Operations Produced by a Query

For beginners, the best way to determine the pipeline of operations produced by a Query expression is to run Normal on it. Let's look at my previous example.

Normal shows the order of operations resulting from a Query expression:

In[∘]:= `Normal [ Query [ u, v ] ]`

Out[∘]= `Map [ v ] / * u`

Notice two things. First, the Query can exist without regard to any data structure. It is essentially a recipe for building a function. Although this concept is sometimes difficult for newcomers to functional programming or the Wolfram Language, it's really no different than writing a function $x \mapsto x^2$ or the function Map [Sqrt]. Those functions can exist perfectly well without ever seeing any data.

Second, notice that the Wolfram Language kernel returns a RightComposition of functions. First, the v function is mapped over the data. Then the u function is applied to the result.

Here's another example. I pick this one because, without reading either the rest of this chapter or the Wolfram Language documentation, you might not intuit the order in which operations are done. This is why Normal is so helpful. The operation is extremely fast even when working with big data: it doesn't need the data on which the Query will ultimately be performed. It thus lets one learn by experimentation and practice.

GroupBy in a Query produces a different order of operations in the pipeline than might naively be expected:

In[∘]:= **Normal [Query [GroupBy [f] , g, h]]**

Out[∘]= GroupBy [f] / * Map [Map [h] / * g]

This response is a little hard to read because of the nested Map statements. The idea, however, is that first the grouping is performed. Then the function h is mapped over the prior result at level {2}, and then the function g is mapped over the prior result. Although Normal when applied to Query does not make use of ResourceFunctions to express its output, if it did, the output from the previous Query might look like the following output.

A Map that contains a pipeline that itself contains a Map can be "flattened" with use of the MapLevel ResourceFunction:

In[∘]:= **GroupBy [f] / ✶ [◦] MapLevel ⊹ [h, { 2 }] / ✶ Map [g];**

I cannot say this too often—when in doubt, apply Normal to the Query and study the resulting pipeline. Although the Normal of a Query is not quite a perfect replica of the actual Query, the order of operations for the two is *always* the same. Indeed, it would be rational to skip the following subsection of the book, which attempts to explain the intricacies of order of operations with Query, and just decide to check your Query with Normal every time you use it. It would be better, however, to read the following subsection because it's intrinsically interesting and because a good theoretical understanding can save time.

Visualizing a Query

You can also visualize a Query itself in TreeForm. Here I make use of the ResourceFunction QueryTreeForm to visualize the order of operations in a Query expression. It presents the order of operations the same as a tree descended on a depth-first basis. I've written some simple code that does some decoration. It labels the tree with the original Query expression on top and the Normal representation of that Query expression on the bottom.

Visualize the pipeline produced by Query as a tree:

In[∘]:= **labeledQueryTreeForm [q_Query, opts : OptionsPattern [[◦] QueryTreeForm ⊹]] :=**
    [◦] QueryTreeForm ⊹ [q, opts] / /
        (Labeled [♯, { q, Normal [q] }, { Top, Bottom }] &)

In[•]:= **labeledQueryTreeForm [Query [u, v]] / / Framed**

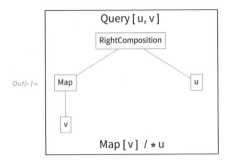

Out[•]=

Query has constructed a pipeline of functions in which, first, the v function is mapped over the data and then the u function is applied to the result. Normal outputs the result as a RightComposition—which I think is a good thing, but just be aware that it could equally well have returned the result as a Composition, u @* Map [v] . This, by the way, is why I emphasized RightComposition so much in the preceding chapters. It may be thought by some users of the Wolfram Language to be a peculiar or obscure focus, but a good understanding of RightComposition ends up being crucial to understanding Query and interpreting its output when things go wrong.

Order of Operations in Query

Learning Strategies

The hardest part of Query is mastering order of operations. Why, for example, was the previous pipeline Map [v] / * u instead of u / * Map [v]? There are three ways of learning this order. The first is the one I already suggested. Just experiment using Normal. One can learn a lot by playing around. Sometimes, however, repeated experimentation with Normal on different Query expressions devolves into hopeless floundering. It's often useful and more elegant to get the Query expression right the first time. I now thus present two design principles that, along with the details contained in the official documentation, should help you quickly generate efficient queries.

LIFO: The General Rule

Here's the first principle. It's LIFO. Last in, first out. The order of operations is generally in the opposite order of the arguments to Query. By way of example, in the previous Query, the v function is the second argument to Query, so it is put in the pipeline before the u function, which is the first argument.

LIFO isn't an arbitrary convention. It makes a lot of sense. The operations generally have to start at the lowest level instead of the highest level because a function applied higher in an expression could eliminate subexpressions at lower levels. And if that happened, subsequently applied functions would then have no input on which to operate.

Let's look at more complicated examples of this general principle. Here is a visualization of Query [u, v, w].

Visualize the pipeline produced by a three-level Query as a tree:

In[ ]:= **labeledQueryTreeForm [Query [u, v, w]] / / Framed**

Out[ ]=

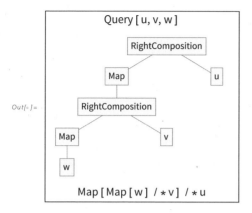

You can see a nested RightComposition of operators. The first thing that happens is that the kernel forms a lower-level RightComposition in which w is mapped over data and then v is applied to the result. The mapping of w comes before the application of v because w is the third argument and v is the second argument. In short, the inner composition is Map [w] / * v. That composed function is itself the first component of a higher-level composition in which the mapping of the lower-level composition is the first component and the function u is the second component. The mapping of the lower-level composition comes first because of the LIFO convention: the function u is before the functions v or w in the arguments to Query, so u is applied after v and w have done their work.

The functions within Query can themselves be compositions. Look at this one.

Visualize a Query pipeline produced with composed operators:

In[ ]:= **labeledQueryTreeForm [Query [u1 / * u2, v, w]] / / Framed**

Out[ ]=

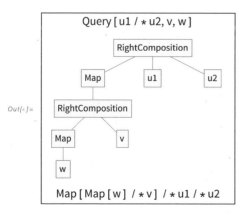

Now notice that although u1 comes before u2, u1 is the first element in the right composition and u2 is the second element. If more than one function is part of the same argument to Query, the functions are right composed in the order provided, not in reverse order. The reverse ordering convention described previously applies only with respect to differently positioned arguments to Query.

Here's what happens when I apply this Query to some data. I'll show the results using TreeForm.

Visualize the results of a Query that itself contains composed operators:

In[ ]:=   **TreeForm [Query [u1 / ∗ u2, v, w] [g [8, h [x, y, 9]]]] / / Framed**

Out[ ]=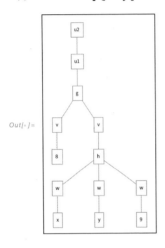

You can see the composition as u1 is first applied at the top level and then u2 is applied.

Here's a yet more baroque Query. I wish I could tell you that we never do things this complicated, but as you will see, we do. So it's crucial to understand the order of operations.

Visualize a Query making extensive use of composed operators:

In[ ]:=   **labeledQueryTreeForm [**
              Query [u1 / ∗ u2, v1 / ∗ v2 / ∗ v3, w1 / ∗ w2] , ImageSize → 420] / / Framed

Out[ ]=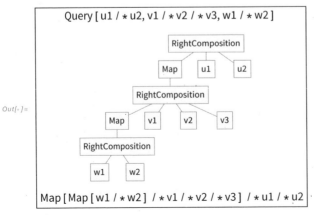

Here the w1 / * w2 RightComposition comes first and is at the lowest level of the Query tree. The mapping of that composition then is the first element in a RightComposition with v1, v2, and v3. That intermediate level is then itself the first element in a top-level RightComposition with u1 and u2. It's that last, top-level composition that is applied to the data.

Again, let's look at it with data. You can see the stacking of the operators. The functions w1 and w2 are serially applied to the data at the lowest level. Then v1, v2, and v3 are applied to the intermediate results, and then u1 and u2 are applied to the top-level results. By the way, it's almost as if we take the operators that appear horizontally in the diagram of the previous pure Query and rotate them 90 degrees counterclockwise to see how they apply to the data.

Visualize the results of a Query making extensive use of composed operators:

In[•]:= **TreeForm [Query [u1 / * u2, v1 / * v2 / * v3, w1 / * w2] [g [8, h [x, y, 9]]]] / / Framed**

Out[•]=

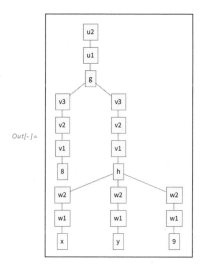

Query, of course works with Associations, and, as will be discussed in the next chapter, Datasets.

Here I use a Part function inside Query to get the age of the first three passengers from a data structure (a List of Associations):

In[•]:= **dinghy = ResourceData [ro, "Dinghy List of Associations"]**

Out[•]= { <| class → 3rd, age → 16, sex → female, survived → True |>,
  <| class → 1st, age → 65, sex → male, survived → False |>,
  <| class → 3rd, age → 2, sex → female, survived → False |>,
  <| class → 3rd, age → Missing [ ] , sex → female, survived → True |>,
  <| class → 3rd, age → 18, sex → female, survived → False |> }

In[•]:= **Query [⌗ ⟦ { 1, 2, 3 } ⟧ &, ⌗age &] [dinghy]**

Out[•]= { 16, 65, 2 }

Beyond LIFO: Descending and Ascending Operators

The second principle is that Query doesn't insist on LIFO where there is good reason to believe that doing things out of LIFO order will be efficient and will not wreck anything. This principle is consistent with the reasoning behind the LIFO presumption. One generally operates first at the lowest level because one worries that doing otherwise could destroy data in a way that would make operations at higher levels meaningless. But there are operations whose form gives one confidence that they will not destroy data. Query constructs a pipeline that puts those operations first because doing so is faster and can often save memory. For example, suppose that one wasn't talking about a little dinghy but the full ocean liner Titanic. It would be wasteful to go through the entire data structure to get the age of every single passenger and then select the age of just the first three. It would be smarter to get the first three passengers and then determine their age.

"Do things that are efficient and won't wreck things" is not really a rule that the kernel can implement. Determination of which operators are put first in the pipeline is based on their form, not necessarily their function. So these principles are implemented—pretty well but not perfectly—by imagining the kernel as moving through the expression tree, first going down in a breadth-first manner and then coming back up. (Expression trees generally grow upside down in the computer world.) Only the few operators labeled as descending are executed on the way down. Otherwise, the kernel works in the normal way set forth in its documentation: starting with the leaves of the expression and working its way up the tree. Operators that aren't descending are called ascending. When in doubt, assume an operator is ascending.

Here's a picture that may help. Here's a TreeForm of Query[f, g] applied to the List of Lists {{3,4}, {5,6}}. Ordinarily, if the resulting structure wasn't the result of a Query, the deepest levels would be evaluated first. That is, think of a little creature wandering the (upside down) tree. It keeps heading down, and when it can't get any further, it goes back up until it can go down over previously untraversed paths. On the way up—but *not* on the way down—when it finds an expression it can transform, it does so, so here the kernel would keep going down to, say 3, come up to List, go down to 4, come up to List, come up to g and say, "Wait, I can evaluate g[{3,4}]; I'll do that now." The creature would wander further and ultimately hit g[{5,7}] and evaluate that. Then it would pass the resulting expression to List (which wouldn't do anything) and then pass the resulting expression to f.

Using TreeForm to demonstrate the order of kernel evaluations:

In[•]:= **TreeForm [Query [f, g] [{ { 3, 4 }, { 5, 7 } }]] // Framed**

Out[•]=

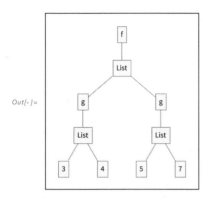

You can see this if I take the Normal form of the Query and Trace it. First, it takes the RightComposition and converts it to a traditional expression. Then it maps g over the List { {3, 4}, {5, 6} }, and it takes that result and passes it to f.

Use Trace to see how the Normal form of a Query works:

In[•]:= **Column @ With [{ nq = Normal [Query [f, g]] }, Trace [nq [{ { 3, 4 }, { 5, 7 } }]]]**

Out[•]=
```
( Map [ g ] / * f ) [ { { 3, 4 }, { 5, 7 } } ]
f [ Map [ g ] [ { { 3, 4 }, { 5, 7 } } ] ]
{ Map [ g ] [ { { 3, 4 }, { 5, 7 } } ], { g [ { 3, 4 } ], g [ { 5, 7 } ] } }
f [ { g [ { 3, 4 } ], g [ { 5, 7 } ] } ]
```

The next example makes clear that form matters. There are two pieces of code that are functionally equivalent in most contexts. They both grab the first three parts of a data structure. One does it using a Part function. The other does it using Span. When the Part function is used, the kernel doesn't recognize it as necessarily non-destructive, so it puts it last in the pipeline. But when Span is used, the kernel recognizes it as non-destructive and elevates its priority.

Compare Span, which is recognized as a non-destructive operator and thus comes first, with the Part function, which is not so recognized and thus comes last (LIFO):

In[•]:= **Map [Normal, { Query [#〚 { 1, 2, 3 } 〛 &, ♯age &], Query [1 ;; 3, ♯age &] }]**

Out[•]= { Map [♯age &] / * (#1〚 { 1, 2, 3 } 〛 &), GeneralUtilities ` Slice [1 ;; 3] / * Map [♯age &] }

Descending Operators

I will now discuss some of the most common "descending operators" that cut in line in the operator pipeline formed by Query. Select is a common example. It makes sense to select data first because then the pipeline doesn't have to process as much at the lower levels. Moreover, Select won't change the content of the expressions it encounters. It just keeps some while discarding others.

Here's the result of a Query whose first argument selects values whose total is even and whose second argument maps the addition of 1 to the second part of each of the expressions it confronts. If the conventional LIFO order prevailed, the kernel would first perform ♯ + 1 & on each of the second parts of { {3, 4}, {5, 7} } and produce { {3, 5}, {5, 8} }. Then Select would realize that only {3, 5} has an even total. The result of the Query would be {3, 5}.

However, that's not what happens. Instead, Select gets precedence. It identifies {5, 7} but not {3, 4} as having a total that is even, so we are left with just { {5, 7} }. We then add 1 to the second position of each element of that intermediate result and are left with { {5, 8} }.

The Select in this Query gets executed first, even though it is the first argument to Query:

In[•]:= **Query [Select [EvenQ [Total [♯]] &] , MapAt [♯ + 1 &, {2}]] [{ {3, 4}, {5, 7} }]**

Out[•]= **{ {5, 8} }**

Trace again shows what is going on. Although it's a little involved, you should be able to see that Select is being performed before MapAt.

Trace shows the exact order of operations in executing the Query:

In[•]:= **Column @ With [**
{ nq = Normal [Query [Select [EvenQ [Total [♯]] &] , MapAt [♯ + 1 &, {2}]]] },
Trace [nq [{ {3, 4}, {5, 7} }]]]

Out[•]=
(Select [EvenQ [Total [♯1]] &] / * MapAt [♯1 + 1 &, {All, 2}]) [{ {3, 4}, {5, 7} }]
MapAt [♯1 + 1 &, {All, 2}] [Select [EvenQ [Total [♯1]] &] [{ {3, 4}, {5, 7} }]]
{ Select [EvenQ [Total [♯1]] &] [{ {3, 4}, {5, 7} }],
   { (EvenQ [Total [♯1]] &) [{3, 4}] , EvenQ [Total [{3, 4}]] ,
      {Total [{3, 4}] , 7} , EvenQ [7] , False} , { (EvenQ [Total [♯1]] &) [{5, 7}] ,
      EvenQ [Total [{5, 7}]] , {Total [{5, 7}] , 12} , EvenQ [12] , True} , { {5, 7} } }
MapAt [♯1 + 1 &, {All, 2}] [{ {5, 7} }]
{ {5, (♯1 + 1 &) [7] } }
{ { (♯1 + 1 &) [7], 7 + 1, 8} , {5, 8} }
{ {5, 8} }

Here are some other common descending operators that Query inserts early in the operator pipeline it constructs.

Slice Operators

There are a number of built-in Wolfram Language functions that get converted into a special operator: GeneralUtilities`Slice. ` functions that get converted include Span, Take, and Key. The ResourceFunction Slice also gets converted. Anything that gets converted into this form is a descending operator; Query inserts it early in the pipeline. This early insertion makes sense because these operators just filter out unwanted items in a data structure. Here's a demonstration.

Operators that are transformed into Slice are descending and get precedence:

In[•]:= { Normal [Query [1 ;; 3]],
    Normal [Query [Take [5]]], Normal [Query [Key [imakey]]] }

Out[•]= { GeneralUtilities ` Slice [1 ;; 3],
    GeneralUtilities ` Slice [ 5 ], GeneralUtilities ` Slice [Key [imakey]] }

When one uses a string as an argument to Query, the kernel assumes one means to use it as a Key. It is thus converted into a GeneralUtilities ` Slice and placed early in the pipeline.

Query treats a string argument as if wrapped by Key and converts into a GeneralUtilities ` Slice:

In[•]:= **Normal [Query ["a", f]]**

Out[•]= GeneralUtilities ` Slice [a] / * f

A Query that extracts the value associated with the "a" key and applies the function f to the result:

In[•]:= **Query ["a", f] [Association ["a" → 3, "b" → 4]]**

Out[•]= f [3]

Variants of Select (SelectFirst, KeySelect, MaximalBy, MinimalBy) likewise just prune out data, so they are "descending," getting applied on the way down.

Select, KeySelect, and similar operators get precedence:

In[•]:= { Normal [Query [Select [EvenQ], g]],
    Normal [Query [SelectFirst [EvenQ], g]], Normal [Query [KeySelect [EvenQ], g]],
    Normal [Query [MaximalBy [Last], g]], Normal [Query [MinimalBy [Last], g]] }

Out[•]= { Select [EvenQ] / * Map [g], SelectFirst [EvenQ] / * g, KeySelect [EvenQ] / * Map [g],
    MaximalBy [Last] / * Map [g], MinimalBy [Last] / * Map [g] }

Deletes

Included among "descending operators" are certain functions that delete, such as DeleteDuplicatesBy and DeleteMissing. These functions are also filters, except that instead of specifying what one wants to keep, one specifies what one wants to get rid of. By getting rid of data, these filtering functions tend to accelerate the execution of subsequent commands.

DeleteDuplicates and basic versions of DeleteMissing get precedence:

In[•]:= **Map [Normal, { Query [DeleteDuplicatesBy [EvenQ], g], Query [DeleteMissing, g] }]**

Out[•]= { DeleteDuplicatesBy [EvenQ] / * Map [g], DeleteMissing / * Map [g] }

Cases

At least in some circumstances, Cases is treated as a descending operator. When used at the first level, Cases does not tend to destroy structure.

The basic use of Cases gets precedence:

In[•]:= **Normal [Query [Cases [{ _, _ }], g]]**

Out[•]= Cases [{ _, _ }] / * Map [g]

Thus, the following Query does not take the first element of each sublist and then see whether the result has just two values. Instead, it first sees which sublists have two values and then finds the first part of the result.

A more complicated instance demonstrating Cases and precedence:

In[•]:= **Query [Cases [{ _, _ }], First] [{ { 3, 4 }, { 5, 6, 7 }, { 8, 9 } }]**

Out[•]= { 3, 8 }

Sorting Operators

Certain forms of various sorting functions, such as Sort, SortBy, ReverseSort, ReverseSortBy, and KeySortBy, are descending operators. They are put toward the front of the pipeline.

Query puts these sorting operations first:

In[•]:= **Map [Normal, { Query [Sort, g], Query [SortBy [f], g], Query [ReverseSort, g],**
Query [ReverseSortBy [f], g], Query [KeySortBy [f], g] }]

Out[•]= { Sort / * Map [g], SortBy [f] / * Map [g], ReverseSort / * Map [g],
ReverseSortBy [f] / * Map [g], KeySortBy [f] / * Map [g] }

Notice, again, that form matters. Here I write SortBy, ReverseSortBy, and KeySortBy as anonymous functions. They are not treated as descending operators even though the code functions the same way as it did previously.

When sorting operations are performed using an anonymous function, Query generally does not recognize them as descending operators:

In[•]:= **Map [Normal, { Query [SortBy [#, f] &, g],**
Query [ReverseSortBy [#, f] &, g], Query [KeySortBy [#, f] &, g] }]

Out[•]= { Map [g] / * (SortBy [#1, f] &),
Map [g] / * (ReverseSortBy [#1, f] &), Map [g] / * (KeySortBy [#1, f] &) }

Here's an example showing more concretely the importance of form in Query arguments. I show two variants of Sort that might appear identical. The first time, I use Sort. The second time I use Sort [#] &. The results differ because the order of operations is different.

Take a matrix. The order in which Total is applied to the rows depends on whether Sort or Sort [♯] & is used:

In[ ]:= **matrix = { {2, 11}, {7, 0}, {−1, 9}, {4, 5}, {1, 16} };**
{ Query [Sort, Total] [matrix] , Query [Sort [♯] &, Total] [matrix] }

Out[ ]= { {8, 17, 13, 9, 7}, {7, 8, 9, 13, 17} }

Several other sorting operators, including KeySort, AlphabeticSort, and LexicographicSort, are not "descending" and thus do not get promoted in the pipeline produced by Query.

The specialized sorting operators AlphabeticSort and LexicographicSort are not descending. Neither is KeySort:

In[ ]:= **Map [Normal,**
{ Query [KeySort, g] , Query [AlphabeticSort, g] , Query [LexicographicSort, g] }]

Out[ ]= { Map [g] / * KeySort, Map [g] / * AlphabeticSort, Map [g] / * LexicographicSort}

Values

Values is a function that strips the keys off Associations. Perhaps because stripping off the keys can make things go faster, Values is applied early as a "descending operator."

Query treats Values as a descending operator and therefore prioritizes it in the operator pipeline:

In[ ]:= **Normal [Query [Values, g]]**

Out[ ]= Values / * Map [g]

DescendingQ

In cases of doubt, there is a function tucked away in the Dataset` context that can help you determine whether a single operator will be descending or not: Dataset`DescendingQ. (Don't use this on composed operators.) Here's an example of how that function works.

Use Dataset`DescendingQ to know for sure if an operator is descending:

In[ ]:= **Needs ["Dataset`"]**

In[ ]:= **AssociationMap [Dataset`DescendingQ, { Select [f] , ♯age &, Sqrt,**
SortBy [♯age &] , Take [5] , DeleteMissing, DeleteMissing [♯, 1, 2] &}]

Out[ ]= <| Select [f] → True, (♯age &) → False, Sqrt → False, SortBy [♯age &] → True,
5 → True, DeleteMissing → True, (DeleteMissing [♯1, 1, 2] &) → False |>

Again, notice that form matters. While DeleteMissing itself is descending, more complex variants of it, such as DeleteMissing [♯, 1, 2] &, are not. This is why one has to be very careful before assuming that an operator is descending. Moral: use Normal to check the pipeline structure or use Dataset`DescendingQ to check on a particular operator.

Four Complications

I will now deal with four complications: (1) composed operators; (2) GroupBy; (3) subqueries; and (4) "Part Specification-Rule" notation for MapAt.

Complication 1: Compositions of Ascending and Descending Operators

One can have a composed function as an argument to Query, such as f / * g or Select [f] / * g or g / * Select [f] or f / * g / * h or an infinite number of other compositions. If the operators within the composition are *all* ascending or *all* descending, then it's easy. If they are all ascending, then they are applied in the usual way as the kernel heads back up the tree. If they are all descending, then they all are applied early as the kernel heads down the tree.

But what if the composed operators are a mix between ascending and descending operators?

If all the descending operators in a mixed composition come before any ascending operators, the kernel applies all the descending operators first. Then it proceeds in the normal way, which would mean it applies operators in subsequent arguments to Query and only then comes back to apply the remaining operators in the prior arguments. Here's an example.

Descending operators sometimes stay descending even if RightComposed with ascending operators:

In[·]:= **Normal [Query [(Select [f] / * SortBy [g] / * h / * i) , j]]**

Out[·]= Select [f] / * SortBy [g] / * Map [j] / * h / * i

Notice that all of the descending operators in the RightComposition in the first argument to Query come before any of the ascending operators (f and g). So it first applies the two descending operators Select [f] and SortBy [g]. Then it skips the remaining two ascending operators h and i in the RightComposition and goes to the end to apply j. Then it comes back and applies h and i.

However, that's the only circumstance in which any of the operators in a mixed RightComposition are privileged to come first. Here, I've stuck SortBy [h], a descending operator, to the right of g, an ascending operator, in the RightComposition. The RightComposition is now "contaminated," and evaluation proceeds as if none of the operators were descending.

Usually, descending operators lose their privilege if they mix with ascending operators in a Composition or RightComposition:

In[·]:= **Normal [Query [(Select [f] / * g / * SortBy [h]) , j]]**

Out[·]= Map [j] / * Select [f] / * g / * SortBy [h]

Again, when in doubt or when the results from your Query produce errors or just don't make sense, just Normal the Query before running it. Doing so seldom takes long at all.

Complication 2: GroupBy

GroupBy[f] is a special case. This function definitely changes the structure of its argument. It doesn't tend to reduce the amount of data to be processed. Nonetheless, it's a descending operator.

You can see this with an example. If the following Query were evaluated in the LIFO way, first it would Map Length over the List of Associations and get a bunch of numbers. It would then try to group those numbers by ♯ sex &, but I'd then get an error message because numbers don't have a sex. The situation is saved by the Query treating GroupBy as descending. It gets applied first. Since there is one male and four females on the dinghy and I am now mapping Length to an Association, I get an Association with the same keys and values of 4 for female and 1 for male.

GroupBy [f] is a descending operator that inserts a level into the data on which the Query is being applied:

In[∘]:= **dinghy**

Out[∘]= { <| class → 3rd, age → 16, sex → female, survived → True |>,
      <| class → 1st, age → 65, sex → male, survived → False |>,
      <| class → 3rd, age → 2, sex → female, survived → False |>,
      <| class → 3rd, age → Missing [ ] , sex → female, survived → True |>,
      <| class → 3rd, age → 18, sex → female, survived → False |> }

In[∘]:= **Query [GroupBy [♯sex &] , Length] [dinghy]**

Out[∘]= <| female → 4, male → 1 |>

One can think of Query with GroupBy[f] as increasing the depth of the expression on which it is going to act. (The f in the preceding sentence is just a shorthand for some arbitrary function.) It can be thought of as inserting a layer into the target expression. Thus, a Query with three arguments, the first of which is a GroupBy[f], creates a pipeline that performs the GroupBy[f] first. If the GroupBy[f] is composed with further operators at the same level, they are then performed on the entirety of the data structure according to the usual order of operations.

Here's an example. I'm trying to get the mean age for each sex (gender) of the passengers. If I were to run this Query, I would get an error because when GroupBy is written as a function, it is not recognized as an operator.

A failed attempt at grouping using a function involving GroupBy:

In[ ]:= **Query [Function [passenger , GroupBy [passenger , ♯sex &]] , Mean, ♯age &] [dinghy]**

Out[ ]= Failure[

> ⚠ Message: (♯age &)[3rd] is expected to have an Association as the first argument.
>   Tag: Function

]

Running Normal on the Query confirms that the order of operations is not correct:

In[ ]:= **Normal [Query [Function [passenger , GroupBy [passenger , ♯sex &]] , Mean, ♯age &]]**

Out[ ]= Map [Map [♯age &] / * Mean] / * Function [passenger, GroupBy [passenger, ♯sex &]]

But if I write GroupBy [f] as an operator, I get the desired behavior:

In[ ]:= **Query [GroupBy [♯sex &] , Mean, ♯age &] [dinghy]**

Out[ ]= <| female → 12, male → 65 |>

A digression. Do you remember how I said earlier in the chapter that the Normal of a Query is not exactly the same thing as the Query? The code in the previous input provides an example of this subtlety.

Here, I Normal the Query before executing it:

In[ ]:= **Normal [Query [GroupBy [♯sex &] , Mean, ♯age &]] [dinghy]**

Out[ ]= $\left\langle \middle| \text{female} \to \frac{1}{4} (36 + \text{Missing} [ ]), \text{male} \to 65 \middle| \right\rangle$

The result is probably not what one would want. Because the age of one of the female passengers is Missing, the Mean function won't compute a purely numeric value. By contrast, the un-normalized version of Query produces the result one would want most of the time. It works because Query has built-in capabilities for dealing with Missing values. As discussed later, setting the MissingBehavior option to None lets one turn that behavior off.

Now the behavior of Query is the same as when I applied Normal:

In[ ]:= **Query [GroupBy [♯sex &] , Mean, ♯age &, MissingBehavior → None] [dinghy]**

Out[ ]= $\left\langle \middle| \text{female} \to \frac{1}{4} (36 + \text{Missing} [ ]), \text{male} \to 65 \middle| \right\rangle$

Other operator forms of GroupBy likewise are also treated as descending and promoted in the operator pipeline. Here's the version of GroupBy that takes a rule between functions as its argument.

GroupBy retains descending status even when its argument is a rule between functions:

In[ ]:= **Normal [Query [GroupBy [(⌗sex &) → (⌗age &)] , Mean / ∗ N]]**

Out[ ]= GroupBy [(⌗sex &) → (⌗age &)] / ∗ Map [Mean / ∗ N]

In[ ]:= **Query [GroupBy [(⌗sex &) → (⌗age &)] , Mean / ∗ N] [dinghy]**

Out[ ]= ⟨| female → 12., male → 65. |⟩

Complication 3: Subqueries

Suppose one wants to convert a descending operator into an ascending one. One wants, for example, a Select [f] operator to be applied in the usual LIFO way. One can change the order of operations produced by Query by wrapping what would otherwise be a descending operator in (another) Query. One could term these wrapped queries as "subqueries."

The following list shows how wrapping a descending Select operator in Query turns it into an ascending operator that is applied last.

Use nested Query functions to try and change the order of operations:

In[ ]:= **Map [Normal, { Query [Select [f] , g] , Query [Query [Select [f]] , g] }]**

Out[ ]= { Select [f] / ∗ Map [g] , Map [g] / ∗ Select [f] }

Complication 4: Syntactic Sugar for MapAt

Suppose one wants to apply a function only to one position with a Wolfram Language expression. The functional programming construct to do this is MapAt.

Apply the f function to the third element of dinghy:

In[ ]:= **MapAt [f, 3] [dinghy]**

Out[ ]= { ⟨| class → 3rd, age → 16, sex → female, survived → True |⟩,
　　　　⟨| class → 1st, age → 65, sex → male, survived → False |⟩,
　　　　f [⟨| class → 3rd, age → 2, sex → female, survived → False |⟩],
　　　　⟨| class → 3rd, age → Missing [ ] , sex → female, survived → True |⟩,
　　　　⟨| class → 3rd, age → 18, sex → female, survived → False |⟩ }

Or, if one wants to apply f to every age value within the List of Associations, one writes the following code.

Use All in combination with key names in the Part specification to MapAt in order to operate on columns:

In[•]:= **MapAt [f, { All, "age" }] [dinghy]**

Out[•]= { <| class → 3rd, age → f [16] , sex → female, survived → True |> ,
   <| class → 1st, age → f [65] , sex → male, survived → False |> ,
   <| class → 3rd, age → f [2] , sex → female, survived → False |> ,
   <| class → 3rd, age → f [Missing [ ]] , sex → female, survived → True |> ,
   <| class → 3rd, age → f [18] , sex → female, survived → False |> }

If one knew age was the second key-value pair, one could write the code using an integer part number. (Yes, I know this is against the whole philosophy of Association, but it can be done.)

Use All in combination with integers in the Part specification to MapAt in order to operate on columns:

In[•]:= **MapAt [f, { All, 2 }] [dinghy]**

Out[•]= { <| class → 3rd, age → f [16] , sex → female, survived → True |> ,
   <| class → 1st, age → f [65] , sex → male, survived → False |> ,
   <| class → 3rd, age → f [2] , sex → female, survived → False |> ,
   <| class → 3rd, age → f [Missing [ ]] , sex → female, survived → True |> ,
   <| class → 3rd, age → f [18] , sex → female, survived → False |> }

Although this notation is fine, it can be somewhat cumbersome when one wants to apply different functions to different parts of the data. Consider, for example, how one would need to write an operation that mapped the function f onto the age column, the function g onto the sex column, and the function h onto the survived column. One can imagine doing this if one had different rules for cleaning up each column of data, but doing so is a bit cumbersome.

The composition of MapAts permits different functions to be applied to different columns:

In[•]:= **(MapAt [f, { All, "age" }] / ***
   MapAt [g, { All, "sex" }] / * MapAt [h, { All, "survived" }]) [dinghy]

Out[•]= { <| class → 3rd, age → f [16] , sex → g [female] , survived → h [True] |> ,
   <| class → 1st, age → f [65] , sex → g [male] , survived → h [False] |> ,
   <| class → 3rd, age → f [2] , sex → g [female] , survived → h [False] |> ,
   <| class → 3rd, age → f [Missing [ ]] , sex → g [female] , survived → h [True] |> ,
   <| class → 3rd, age → f [18] , sex → g [female] , survived → h [False] |> }

Within Query, however, there is an alternative syntax for MapAt: Part Specification-Rule notation. One puts the part (or key) number as the left-hand side of a Rule and the function to be applied as the right-hand side, and one wraps it all up in a List.

There's syntactic sugar for MapAt. One can "speak" the code below as "apply f to the third part":

In[•]:= **Normal [Query [{ 3 → f }]]**

Out[•]= MapAt [f, 3]

In[•]:= **Query [{ 3 → f }] [dinghy]**

Out[•]= { <| class → 3rd, age → 16, sex → female, survived → True |>,
  <| class → 1st, age → 65, sex → male, survived → False |>,
  f [<| class → 3rd, age → 2, sex → female, survived → False |>],
  <| class → 3rd, age → Missing [ ], sex → female, survived → True |>,
  <| class → 3rd, age → 18, sex → female, survived → False |> }

To apply the function only to the "age" key-value pair within every Association, I write the following code:

In[•]:= **Query [All, { "age" → f }] [dinghy]**

Out[•]= { <| class → 3rd, age → f [16], sex → female, survived → True |>,
  <| class → 1st, age → f [65], sex → male, survived → False |>,
  <| class → 3rd, age → f [2], sex → female, survived → False |>,
  <| class → 3rd, age → f [Missing [ ]], sex → female, survived → True |>,
  <| class → 3rd, age → f [18], sex → female, survived → False |> }

Notice how when Normal is applied to this Query, one gets a MapAt operator with a two-argument Part specification, the first argument of which is All (meaning all of the rows).

For example:

In[•]:= **Normal [Query [All, { "age" → f }]]**

Out[•]= MapAt [f, { All, age }]

One can use this same syntactic sugar to perform RightComposition of multiple MapAt statements, each operating on different parts.

Here I apply the function f to the age values and the function g to the sex values:

In[•]:= **Query [All, { "age" → f, "sex" → g }] [dinghy]**

Out[•]= { <| class → 3rd, age → f [16], sex → g [female], survived → True |>,
  <| class → 1st, age → f [65], sex → g [male], survived → False |>,
  <| class → 3rd, age → f [2], sex → g [female], survived → False |>,
  <| class → 3rd, age → f [Missing [ ]], sex → g [female], survived → True |>,
  <| class → 3rd, age → f [18], sex → g [female], survived → False |> }

A Normal of the Query shows that it literally constructs a RightComposition of MapAts:

In[•]:= **Normal [Query [All, { "age" → f, "sex" → g }]]**

Out[•]= MapAt [g, { All, sex }] / ∗ MapAt [f, { All, age }]

Solve Sample Problems with Query

Let's now further explore Query by redoing the examples from the preceding chapter. The material in Example 1 is particularly important for understanding the remainder of this book.

Example 1 Redone Using Query

In Example 1 from the preceding chapter, we wanted to get the genders of persons over the age of 70 on the Titanic. Here's a traditional approach to retrieving that information.

Retrieve the Titanic data:

In[•]:= **titanic = ResourceData [ro, "Titanic List of Associations"]**

Out[•]=
{ <| class → 1st, age → 29, sex → female, survived → True |>,
  <| class → 1st, age → 1, sex → male, survived → True |>, ⟨··· 1305 ···⟩,
  <| class → 3rd, age → 27, sex → male, survived → False |>,
  <| class → 3rd, age → 29, sex → male, survived → False |> }

Full expression not available   (original memory size: 1 MB   )   ⚙

Get the genders of everyone over the age of 70:

In[•]:= **Map [♯sex &, Select [titanic, ♯age > 70 &]]**

Out[•]= { male, male, female, male, male, male }

Here's the pipeline version I construct without use of Query. First I create a Select operator using the function ♯ age > 70 &. I take the output from that operation and map ♯ sex & over it.

As in the previous chapter, I can name the pipeline oldGenders and apply it to the data stored in titanic:

In[•]:= **oldGenders = Select [♯age > 70 &] / ∗ Map [♯sex &]**

Out[•]= Select [♯age > 70 &] / ∗ Map [♯sex &]

In[•]:= **oldGenders [titanic]**

Out[•]= { male, male, female, male, male, male }

Here's how I could do the same thing using Query. The Select [♯ age > 70 &] operator will be applied first. The ♯ sex & function will be applied second but automatically mapped over the result due to its position in the Query arguments. It's cleaner code, in my opinion.

Construct a Query in which a Select function is the first argument and an anonymous function is the second argument:

In[ ]:=   **Query [Select [♯age > 70 &] , ♯sex &] [titanic]**

Out[ ]=   { male, male, female, male, male, male }

It is interesting, by the way, that there were so few passengers over the age of 70. Perhaps it was because of a combination of people not living as long at the start of the twentieth century and the elderly generally not making sea voyages in the Atlantic chill of mid-April.

Example 2 Redone Using Query

Suppose I want to count the number of women in each cabin class. Here are some ways I did so in the previous chapter without the benefit of Query.

A traditional approach to counting the number of women passengers in each cabin class:

In[ ]:=   **Counts [Map [♯class &, Select [titanic, ♯sex === "female" &]]]**

Out[ ]=   <| 1st → 144, 2nd → 106, 3rd → 216 |>

A more operator-oriented form:

In[ ]:=   **Counts [Map [♯class &] [Select [♯sex === "female" &] [titanic]]]**

Out[ ]=   <| 1st → 144, 2nd → 106, 3rd → 216 |>

Using RightComposition:

In[ ]:=   **womenCountByCabin = Select [♯sex === "female" &] /* Map [♯class &] /* Counts**

Out[ ]=   Select [♯sex === female &] /* Map [♯class &] /* Counts

Now I write the code taking advantage of Query. The filtering Select operator and the Counts operator work on the entirety of the data, so they go at the top level. The cabin class determination works on each passenger, so it goes at a lower level.

Get the number of women broken down by cabin class:

In[ ]:=   **womenCountByCabinQuery =**
  Query [Select [♯sex === "female" &] /* Counts, ♯class &]

Out[ ]=   Query [Select [♯sex === female &] /* Counts, ♯class &]

The use of Normal shows that the Query is converted into a right composition of operators: first it selects the women *and then* it maps ♯ class & over those remaining *and then* it applies Counts on the result. Query produces pipelines of right-composed operators.

Using **Normal** shows how the **Query** will work:

In[•]:= **Normal [womenCountByCabinQuery]**

Out[•]= Select [⌗sex === female &] / * Map [⌗class &] / * Counts

The Query is now applied to titanic. It works!

Get the number of women on the Titanic broken down by cabin class:

In[•]:= **womenCountByCabinQuery [titanic]**

Out[•]= <| 1st → 144, 2nd → 106, 3rd → 216 |>

The order of operations produced by Query is precisely as advertised in the preceding material. Select is a descending operator so it gets promoted, but Counts is not. So, even when composed with a descending operator, Counts doesn't itself become descending. So basically, Query uses the default LIFO order but sticks the Select operator at the head of the pipeline.

Example 3 Redone Using Query

I will now redo the third example from the previous chapter in which I obtain the mean age of the passengers in each cabin class. You may recall that the existence of missing data required some special handling.

Write a function that takes the mean of the numeric data and maps it over the age values of passengers on the Titanic grouped by cabin class:

In[•]:= **filteredMean = N [Mean [Select [NumericQ] [⌗]]] &;**

In[•]:= **Map [filteredMean, Map [⌗age &, GroupBy [titanic, ⌗class &], {2}]]**

Out[•]= <| 1st → 39.1655, 2nd → 29.5172, 3rd → 24.8483 |>

I also showed how one could dispense with the level specification on Map and write the following (ugly) code.

Create an operator pipeline with nested **Map** statements and the function for handling missing data:

In[•]:= **meanAgeByCabin = GroupBy [⌗class &] / * Map [Map [⌗age &] / * filteredMean] ;
meanAgeByCabin [titanic]**

Out[•]= <| 1st → 39.1655, 2nd → 29.5172, 3rd → 24.8483 |>

Using Query yields cleaner code. There's no need to write a custom mean function to get rid of missing values. We don't write obscure nested Maps. Query does that work by default.

Get the mean age of passengers broken down by cabin class:

In[ ]:= **meanAgeByCabinQuery = Query [GroupBy [⌗class &] , Mean / ∗ N, ⌗age &];**
meanAgeByCabinQuery [titanic]

Out[ ]= **‹| 1st → 39.1655, 2nd → 29.5172, 3rd → 24.8483 |›**

Here's the Normal form. It looks, by the way, exactly like the pipeline I constructed by hand in the previous chapter and in the code immediately prior to this.

Wrap Normal around a Query to see the pipeline of operators:

In[ ]:= **Normal [meanAgeByCabinQuery]**

Out[ ]= **GroupBy [⌗class &] / ∗ Map [Map [⌗age &] / ∗ Mean / ∗ N]**

Example 4 Redone Using Query

Let's redo the median survival analysis from the preceding chapter. The idea was to find the median age of Titanic passengers (restricted to those under the age of 50) based on whether the passenger survived. Here's what I did.

Use conventional programming techniques to compute the median age of Titanic passengers (restricted to those under the age of 50) based on whether the passenger survived:

In[ ]:= **Map [Median,**
Map [⌗age &, GroupBy [Select [titanic, ⌗age < 50 &] , ⌗survived &] , {2}]]

Out[ ]= **‹| True → 26, False → 27 |›**

Or if I preferred a pipeline style of program, I could write out the following RightComposition of operators.

Create an operator pipeline by hand and then apply it to titanic to do the same computation:

In[ ]:= **medianSurvival = Select [⌗age < 50 &] / ∗**
GroupBy [⌗survived &] / ∗ Map [Map [⌗age &] / ∗ Median];
medianSurvival [titanic]

Out[ ]= **‹| True → 26, False → 27 |›**

Query again permits the code to be more lucid. I use three arguments. The first accomplishes filtering and grouping on the entire set of data. The third argument applies a function (⌗ age &) to each member of each resulting group. And the second argument specifies what to do (Median) with each group after the function in the third argument is applied.

A Query operator is constructed from three arguments:

In[ ]:= **medianSurvivalQuery =**
Query [Select [⌗age < 50 &] / ∗ GroupBy [⌗survived &] , Median, ⌗age &];
medianSurvivalQuery [titanic]

Out[ ]= **‹| True → 26, False → 27 |›**

Here's the Normal version of what's going on:

In[•]:= **Normal [medianSurvivalQuery]**

Out[•]= Select [⌗age < 50 &] / * GroupBy [⌗survived &] / * Map [Map [⌗age &] / * Median]

Notice that we did not have to deal with passengers whose ages were missing. The default behavior of Query (set by the default option MissingBehavior → Automatic) is to drop or ignore missing values presented to certain aggregation functions such as Total, Mean, Median, Min, Max, and others. I'll discuss how Query deals with missing values in more detail later.

Example 5 Redone Using Query

Often in data analysis, one needs to join two sets of data together using some common column to perform the assembly. In the previous chapter, I showed how to use JoinAcross to accomplish this goal.

Use JoinAcross to join two sets of data:

In[•]:= **joined = JoinAcross [titanic, titanicCabins, "class"]**

Out[•]=
{ <| class → 1st, age → 29, sex → female, survived → True, squarefeet → 300,
   window → True, decklocations → { 1, 2 } |>, ⸋ 1307 ⸋ , <| class → 3rd, age → 29, sex → male,
   survived → False, squarefeet → 100, window → False, decklocations → { 4, 5, 6 } |> }

Full expression not available   (original memory size: 1.5 MB   )   ⚙

While this joining could be done using Query as shown next, there's really no point. Although Query is a wonderful functional programming construct, one doesn't have to use it every time one wants to do data analysis.

Combine Query with an anonymous function based on JoinAcross to join information on the dinghy passengers with information on Titanic cabins:

In[•]:= **Query [JoinAcross [titanic, ⌗, "class"] &] [titanicCabins]**

Out[•]=
{ <| class → 1st, age → 29, sex → female, survived → True, squarefeet → 300,
   window → True, decklocations → { 1, 2 } |>, ⸋ 1307 ⸋ , <| class → 3rd, age → 29, sex → male,
   survived → False, squarefeet → 100, window → False, decklocations → { 4, 5, 6 } |> }

Full expression not available   (original memory size: 1.5 MB   )   ⚙

Now Query will come in handy for doing data analysis on the resulting data. Recall that before I wanted the mean square footage of cabins on the Titanic, but I wanted it broken down by the sex of its occupying passenger.

Here's essentially how I did it with a pipeline of operators:

In[•]:= **(GroupBy [⌗sex &] / * Map [Map [⌗squarefeet &] / * Mean / * N]) [joined]**

Out[•]= <| female → 184.549, male → 162.752 |>

And with the useful MapLevel ResourceFunction, I could have written it this way to avoid the ugly nested Map statements:

In[·]:= (GroupBy [⌗sex &] / * [▪] MapLevel ₊ [⌗squarefeet &, { 2 }] / * Map [Mean / * N]) [joined]

Out[·]= <| female → 184.549, male → 162.752 |>

With Query, the code is simpler:

In[·]:= Query [GroupBy [⌗sex &] , Mean / * N, ⌗squarefeet &] [joined]

Out[·]= <| female → 184.549, male → 162.752 |>

How to Do Nothing: All or Identity

I now want to go through many of the frequently used operators that tend not to alter structure. Executing these operators sooner rather than later is likely to be efficient.

Sometimes, one does not wish to do anything at a particular level of an expression. One wants to leave it as is. Suppose, for example, you just want the age and sex of everyone in the dinghy. You can't do this by putting a Null as an argument to Query (unlike some other languages where this is permissible: Query [, { "age", "sex" }] [dinghy]).

To fix this, use All or Identity as a kind of placeholder that tells the kernel to do nothing. The Identity function just returns its argument unchanged. Query appears to convert All into Identity, so it should not make any difference whether one uses All or Identity in a Query.

Use All or Identity to tell the Query effectively to do nothing at a given level:

In[·]:= Query [All, { "age", "sex" }] [dinghy]

Out[·]= { <| age → 16, sex → female |>, <| age → 65, sex → male |>, <| age → 2, sex → female |>, <| age → Missing [ ] , sex → female |>, <| age → 18, sex → female |> }

In[·]:= Query [Identity, { "age", "sex" }] [dinghy]

Out[·]= { <| age → 16, sex → female |>, <| age → 65, sex → male |>, <| age → 2, sex → female |>, <| age → Missing [ ] , sex → female |>, <| age → 18, sex → female |> }

Queries with Deeply Nested Datasets

One useful feature of the Wolfram Language is its support for hierarchical data, deeply nested Lists, Associations, and Datasets. One is not limited to simple two-dimensional tables as might be the case in systems based, for example, on SQL. Here's an example: the planets Dataset (put in Normal form since I haven't shown you the Dataset wrapper yet). Basically, it's an Association whose outer keys are the names of the planets. Each value is data on the mass, radius, and moons of that planet, but the moons data is itself an Association in which the keys are the names of the moons and the values are Associations in which the keys are the mass of the moon and its radius.

Get the planets data in Association form from the ResourceObject for this book:

In[ ]:= **(planets = ResourceData [ro, "Planets Deeply Nested Structure"]) / / [■] Terse + [5]**

Out[ ]//Short= ⟨| Mercury → ⟨| Mass → 3.30104×10^{23} kg , Radius → 2439.7 km , Moons → ⟨| |⟩ |⟩,

≪6≫, Neptune → ⟨| Mass → 1.02410×10^{26} kg , Radius → 24553. km ,

Moons → ⟨| Naiad → ⟨| Mass → 1.9×10^{17} kg , Radius → 33. km |⟩,

Thalassa → ⟨| Mass → 3.7×10^{17} kg , Radius → 41. km |⟩,

≪10≫, Neso → ⟨| Radius → 30. km |⟩ |⟩ |⟩ |⟩

Suppose I want the radius of Phobos, a moon of Mars. I could just use a Query that picked out keys at different levels.

Use Query with lots of arguments to access deeply nested data:

In[ ]:= **Query ["Mars", "Moons", "Phobos", "Radius"] [planets]**

Out[ ]= 11.1 km

Or suppose I want the mean mass of the moons of Mars, a tongue twister as well as a Query.

The mean mass of the moons of Mars:

In[ ]:= **Query ["Mars", "Moons", Mean, "Mass"] [planets]**

Out[ ]= 6.10×10^{15} kg

Or the total mass of the moons for each planet:

In[ ]:= **Query [All, "Moons", Total, "Mass"] [planets]**

Out[ ]= ⟨| Mercury → 0, Venus → 0, Earth → 7.3459×10^{22} kg ,

Mars → 1.22×10^{16} kg , Jupiter → 3.9301×10^{23} kg , Saturn → 1.4051×10^{23} kg ,

Uranus → 9.14×10^{21} kg , Neptune → 2.1487×10^{22} kg |⟩

Essentially, working with deeply nested Associations is no different than working with less nested ones.

Functions That Create Queries

One of the signature features of the Wolfram Language, along with other descendants of LISP, is the ability to write functions that create functions. You can thus write a function that generates a Query. This is a major advantage of the Wolfram Query framework over constructs such as SQL, which is not built for symbolic query construction. Here, for example, I write a function, medianGrouper, that groups its arguments according to some function f and then finds, for each grouping, the median of the mapping of the function g over each grouping.

Use a function to symbolically construct a Query:

In[ ]:= **medianGrouper [f_ , g_] := Query [GroupBy [f] , Median, g]**

Here, I use medianGrouper to form a Query named mga. It groups data by a combination of its sex and class and then computes the median age of each grouping.

Use a function to build a Query that will group data by sex and class and then compute the median age for each grouping:

In[ ]:= **mga = medianGrouper [{⌗sex , ⌗class } &, ⌗age &]**

Out[ ]= Query [GroupBy [{⌗sex, ⌗class} &] , Median, ⌗age &]

I apply the resulting function to the Titanic data.

The median ages of sex, cabin combinations on the Titanic:

In[ ]:= **mga [titanic]**

Out[ ]= $\langle |$ {female, 1st} → 36, {male, 1st} → 42, {male, 2nd} → $\dfrac{59}{2}$,

{female, 2nd} → 28, {male, 3rd} → 25, {female, 3rd} → 22 $| \rangle$

Debugging Queries That Go Wrong

Unless you are an extraordinary programmer, your queries will create errors. An important skill in working with data is relaxing when these errors occur, being able to diagnose the root cause, and developing a fix. Of course, all the skills you've learned in other parts of Wolfram Language programming (and programming generally) apply here. Thus, techniques like reading the error message carefully, checking the spelling of your code (including capitalization), reading the documentation, looking up the error message in a search engine, and breaking the program up into pieces are all extremely useful. There are, however, some common and special errors associated with Query that are useful to identify and study. There are further errors that can occur when the data is part of a Dataset, but I will defer examination of those errors until the Dataset chapter.

Results That Make No Sense

Suppose I want to group my dinghy data by passenger class, get the ages of the passengers, and then sort the list of ages within each passenger group. Here's my first (flawed) attempt.

Errors can occur if one forgets that Sort is a descending operator:

In[•]:= **Query [GroupBy [♯class &] / * Sort, All, ♯age &] [dinghy]**

Out[•]= ‹| 1st → { 65 } , 3rd → { 16, 2, Missing [ ] , 18 } |›

This Query works, but it gets the wrong answer. The ages are not sorted properly. Very frequently, in my experience, Query errors result from misunderstandings about order of operations.

I'll do a Normal transformation of the Query and see what is going on:

In[•]:= **Normal [Query [GroupBy [♯class &] / * Sort, All, ♯age &]]**

Out[•]= GroupBy [♯class &] / * Sort / * Map [Map [♯age &]]

We can see that at the time the Sort operation occurs, the kernel has not isolated the age column, so Associations are being sorted as a whole rather than on just their age component. I now realize I need to change the order of operations. We've looked at several techniques in this chapter about how to do so. Here's a simple fix: subordinate the precedence of Sort by wrapping Query around it.

Change the order of operations by moving the position of the operands to Query:

In[•]:= **Normal [Query [GroupBy [♯class &] , Query [Sort] , ♯age &]]**

Out[•]= GroupBy [♯class &] / * Map [Map [♯age &] / * Sort]

In[•]:= **Query [GroupBy [♯class &] , Query [Sort] , ♯age &] [dinghy]**

Out[•]= ‹| 3rd → { 2, 16, 18, Missing [ ] } , 1st → { 65 } |›

The Failure to Obtain Any Result at All

Sometimes a Query will not produce a result at all. Instead, one obtains a Failure object. Here's one where I use IntegerDigits to obtain the second digit of the passengers' ages. This would seem to work—at least so long as the passengers' ages have two digits.

By default, if Query finds any errors, it returns a Failure object:

In[•]:= **Query [All, IntegerDigits [♯age] [[2]] &] [titanic]**

Out[•]= Failure[⚠ Message: Part 2 of {1} does not exist.
                      Tag: Part   ]

This Query fails for two reasons. The second will be discussed later. The first is that some of the passengers are less than 10 years old; there is no second base-10 digit to their age. As it happens, I could eliminate this particular problem by writing the Query as shown.

Using Last lets the Query succeed when there is only one item in the list of digits:

In[•]:= **Query [All, (IntegerDigits [⌗age] &) / * Last] [titanic] / /** ⸢•⸣ **Terse** ₊ **[5]**

Out[•]//Short= {9, 1, 2, 0, 5, 8, 3, 9, 3, 1, 7, 8, 4, 6, 0, Missing [ ], 4, 0, 2, 6, 7, 7, 6, 2, 9, ≪1259≫, Missing [ ], 3, 8, 1, 8, 1, 7, Missing [ ], Missing [ ], Missing [ ], 9, 1, 7, Missing [ ], 6, 7, 5, 6, Missing [ ], Missing [ ], 5, Missing [ ], 7, 7, 9}

But suppose I did not know the data well enough to realize this problem? Or suppose the error was more subtle?

First, I might want to just ram through the Query and get it to work on as much of the data as possible. That is, maybe 99% of the rows work just fine and that's all I care about. A Failure object can be annoying in these circumstances. To ignore the failed items, I add an option at the end of the Query, FailureAction → None. One of the things that makes Queries different from their Normal form is that Query has error handling built in. The default option means that the computation generates a Failure object when an error occurs. There's no "partial credit."

In this instance, shutting off the error checking is fairly helpful. I can see more clearly that the code is trying to take the second part of lists that have just one part.

Avoid Failure returns by setting FailureAction → None as an option to Query:

In[•]:= **(Query [All, IntegerDigits [⌗age] ⟦2⟧ &, FailureAction → None] [titanic]) / /** ⸢•⸣ **Terse** ₊ **[5]**

⸢⋯⸣ Part : Part 2 of {1} does not exist.

⸢⋯⸣ Part : Part 2 of {2} does not exist.

⸢⋯⸣ Part : Part 2 of IntegerDigits [Missing []] does not exist.

⸢⋯⸣ General : Further output of Part::partw will be suppressed during this calculation.

Out[•]//Short= {9, {1} ⟦2⟧, {2} ⟦2⟧, 0, 5, 8, 3, 9, 3, 1, 7, ≪1287≫, 6, 7, 5, 6, IntegerDigits [Missing [ ]] ⟦2⟧, IntegerDigits [Missing [ ]] ⟦2⟧, 5, IntegerDigits [Missing [ ]] ⟦2⟧, 7, 7, 9}

I might decide at that point that I don't want the results that have problems; I just want the error-free components of the result. To do this, I set the FailureAction option to "Drop". (Make sure to put "Drop" in quotes; it's a string.) Now I get a clean response that does not generate any error messages and that appears free of errors.

Setting FailureAction → "Drop" avoids error messages and just keeps "the good stuff":

In[•]:= **Query [All, IntegerDigits [♯age] 〚2〛 &, FailureAction → "Drop"] [titanic] / /**
[•] Terse + [5]

Out[•]//Short= {9, 0, 5, 8, 3, 9, 3, 1, 7, 8, 4, 6, 0, 4, 0, 2, 6, 7, 7, 6, 2, 9, 5, 5, 9, 5, 8, 5,
0, 0, 8, 2, 5, 2, 1, 8, 4, 9, 0, 1, 5, 2, 3, ≪878≫, 2, 1, 4, 5, 9, 6, 8, 3, 2, 1, 0, 6,
0, 3, 8, 8, 7, 8, 1, 6, 1, 2, 0, 4, 2, 2, 3, 8, 1, 8, 1, 7, 9, 1, 7, 6, 7, 5, 6, 5, 7, 7, 9}

This is a mixed virtue. On the one hand, I get a clean-looking result; on the other hand, I may have masked serious problems with my understanding of the data that come back to produce more problems with future queries. Worse, we might have undetected, substantive errors in the results. Still, sometimes, just dropping the bad items is a reasonable fix to a Query problem.

A slightly less drastic approach than just dropping the problem data is to replace the problem results with something either more attractive or something clearer. If I use "Replace" as the value of the FailureAction option, I get Missing [Failed] instead of expressions such as {1} 〚2〛. While there may be no advantage here to that substitution, in other settings, where the problem data is more elaborate, a simple Missing [Failed] may make your life—and that of the Wolfram Language front end—much more pleasant.

Use FailureAction → "Replace" to generate clean Missing values for problematic applications of the Query function to parts of the data:

In[•]:= **Query [All, IntegerDigits [♯age] 〚2〛 &, FailureAction → "Replace"] [titanic] / /**
[•] Terse + [5]

Out[•]//Short= {9, Missing [Failed] , Missing [Failed] , 0, 5, 8, 3, 9, 3, 1, 7, 8,
4, 6, 0, Missing [Failed] , ≪1278≫, 9, 1, 7, Missing [Failed] , 6, 7, 5,
6, Missing [Failed] , Missing [Failed] , 5, Missing [Failed] , 7, 7, 9}

One can also generate a custom response to failure by adding a second argument to "Replace". The Wolfram Language documentation, for example, has a reasonable idea: set the FailureAction option to {"Replace", Print}. The kernel will then spit out a Print cell each time it encounters an error. The output will have Null instead of Missing [Failed] as the placeholder for the problem results because Print is a function that has side effects (it prints stuff out) but returns Null as a value. The next example demonstrates this method on the first 20 rows of titanic. I restrict myself to the first 20 rows because I would otherwise generate dozens of Print cells. Generating hundreds of Print cells with error messages is generally not helpful.

Use Wolfram commands to generate custom behavior when an error is confronted:

In[·]:= **Query [1 ;; 20, IntegerDigits [⌗age] ⟦2⟧ &, FailureAction → { "Replace", Print }] [
titanic] / /** [▪] **Terse** ₊ **[5]**

Out[·]//Short= { 9, Null, Null, 0, 5, 8, 3, 9, 3, 1, 7, 8, 4, 6, 0, Null, 4, 0, 2, 6 }

If one is worried that the use of { "Replace", Print } as the option to FailureAction might result in a notebook now stuffed with error messages, there is a hack to avoid the problem. It is shown next. Basically, you preface Query with a counter. Then each time you encounter the error, the kernel increments the counter by one. You then condition the printing of the error message on the error counter being less than some ceiling value. It's not elegant, but it's a lot more elegant than having a notebook with a million-row set of data coming to a halt or crashing because the kernel generates one million print cells that choke the Wolfram Language front end!

Custom behavior on confronting errors can be elaborate:

In[·]:= **(errorCount = 0;**
Query [1 ;; 20, IntegerDigits [⌗age] ⟦2⟧ &,
FailureAction → { "Replace", (errorCount + +;
If [errorCount ≤ 2, (Print [⌗];
⌗⟦2⟧)]) & }] [titanic]) / / [▪] **Terse** ₊ **[6]**

| Failure[| ⚠ | Message:
Tag: | Part 2 of {1} does not exist.
Part |] |

| Failure[| ⚠ | Message:
Tag: | Part 2 of {2} does not exist.
Part |] |

Out[·]//Short= { 9, <| MessageTemplate :→ Part::partw, MessageParameters → { 2, {1} } |>,
<| MessageTemplate :→ Part::partw, MessageParameters → { 2, {2} } |>,
0, 5, 8, 3, 9, 3, 1, 7, 8, 4, 6, 0, Null, 4, 0, 2, 6 }

Perhaps the most conservative approach to detecting the source of error is to use "Encapsulate" as the value of FailureAction. The following code shows what it does. I'm only going to look at the first 20 Titanic passengers to keep the output short.

Use FailureAction → "Encapsulate" to insert the Failure objects into the result:

```
In[ ]:= Query[1 ;; 20, IntegerDigits[#age][[2]] &, FailureAction → "Encapsulate"] [titanic] //
        Terse[]

Out[ ]//Short= {9, Failure[ ⚠ Message: Part 2 of {1} does not exist.
                             Tag:     Part ],
               Failure[ ⚠ Message: Part 2 of {2} does not exist.
                           Tag:     Part ], 0, 5, ≪11≫, 4, 0, 2, 6}
```

Now, instead of having Missing[Failed] as the output, which is short but not particularly informative, one gets the whole glorious Failure object embedded within the answer. You can already see from the output here that, actually, there are two kinds of errors being made in the Query. The first, as mentioned previously, is that some of the ages may have only one digit, so asking for the second digit won't work. The second error, however, is that some of the passengers don't have age information at all, so asking for IntegerDigits[Missing[]] is a nonstarter. The disadvantage of "Encapsulate" is that the output can be quite involved if the failures are frequent or complex.

There are a couple of ways to clean up the Query. One is to use a Switch statement as shown here. If the age is missing, it outputs Missing[]. Otherwise it outputs the last digit of the age.

Use Switch to clean up the Query:

```
In[ ]:= Query[All, Switch[#age, _Missing, Missing[], _, Last[IntegerDigits[#age]]] &] [
          titanic] // Short

Out[ ]//Short= {9, 1, 2, 0, 5, 8, ≪1297≫, Missing[], 5, Missing[], 7, 7, 9}
```

A more informative method, but one that would be less amenable to subsequent processing, would be to generate some text. Here I do so by using StringTemplate and Style to generate an error message that may be more interpretable by humans.

Combine custom programs with FailureAction → "Encapsulate" to generate custom responses when the operators inside Query encounter problems:

```
In[ ]:= Query[All, If[#age ≥ 10, IntegerDigits[#age][[2]],
            Style[StringTemplate["`1` is not a 2 digit number"][#age], Pink]] &,
          FailureAction → "Encapsulate"] [titanic] // Terse[5]

Out[ ]//Short= {9, 1 is not a 2 digit number, 2 is not a 2 digit number, 0, ≪1302≫, 7, 7, 9}
```

Dealing with Missing Parts

There is another option to Query that deals with a particular problem that can arise: missing data. Consider, for example, what happens when I want the fourth part of each row but at least some of the expressions don't have a fourth part. I first modify my dinghy to get rid of the "survived" key-value pair in the third row. This means that the third row no longer has four parts; it has only three.

Create a variant of dinghy that omits a key-value pair:

In[ ]:= **dinghya = Delete [dinghy, { 3, "survived" }]**

Out[ ]= { <| class → 3rd, age → 16, sex → female, survived → True |>,
     <| class → 1st, age → 65, sex → male, survived → False |>,
     <| class → 3rd, age → 2, sex → female |>,
     <| class → 3rd, age → Missing [ ] , sex → female, survived → True |>,
     <| class → 3rd, age → 18, sex → female, survived → False |> }

So what happens when I use Query to get the fourth part of each row, even the row that doesn't have a fourth part anymore?

Query can return results even when it is asked to find Parts that don't exist:

In[ ]:= **Query [All, 4] [dinghya]**

Out[ ]= { True, False, Missing [PartAbsent, 4] , True, False }

The good news is that in certain cases the kernel doesn't skip a beat and doesn't generate a potentially annoying error message. Instead, it just wraps the third part of the output in Missing. The bad news is that if this were a 100,000-element set of data and every row was supposed to have a "survival" key value, we might never notice the problem. Query's lenity in certain cases would obscure the matter.

This lenity appears to extend to all methods of data retrieval that rely on Slice. Here are two additional examples.

Query ignores the absence of top-level missing parts:

In[ ]:= **Query [1 ;; 10 000] [dinghy]**

Out[ ]= { <| class → 3rd, age → 16, sex → female, survived → True |>,
     <| class → 1st, age → 65, sex → male, survived → False |>,
     <| class → 3rd, age → 2, sex → female, survived → False |>,
     <| class → 3rd, age → Missing [ ] , sex → female, survived → True |>,
     <| class → 3rd, age → 18, sex → female, survived → False |> }

Query wraps Missing around Slices that do not exist:

In[•]:= **Query [All, "survived"] [dinghya]**

Out[•]= { True, False, Missing [KeyAbsent, survived] , True, False }

The lenity extends only to methods of retrieval that ultimately may rely on Slice. If I'd asked for the survival value using an anonymous function with named slots (such as ♯ survived &), I'd get an error.

But using an anonymous function with key arguments to retrieve missing data yields Failure objects:

In[•]:= **Query [All, ♯survived &] [dinghya]**

Out[•]= Failure[⚠ Message: Named Slot survived in ♯survived & cannot be filled from <|class → 3rd, age → 2, sex → female |>. Tag: Function]

I can force the kernel to be more strict by setting the PartBehavior option to None. Now, I get a failed Query.

Make Query intolerant of nonexistent parts by setting PartBehavior → None:

In[•]:= **Query [All, 4, PartBehavior → None] [dinghya]**

Out[•]= Failure[⚠ Message: Part 4 of <|class → 3rd, age → 2, sex → female |> does not exist. Tag: Part]

With the problem no longer masked, I can use the debugging techniques discussed in the previous subsection to isolate and solve the problem.

Combine intolerance of nonexistent parts with explicit error messages:

In[•]:= **Query [All, "survived", PartBehavior → None, FailureAction → "Encapsulate"] [dinghya]**

Out[•]= { True, False, Missing [KeyAbsent, survived] , True, False }

Now I see that the problem must be that the third row doesn't have a key-value pair with the "survived" key. I fix the problem using Insert.

Use Insert to restore a lost key-value pair:

In[•]:= **dinghyb = Insert [dinghya, "survived" → Missing [ ] , { { 3, −1 } }]**

Out[•]= { <|class → 3rd, age → 16, sex → female, survived → True |>,
        <|class → 1st, age → 65, sex → male, survived → False |>,
        <|class → 3rd, age → 2, sex → female, survived → Missing [ ] |>,
        <|class → 3rd, age → Missing [ ] , sex → female, survived → True |>,
        <|class → 3rd, age → 18, sex → female, survived → False |> }

Now everything works:

In[ ]:= **Query [All, "survived", PartBehavior → None, FailureAction → "Encapsulate"] [dinghyb]**

Out[ ]= { True, False, Missing [ ] , True, False }

Of course, now that I recognize these issues with the data, it might be better to go back and clean the data *before* I ever start with more substantive analysis. Here's the kind of code that would help.

Use AssociationThread to construct an Association with the same keys as the passengers in dinghya but in which all the values are Missing [ ] :

In[ ]:= **fix = AssociationThread [{ "class", "age", "sex", "survived" } , Missing [ ]]**

Out[ ]= <| class → Missing [ ] , age → Missing [ ] , sex → Missing [ ] , survived → Missing [ ] |>

Exploit the fact that when joined, Associations have duplicate keys and the last value encountered is the output:

In[ ]:= **fixFunction = Join [fix, ♯] &**

Out[ ]= Join [fix, ♯1] &

Use fixFunction as the second argument to a Query to map it over each passenger in the data:

In[ ]:= **fixedDinghya = Query [All, fixFunction] [dinghya]**

Out[ ]= { <| class → 3rd, age → 16, sex → female, survived → True |>,
    <| class → 1st, age → 65, sex → male, survived → False |>,
    <| class → 3rd, age → 2, sex → female, survived → Missing [ ] |>,
    <| class → 3rd, age → Missing [ ] , sex → female, survived → True |>,
    <| class → 3rd, age → 18, sex → female, survived → False |> }

Now I can sensibly compute survival for each passenger or whatever else I am interested in:

In[ ]:= **{ Query [All, ♯survived &] [fixedDinghya] ,
    Query [Counts, ♯survived &] [fixedDinghya] }**

Out[ ]= { { True, False, Missing [ ] , True, False }, <| True → 2, False → 2, Missing [ ] → 1 |> }

Dealing with Missings

I briefly discussed earlier how Query deals with missing values in certain contexts. I now want to engage in a deeper dive. The first principle is that the treatment of missing data can depend on the value of the MissingBehavior option to Query. One possible value for that option is None. It's not the default value, but one can use it. Setting MissingBehavior → None has the virtue of simplicity: one essentially gets the same behavior as if one applied the function entirely outside the Query context or if one used the Normal of the Query. Here's an example.

The behavior of Query with MissingBehavior → None is essentially the same as with the Normal of the Query:

```
In[ ]:=   { Query [ Total, MissingBehavior → None ] [ { 3, 4, Missing [ ] } ],
             Normal [ Query [ Total ] ] [ { 3, 4, Missing [ ] } ] }
Out[ ]=   { 7 + Missing [ ] , 7 + Missing [ ] }
```

Where things get more complicated is when one leaves (or sets) the value of the MissingBehavior option to be Automatic. There are four possibilities I want to address here. The first, which occurs quite frequently, is that Query doesn't do anything special. The result is the same as if you set MissingBehavior → None.

Except for certain functions, Query operators, when used on data with missing values, do whatever the Normal of the Query would do:

```
In[ ]:=   Query [ f ] [ { 3, 4, Missing [ ] } ]
Out[ ]=   f [ { 3, 4, Missing [ ] } ]
```

The second possibility is that Query will drop or ignore the missing values. This occurs when one uses functions such as Total, Mean, Median, Min, or Max where one generally wants to engage in some form of mathematical aggregation.

Query drops the missing values and computes the mean of { 3, 4, 6, 11 }:

```
In[ ]:=   Query [ Mean ] [ { 3, 4, Missing [ ] , 6, 11, Missing [ ] } ]
Out[ ]=   6
```

One needs to be aware that the scope of this default treatment is limited. In the following code, for example, the Mean function is wrapped inside another function. Query, which emphasizes form, sees that as a different operation and thus fails to drop missing values.

Query sees this as a different operation and thus fails to drop Missings:

```
In[ ]:=   Query [ N [ Mean [ # ] ] &, #age &] [ dinghy ]
Out[ ]=   0.2 ( 101. + Missing [ ] )
```

Moreover, all numeric aggregation functions do not result in dropped missing values.

Query with TrimmedMean does not delete missing values:

```
In[ ]:=   Query [ TrimmedMean ] [ Append [ Range [ 200 ] , Missing [ ] ] ]
```

```
In[ ]:=   Failure [  ⚠   Message:   The first argument   {1, 2, 3, 4, 5, 6, 7, 8, 9, 10,   ≪191≫ }   ]
                                     is expected to be a real numeric vector or matrix.
                      Tag:          TrimmedMean
```

A third possibility occurs when one uses statistical functions on data that does not have enough elements to perform the computation. To compute a StandardDeviation, for example, one should have at least one piece of data.

Outside of Query, attempting to compute the StandardDeviation of an empty List will produce a warning and will yield StandardDeviation [{ }] :

In[◦]:= **StandardDeviation [{ }]**

⋯ StandardDeviation : The argument {} should have at least two elements.

Out[◦]= StandardDeviation [{ }]

That could be annoying if one had thousands of rows of data in some large data structure and only one of the rows was an empty list.

With MissingBehavior → None, StandardDeviation mapped over data that includes even one empty list produces a Failure object:

In[◦]:= **Query [All, StandardDeviation, MissingBehavior → None] [**
{ {3, 4}, {5, 8}, { }, {4, 11} }]

Out[◦]= Failure[⚠ Message: The argument {} should have at least two elements.
Tag: StandardDeviation]

By using the default MissingBehavior → Automatic, StandardDeviation applied to an empty List produces Missing[Indeterminate] and, critically, no error message:

In[◦]:= **Query [All, StandardDeviation] [{ {3, 4}, {5, 8}, { }, {4, 11} }]**

Out[◦]= $\left\{ \dfrac{1}{\sqrt{2}}, \dfrac{3}{\sqrt{2}}, \text{Missing [Indeterminate]}, \dfrac{7}{\sqrt{2}} \right\}$

A fourth possibility occurs when one tries to perform certain arithmetic operations on missing data. Here's what happens outside the Query world.

Power applied to a missing just treats that missing the same as any other Wolfram Language expression:

In[◦]:= **Power [Missing [ ] , 3]**

Out[◦]= Missing [ ] ^{3}

This treatment might be very undesirable if we were subsequently hunting for missing data. So, here is what Query does by default.

Query with Power [♯, 3] & produces another Missing object, but this one has the reason as its argument:

In[◦]:= **Query [All, Power [♯, 3] &] [{ 2, 3, Missing [ ] }]**

Out[◦]= { 8, 27, Missing [Indeterminate] }

Find the position(s) of problematic data:

In[*]:= **Position [%, _Missing]**

Out[*]= **{ { 3 } }**

Similar behavior occurs by default for many other arithmetic functions, such as Times and Minus:

In[*]:= **{ Query [All, Times [4, ⌗] &] [{ 3, 5, Missing [ ] }],**
Query [All, Minus [⌗] &] [{ 3, 5, Missing [ ] }] }

Out[*]= **{ { 12, 20, Missing [Indeterminate] }, { −3, −5, Missing [Indeterminate] } }**

But Query doesn't by default fix all numeric operations on missing values. Here I use a Log function on the age value instead of a squaring function.

In this case, Query does not know that Log of Missing really makes no sense:

In[*]:= **Query [All, Log [⌗age] &] [dinghy]**

Out[*]= **{ Log [16], Log [65], Log [2], Log [Missing [ ]], Log [18] }**

The fifth possibility is when one runs functions such as Counts, GroupBy and Map on just a single Missing [ ] piece of data. Here's what happens outside of Query or if I switch to MissingBehavior → None.

Counts of a single Missing [ ] produces an error:

In[*]:= **Query [All, Counts, MissingBehavior → None] [{ { "a", "a", "b" }, Missing [ ] }]**

Out[*]= Failure[⚠ Message: The argument Missing   [] is not a list.
                      Tag: Counts   ]

The default behavior of Query avoids Failure:

In[*]:= **Query [All, Counts] [{ { "a", "a", "b" }, Missing [ ] }]**

Out[*]= **{ <| a → 2, b → 1 |>, Missing [ ] }**

Even if most elements can properly be grouped, a single Missing [ ] results in Failure:

In[*]:= **Query [All, GroupBy [EvenQ], MissingBehavior → None] [**
{ { 4, 5, 6 }, { 10, 11, 13 }, Missing [ ] }]

Out[*]= Failure[⚠ Message: The argument Missing   [] is not a
                      valid list of Associations or rules or lists of rules.
                      Tag: GroupBy   ]

The default behavior of Query avoids Failure:

In[*]:= **Query [All, GroupBy [EvenQ]] [{ { 4, 5, 6 }, { 10, 11, 13 }, Missing [ ] }]**

Out[*]= **{ <| True → { 4, 6 }, False → { 5 } |>, <| True → { 10 }, False → { 11, 13 } |>, Missing [ ] }**

Exercises

For all of the exercises in this chapter, try first to use Query. Often it's the most concise way of representing the question, but there's no shame in just coding directly without it.

4.1   Get the first and fourth passenger from dinghy.

4.2   Did the third passenger on the dinghy survive?

4.3   Recall the planets data (ResourceData [ro, "Planets Deeply Nested Structure"]). What is the median mass of the moons of Jupiter?

4.4   Provide a breakdown of the survival of Titanic passengers (the whole ship, not just the small sample) by the sex of the passenger.

4.5   Find the male passengers on the Titanic over age 40. Break down whether they survived based on their cabin class. Hint 1: You may want to read the documentation on the And function. Present the results so that the False response always appears before the True response. For extra credit, sort the classes according to the fraction that died. Hint 2: You might want to reread the material in the preceding chapter on Boolean keys and read up on the ToString function. Hint 3: Think hard about order of operations in your Sort and whether one or two Queries might be better here.

4.6   Do all exercises 3.1 through 3.3 from the preceding chapter using Query.

4.7   Use Query to compute the median age of the passengers on the Titanic broken down by cabin class.

4.8   Use MeanAround instead of Mean to break down the approximate mean age of Titanic passengers by sex. Hint: Does MeanAround deal with Missings the same way as Mean? If not, how might a function with DeleteMissing be inserted into the pipeline to fix matters. Note: MeanAround was introduced in Version 12; you can't do this with earlier versions.

Tech Notes

- Query is most useful when one wishes to apply operators at different levels of the data. If one wishes simply to work with the top level of the data, i.e. have a single-argument Query, it is often simpler just to write the function and not bother with the Query apparatus. One can apply the function directly, or if application occurs at a lower level, one can use Map with the appropriate level specification. However, if one wishes to apply operators at multiple levels of the data structure, Query can be quite useful. Indeed, Query could have been called MultilevelFunction or MultilevelMap. Fortunately, that path was not taken.

- There is a ResourceFunction MapLevel that somewhat clarifies what is going on with the Normal form of Query. Basically, instead of writing something like Map [Map [f] / *g] in which there is a nested Map, one would write MapLevel [f, { 2 }] / *g with the { 2 } as the second argument to MapLevel denoting that the function should be applied only at level { 2 } of the expression. Perhaps in some future version of the Wolfram Language, MapLevel will become integrated into the language and the presentation of the Normal form of a Query will be simplified.

- Other querying languages, such as dplyr from the R "tidyverse," also produce a pipeline of operators.

- One gets the sense that some very smart developers figured out a way to unify a bunch of Wolfram Language commands such that "legacy" functions such as Part, Take, and Span would just be special cases of a more general information extraction operation. At the moment, though, this superfunction GeneralUtilities`Slice sits in an less convenient context, perhaps waiting its turn to become part of the System` context, perhaps under a different name.

- Notice that when the argument to Take is not a number but something that needs to be computed, it is not a special case of GeneralUtilities`Slice and thus is no longer treated as a descending operator.

In[ ]:=   **Normal [Query [Take [UpTo [5]] , g]]**

Out[ ]=   Map [g] /* UpTo [5]

- If one uses anonymous functions at lower levels, the All function or Identity function at a higher level does nothing and Query just produces a mapping at a lower level. Whereas, if one creates a Query in which the parts at the lower level are denoted via their keys, Query produces an advanced form of GeneralUtilities`Slice.

In[ ]:=   **{ Normal [Query [Identity, { ♯age, ♯sex } &]] ,**
   Normal [Query [Identity, { "age", "sex"}]] }

Out[ ]=   { Map [{♯age, ♯sex} &] , GeneralUtilities`Slice [All, { age, sex}] }

- There are two additional ways to perform multiple MapAts. The first is efficient but really obscure. One uses functional programming to construct the RightComposition of MapAt operators rather than writing it out directly.

In[ ]:=   **RightComposition @@**
   MapThread [MapAt [♯1, {All, ♯2 }] &, { {f, g, h}, { "age", "sex", "survived"} }]

Out[ ]=   MapAt [f, {All, age}] /* MapAt [g, {All, sex}] /* MapAt [h, {All, survived}]

The second way is to use the ResourceFunction MapAtKey. It has a more pleasing syntax. I show it here, applying three different functions to three different columns in dinghy⟦1⟧.

In[ ]:=   [▣] **MapAtKey** + **[{ "age" → f, "sex" → g, "survived" → h}, dinghy⟦1⟧]**

Out[ ]=   <| class → 3rd, age → f [16] , sex → g [female] , survived → h [True] |>

- However, there are several limitations of MapAtKey. First, the part specification does not accept All. Thus, if I want to perform this set of operations on all rows of dinghy, I have to Map the MapAtKey function.

In[ ]:=   **Map [[▣] MapAtKey + [{ "age" → f, "sex" → g, "survived" → h}, ♯] &, dinghy]**

Out[ ]=   { <| class → 3rd, age → f [16] , sex → g [female] , survived → h [True] |>,
      <| class → 1st, age → f [65] , sex → g [male] , survived → h [False] |>,
      <| class → 3rd, age → f [2] , sex → g [female] , survived → h [False] |>,
      <| class → 3rd, age → f [Missing [ ]] , sex → g [female] , survived → h [True] |>,
      <| class → 3rd, age → f [18] , sex → g [female] , survived → h [False] |> }

Second, at present, there is no built-in operator form. I would like to be able to write
Map [MapAtKey [{ "age"→f, "sex"→g, "survived"→h}] , dinghy] , but that does not work, and third,
MapAtKey works only on Associations. Unlike MapAt, it does not work on expressions without keys.

- At present, the best way to do multiple transformations of the values of an **Association** is to use the Part Specification-Rule notation described previously.

- Advanced or particularly curious users may want to perform **Trace** on a **Query**. This should be done with some care as the output can be gargantuan, but here's an example that shows the last components of **Trace**. If one omits the **Part** specifications in this code, the output is very large but shows the very elaborate process by which the kernel compiles the **Query** and then, with the various options in mind, evaluates it.

In[ ]:= **Trace [Query [f, g] [{ { 3, 4 }, { 5, 6 } }]] ⟦−2, −2, 2, 2⟧**

Out[ ]= { (Map [g] / ∗ f) [{ { 3, 4 }, { 5, 6 } }], f [Map [g] [{ { 3, 4 }, { 5, 6 } }]],
    { Map [g] [{ { 3, 4 }, { 5, 6 } }], { g [{ 3, 4 }], g [{ 5, 6 }] } },
    f [{ g [{ 3, 4 }], g [{ 5, 6 }] }] } }

References

H. Wickham and G. Grolemun, *R for Data Science*, Boston: O'Reilly, 2017. r4ds.had.co.nz.

5 | The Dataset

This chapter uses a data resource from the Wolfram Data Repository (wolfr.am/WDR). To access the data, evaluate the following code.

Acquire the ResourceObject from the Wolfram Data Repository:

In[∘]:= **ro = ResourceObject ["Sample Data for Query Book"]**

Out[∘]= ResourceObject[⊞ 🏛 Name: Sample Data for Query Book »
Type: DataResource
Description: Data to support the Wolfram Media book Query:
Getting Information from Data wit...]

I am also going to ask you to run a piece of code that you may well not understand now but that will be explained at the end of the chapter. It alters the default number of rows displayed in a Dataset and thus improves pagination of the print version of this book.

Use SetOptions to change the default number of rows displayed in a Dataset from 20 to 8:

In[∘]:= **SetOptions [Dataset, MaxItems → 8] ;**

Introduction

So far, I have shown how Wolfram Language data structures such as Lists, Associations, and Lists of Associations can combine with Query to produce information. This all works just fine. But there are at least three reasons to wrap these structures in something called Dataset. It's incredibly easy to do. Here, I show the lifeboat as a List of Associations and then as a Dataset.

Retrieve the lifeboat data from the repository. Shorten the presentation of each item using the Terse ResourceFunction:

In[∘]:= **(lifeboat = ResourceData [ro, "Lifeboat List of Associations"]) / / [∘] Terse + [5]**

Out[∘]//Short= { <| class → 3rd, age → 16, sex → female, survived → True |>,
    <| class → 1st, age → 65, sex → male, survived → False |>, «19»,
    <| class → 2nd, age → 50, sex → female, survived → True |> }

I then apply Dataset to the data structure.

Convert a List of Associations into a dataset:

In[·]:= **lifeboatDS = Dataset [lifeboat]**

Out[·]=

class	age	sex	survived
3rd	16	female	True
1st	65	male	False
3rd	2	female	False
3rd	—	female	True
3rd	18	female	False
3rd	—	male	False
3rd	22	female	True
2nd	48	female	True

rows 1–8 of **22**

That's it! Of course, just because it's easy, doesn't mean it should be done. I thus will now address why it's often a good idea to wrap expressions, particularly data that is similar to a table or spreadsheet (or tabbed spreadsheet), in Dataset.

Visualization

One reason to wrap data structures in Dataset is visualization. When you wrap a data structure in Dataset and use the Wolfram Language front end, you get a dynamic and attractive interface for visualizing the data. The interface lets you scroll through large amounts of data or drill down into nested data. The Wolfram Language front end bears the memory burden of carrying these elaborate dynamic structures, but, generally, it is one that it is able to bear. Other clients, such as the Jupyter Notebook, will not have the capability to bear this memory burden.

Note: I use the term "wrap" in this chapter to denote what the user does. The user simply treats Dataset like any other Wolfram Language function that takes arguments. But Dataset is not an inert wrapper. It doesn't just leave intact the data structure to which it applies. It's not like List or some abstract function f. Instead, Dataset converts the data structure into a more elaborate expression containing, among other things, information on the types of data it holds.

If you are reading the notebook version of this book, you can take advantage of the Dataset dynamic interface. If you position your mouse over either a row header, column header, or element within a dataset, you'll see the indication of the applicable part specification immediately below the cell holding the dataset. So, if in the lifeboat dataset, I move my mouse over the "sex" column, I get "All > sex" displayed immediately below the cell containing the dataset. That can help me figure out how to specify that column programmatically. If I move it over False in the survived column of the third row, it displays "3 > survived", again telling me how to specify that cell programmatically.

Any column headers or row headers are left and right clickable. Try left clicking the "age" heading in the previous representation. What you should see is something like the following picture: the values for all the ages. This is particularly helpful where, as sometimes occurs, the data in a row or column is sufficiently long or baroque that Dataset decides to display it in some elided form, such as a List with just an ellipsis inside. Clicking the row or column containing these elided forms often provides a full display of what is actually contained inside.

⊞ › All › age

| 16 | 65 | 2 | — | 18 | — | 22 | 48 | 14 | 44 | 33 |
| 39 | 19 | 29 | 46 | — | — | 22 | 22 | 56 | — | 50 |

If you then click back on the little grid in the upper-left corner, you get your original Dataset restored. The dynamic interface is even more useful for datasets that have more deeply nested structures. Here, I show what happens when I click through the planets Dataset to get information on Uranus's moon Cordelia. It's kind of a little moon.

⊞ › Uranus › Moons › Cordelia

Mass	Radius
4.5×10^{16} kg	20.1 km

You can also right click the row or column headers. Doing so yields a context menu. Now you can copy to the clipboard either the position (part specification) of that element or the Normal form of the appropriate data. Alternatively, you can paste the same elements into a new cell below where you are clicking.

Syntactic Sugar for Queries

A second reason to wrap data structures with Dataset is to get access to syntactic sugar. Instead of writing Query [f, g] [ds] (where ds is a dataset), you can write ds [f, g]; you don't need to use the word Query anymore. The code ds [f, g] in effect constructs Query [f, g] [ds]. Syntactically, it looks as if the dataset or other structure has become a function.

This code, for example, containing a List of Associations, does not produce the desired results because it is not a dataset.

Implicit Queries don't work on expressions that aren't datasets:

```
In[·]:= {Association ["a" → 4], Association ["a" → 4] } [All, "a"]

Out[·]= { <|a → 4|>, <|a → 4|> } [All, a]
```

To get all of the values with the key "a", you would need to use an explicit Query or use Part notation.

For Lists of Associations, use Query or use Part notation:

In[•]:= { Query [All, "a"] [{ Association ["a" → 4] , Association ["a" → 4] }] ,
　　　　{ Association ["a" → 4] , Association ["a" → 4] } [[All, "a"]] }

Out[•]= { { 4, 4 } , { 4, 4 } }

But this code, containing a Dataset made from a list of Associations, works just fine. Again, notice that the output is still a Dataset but that the orientation is vertical. I'll discuss orientation later in the chapter.

Implicit Queries work on datasets:

In[•]:= **Dataset [{ Association ["a" → 4] , Association ["a" → 4] }] [All, "a"]**

Out[•]=

4
4

Here's an example using the Dataset involving Titanic passengers that emphasizes the point.

Retrieve information for the 1309 passengers on the Titanic as a Dataset:

In[•]:= **titanic = ResourceData [ro, "Titanic List of Associations Dataset"]**

Out[•]=

class	age	sex	survived
1st	29	female	True
1st	1	male	True
1st	2	female	False
1st	30	male	False
1st	25	female	False
1st	48	male	True
1st	63	female	True
1st	39	male	False

rows 1–8 of 1309

And I could write the following explicit Query.

An explicit Query to break down survival on the Titanic by gender:

In[•]:= **Query [GroupBy [⌗sex &] ,**
   GroupBy [ToString [⌗survived] &] / ∗ KeySort, Length] [titanic]

	False	True
female	127	339
male	682	161

Out[•]=

But I could equally well write the following code in which titanic, a Dataset, now looks like a function with a bunch of functions or function compositions as arguments. The Query is implicit.

An implicit Query to break down survival on the Titanic by gender:

In[•]:= **titanic [GroupBy [⌗sex &] , GroupBy [ToString [⌗survived] &] / ∗ KeySort, Length]**

	False	True
female	127	339
male	682	161

Out[•]=

It's all a little like writing Map [f, x] or f / @ x. They are the same thing. Which to use is mostly a matter of aesthetics and programming workflow preferences. For what it's worth, perhaps merely as a matter of habit or code transparency, I prefer using the explicit Query and tend not to rely on the implicit Query syntactic sugar. I have seen very respectable programmers choose otherwise.

Optimization for Queries

The third current advantage is that the Wolfram Language kernel may engage in some optimizations of the data structure that sometimes accelerate subsequent queries on it. This optimization occurs primarily because in the course of embedding the data in a dataset, the kernel analyzes the structure of the data to find regularities—the first column is all integers and the keys of the second column are all either "male" or "female", for example. The kernel may then exploit these regularities to compress the data and optimize future Queries.

Inside the Datasets

It's worth looking at least one time inside a Dataset object. Knowledge of the internal structure can help you fix or understand presentation issues that sometimes arise. You can't use traditional methods such as Part because conventional Wolfram Language "de-referencing" functions will only access the data within the Dataset, not its internal "meta"-information. (Dataset responds True to AtomQ, which indicates that Part will not work in a typical fashion.) You can, however, access the internals in several ways. The simplest is to get the InputForm of the dataset. You can also see this internal structure if you access the Wolfram Language through something other than the Wolfram Language front end, for example, the Jupyter interface. Here, I show the internal form of the dinghy dataset, an imaginary dinghy launched from the Titanic with five passengers.

Get the InputForm of a small dataset:

In[∘]:= (dinghyDS = ResourceData [ro, "Dinghy List of Associations Dataset"]) / / InputForm

Out[∘]//InputForm= Dataset [{ < | "class" −> "3rd", "age" −> 16,
    "sex" −> "female", "survived" −> True | >,
    < | "class" −> "1st", "age" −> 65,
    "sex" −> "male", "survived" −> False | >,
    < | "class" −> "3rd", "age" −> 2,
    "sex" −> "female", "survived" −> False | >,
    < | "class" −> "3rd", "age" −> Missing [ ],
    "sex" −> "female", "survived" −> True | >,
    < | "class" −> "3rd", "age" −> 18,
    "sex" −> "female", "survived" −> False | > },
  TypeSystem ` Vector [ TypeSystem ` Struct [
  { "class", "age", "sex", "survived" },
  { TypeSystem ` Atom [ TypeSystem ` Enumeration [
  "1st", "3rd"]], TypeSystem ` Atom [Integer],
  TypeSystem ` Atom [ TypeSystem ` Enumeration [
  "female", "male"]], TypeSystem ` Atom [
  TypeSystem ` Boolean] }]], 5], < | | >]

What you see is a sequence of information. The first item is the original data. You can recover this directly with the Normal function or the Dataset ` GetData function.

Use Dataset ` GetData to retrieve the data inside the dataset:

In[∘]:= Dataset ` GetData [dinghyDS]

Out[∘]= { <| class → 3rd, age → 16, sex → female, survived → True |>,
    <| class → 1st, age → 65, sex → male, survived → False |>,
    <| class → 3rd, age → 2, sex → female, survived → False |>,
    <| class → 3rd, age → Missing [ ], sex → female, survived → True |>,
    <| class → 3rd, age → 18, sex → female, survived → False |> }

The second item inside Dataset provides information on the types of data it contains. This information, which can be obtained with the Dataset ` GetType function, is used by the Wolfram Language front end to format the presentation of the data and to optimize queries used on the data. Here, the data, which was formatted as vertically stacked pieces of information on each passenger, is identified as a Vector whose elements are all of type Struct. Again, I'll discuss later how to use type structure to master the presentation of information, but for now, it's just worth seeing that Dataset, deep inside, contains information on the structure of the data it contains.

Load the TypeSystem` package. Use Dataset`GetType to retrieve type information inside the dataset:

In[∘]:= **Needs ["TypeSystem` "]**

In[∘]:= **Dataset`GetType [dinghyDS]**

Out[∘]= Vector [Struct [{ class, age, sex, survived } , { Atom [Enumeration [1st, 3rd]] ,
      Atom [Integer] , Atom [Enumeration [female, male]] , Atom [Boolean] }] , 5]

Dataset Presentation

If you are working with Version 13 (or later) of the Wolfram Language, there are many opportunities to format Dataset objects to make them more attractive or useful. I present several of them here. The basic ideas, however, are as follows:

> Dataset has many presentation options that are controlled by a "specification list."

> Item and header presentations can be "content aware."

> Datasets derived from other Datasets generally do not inherit styling options, but inheritance and/or restyling can be accomplished through the FormatDataset ResourceFunction or the DatasetQuery ResourceFunction.

> The Wolfram Language front end handles vertical versus horizontal orientation of the successive levels of hierarchical data in derivative Datasets, but one can generally alter that orientation through KeySort and other functions in one's Query.

> The Wolfram Language front end elides full presentation of large items, but one can, in many cases, override those elisions.

Dataset Options

Let's start with a plain vanilla Dataset. I'll label the underlying data as dinghyAssociations and the Dataset I create as vanillaDS.

Retrieve a List of Associations from the Wolfram Data Repository:

In[∘]:= **dinghyAssociations = ResourceData [ro, "Dinghy List of Associations"]**

Out[∘]= { <| class → 3rd, age → 16, sex → female, survived → True |>,
      <| class → 1st, age → 65, sex → male, survived → False |>,
      <| class → 3rd, age → 2, sex → female, survived → False |>,
      <| class → 3rd, age → Missing [ ] , sex → female, survived → True |>,
      <| class → 3rd, age → 18, sex → female, survived → False |> }

Convert the List of Associations into a Dataset by wrapping Dataset around it:

In[ ]:=   **vanillaDS = Dataset [dinghyAssociations]**

Out[ ]=

class	age	sex	survived
3rd	16	female	True
1st	65	male	False
3rd	2	female	False
3rd	—	female	True
3rd	18	female	False

DatasetTheme for Simple Presentation Tasks

The presentation is reasonably attractive. But perhaps it isn't what you really want.
Probably the simplest way to format a Dataset is using the DatasetTheme option.
Here's an example using the "Business" theme. The documentation for DatasetTheme
shows several other of these "comprehensive design themes" (my term) that alter
many aspects of the presentation in ways thought to be artistically coherent.

Set the DatasetTheme to "Business":

In[ ]:=   **businessDinghy = Dataset [dinghyAssociations, DatasetTheme → "Business"]**

Out[ ]=

class	age	sex	survived
3rd	16	female	True
1st	65	male	False
3rd	2	female	False
3rd	—	female	True
3rd	18	female	False

Here's the same data using the "Web" comprehensive design theme.

Set the DatasetTheme to "Web":

In[ ]:=   **webDinghy = Dataset [dinghyAssociations, DatasetTheme → "Web"]**

Out[ ]=

class	age	sex	survived
3rd	16	female	True
1st	65	male	False
3rd	2	female	False
3rd	—	female	True
3rd	18	female	False

These comprehensive design themes, such as "Business" or "Web", have subthemes that control limited aspects of the presentation. Suppose, for example, that you generally like the "Business" theme but you wish the column dividers were visible and that the column headers were vertical. You can make the value of the DatasetTheme option a List containing special strings and accommodate many of the typical formatting desires. Presentation details you can adjust by combining comprehensive design themes with special strings include fonts, dividers, backgrounds, and header orientation.

DatasetTheme can take a List of specifications that customize (within limits) the presentation of Datasets; the order of strings within the List does not generally matter:

In[ ]:= **businessDinghy = Dataset [dinghyAssociations,**
      DatasetTheme → { "ColumnDividers", "VerticalColumnHeaders", "Business" }]

Out[ ]=

class	age	sex	survived
3rd	16	female	True
1st	65	male	False
3rd	2	female	False
3rd	—	female	True
3rd	18	female	False

You can also use these special strings without specifying an underlying DatasetTheme such as "Business". Indeed, for some formatting options, such as dividers, the only documented way to control them as of Version 13.1 is through these special strings.

Use special strings without a comprehensive design theme:

In[ ]:= **Dataset [dinghyAssociations, DatasetTheme → { "ColumnDividers",**
      "VerticalColumnHeaders", "AlternatingRowBackgrounds", "Sans" }]

Out[ ]=

class	age	sex	survived
3rd	16	female	True
1st	65	male	False
3rd	2	female	False
3rd	—	female	True
3rd	18	female	False

Several of the special strings used within DatasetTheme accept parameters. Here, for example, I specify that the "ColumnDividers" are to be thick and Purple and that the "AlternatingRowBackgrounds" are to cycle through Pink, Green, and Brown. When using multiple parameterized special strings, it is important to clarify their scope with the use of braces. The result here is admittedly hideous, but the point is that DatasetTheme gives you a great deal of artistic license to use (or abuse).

Parameterize special strings within the DatasetTheme option by delimiting them with braces and then specifying various design details:

In[•]:= **hideousDinghy = Dataset [dinghyAssociations,**
DatasetTheme → { { "ColumnDividers", { AbsoluteThickness [3] , Purple } },
{ "AlternatingRowBackgrounds", { Pink, Green, Brown } },
"VerticalColumnHeaders", "Business" }]

Out[•]=

class	age	sex	survived
3rd	16	female	True
1st	65	male	False
3rd	2	female	False
3rd	—	female	True
3rd	18	female	False

Custom Dataset Presentation Basics

DatasetTheme can't do everything, however. For some forms of custom control, you need to augment or dispense with themes and just set options yourself. Suppose, for example, you want the background of the entire Dataset to be Yellow and want the column headers to appear in a large italicized font. Here's how to do it.

Set the Background option and HeaderStyle option to control Dataset presentation:

In[•]:= **Dataset [dinghyAssociations, Background → Yellow, HeaderStyle → Directive [Italic, 24]]**

Out[•]=

class	*age*	*sex*	*survived*
3rd	16	female	True
1st	65	male	False
3rd	2	female	False
3rd	—	female	True
3rd	18	female	False

Or perhaps you just wants three rows to appear and to elide presentation of the "class" and "age" columns.

Use MaxItems to alter the number of top-level elements (rows) presented and HiddenItems to suppress the presentation of certain columns:

In[ ]:= **Dataset [dinghyAssociations, MaxItems → 3, HiddenItems → { "class", "age" }]**

Out[ ]=

+	+	sex	survived
•	•	female	True
•	•	male	False
•	•	female	False

rows 1–3 of **5**

In Version 12 and earlier, instead of using MaxItems to alter the number of rows displayed, you need to alter a system variable: Dataset`$DatasetTargetRowCount. Other formatting options, however, are not realistically available in Version 12 or earlier.

You can also mix DatasetTheme with custom options. Here, I compare the use of the "Web" theme without any overrides and a "Web" theme in which I override the HeaderBackground so that it is Cyan.

Combine DatasetTheme with HeaderBackground to show that HeaderBackground takes precedence:

In[ ]:= **{ Dataset [dinghyAssociations, DatasetTheme → "Web"] ,**
   Dataset [dinghyAssociations, DatasetTheme → "Web", HeaderBackground → Cyan] }

Out[ ]=

class	age	sex	survived
3rd	16	female	True
1st	65	male	False
3rd	2	female	False
3rd	—	female	True
3rd	18	female	False

class	age	sex	survived
3rd	16	female	True
1st	65	male	False
3rd	2	female	False
3rd	—	female	True
3rd	18	female	False

Level-Specific Dataset Presentation

Thus far, I've shown how to apply presentation options to the entire Dataset. To do so, I've just made the option value the right-hand side of a Rule. But there may be times when you just want to apply presentations to a particular row, column, or other level, such as an individual item. You might also want the presentation to be content or position aware, perhaps only turning a number red if its value is negative. The Wolfram Language gains this flexibility with an elaborate syntax that can be used for many of the Dataset presentation options.

The general idea is to set the option value to a List in which each successive element corresponds to a specification for each successive level of the Dataset. I'll call this list the "specification list." One uses None (or, occasionally, All) as a placeholder in the specification list for situations in which one doesn't want to override the default presentation for a particular level. Suppose, for example, I want to override the default background for the first two rows. I want the first row to be LightBlue, the second row to be Yellow, the third and fourth rows to assume the default background, and the fifth row to be Orange. I don't want any background based on the column. Here's the syntax. I have a specification list that contains two elements. The first element of the level list governs the background based on the top level of the underlying data (the rows). The second element of the level list governs the background based on the next level of the underlying data (the columns). Thus, in the first position of my level list, which governs the rows, I have {LightBlue, Yellow, None, None, Orange}. In the second position of my specification list, I use None because I don't want any special background based on the second level.

Write a specification list consisting of two elements, then apply that specification list as the value of the Background for a Dataset that has two levels:

In[•]:= **speclist = { { LightBlue, Yellow, None, None, Orange }, None };**

In[•]:= **Dataset [dinghyAssociations, Background → speclist]**

Out[•] =

class	age	sex	survived
3rd	16	female	True
1st	65	male	False
3rd	2	female	False
3rd	—	female	True
3rd	18	female	False

I can simplify this specification of the option value. In particular, I can omit None if there are no values of interest that follow. Thus, if I only wanted the first row to be LightBlue and the second row to be Yellow, I can specify the background as set forth in this next example.

Eliminate trailing Nones within a specification level to simplify specification:

In[∘]:= **Dataset [dinghyAssociations, Background → { {LightBlue, Yellow}, None}]**

Out[∘]=

class	age	sex	survived
3rd	16	female	True
1st	65	male	False
3rd	2	female	False
3rd	—	female	True
3rd	18	female	False

If I did want that final row to be **Orange**, I would either have to retain the intermediate Nones or use positional overrides as discussed later in this chapter.

Indeed, I can simplify the specification list for **Background** still further. Not only do I not need Nones for trailing elements within the first level, I don't need the **None** to specify the second level at all. Basically, the Wolfram Language assumes that if I don't specify anything for subsequent levels, I mean **None**. More precisely, for an *n*-level Dataset where only *n–k* elements of a presentation option are given, the Wolfram Language assumes the remaining *k* elements are **None**.

Use only one level specification, deleting all trailing Nones:

In[∘]:= **Dataset [dinghyAssociations, Background → { {LightBlue, Yellow} }]**

Out[∘]=

class	age	sex	survived
3rd	16	female	True
1st	65	male	False
3rd	2	female	False
3rd	—	female	True
3rd	18	female	False

What if I wanted the rows to cycle between **LightBlue** and **Yellow**? I could, I suppose, just do something like the following.

Create a List of colors to give a background color to each row:

In[•]:= **Dataset [dinghyAssociations,**
 Background → { { LightBlue, Yellow, LightBlue, Yellow, LightBlue } }]

Out[•]=

class	age	sex	survived
3rd	16	female	True
1st	65	male	False
3rd	2	female	False
3rd	—	female	True
3rd	18	female	False

If I knew there were only five rows, that specification wouldn't be too awful, but imagine I had one thousand rows or an unknown number of rows. Identifying a background color for every row would then be ugly and tedious. The Wolfram Language thus provides an elaborate cycling language. The idea is to designate cycling by wrapping the cycling elements in a List. Here's how to exploit that syntax and better specify that the rows should cycle between LightBlue and Yellow.

Create a cycle specification with a nested two-element List of cycle elements:

In[•]:= **cycle2 = { { LightBlue, Yellow } };**

Use that cycle specification as a level specification for the Background option:

In[•]:= **Dataset [dinghyAssociations, Background → { cycle2 }]**

Out[•]=

class	age	sex	survived
3rd	16	female	True
1st	65	male	False
3rd	2	female	False
3rd	—	female	True
3rd	18	female	False

It doesn't have to be two elements in the cycle. I could ask that the rows cycle between LightBlue, Yellow, and Green.

Create a cycle specification with a nested three-element list of cycle elements:

In[•]:= **cycle3 = { { LightBlue, Yellow, Green } };**

Use that cycle specification as a level specification for the Background option:

In[•]:= **Dataset [dinghyAssociations, Background → { cycle3 }]**

Out[•]=

class	age	sex	survived
3rd	16	female	True
1st	65	male	False
3rd	2	female	False
3rd	—	female	True
3rd	18	female	False

Notice also that the cycling doesn't have to occur only within the first level. What if I want the columns (rather than the rows) to cycle between LightBlue and Yellow. I just make the cycle the second element of a specification in which the first element is None, which basically acts as a placeholder. Here, I can't omit the None because, if I were to do so, the Wolfram Language would assume I meant for the lone element of the specification list to apply to the top level and assume the remaining level specifications were Nones.

Use None as the first element in a specification list to specify that no formatting is to occur at the top level:

In[•]:= **Dataset [dinghyAssociations, Background → { None, cycle2 }]**

Out[•]=

class	age	sex	survived
3rd	16	female	True
1st	65	male	False
3rd	2	female	False
3rd	—	female	True
3rd	18	female	False

I could also finish (or preface) an element of my specification list with non-cycling elements. Here, I cycle at the top level through LightBlue and Yellow but make the last row Orange.

Mix a cycle specification with a non-cycling element within a level specification:

In[•]:= **Dataset [dinghyAssociations, Background → { { { LightBlue, Yellow }, Orange } }]**

Out[•]=

class	age	sex	survived
3rd	16	female	True
1st	65	male	False
3rd	2	female	False
3rd	—	female	True
3rd	18	female	False

You can also override the specification for a particular item. Suppose, for example, I generally want the row backgrounds to alternate between Yellow and LightPurple but want to highlight that the 65-year-old male in the second row did not survive. I also want to highlight in a different way that the 18-year-old in the last row (who did not survive) is a female. I do so by adding an extra element to the specification list for the Background option. That extra element is a List of Rules in which the left-hand sides are position specifications and the right-hand sides are values.

Create a List of overrides in which the left-hand side of each is itself a List of an index into a List (of Associations) and a key for an Association:

In[•]:= **overrides = { { 2, "survived" } → Red, { 5, "sex" } → LightBlue };**

Make the List of positional overrides the last element of a specification List:

In[•]:= **Dataset [dinghyAssociations,**
Background → { { { Yellow, LightPurple } }, None, overrides }]

Out[•]=

class	age	sex	survived
3rd	16	female	True
1st	65	male	False
3rd	2	female	False
3rd	—	female	True
3rd	18	female	False

Moreover, if all I want is to override the default values, I can get away with a truncated specification list. If I provide a list of Rules, the Wolfram Language assumes the preceding elements of the specification list are Nones.

Make the only value of a presentation option a List of positional overrides:

In[*]:= **Dataset [dinghyAssociations, Background → overrides]**

Out[*]=

class	age	sex	survived
3rd	16	female	True
1st	65	male	False
3rd	2	female	False
3rd	—	female	True
3rd	18	female	False

What I am describing is a system of specifying formatting option values by a series of specifications corresponding to the levels of the underlying data or according to specific positions in the data. This system also works in a somewhat similar way with Grid. Data considered to be at one level in a **Dataset** may be at a different level, however, when similar data is inside a Grid.

Create a common background specification:

In[*]:= **commonBackground = { None, { { Yellow, LightPurple } } };**

When the common background specification is used inside a **Dataset**, the color of the columns alternates; when the same common background specification is used inside a Grid, the color of the rows alternates:

In[*]:= **{ Dataset [dinghyAssociations, Background → commonBackground] ,**
Grid [{ { "3rd", 16, "female", True }, { "1st", 65, "male", False },
{ "3rd", 2, "female", False }, { "3rd", Missing [ ] , "female", True },
{ "3rd", 18, "female", False } }, Background → commonBackground] }

Out[*]=

class	age	sex	survived
3rd	16	female	True
1st	65	male	False
3rd	2	female	False
3rd	—	female	True
3rd	18	female	False

3rd	16	female	True
1st	65	male	False
3rd	2	female	False
3rd	Missing [ ]	female	True
3rd	18	female	False

Using Functions to Specify Dataset Presentation

We can have position- and content-aware backgrounds. That is, instead of designating the background elements explicitly, I can do so with a function. The function can accept up to three positional arguments: the first argument is the item itself, the second argument is the item's position, and the third argument is the expression inside the Dataset itself. I will refer to these functions as IPD functions (Item-Position-Dataset).

Let's start with a simple example IPD function in which only the position matters. If the position has "age" as its second element or is the fourth row, apply a Red background; otherwise, apply a LightBlue background.

Use a polymorphic description of a function so that generally the result is LightBlue but where the result is Red for two alternative values of the second argument:

In[•]:= **backgroundFunction [_, { _, "age"} | {4, _}, _] := Red;**
       backgroundFunction [_, _, _] := LightBlue

Set the value of the Background option to backgroundFunction with three arguments:

In[•]:= **Dataset [dinghyAssociations, Background → (backgroundFunction [#1, #2, #3] &)]**

Out[•]=

class	age	sex	survived
3rd	16	female	True
1st	65	male	False
3rd	2	female	False
3rd	—	female	True
3rd	18	female	False

Notice that simply using backgroundFunction without specifying that it accepts three arguments will not work as desired:

In[•]:= **Dataset [dinghyAssociations, Background → backgroundFunction]**

Out[•]=

class	age	sex	survived
3rd	16	female	True
1st	65	male	False
3rd	2	female	False
3rd	—	female	True
3rd	18	female	False

Here's an IPD function in which only the value matters. I use the Hash function, which takes any Wolfram Language expression and turns it into a fixed-length number. If the Hash of the value is even, the background is Yellow; otherwise, it is LightBlue.

Use If to create a function that yields Yellow if the Hash of its first argument is even and otherwise yields LightBlue:

In[•]:= **backgroundFunction2 [item_, __] := If [EvenQ [Hash [item]], Yellow, LightBlue]**

In[ ]:= **Dataset [dinghyAssociations, Background → (backgroundFunction2 [⌗1 , ⌗2 , ⌗3] &)]**

Out[ ]=

class	age	sex	survived
3rd	16	female	True
1st	65	male	False
3rd	2	female	False
3rd	—	female	True
3rd	18	female	False

Finally, here's an admittedly contrived IPD function in which the background colors depend on the value, the position, and the contents of the Dataset itself. Generally, the background color is LightBlue. But if the Hash of the item is even and it is in either the "age" column or the second row, the background color changes. The particular color in that instance depends on the median age of the passengers in the Dataset itself.

Create an IPD function that generally yields LightBlue but yields a color that depends on the Median of the age value in the Dataset if the Hash of an item is even and the position of that item matches one of two alternative patterns:

In[ ]:= **backgroundFunction3 [_, _, _] := LightBlue;**
 backgroundFunction3 [item_ /; EvenQ [Hash [item]], { _, "age"} | {2, _},
  ds_] := Hue [Rescale [Query [Median, ⌗age &] [ds], {0, 80}, {0, 1}]]

In[ ]:= **Dataset [dinghyAssociations, Background → (backgroundFunction3 [⌗1 , ⌗2 , ⌗3] &)]**

Out[ ]=

class	age	sex	survived
3rd	16	female	True
1st	65	male	False
3rd	2·	female	False
3rd	—	female	True
3rd	18	female	False

Good news! You can transfer your understanding of how the Background option works in Dataset to many other Dataset options as well: Alignment, HeaderAlignment, HeaderBackground, HeaderDisplayFunction, HeaderSize, HeaderStyle, ItemDisplayFunction, ItemSize, and ItemStyle. Here, for example, I use the syntax just described to customize values for several of these options. The result is aesthetically hideous, but it does show the immense flexibility of the Dataset presentation options.

I examine the HeaderDisplayFunction and ItemDisplayFunction options later in this chapter. Those options pose additional complications.

Add numerous presentation options with level specifications to Dataset to customize its appearance:

In[ ]:= **Dataset [dinghyAssociations,**
    Alignment → { { 3, "survived" } → Right, { 4, "sex" } → Top },
    HeaderAlignment → { None, { { Left, Right } } },
    HeaderBackground → { None, { { Yellow, LightBrown } } },
    HeaderSize → { None, { 4, { 7 }, 9 } },
    HeaderStyle → { None, Black, { All, "survived" } → Red },
    ItemSize → { None, 5, 3 → 1 },
    ItemStyle → { None, { { Brown, Purple } }, { 2, "sex" } → Directive [{ 24, Blue }] }]

Out[ ]=

class	age	sex	survived
3rd	16	female	True
1st	65	male	False
3rd	2	female	False
3rd	—	female	True
3rd	18	female	False

I can use IPD functions with these other options as well. Here, the headers are colored according to the last digit of the Hash of the header value and position. The font size of the items is determined according to the first digit of the Hash of the List of the item position and the expression inside the Dataset itself.

Use IPD functions to control HeaderStyle and ItemStyle:

In[ ]:= **Dataset [dinghyAssociations,**
    HeaderStyle → (Hue [Last [IntegerDigits [Hash [{ #1, #2 }]]] / 10] &),
    ItemStyle → (6 * First [IntegerDigits [Hash [{ #2, #3 }]]] &)]

Out[ ]=

class	age	sex	survived
3rd	16	female	True
1st	65	male	False
3rd	2	female	False
3rd	—	female	True
3rd	18	female	False

Specification Conflict in Dataset Presentation

I need to address one additional matter. What happens when there are specification lists that appear to conflict? Suppose, for example, I specify that the ItemStyle at the top level is Directive [{Blue, 6}] and specify that the ItemStyle at the next level is Directive [{Red, 18}]? Do I get little blue print or big red print?

ItemStyle specifications at two different levels conflict:

In[ ]:= **Dataset [dinghyAssociations,**
    ItemStyle → { Directive [{Blue, 6}] , Directive [{Red, 18}] }]

Out[ ]=

class	age	sex	survived
3rd	16	female	True
1st	65	male	False
3rd	2	female	False
3rd	—	female	True
3rd	18	female	False

As you can see, the specification at the lowest level prevails. There is an exception, however, for the Background option. For Background, the conflicting colors blend. So, if I specify LightBlue as the top-level background color and LightRed as the next-level background color, the result is Blend [{LightBlue, LightRed}], which is LightPurple.

Use a specification list for Background in which LightBlue applies at the first level and LightRed applies at the second level:

In[ ]:= **Dataset [dinghyAssociations, Background → {LightBlue, LightRed}]**

Out[ ]=

class	age	sex	survived
3rd	16	female	True
1st	65	male	False
3rd	2	female	False
3rd	—	female	True
3rd	18	female	False

Notice that there is no blending with HeaderBackground. That's because there is no conflict. Each header gets its own style according to the specification list.

Use GroupBy on lifeboat to create a two-level Dataset:

In[ ]:= **genderSurvival = Query [GroupBy [♯sex &] ,**
　　　GroupBy [ToString [♯survived] &] / ∗ KeySort, Length] [lifeboat]

Out[ ]= ⟨| female → ⟨| False → 3, True → 7 |⟩ , male → ⟨| False → 10, True → 2 |⟩ |⟩

Use a specification list for HeaderBackground in which LightBlue applies at the first level and Red applies at the second level:

In[ ]:= **Dataset [genderSurvival, HeaderBackground → { LightBlue, Red }]**

Out[ ]=

	False	True
female	3	7
male	10	2

ItemDisplayFunction and HeaderDisplayFunction

Basic Use

Although you can change the presentation of items and headers in the Dataset with use of the options just examined, sometimes you need something more flexible. Suppose, for example, that you want to (1) map genders to some classical icons such as ♀ and ♂, (2) round ages to the nearest five years, and (3) remove vowels from any headers that are strings. You can't do this with ItemStyle or HeaderStyle because you are not really applying a style to the items or headers. Instead, although you are not, in fact, changing the contents of the Dataset, you are making the items and headers display *as if* they held different values. The options you need in this instance are ItemDisplayFunction or HeaderDisplayFunction. Option values should be IPD functions, such as those I described previously, used for other presentation options such as Background or ItemStyle. To reiterate, the arguments for an IPD function are (1) the item itself, (2) the position of the item in the Dataset, and (3) the Dataset itself.

Most of the time, you will need to place the IPD functions in a specification list just as you did when you were using functions in ItemStyle and HeaderStyle.

Write a function vowelRemove that does nothing if its argument is not a string but that deletes vowels if it is:

In[ ]:= **vowelRemove = If [StringQ [♯] , StringDelete [♯, "a" | "e" | "i" | "o" | "u"] , ♯] &;**

Write a function that yields Missing [ ] if its argument satisfies MissingQ but otherwise tries to round its value to the nearest five:

In[ ]:= **round5 = If [MissingQ [♯] , Missing [ ] , Round [♯, 5]] &;**

Write a function genderSymbol that yields a gender-related string based on its argument:

In[ ]:= **genderSymbol = Which [♯ == "female", "♀", ♯ == "male", "♂", True, "⚥"] &;**

Use positional overrides to apply the round5 IPD function to "age" and the genderSymbol IPD function to "sex" for items and then use the vowelRemove IPD function for headers.

Add a List of Rules to the value of the ItemDisplayFunction option to map specific positions to different IPD functions:

In[ ]:= **Dataset [dinghyAssociations,**
　　　　ItemDisplayFunction → { None, None, { "age" → round5, "sex" → genderSymbol } },
　　　　HeaderDisplayFunction → vowelRemove]

Out[ ]=

clss	g	sx	srvvd
3rd	15	♀	True
1st	65	♂	False
3rd	0	♀	False
3rd	Missing[]	♀	True
3rd .	20	♀	False

Just as before, Nones can be eliminated where a List of Rules follows:

In[ ]:= **Dataset [dinghyAssociations,**
　　　　ItemDisplayFunction → { "age" → round5, "sex" → genderSymbol },
　　　　HeaderDisplayFunction → vowelRemove]

Out[ ]=

clss	g	sx	srvvd
3rd	15	♀	True
1st	65	♂	False
3rd	0	♀	False
3rd	Missing[]	♀	True
3rd	20	♀	False

You might notice that the dash in the "age" column of the fourth row has turned into Missing [ ] . I'll discuss how to change that in the subsection on custom elision.

Interaction of Style and DisplayFunction Options in Dataset

Both ItemStyle and ItemDisplayFunction can affect the presentation of items in a Dataset, and both HeaderStyle and HeaderDisplayFunction can affect the presentation of headers. I will now discuss the interaction of these two options.

In case of a direct conflict, the display function option (ItemDisplayFunction, HeaderDisplayFunction) prevails over the style option (ItemStyle, HeaderStyle). This is true regardless of the order in which the options are specified.

Create conflicting directives for items and headers with ItemDisplayFunction, ItemStyle, HeaderDisplayFunction, and HeaderStyle:

In[•]:= **Dataset [dinghyAssociations,**
   ItemDisplayFunction → (Style [⌗ , Blue] &) , ItemStyle → Red,
   HeaderDisplayFunction → (Style [⌗ , Purple] &) , HeaderStyle → Green]

Out[•]=

class	age	sex	survived
3rd	16	female	True
1st	65	male	False
3rd	2	female	False
3rd	Missing[]	female	True
3rd	18	female	False

Often, however, the two work cumulatively. Here, the style options change the font color of the item or header and the display function options change the font size.

Create non-conflicting directives for items and headers with ItemDisplayFunction, ItemStyle, HeaderDisplayFunction, and HeaderStyle:

In[•]:= **Dataset [dinghyAssociations, ItemDisplayFunction → (Style [⌗ , 24] &) ,**
   ItemStyle → Red, HeaderDisplayFunction → (Style [⌗ , 24] &) , HeaderStyle → Green]

Out[•]=

class	age	sex	survived
3rd	16	female	True
1st	65	male	False
3rd	2	female	False
3rd	Missing[]	female	True
3rd	18	female	False

Reformatting Pre-existing Datasets

Thus far, I've taken data that isn't already a Dataset and shown how you can convert it into a Dataset with customized presentation features. But what if you already has a Dataset and want to change its presentation? What if you already have, for example, vanillaDS, as created previously, perhaps created with considerable computational effort, and decide to make changes. There are several methods for doing this.

One option is to undo the Dataset wrapper and rewrap the underlying data in Dataset but this time include the desired formatting options. Here are several ways of unwrapping the Dataset.

Use Normal to extract just the underlying data from a Dataset:

In[ ]:= **Normal [vanillaDS]**

Out[ ]= { <| class → 3rd, age → 16, sex → female, survived → True |>,
     <| class → 1st, age → 65, sex → male, survived → False |>,
     <| class → 3rd, age → 2, sex → female, survived → False |>,
     <| class → 3rd, age → Missing [ ] , sex → female, survived → True |>,
     <| class → 3rd, age → 18, sex → female, survived → False |> }

Alternatively, use Dataset`GetData to extract just the underlying data from a Dataset:

In[ ]:= **Dataset`GetData [vanillaDS]**

Out[ ]= { <| class → 3rd, age → 16, sex → female, survived → True |>,
     <| class → 1st, age → 65, sex → male, survived → False |>,
     <| class → 3rd, age → 2, sex → female, survived → False |>,
     <| class → 3rd, age → Missing [ ] , sex → female, survived → True |>,
     <| class → 3rd, age → 18, sex → female, survived → False |> }

And now let's combine that unwrapping with a re-conversion.

Extract the data from an underlying Dataset and then convert it into a Dataset with presentation options:

In[ ]:= **Dataset [Normal [vanillaDS] , Background → Orange,
     HeaderBackground → { None, Black } , HeaderStyle → White]**

Out[ ]=

class	age	sex	survived
3rd	16	female	True
1st	65	male	False
3rd	2	female	False
3rd	—	female	True
3rd	18	female	False

A second way to reformat a Dataset is to use the FormatDataset ResourceFunction, which creates an operator that can then operate on the data. Behind the scenes, FormatDataset is automating the process described immediately prior to this.

Use FormatDataset with presentation option arguments and then apply that function to a Dataset:

In[•]:= [•] **FormatDataset** ◆ **[Background → RGBColor ["#DC143C"] ,**
     HeaderBackground → { None, Black } , HeaderStyle → White] [vanillaDS]

Out[•]=

class	age	sex	survived
3rd	16	female	True
1st	65	male	False
3rd	2	female	False
3rd	—	female	True
3rd	18	female	False

Option Inheritance

Operations on Datasets pose their own set of issues for formatting. Suppose, for example, I have the businessDinghy Dataset and want to look at only women. What you can see is that, at least through Version 13.1, the derivative Dataset does not inherit options from its parent.

Compare the original Dataset with formatting to the derived Dataset in which formatting is lost:

In[•]:= **{ businessDinghy, Query [Select [#sex == "female" &]] [businessDinghy] }**

Out[•]= {

class	age	sex	survived
3rd	16	female	True
1st	65	male	False
3rd	2	female	False
3rd	—	female	True
3rd	18	female	False

,

class	age	sex	survived
3rd	16	female	True
3rd	2	female	False
3rd	—	female	True
3rd	18	female	False

}

I can replicate the formatting of the original, however, without too much difficulty by using Options to grab the format settings from the underlying Dataset and then using them as arguments to the FormatDataset ResourceFunction.

Use Options to yield the presentation options from the businessDinghy Dataset:

In[•]:= **bdOpts = Options [businessDinghy]**

Out[•]= { DatasetTheme → { ColumnDividers, VerticalColumnHeaders, Business } }

Use Query with Select to get just the female passengers in businessDinghy; use FormatDataset to format the result using options from the original Dataset:

In[•]:= **Query [Select [♯sex == "female" &]] [businessDinghy] / /**
       [•] FormatDataset + [bdOpts]

Out[•]=

class	age	sex	survived
3rd	16	female	True
3rd	2	female	False
3rd	—	female	True
3rd	18	female	False

For pedagogical purposes, I use two lines of code to accomplish inheritance, but you could write this as a one-liner:

In[•]:= **Query [Select [♯sex == "female" &]] [businessDinghy] / /**
       [•] FormatDataset + [Options [businessDinghy]] ;

You don't have to grab all of the options from the parent Dataset. You can use them as a baseline and then use typical Wolfram Language programming techniques to subtract from and add to the parent options.

Delete the "VerticalColumnHeaders" from the inherited options and hide the "age" column:

In[•]:= **With [{ formats = Append [DeleteCases [Options [businessDinghy],**
         "VerticalColumnHeaders", ∞] , HiddenItems → { "age" }] },
       Select [♯sex == "female" &] [businessDinghy] / / [•] FormatDataset + [formats]
       ]

Out[•]=

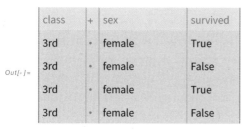

class	+	sex	survived
3rd	•	female	True
3rd	•	female	False
3rd	•	female	True
3rd	•	female	False

An alternative and often simpler vehicle for inheriting formatting options is to use the DatasetQuery ResourceFunction. You write the query the same way as if you were using Query.

By default, DatasetQuery preserves all formatting options from the original Dataset:

In[ ]:=   [▪] **DatasetQuery** ⟳ **[Select [⌗sex == "female" &]] [businessDinghy]**

Out[ ]=

class	age	sex	survived
3rd	16	female	True
3rd	2	female	False
3rd	—	female	True
3rd	18	female	False

You can override inheritance by setting the "Inheritance" option to an Association with "Addition" and/or "Deletion" key-value pairs.

Override the original style using a DatasetTheme and ItemStyle in the "Additions" key to the "Inheritance" option of DatasetQuery:

In[ ]:=   [▪] **DatasetQuery** ⟳ **[Select [⌗sex == "female" &] , "Inheritance" →**
⟨| "Additions" → { DatasetTheme → { "Business", "AlternatingRowBackgrounds" } ,
ItemStyle → ■} |⟩] [businessDinghy]

Out[ ]=

class	age	sex	survived
3rd	16	female	True
3rd	2	female	False
3rd	—	female	True
3rd	18	female	False

More elaborate examples and issues associated with the DatasetQuery ResourceFunction are contained in its documentation.

Header Ordering

Often times, a data restructuring operation, particularly one involving grouping, results in the order of groups being other than desired. Suppose, for example, that I were to break down survival on the Titanic by cabin class and sex. To make the problem appear, I'm going to do something not too nasty, which is just to jumble the Titanic data.

Jumble the Titanic data; get counts by cabin class and sex:

In[•]:= (SeedRandom [20 220 702] ;
titanic2 = RandomSample [titanic] ;
breakdown1 = Query [GroupBy [#class &] , GroupBy [#sex &] , Length] [titanic2])

Out[•]=

3rd	male	493
	female	216
2nd	female	106
	male	171
1st	female	144
	male	179

The output is unpleasant for several reasons. First, the ordering of the class headers is odd. The only reason third class comes first is that, as it happens, the first person it encountered in the jumbled data came from third class. Second, the sex order is sometimes male-female and other times female-male. This inconsistency makes the result difficult to comprehend. Third, I have effectively a 6 × 1 table. The male vs. female groupings are presented vertically, in the same orientation as the class groupings. I would prefer a 3 × 2 conventional table in which cabin class is in the rows and sex is in the columns. I'd like the male vs. female groupings to be presented horizontally in the opposite orientation as the class groupings. In short, I want to change the relative orientation of the different levels of the Dataset.

One fix is to compose a KeySort with both of the grouping operations. After having done so, the cabin classes are sorted alphabetically and the sex sub-groupings are consistently sorted alphabetically. The latter sorting has a fringe benefit. Because the order of the "sex" keys in the key-value pairs is the same, the kernel is smart enough to realize that it can internally compress the data as something known internally as a Struct. And when the Wolfram Language front end sees a Struct, it can (subject to various complications) present the data in an orientation opposite that of the preceding groupings.

Use KeySort to force a consistent ordering of the keys and thereby induce the orientation of the second level of the resulting Dataset to differ from that of the preceding level:

In[•]:= **breakdown2 = Query [GroupBy [#class &] / * KeySort,**
GroupBy [#sex &] / * KeySort, Length] [titanic2]

Out[•]=

	female	male
1st	144	179
2nd	106	171
3rd	216	493

This technique generalizes to Datasets that have more than two levels.

Use KeySort to force a consistent ordering of the keys and thereby induce the orientation of each successive level of the resulting Dataset to differ from that of the preceding level:

In[•]:= **breakdown3 = Query [GroupBy [⌗class &] / * KeySort, GroupBy [⌗sex &] / * KeySort, GroupBy [If [⌗age ≤ 18, "child", "adult", Missing [ ]] &] / * KeySort, Length] [titanic2]**

Out[•]=

		female		male	
1st	adult	120	adult	143
	child	13	child	8
	—	11	—	28
2nd	adult	82	adult	137
	child	21	child	21
	—	3	—	13
3rd	adult	94	adult	277
	child	58	child	72
	—	64	—	144

I can use KeyTake or the ResourceFunction KeySortLike to get further control over the order of the groupings. Suppose for some reason I want the order of the cabin classes to be "2nd", "3rd", and "1st" and the order of the sexes to be (consistently) "male", "female".

Use KeyTake to force a particular order on the keys in a Dataset resulting from a Query:

In[•]:= **Query [GroupBy [⌗class &] / * KeyTake [{ "2nd", "3rd", "1st" }], GroupBy [⌗sex &] / * KeyTake [{ "male", "female" }], Length] [titanic2]**

Out[•]=

	male	female
2nd	171	106
3rd	493	216
1st	179	144

Or, suppose I really don't care about the ordering of people in "3rd" or "1st" class. All I really care about is that people who were in "2nd" class get listed first. I can use KeySortLike as a simple way to fulfill this desire.

Use the KeySortLike ResourceFunction to force a particular order on the keys in a Dataset resulting from a Query:

In[ ]:= **Query [GroupBy [#class &] / * ⊡ KeySortLike + [{ "2nd" }] ,**
  GroupBy [#sex &] / * KeyTake [{ "male", "female" }] , Length] [titanic2]

Out[ ]=

	male	female
2nd	171	106
3rd	493	216
1st	179	144

All of this may well be enough for most people most of the time, and those people may safely skip the next few paragraphs. If, however, you are curious as to why sorting alters the orientation of the presentation, I will now expose some internals of Dataset. Doing so efficiently requires Wolfram Language 13.1 (or, presumably, any later versions). I do not provide a comprehensive explanation of orientation but provide a glimpse into what is going on behind the scenes.

The type information for the first Dataset generated previously (breakdown1) in which the orientation of the sexes was vertical shows that the first grouping is an Enumeration for which the permissible values are "1st", "2nd", and "3rd". The second grouping is an Association in which the keys are an Enumeration for which the permissible values are "female" and "male". It appears that when an Enumeration is needed to store the data, the orientation does not change from that of the preceding level.

Load the "TypeSystem`" package:

In[ ]:= **Needs ["TypeSystem`"]**

Use ExpressionTree and Dataset`GetType to show the internal structure of a Dataset in which the keys were not sorted:

In[ ]:= **ExpressionTree [Dataset`GetType [breakdown1] , ImageSize → 350]**

Out[ ]=

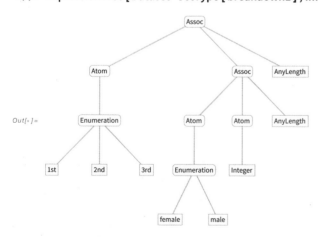

Now look at the type information for the second **Dataset** generated previously (breakdown2) in which the orientation of the sexes was vertical. You can see that, as before, the first grouping is an **Enumeration** for which the permissible values are "1st", "2nd", and "3rd". The second grouping is now different, however. It is a **Struct** in which the keys are a **List** for which the permissible values are "female" and "male". Since Version 13.1, when a **Struct** is available to store the data within a level, the orientation of that level changes from that of the previous level.

Use **ExpressionTree** and **Dataset`GetType** to show the internal structure of a **Dataset** in which the keys were sorted:

In[ ]:= **ExpressionTree [Dataset`GetType [breakdown2] , ImageSize → 350]**

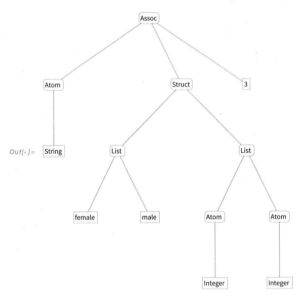

Customizing Elision

Sometimes, the values inside a **Dataset** item could take up a great deal of space to display. Here's a trivial example.

Construct a **Dataset** in which one of the values is a **List** of 10 numbers:

In[ ]:= **elided = Dataset [Association ["a" → Range [4] , "b" → Range [10]]]**

Out[ ]=

a	{1, 2, 3, 4}
b	{...10}

The front end has elided presentation of the full **List** associated with the "b" key. Although this may well be a very sensible decision 90% of the time, there may be special cases where you really want to see all of the values. Here is one way of overriding the front end's valiant effort to use sensible heuristics. You can **Map** something like **OutputForm** onto the values that are being elided. You can do so directly or using **Query**.

OutputForm prevents elision of long outputs:

In[ ]:= **notElided = Query [All, OutputForm] [**
     Dataset [Association ["a" → Range [4] , "b" → Range [10]]]]

a	{1, 2, 3, 4}
b	{1, 2, 3, 4, 5, 6, 7, 8, 9, 10}

Out[ ]=

This "fix" is risky, however. It does not just change the presentation of the Dataset; it actually changes the underlying data, which can have side effects if you then try to use the results.

Use of OutputForm to prevent elision may prevent subsequent operations on the Dataset from working as expected:

In[ ]:= **{ Query [All, Mean] [elided] , Query [All, Mean] [notElided] }**

Out[ ]=
$\Bigl\{$
a	5/2
b	11/2
,
a	Mean$\bigl[$ {1, 2, 3, 4} $\bigr]$
b	Mean$\bigl[$ {1, 2, 3, 4, 5, 6, 7, 8, 9, 10} $\bigr]$
$\Bigr\}$

A better fix would be to use an IPD function that contains OutputForm:

In[ ]:= **formatted =** ⊡ **FormatDataset** ⊹ **[ItemDisplayFunction → (OutputForm [#1] &)] [**
     Dataset [Association ["a" → Range [4] , "b" → Range [10]]]]

a	{1, 2, 3, 4}
b	{1, 2, 3, 4, 5, 6, 7, 8, 9, 10}

Out[ ]=

Because the underlying data has not changed, subsequent operations on the data work as expected.

Compute the Mean of the data in the formatted Dataset:

In[ ]:= **Query [All, Mean] [formatted]**

a	5/2
b	11/2

Out[ ]=

Here's another example in which the default behavior of Dataset, although perfectly sensible most of the time, might not be what you desire. Suppose I have a Graphics expression such as that produced by ListLinePlot. Notice that it is decorated with ticks on the axes (by default) as well as with a Callout and PlotMarkers that I have added.

Generate a Graphics object with Callout details and (by default) Ticks:

In[ ]:= **lp = ListLinePlot [Callout [{ 1, 3, 4, 6 } , "trend"] , PlotMarkers → Automatic]**

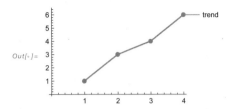

When I make the Graphics expression lp the value of an Association and convert the result to a Dataset, however, visualization of the plot is simplified. Again, many times, that is the smart decision. You often won't want clutter inside the visualization of a Dataset, just a kind of clue as to what really might be inside.

Create a Dataset that includes a decorated Graphics object with the default value for the ItemDisplayFunction option:

In[ ]:= **lpds = Dataset [Association ["a" → lp, "b" → Range [10]]]**

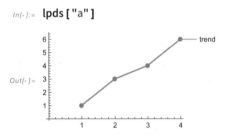

And you can recover the full plot easily using the techniques discussed in this book.

Retrieve the value of the "a" key from the Dataset lpds:

In[ ]:= **lpds ["a"]**

But what if you really do want the Graphics object to appear as an item in the Dataset with its details preserved? The answer is again an IPD function. You adjust the ItemDisplayFunction so that the Graphics expression in question is wrapped with the simple "do-nothing" IPD function # 1 &, which presumably overrides whatever default display function the Wolfram Language front end had in mind for that Graphics expression.

Use of the simple ItemDisplayFunction preserves the appearance of the graphic:

In[•]:= [•] **FormatDataset** ₊ **[ItemDisplayFunction → (#1 &)] [lpds]**

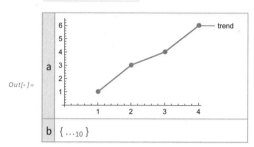

Out[•]=

Indeed, you can exploit IPD functions to further manipulate the display of the Graphics expression.

Use FormatDataset to reformat a Graphics item associated with the "a" key by making its background Yellow:

In[•]:= [•] **FormatDataset** ₊ **[ItemDisplayFunction →**
{ "a" → (Graphics [First [#] , Background → Yellow, Options [#]] &) }] [lpds]

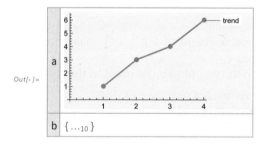

Out[•]=

And if the Graphics or another troublesome expression is just one item in a complex Dataset, you can combine IPD functions that work at a particular level with overriding IPD functions that work on particular positions in the Dataset. Here, I specify that the IPD function Framed [#, FrameStyle → Red] & applies generally to Dataset items at level 2. I also specify position overrides with a series of Rules in which the right-hand sides are IPD functions.

Assign to idf a level specification list in which the first element is None (for level 1), the second element is an IPD function calling for a red frame (for level 2), and the third element is a list of positional overrides:

In[•]:= **idf = { None, Framed [#1, FrameStyle → Red] &,**
{ { "a", "♀" } → (Graphics [First [#1] , Background → Yellow, Options [#1]] &) ,
{ "b", "♂" } → (Graphics [First [#1] , Background → Orange,
AxesLabel → { "x", "y" } , Options [#1]] &) } };

In[ ]:= **Dataset [Association ["a" → Association ["♀" → lp, "♂" → 4] ,**
"b" → Association ["♀" → 7, "♂" → lp]] , ItemDisplayFunction → idf]

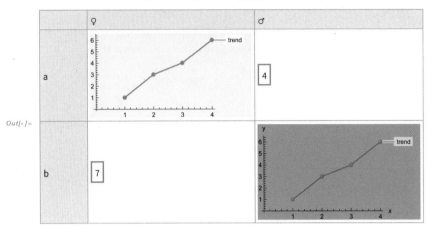

Out[ ]=

You could alternatively use a more general IPD function to achieve this goal.

Write an IPD function idf2 that frames any item that is not a Graphics object:

In[ ]:= **idf2 [item : Except [_Graphics] , pos_, _] := Framed [item, FrameStyle → Red]**

If the item is a Graphics object and the position matches { "a", "♀" } , make the background Yellow; If the item is a Graphics object and the position matches { "b", "♂" } , make the background Orange:

In[ ]:= **idf2 [item _Graphics, { "a", "♀" }, _] :=**
Graphics [First [item] , Background → Yellow, Options [item]] ;
idf2 [item _Graphics, { "b", "♂" }, _] := Graphics [First [item] ,
Background → Orange, AxesLabel → { "x", "y" }, Options [item]] ;

Use idf2 as the value of the ItemDisplayFunction for the Dataset:

In[ ]:= **Dataset [Association ["a" → Association ["♀" → lp, "♂" → 4] ,**
"b" → Association ["♀" → 7, "♂" → lp]] ,
ItemDisplayFunction → (idf2 [#1, #2, #3] &)]

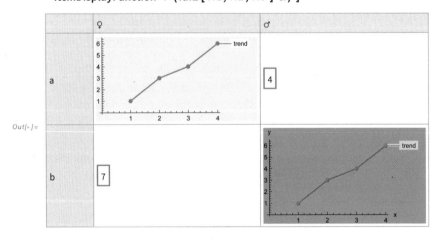

Out[ ]=

Resetting Dataset Visualization

Almost all of the time, particularly since Version 13, operations on Dataset result either in perfectly sensible presentations of the data or presentations that can be fixed with the simple KeySort (and similar) expedients described previously. Even Version 13.1 is still not perfect, however. And if you are using an older version of the Wolfram Language, you may find more frequently that Dataset operations can result in undesired presentations. There is a fix that sometimes works. It basically forces the Wolfram Language front end to rethink how to present the data. Use the ResetDataset ResourceFunction.

To show the problem, I want to look at a computation similar to one I performed previously. Here's what I start with. Notice that the missing age of one of the passengers is represented with an attractive dash.

Convert dinghyAssociations to a Dataset:

In[ ]:= **Dataset [dinghyAssociations]**

Out[ ]=

class	age	sex	survived
3rd	16	female	True
1st	65	male	False
3rd	2	female	False
3rd	—	female	True
3rd	18	female	False

Now let's add an ItemDisplayFunction option to preserve the fact that some of the age data is missing. In other words, the IDF function would appear to do nothing:

In[ ]:= **withExplicitMissing = Dataset [dinghyAssociations,**
ItemDisplayFunction → { "age" → (If [MissingQ [♯], Missing [ ], ♯] &) }]

Out[ ]=

class	age	sex	survived
3rd	16	female	True
1st	65	male	False
3rd	2	female	False
3rd	Missing[]	female	True
3rd	18	female	False

Even though I essentially did nothing, the pleasant dash is gone and a literal Missing [ ] is present—not as attractive, in my view. And this change occurs even though, as I show in the next example, the data of the original Dataset is exactly the same as the data of the new Dataset and the type of the original Dataset is exactly the same as the type of the new Dataset.

Compare data and type of Dataset [dinghyAssociations] with withExplicitMissing:

In[ ]:=   { Dataset ` GetData [withExplicitMissing] ===
        Dataset ` GetData [Dataset [dinghyAssociations]] ,
      Dataset ` GetType [withExplicitMissing] ===
        Dataset ` GetType [Dataset [dinghyAssociations]] }

Out[ ]=   { True, True }

Fortunately, I can fix the problem with the ResetDataset ResourceFunction.

Use ResetDataset to restore proper formatting:

In[ ]:=   [▪] ResetDataset + [withExplicitMissing]

Out[ ]=

class	age	sex	survived
3rd	16	female	True
1st	65	male	False
3rd	2	female	False
3rd	—	female	True
3rd	18	female	False

Exercises

5.1 Convert a List of the integers from 2 to 11 into a dataset. Assign your result to the variable r10.

5.2 See what r10 looks like in Normal form.

5.3 Find out what types the Dataset uses to describe the elements of r10. You may wish to run Needs ["TypeSystem`"] first.

5.4 Use Query to create a new Dataset whose values are the even elements of r10. (If the orientation is now different than for r10, it is because the data has fewer elements.)

5.5 Use the syntactic sugar (implicit Query method) described in this chapter to write the same "query" as in the prior problem (selecting only the even elements of r10) but without explicitly using the Query function.

5.6 Run the code lifeboat=ResourceData [ro, "Lifeboat List of Associations"] . Create a Dataset named lifeboatW out of the resulting List of Associations that uses the "Web" theme.

5.7 Try and recreate the "Web" theme shown before using various presentation options. You do not have to get the colors exactly correct. Also, you may need to use DatasetTheme in order to get the column dividers.

5.8 Write a Query that retrieves only the survivors in lifeboatW and then drops the "survived" column. See if you can preserve the formatting of lifeboatW. Hint: Using the DatasetQuery ResourceFunction might make this easier.

5.9 Write a Query that retrieves passengers age 50 or older in lifeboatW and then drops the "age" column. Preserve the formatting of lifeboatW except change the HeaderBackground to Yellow.

5.10 In the famous 1997 movie *Titanic*, a main character (portrayed by actress Kate Winslet) is Rose, a 17-year-old girl who travels in first class. Take ExampleData [{ "Dataset", "Titanic" }] and then use either Query or the implicit Query method to find the passengers on the Titanic who meet this description. Assign your result to the variable roses. You should find two possible passengers.

5.11 Get the Major League Soccer (MLS) dataset out of the ResourceObject for this book with the code mls=ResourceData [ro, "MLS List of Associations Dataset"] .

5.12 Get the median guaranteed compensation for players in 2016 broken down by position and sorted from high to low. Hint: The date is stored as a DateObject.

5.13 Display the MLS data so that any dollar figures are rounded to the nearest ten thousand. (You will want to use an IPD function to do so.) Put the last name of the player in 24 point type and the first name of the player in 8-point type. Create alternating row backgrounds of white and very light blue. Instead of displaying the first 20 items and then requiring a new "page" to be chosen, display only the first eight items before a new "page" must be chosen. Hint: The BaseSalary and GuaranteedCompensation are stored as Quantity objects. Here's how one could round $34,343 to the nearest $10,000: Round [Quantity [34343, "USDollars"] , Quantity [10000, "USDollars"] .

5.14 Did you notice that the labeling of positions is inconsistent? Sometimes, for example, a player is listed as playing "M / F", which I am confident means midfielder-forward, and other times, they are listed as playing "M−F", which I am confident means the same thing. It appears that sometimes a "/" is used to designate alternative positions and sometimes a "-" is used for the same purpose. Improve the dataset so that the encoding of the position column is consistent. Use an implicit Query to do this. Call your result mls2. Hint 1: The "Position" column may contain Missings or things that aren't strings. How are you going to handle that? Hint 2: My code uses MapAt.

5.15 Reformat your answer (mls2) so that only six rows display at a time, the headers are red, the column backgrounds alternate in color between orange and pink, and the columns are divided by thick yellow lines.

5.16 Now determine the median salary in 2017 by position using the improved MLS data (mls2). Format your answer so that the rows alternate in color between Gray and Lighter @ Gray. Some soccer experts might agree with me that goalkeepers are underpaid relative to their value in the game. Hint: Remember that dates are stored as DateObjects so that what may appear as 2017 is actually DateObject [{ 2017 }] .

Tech Notes

- You can generate a Query so complicated or meaningless that the system doesn't quite know what to do with it. In these circumstances, you may end up with the Dataset object being converted to its Normal form. Here, I apply f to dinghyDS. The result is an expression with f as its head and whose argument is the Normal form of the input Dataset.

In[∘]:= **dinghyDS [f]**

Out[∘]= f [{ <| class → 3rd, age → 16, sex → female, survived → True |>,
           <| class → 1st, age → 65, sex → male, survived → False |>,
           <| class → 3rd, age → 2, sex → female, survived → False |>,
           <| class → 3rd, age → Missing [ ] , sex → female, survived → True |>,
           <| class → 3rd, age → 18, sex → female, survived → False |> }]

In[◦]:= **dinghyDS [Length]**

Out[◦]= 5

In[◦]:= **Length [dinghyDS]**

Out[◦]= 5

- In the real world, however, where I am not seeking to break Dataset, I find that this sort of thing seldom occurs. So long as you keep your blunders to lower levels of the expression, it's tough to "escape" the Dataset.

In[◦]:= **dinghyDS [All, f]**

Out[◦]=

f [⟨|"class" → "3rd", "age" → 16, "sex" → "female", "survived" → True |⟩]
f [⟨|"class" → "1st", "age" → 65, "sex" → "male", "survived" → False |⟩]
f [⟨|"class" → "3rd", "age" → 2, "sex" → "female", "survived" → False |⟩]
f [⟨|"class" → "3rd", "age" → Missing[], "sex" → "female", "survived" → True |⟩]
f [⟨|"class" → "3rd", "age" → 18, "sex" → "female", "survived" → False |⟩]

- As of Version 13, the type representations used inside Dataset differ from those used by the Wolfram Language compiler. Do not interchange them.

- To see the incredibly complex choices made by the Wolfram Language front end in deciding how to render a Dataset, wrap the function ToBoxes around it. When executed, you will see a ghastly yet impressive expression full of detailed information showing how the Wolfram Language front end constructs the dynamic visualization most users take for granted.

More to Explore

How to Make Use of Associations (wolfr.am/UsingAssociations)

Airline Performance in 2015; Dataset readers may wish to use for practice (wolfr.am/AirlinePerformance)

Dataset vs. an Association of Associations (wolfr.am/DatasetVAssociationOfAssociations)

6 | Basic Recipes

This chapter uses a data resource from the Wolfram Data Repository (wolfr.am/WDR). To access the data, evaluate the following code.

Acquire the ResourceObject from the Wolfram Data Repository:

In[•]:= **ro = ResourceObject ["Sample Data for Query Book"]**

Out[•]= ResourceObject⎡ ⊞ 🏛 Name: Sample Data for Query Book »   ⎤
                                      Type: DataResource
                         Description: Data to support the Wolfram Media book Query:
                                       Getting Information from Data wit...

You can also evaluate this piece of code, which will result in the default number of rows in Datasets being 8 instead of the usual 20:

In[•]:= **SetOptions [Dataset, MaxItems → 8] ;**

Introduction

In this chapter, I provide basic recipes that work on a variety of issues that I have confronted in the real world of data analysis. Some of these you may be able to use almost as is without significant alteration. Others will require some understanding of the underlying concepts presented in this book. I highly recommend that impatient readers "Riffle": interleave review of this chapter with the more generalized knowledge found in earlier chapters. I've broken down the recipes into two chapters. This chapter deals with recipes that tend to be simpler. The next chapter deals with more advanced ones.

The data for this chapter is stored in a ResourceObject named ro that I retrieved at the start of this notebook. I'm going to make extensive use of the imaginary lifeboat from the Titanic. I load it now.

Load the lifeboat data:

In[•]:= **lifeboatDS = ResourceData [ro, "Lifeboat List of Associations Dataset"]**

Out[•]=

class	age	sex	survived
3rd	16	female	True
1st	65	male	False
3rd	2	female	False
3rd	—	female	True
3rd	18	female	False
3rd	—	male	False
3rd	22	female	True
2nd	48	female	True

rows 1–8 of **22**

I also load up the Titanic Dataset, which I will use a lot as well.

Load the Titanic data:

In[•]:= **titanicDS = ResourceData [ro, "Titanic List of Associations Dataset"]**

Out[•]=

class	age	sex	survived
1st	29	female	True
1st	1	male	True
1st	2	female	False
1st	30	male	False
1st	25	female	False
1st	48	male	True
1st	63	female	True
1st	39	male	False

rows 1–8 of **1309**

Get the Dimensions of a Dataset

Use Dimensions to get information on the dimensionality of a Dataset.

Get the dimensions of a Dataset:

In[•]:= **Dimensions [lifeboatDS]**

Out[•]= **{ 22, 4 }**

If the Dataset is "highly regular," meaning that the number of elements at each level is the same and the order of keys in any Association at the lower levels is the same, the dimensions of the Dataset will be the same as the dimensions of the underlying values in the Dataset.

Use Values to convert an Association into a List, use Normal to turn the Dataset into a List of Lists, and get its dimensions:

In[•]:= **Dimensions [Normal [Query [All, Values] [lifeboatDS]]]**

Out[•]= **{ 22, 4 }**

If, however, the Dataset is not highly regular, Dimensions will yield a different result. Here, for example, is a Dataset extremely similar to titanicDS except that the order of the keys in the second row has been scrambled.

Use KeyTake with MapAt to alter the order of key-value pairs in just one of the Associations in a Dataset; show the Normal form of the resulting Dataset:

In[•]:= **(scrambledLifeboatData =**
      Normal [Query [MapAt [KeyTake [{ "age", "survived", "class", "sex" }], 2]] [
      lifeboatDS]]) / / [•] Terse ◆ [5]

Out[•]//Short= { <| class → 3rd, age → 16, sex → female, survived → True |>,
    <| age → 65, survived → False, class → 1st, sex → male |>,
    <| class → 3rd, age → 2, sex → female, survived → False |>, ≪17≫,
    <| class → 2nd, age → Missing [ ], sex → male, survived → False |>,
    <| class → 2nd, age → 50, sex → female, survived → True |> }

I now convert this List of Associations into a Dataset. Notice that the data "looks" regular. The column order is consistent and there are four columns in each row.

Wrap Dataset around the data structure:

In[•]:= **Dataset [scrambledLifeboatData]**

Out[•]=

class	age	sex	survived
3rd	16	female	True
1st	65	male	False
3rd	2	female	False
3rd	—	female	True
3rd	18	female	False
3rd	—	male	False
3rd	22	female	True
2nd	48	female	True

rows 1–8 of 22

But if I take its dimensions now, I get something perhaps unexpected. Because the order of the keys is not consistent, the Wolfram Language does not recognize it as being 22×4.

Use Dimensions to get the dimensionality of the resulting Dataset:

In[∘]:= **Dimensions [Dataset [scrambledLifeboatData]]**

Out[∘]= {22}

Here's another example of where the order of the keys matters in the output of Dimensions on a Dataset. Here, I use Select to retrieve only those passengers on the Titanic for whom the age is known and then use GroupBy to break them down by sex, cabin class and age group ("child", "adult" or missing), but I don't sort the age groupings.

Four arguments to Query produce a dataset with three levels:

In[∘]:= **bySexClassAge = Query [(Select [Not [MissingQ [♯age]] &]) / * GroupBy [♯sex &] ,**
GroupBy [♯class &] / * KeySort,
GroupBy [If [♯age ≤ 18, "child", "adult"] &] , Length] [titanicDS]

		1st		2nd		3rd	
female	adult	120	adult	82	adult	94
	child	13	child	21	child	58
male	child	8	adult	137	adult	277
	adult	143	child	21	child	72

I now take its dimensions. It says it is 2 × 3:

In[∘]:= **Dimensions [bySexClassAge]**

Out[∘]= {2, 3}

If, however, the ages are sorted so that they consistently appear in order as "adult" and "child", the Dataset is found to have Dimensions of $2 \times 3 \times 2$.

Applying KeySort at a low level of the Dataset permits the Wolfram Language kernel to see the dimensions of the result as more regular:

In[∘]:= **Dimensions [Query [All, All, KeySort] [bySexClassAge]]**

Out[∘]= {2, 3, 2}

Rename All of the Columns

The Wolfram Language documentation contains a recommended way of renaming columns. It has the virtue of efficiency but relies on coding constructs whose meanings remain somewhat obscure. The idea is to form an Association in which the keys are the *new* column names and the values are the *old* column names. This is somewhat backwards from the syntax that I (at least) would expect, but once you remember the reverse order, it is simple and useful.

Change the names of the columns to "cabin", "years", "gender", and "survival":

In[•]:= **columnNameChanger = Association ["cabin" → "class",**
"years" → "age", "gender" → "sex", "survival" → "survived"] ;

In[•]:= **Query [All, columnNameChanger] [lifeboatDS]**

Out[•]=

cabin	years	gender	survival
3rd	16	female	True
1st	65	male	False
3rd	2	female	False
3rd	—	female	True
3rd	18	female	False
3rd	—	male	False
3rd	22	female	True
2nd	48	female	True

rows 1–8 of 22

A second method is to rely on the KeyReplace function contained in the Wolfram Function Repository (wolfr.am/WFR). This method has the virtue of a pleasing syntax in which the old name goes on the left-hand side of the rule and the new name goes on the right-hand side. Until such time, if ever, that it becomes part of the built-in language, use of this method does, however, require web access and relies on a non-guaranteed perpetuation of this ResourceFunction.

The KeyReplace ResourceFunction can change column names:

In[•]:= **Query [All, [•] KeyReplace + [{ "class" → "cabin", "age" → "years",**
"sex" → "gender", "survived" → "survival" }]] [lifeboatDS]

Out[•]=

cabin	years	gender	survival
3rd	16	female	True
1st	65	male	False
3rd	2	female	False
3rd	—	female	True
3rd	18	female	False
3rd	—	male	False
3rd	22	female	True
2nd	48	female	True

rows 1–8 of 22

Rename Just Some of the Columns

In the previous example, I renamed all of the columns. Suppose, however, you wanted to rename the "class" column to be "cabin" and the "sex" column to be "gender" but wanted to leave the "age" and "survival" names alone. You could, of course, type out everything as I did previously, and this is fine if there are just a few columns, as is the case in the Titanic **Dataset**. But what if you have hundreds of columns and want to rename just a few? Typing an **Association** from all the new keys to all the old keys is going to be a nuisance. You might naively think the following code would work. As it shows, however, this results in the remaining columns being dropped rather than renamed (or retained).

Code that changes the names of two columns but mistakenly drops the remaining columns:

In[•]:= **Query [All, Association ["cabin" → "class", "gender" → "sex"]] [lifeboatDS]**

Out[•]=

cabin	gender
3rd	female
1st	male
3rd	female
3rd	female
3rd	female
3rd	male
3rd	female
2nd	female

rows 1–8 of 22

Probably the simplest way to rename just some of the columns with built-in functions while keeping the remainder is to use the operator form of **KeyMap** in which the function relies on a list of substitution rules. The idea is that each time **Query** confronts an **Association**, it takes the keys and replaces them using the rules specified. Everything else remains unchanged. So the column names end up being changed but the column order ends up being preserved.

Rename the "class" column "cabin" and the "sex" column "gender"; leave everything else unchanged and preserve the order of the columns (timing will be different depending on your machine):

In[•]:= **rename2Columns = KeyMap [# /. { "class" → "cabin", "sex" → "gender" } &] ;**

In[◦]:= **RepeatedTiming [Query [All, rename2Columns] [lifeboatDS]]**

Out[◦]= $\Big\{0.000849333,$

cabin	age	gender	survived
3rd	16	female	True
1st	65	male	False
3rd	2	female	False
3rd	—	female	True
3rd	18	female	False
3rd	—	male	False
3rd	22	female	True
2nd	48	female	True

rows 1–8 of 22 $\Big\}$

An alternative method for partial column-name replacement is to use the KeyReplace ResourceFunction. It may be a little slower, but I think the syntax is cleaner.

Use the KeyReplace ResourceFunction to change just some of the names in Associations:

In[◦]:= **EchoTiming [**
    Query [All, [▪] KeyReplace + [{ "class" → "cabin", "sex" → "gender" }]] [lifeboatDS]]

⌚ 0.042059

Out[◦]=

cabin	age	gender	survived
3rd	16	female	True
1st	65	male	False
3rd	2	female	False
3rd	—	female	True
3rd	18	female	False
3rd	—	male	False
3rd	22	female	True
2nd	48	female	True

rows 1–8 of 22

If one doesn't care about preserving the order of the keys, there is yet another alternative method. I can run a Query in which, for each row, I augment the Association to include key-value pairs for "cabin" and "gender" and then use KeyDrop to get rid of the old column names. This appears to be the fastest method.

Use **KeyDrop** to rename columns if the order of columns does not matter:

In[•]:= **EchoTiming [Query [All, (Association [#, "cabin" → #class, "gender" → #sex] &) / ∗ KeyDrop [{ "class", "sex" }]] [lifeboatDS]]**

💡 0.00231

Out[•]=

age	survived	cabin	gender
16	True	3rd	female
65	False	1st	male
2	False	3rd	female
—	True	3rd	female
18	False	3rd	female
—	False	3rd	male
22	True	3rd	female
48	True	2nd	female

rows 1–8 of 22

Sort Rows and Columns

Here's an **Association** of Associations wrapped in a **Dataset**.

Construct a **Dataset** by hand using nested Associations:

In[•]:= **passengerCounts = Dataset [<| "3rd" → <| "female" → 5, "male" → 8 |>, "1st" → <| "female" → 1, "male" → 2 |>, "2nd" → <| "female" → 3, "male" → 3 |> |>]**

Out[•]=

	female	male
3rd	5	8
1st	1	2
2nd	3	3

Suppose I want the rows sorted so that they go "1st", "2nd" and "3rd" and I want the males to come before the females. One way I can do this is by creating a **Query** and putting the appropriate KeyTakes as the first and second arguments.

Use KeyTake to impose an order on key-value pairs in an Association:

In[ ]:= **Query [KeyTake [{ "1st", "2nd", "3rd" }] , KeyTake [{ "male", "female" }]] [passengerCounts]**

Out[ ]=

	male	female
1st	2	1
2nd	3	3
3rd	8	5

That works fine if there are just a few columns, but imagine a world in which there are lots of columns. Writing out a custom order of rows and columns can be cumbersome. If, however, there is some function of the keys that determines their order, then you can use KeySort or KeySortBy to order the rows and/or columns. Here, I use KeyTake to sort the rows and KeySortBy [StringLength] to sort the columns so that "male" (four letters) comes before "female" (six letters).

Use KeySortBy with a function to sort key-value pairs in an Association:

In[ ]:= **Query [KeyTake [{ "1st", "2nd", "3rd" }] , KeySortBy [StringLength]] [passengerCounts]**

Out[ ]=

	male	female
1st	2	1
2nd	3	3
3rd	8	5

Recall the effort in an earlier chapter to break down passenger count by class and sex. The women are presented first because "female" precedes "male" alphabetically.

Use KeySort to ensure a consistent ordering of groupings applied at lower levels of an expression:

In[ ]:= **Normal [**
   Query [GroupBy [#class &] , GroupBy [#sex &] / * KeySort, Length] [lifeboatDS]]

Out[ ]= ‹| 3rd → ‹| female → 6, male → 7 |›,
   1st → ‹| female → 1, male → 2 |›, 2nd → ‹| female → 3, male → 3 |› |›

But what if I wanted some other ordering of the columns? Perhaps, for some reason, I want column headers with fewer letters to come ahead of column headers with more letters. I could use KeySortBy to establish an ordering of the column headers.

Break down the lifeboat first by cabin class and then by sex and make sure the columns are sorted by a function of their key, the number of characters in the string that constitutes the key:

In[•]:= **Query [GroupBy [⫲class &] ,**
      GroupBy [⫲sex &] / * KeySortBy [StringLength] , Length] [lifeboatDS]

	male	female
3rd	7	6
1st	2	1
2nd	3	3

Out[•]=

What if I want a custom order of columns such as one in which second class comes before third class comes before first class? I can use the KeyTake operator.

Break down the lifeboat first by cabin class and then by gender and use a custom ordering of the columns:

In[•]:= **Query [GroupBy [⫲sex &] ,**
      GroupBy [⫲class &] / * KeyTake [{ "2nd", "3rd", "1st" }] , Length] [lifeboatDS]

	2nd	3rd	1st
female	3	6	1
male	3	7	2

Out[•]=

One can also sort by value. Here, I sort the lifeboat members by class and then break ties using age.

Sort the rows of a Dataset first by one function and then use a second function to break ties:

In[•]:= **Query [SortBy [{ ⫲class &, ⫲age & }]] [lifeboatDS]**

class	age	sex	survived
1st	19	female	True
1st	46	male	False
1st	65	male	False
2nd	22	male	True
2nd	44	female	False
2nd	48	female	True
2nd	50	female	True
2nd	—	male	False

Out[•]=

rows 1–8 of 22

In theory, one can sort a List of Associations by value as well. The key order now differs from Association to Association (compare, for example, the second to last example to many of the others).

Columns can be sorted by value:

In[•]:= (sortedAssociations = Normal [Query [All, Sort] [lifeboatDS]]) / / [=] Terse ⊹ [8]

Out[•]//Short= { <| age → 16, class → 3rd, sex → female, survived → True |>,
    <| age → 65, class → 1st, sex → male, survived → False |>,
    <| age → 2, class → 3rd, sex → female, survived → False |>,
    <| class → 3rd, sex → female, survived → True, age → Missing [ ] |>,
    <| age → 18, class → 3rd, sex → female, survived → False |>,
    ≪13≫, <| age → 22, class → 2nd, sex → male, survived → True |>,
    <| age → 56, class → 3rd, sex → male, survived → False |>,
    <| class → 2nd, sex → male, survived → False, age → Missing [ ] |>,
    <| age → 50, class → 2nd, sex → female, survived → True |> }

When the same List of Associations is converted into a Dataset, however, the key-value pairs are displayed according to the order of the keys in the first row: "age" always comes first.

The Dataset function creates consistency in the order of the key-value pairs in the List of Associations:

In[•]:= **Dataset [sortedAssociations]**

Out[•]=

age	class	sex	survived
16	3rd	female	True
65	1st	male	False
2	3rd	female	False
—	3rd	female	True
18	3rd	female	False
—	3rd	male	False
22	3rd	female	True
48	2nd	female	True

⊼ ⋀ rows 1–8 of 22 ⋁ ⋎

Sort Groupings

One often wants to group data and sort the names of the resulting groupings. Suppose, for example, that I want to count how many passengers of each sex are on the lifeboat.

How many passengers of each sex are on the lifeboat:

In[•]:= **Query [GroupBy [⌗sex &] , Length] [lifeboatDS]**

Out[•]=

female	10
male	12

Notice that the "female" grouping comes before the "male" grouping. This sorting occurs because the first person in the lifeboat Dataset just happens to be female. I can illustrate this dependency by rotating the original data left and making that 46-year-old male in first class the first person in the Dataset. Now, when the grouping is done, the males come before the females.

The order of the keys in an Association output from GroupBy depends on the order of the values of the grouping function encountered during a parse of the data:

In[•]:= **Query [GroupBy [⌗sex &] , Length] [Query [RotateLeft] [lifeboatDS]]**

Out[•]=

male	12
female	10

But what if I wanted a presentation in which I was assured that, regardless of the ordering of the rows, the data for men was presented first? Again, KeyTake comes to the rescue.

Use KeyTake to force a desired order of groupings:

In[•]:= **Query [GroupBy [⌗sex &] /∗ KeyTake [{ "male", "female" }] , Length] [lifeboatDS]**

Out[•]=

male	12
female	10

I can also perform custom sorts on both the rows and the columns.

Show how many passengers of each sex and of each cabin class are on the lifeboat but make sure that information on males is presented before information on females and that the cabin classes are presented as "2nd", then "3rd", and then "1st":

In[ ]:= **Query [GroupBy [⌗sex &] / ∗ KeyTake [{ "male", "female" }] ,**
GroupBy [⌗class &] / ∗ KeyTake [{ "2nd", "3rd", "1st" }] , Length] [lifeboatDS]

Out[ ]=

	2nd	3rd	1st
male	3	7	2
female	3	6	1

Conceptually, sorting on groupings isn't really any different than sorting on rows or columns.

Sample the Rows

Sometimes one just wants a random sample of the data in a large Dataset. One can use Span to get this. Here, I get every fourth row in the lifeboat Dataset.

Use Span to get a regular sampling of rows in a Dataset:

In[ ]:= **Query [1 ;; −1 ;; 4] [lifeboatDS]**

Out[ ]=

class	age	sex	survived
3rd	16	female	True
3rd	18	female	False
3rd	14	male	False
1st	19	female	True
3rd	—	female	True
2nd	—	male	False

One can also write this as Span [1, All, 4] , 1 ;; All ;; 4 or even 1 ;; ;; 4 (in which there is nothing between the two sequences of semicolons).

I can also use Range, although for long Datasets this can require more memory.

Use Range to get a regular sampling of rows in a Dataset:

In[ ]:= **Query [Range [1, Length [lifeboatDS] , 4]] [lifeboatDS]**

Out[ ]=

class	age	sex	survived
3rd	16	female	True
3rd	18	female	False
3rd	14	male	False
1st	19	female	True
3rd	—	female	True
2nd	—	male	False

Instead of regularly sampling a Dataset, one can do so randomly. Here, I get a random sample of six rows.

Seed the random number generator and then use RandomSample to get a random sample of rows in a Dataset:

In[ ]:= **(SeedRandom [20 230 110] ; Query [RandomSample [⌗ , 6] &] [lifeboatDS])**

Out[ ]=

class	age	sex	survived
3rd	56	male	False
2nd	—	male	False
3rd	—	female	True
1st	46	male	False
3rd	16	female	True
2nd	—	male	False

It would be somewhat unusual to randomly sample columns, but here is how to do it. Remembering that columns can be selected by their position in the Dataset rather than by column names, I take three random numbers from a Range going from 1 to the number of columns in the Dataset. I can use the same technique at even lower levels of a more deeply nested dataset.

Randomly sample lower levels of a Dataset:

In[•]:= (SeedRandom [20 230 110] ;
        Query [All, RandomSample [Range [Dimensions [lifeboatDS] [[2]]] , 3]] [lifeboatDS])

Out[•]=

sex	age	survived
female	16	True
male	65	False
female	2	False
female	—	True
female	18	False
male	—	False
female	22	True
female	48	True

rows 1–8 of **22**

Replace Some Key-Value Pairs in an Association: The Association Override Feature

Let's grab the first row of the lifeboat and call its Normal form passenger1.

Part extracts the first row; Normal lets the result escape the Dataset:

In[•]:= **passenger1 = Normal [lifeboatDS[[1]]]**

Out[•]= <| class → 3rd, age → 16, sex → female, survived → True |>

Suppose I learn there is a mistake and I want to change the age of passenger1 from 16 to 19. Here are several ways I could do it.

I could use ReplacePart:

In[•]:= **ReplacePart [passenger1, "age" → 19]**

Out[•]= <| class → 3rd, age → 19, sex → female, survived → True |>

I could also use what I call the "Association Override Feature." When Association encounters a duplicate key, it takes the last value for the key that it finds:

In[•]:= **Association [passenger1, "age" → 19]**

Out[•]= <| class → 3rd, age → 19, sex → female, survived → True |>

I could combine this with the fact that Association automatically flattens when it evaluates:

In[ ]:= **Association [passenger1, Association ["age" → 19]]**

Out[ ]= <| class → 3rd, age → 19, sex → female, survived → True |>

Append also works, but the order of the keys is changed:

In[ ]:= **Append [passenger1, "age" → 19]**

Out[ ]= <| class → 3rd, sex → female, survived → True, age → 19 |>

Note that none of these versions change the actual value for passenger1. To do that, I need to make an assignment:

In[ ]:= **passenger1 = Association [passenger1, "age" → 19]**

Out[ ]= <| class → 3rd, age → 19, sex → female, survived → True |>

Changing passenger1 doesn't change the first row of lifeboatDS. To do that, I'd have to run the following code. I'm going to comment it out, however, so it doesn't mess up the remainder of this chapter.

Use ReplacePart to change items in a Dataset. The code doesn't execute because it is wrapped in (* ... *), which is how the Wolfram Language denotes comments:

In[ ]:= (*lifeboatDS=ReplacePart[lifeboatDS,1→passenger1] *) ;

Keep and Drop Rows or Columns

Often, one just wants part of a Dataset shown. If the Dataset does not contain an Association at the relevant level, Take and Drop often come in handy. If the Dataset does contain Associations at the relevant levels, the cognate functions KeyTake and KeyDrop are frequently used.

Suppose, for example, I just want the first three rows of lifeboatDS, which is structured as a List of Associations.

The data wrapped in lifeboatDS is a List at its top level:

In[ ]:= **Head [Normal [lifeboatDS]]**

Out[ ]= List

Use Take to get contiguous elements:

In[ ]:= **Take [lifeboatDS, 3]**

Out[ ]=

class	age	sex	survived
3rd	16	female	True
1st	65	male	False
3rd	2	female	False

Use Drop to get rid of the first 17 rows of lifeboatDS:

In[ ]:= **Drop [lifeboatDS, 17]**

Out[ ]=

class	age	sex	survived
3rd	22	male	False
2nd	22	male	True
3rd	56	male	False
2nd	—	male	False
2nd	50	female	True

If the Dataset was structured as Lists rather than Associations at the first level, I could use Take and Drop there too. Here, I take the first four rows and first two columns of the stripped lifeboat Dataset.

Take can be used at multiple levels of a Dataset where the levels are Lists:

In[ ]:= **lifeboat = Query [All, Values] [lifeboatDS]**

Out[ ]=

3rd	16	female	True
1st	65	male	False
3rd	2	female	False
3rd	—	female	True
3rd	18	female	False
3rd	—	male	False
3rd	22	female	True
2nd	48	female	True

rows 1–8 of 22

Take gets the first four rows and then the first two columns:

In[ ]:= **Take [lifeboat, 4, 2]**

Out[ ]=

3rd	16
1st	65
3rd	2
3rd	—

Here, I get rid of the first 18 rows and the last column.

Drop can be used at multiple levels of a Dataset where the levels are Lists:

In[∘]:= **Drop [lifeboat, 18, −1]**

Out[∘]=

2nd	22	male
3rd	56	male
2nd	—	male
2nd	50	female

Now let's work with levels of a Dataset that contain Associations. Here, I get just the "sex" and "age" of the first four lifeboat passengers. There's no operator form of Take, so I use Span, though I could equally well have used Take [#, 4] & or a Range as the first argument to Query.

Use KeyTake to extract key-value pairs from lower levels of the data in a Dataset:

In[∘]:= **Query [1 ;; 4, KeyTake [{ "sex", "age" }]] [lifeboatDS]**

Out[∘]=

sex	age
female	16
male	65
female	2
female	—

Or suppose I wanted the last three passengers, but I didn't want the result to contain their age or survival.

Use KeyDrop to eliminate key-value pairs from lower levels of the data in a Dataset:

In[∘]:= **Query [−3 ;; −1, KeyDrop [{ "age", "survived" }]] [lifeboatDS]**

Out[∘]=

class	sex
3rd	male
2nd	male
2nd	female

If I wanted all the passengers without "age", I would write the following.

Delete the "age" column in lifeboatDS:

In[∘]:= **Query [All, KeyDrop ["age"]] [lifeboatDS]**

Out[∘]=

class	sex	survived
3rd	female	True
1st	male	False
3rd	female	False
3rd	female	True
3rd	female	False
3rd	male	False
3rd	female	True
2nd	female	True

rows 1–8 of **22**

Suppose I want to find rows in titanicDS where the person is male and in first class. I can use Select in conjunction with an anonymous function as follows.

Use Select at the top level to find Associations with certain key-value combinations:

In[∘]:= **Query [Select [⌗class === "1st" && ⌗sex === "male" &]] [titanicDS]**

Out[∘]=

class	age	sex	survived
1st	1	male	True
1st	30	male	False
1st	48	male	True
1st	39	male	False
1st	71	male	False
1st	47	male	False
1st	80	male	True
1st	—	male	False

rows 1–8 of **179**

Another way, however, is to create a pattern that conforms to the desired output. Here, I create a pattern that corresponds to males in first class. I don't care what the other values are.

Create a key-value pattern that can be used by Cases to find data:

In[•]:= **male1st =**
    AssociationThread [{ "class", "age", "sex", "survived" }, { "1st", _, "male", _ }]

Out[•]= **<| class → 1st, age → _, sex → male, survived → _ |>**

If you don't like AssociationThread, you can also just write the pattern directly as
<| class → 1st, age →_, sex → male, survived →_ |> .

Now I use that pattern as an argument to Cases. I wrap it in Query here, but one doesn't really need to do so.

Use Cases in combination with a key-value pattern to find data in a Dataset:

In[•]:= **Query [Cases [male1st]] [titanicDS]**

Out[•]=

class	age	sex	survived
1st	1	male	True
1st	30	male	False
1st	48	male	True
1st	39	male	False
1st	71	male	False
1st	47	male	False
1st	80	male	True
1st	—	male	False

rows 1–8 of 179

Or I can combine Select and an operator form of MatchQ. Here, I show it without the Query wrapping, although I could wrap it in Query.

Select with MatchQ can likewise be used with a key-value pattern to find data in a Dataset:

In[•]:= **Select [MatchQ [male1st]] [titanicDS]**

Out[•]=

class	age	sex	survived
1st	1	male	True
1st	30	male	False
1st	48	male	True
1st	39	male	False
1st	71	male	False
1st	47	male	False
1st	80	male	True
1st	—	male	False

rows 1–8 of 179

If I trust that the keys in various associations are in the same order, I can do something even simpler. Here, I get the surviving females on the Titanic over age 60 for which we have information on cabin class.

Select can combine with MatchQ on the Values of an Association to find an Association whose Values follow a pattern:

In[•]:= **Select [MatchQ [Values [#] , { _String, x_ /; x > 60, "female", True }] &] [titanicDS]**

Out[•]=

class	age	sex	survived
1st	63	female	True
1st	76	female	True
1st	64	female	True
1st	64	female	True
1st	62	female	True
3rd	63	female	True

Join Columns Based on Precomputed Data

Here's some additional data about the passengers on the lifeboat. It's in the form of a List of Associations in which the keys are "id" and "weight".

Load in ID and weight information on lifeboat passengers:

In[•]:= **preComputedAssociationData = ResourceData [ro, "IDWeight List of Associations"]**

Out[•]= { <| id → 1, weight → 111 |>, <| id → 2, weight → 92 |>,
  <| id → 3, weight → 163 |>, <| id → 4, weight → 95 |>, <| id → 5, weight → 128 |>,
  <| id → 6, weight → 163 |>, <| id → 7, weight → 200 |>, <| id → 8, weight → 180 |>,
  <| id → 9, weight → 149 |>, <| id → 10, weight → 145 |>, <| id → 11, weight → 140 |>,
  <| id → 12, weight → 144 |>, <| id → 13, weight → 110 |>, <| id → 14, weight → 167 |>,
  <| id → 15, weight → 169 |>, <| id → 16, weight → 144 |>, <| id → 17, weight → 186 |>,
  <| id → 18, weight → 174 |>, <| id → 19, weight → 175 |>, <| id → 20, weight → 153 |>,
  <| id → 21, weight → 200 |>, <| id → 22, weight → 192 |> }

Assume that the ordering of the rows in this precomputed data corresponds to the ordering of the rows of data we have already seen about the lifeboat. I'd like to join the two pieces of information together into a single data structure. You might think I could use JoinAcross, but that won't work because there's no column in lifeboatDS whose meaning corresponds with a column in the new data.

When there's no common column among the datasets but I know from external information that the rows of the data are in the same order, I can use Join at level 2 to put the pieces together. I do so by wrapping Dataset around the List of Associations in preComputedAssociationData to make sure that both Joined expressions have the same Head.

Join Datasets that are each Lists of Associations where the Length of each List is the same:

In[•]:= **augmentedDsLifeboat = Join [lifeboatDS, Dataset [preComputedAssociationData] , 2]**

Out[•]=

class	age	sex	survived	id	weight
3rd	16	female	True	1	111
1st	65	male	False	2	92
3rd	2	female	False	3	163
3rd	—	female	True	4	95
3rd	18	female	False	5	128
3rd	—	male	False	6	163
3rd	22	female	True	7	200
2nd	48	female	True	8	180

rows 1–8 of 22

Alternatively, I could have converted lifeboatDS into a List of Associations and then joined it with the List of Associations in preComputedAssociationData.

Join Lists of Associations where the Length of each List is the same:

In[•]:= **augmentedDsLifeboat =**
   Dataset [Join [Normal@lifeboatDS, preComputedAssociationData, 2]]

Out[•]=

class	age	sex	survived	id	weight
3rd	16	female	True	1	111
1st	65	male	False	2	92
3rd	2	female	False	3	163
3rd	—	female	True	4	95
3rd	18	female	False	5	128
3rd	—	male	False	6	163
3rd	22	female	True	7	200
2nd	48	female	True	8	180

rows 1–8 of 22

I could also Join the values of lifeboatDS with the values of the preComputed··. AssociationData. Join at level 2 works just fine when both data structures are Lists of Lists with the same number of rows.

Strip the precomputed data of its keys and turn it into a nested List:

In[ ]:= **preComputedDataList = Map [Values, preComputedAssociationData]**

Out[ ]= { {1, 111}, {2, 92}, {3, 163}, {4, 95}, {5, 128}, {6, 163}, {7, 200}, {8, 180},
{9, 149}, {10, 145}, {11, 140}, {12, 144}, {13, 110}, {14, 167}, {15, 169},
{16, 144}, {17, 186}, {18, 174}, {19, 175}, {20, 153}, {21, 200}, {22, 192} }

Strip the existing information on the passengers in the lifeboat of its keys and combine it
with the nested List of precomputed data:

In[ ]:= **Join [Map [Values, lifeboatDS] , preComputedDataList, 2] / / ⟦▪⟧ Terse + [5]**

Out[ ]//Short= { {3rd, 16, female, True, 1, 111}, {1st, 65, male, False, 2, 92},
{3rd, 2, female, False, 3, 163}, {3rd, Missing [ ] , female, True, 4, 95},
{3rd, 18, female, False, 5, 128}, ≪12≫, {3rd, 22, male, False, 18, 174},
{2nd, 22, male, True, 19, 175}, {3rd, 56, male, False, 20, 153},
{2nd, Missing [ ] , male, False, 21, 200}, {2nd, 50, female, True, 22, 192} }

Join a Column to a Dataset Based on Values in the Existing Columns

To join a column to a Dataset based not on external data but—as is often the case in
spreadsheets—on the values in one or more existing columns, one simply applies a
function to the rows as shown in the following code.

Add columns to a Dataset whose values derive from existing columns:

In[ ]:= **Query [All,**
Association [#1 , "over50Q" → TrueQ [#age > 50] , "childQ" → TrueQ [#age ≤ 18] ,
"girlQ" → TrueQ [#age < 18 && #sex === "female"]] &] [lifeboatDS]

Out[ ]=

class	age	sex	survived	over50Q	childQ	girlQ
3rd	16	female	True	False	True	True
1st	65	male	False	True	False	False
3rd	2	female	False	False	True	True
3rd	—	female	True	False	False	False
3rd	18	female	False	False	True	False
3rd	—	male	False	False	False	False
3rd	22	female	True	False	False	False
2nd	48	female	True	False	False	False

rows 1–8 of 22

There are three features of that code that I want to highlight.

1. Notice that I can use functions that rely on only one column of the data (over50Q and childQ) or that rely on multiple columns of the data (girlQ).

2. I can wrap Association around the original Association and then just splice in a sequence of key-value pairs. I don't need Append or Join or other such constructs. This technique works because Association behaves as if it has the attribute Flat. As set forth in the Wolfram Language documentation, for a symbol f with attribute Flat, f [f [a, b] , f [c]] is automatically reduced to f [a, b, c].

3. Use of TrueQ prevents propagation of Missing values. If the row does not contain information on age, the comparison operations now yield "False."

Sometimes, one wants columns in a Dataset to be based not on the original columns but on computed columns. One can use localizing functions, such as With or Module, to get doubly derived columns in a single pass through the data.

For efficiency, use With or Module to create local variables within a Query:

In[•]:=   **Query [All, With [{ over40 = TrueQ [#age > 40] } , Association [#1, "over40Q" → over40, "oldSurvivor" → TrueQ [over40 && #survived]]] &] [lifeboatDS]**

Out[•]=

class	age	sex	survived	over40Q	oldSurvivor
3rd	16	female	True	False	False
1st	65	male	False	True	False
3rd	2	female	False	False	False
3rd	—	female	True	False	False
3rd	18	female	False	False	False
3rd	—	male	False	False	False
3rd	22	female	True	False	False
2nd	48	female	True	True	True

rows 1–8 of 22

If I want to add an additional column and take only some existing columns or, equivalently, drop some existing columns, I can combine this technique with the recipe for Keep and Drop Rows or Columns, discussed in a previous section in this chapter. Suppose, for example, I want the new columns over40Q, childQ and girlQ as before but, in light of that data, I no longer want to keep "sex" and "age". I use KeyDrop inside the Association as follows. Notice I can no longer use the operator form of KeyDrop because it is inside another function.

Combine KeyDrop with the fact that Association behaves as if it is Flat to retain some old columns and compute new ones:

In[*]:= **Query [All, Association [KeyDrop [⌗, {"sex", "age"}] ,**
"over40Q" → TrueQ [⌗age > 40] , "childQ" → TrueQ [⌗age ≤ 18] ,
"girlQ" → TrueQ [⌗age < 18 && ⌗sex === "female"]] &] [lifeboatDS]

Out[*]=

class	survived	over40Q	childQ	girlQ
3rd	True	False	True	True
1st	False	True	False	False
3rd	False	False	True	True
3rd	True	False	False	False
3rd	False	False	True	False
3rd	False	False	False	False
3rd	True	False	False	False
2nd	True	True	False	False

rows 1–8 of **22**

Change the Value of an Existing Column: Row-Wise

Remember the Association Override Feature: Associations cannot have duplicate keys, so when a duplicate key is encountered, the kernel just tosses out the old key-value pair and keeps the latest one. One can exploit the Association Override Feature to redefine the values in a column. Here, I age everyone in the lifeboat by one year. Remember, though, that this operation won't change the values of lifeboatDS. For that, I would need to assign the result to some variable.

Change the values in an existing column by exploiting the Association Override Feature:

In[*]:= **Query [All, Association [⌗, "age" → ⌗age + 1] &] [titanicDS]**

Out[*]=

class	age	sex	survived
1st	30	female	True
1st	2	male	True
1st	3	female	False
1st	31	male	False
1st	26	female	False
1st	49	male	True
1st	64	female	True
1st	40	male	False

rows 1–8 of **1309**

I could also use MapAt as the second argument to Query. This method can sometimes be a little faster.

Use MapAt to change the values in various parts of a Dataset:

In[◦]:= **Query [All, MapAt [⌗ + 1 &, "age"]] [titanicDS]**

Out[◦]=

class	age	sex	survived
1st	30	female	True
1st	2	male	True
1st	3	female	False
1st	31	male	False
1st	26	female	False
1st	49	male	True
1st	64	female	True
1st	40	male	False

rows 1–8 of **1309**

Add Row Headers (Indexing)

Sequential Integer Headers

Suppose one wants to add row headers to a Dataset that does not have them already. One might want to do this to clarify the meaning of each row. Or, as discussed later, one might want to do this, whether the data is wrapped in Dataset or not, to retrieve information more swiftly.

If the row headers are going to be sequential values, there are several ways to do it. One way is to RightComposition a MapIndexed operator with Association. Remember that MapIndexed produces part specifications wrapped in a List, so if you want just an integer, you need to just take the first part of the List. This is why the function is ⌗2[[1]] → ⌗1& and not ⌗2 → ⌗1&.

Use MapIndexed to create integer row keys (headers) in a Dataset:

In[◦]:= **Query [MapIndexed [⌗2[[1]] → ⌗1 &] /* Association] [lifeboatDS]**

Out[◦]=

	class	age	sex	survived
1	3rd	16	female	True
2	1st	65	male	False
3	3rd	2	female	False
4	3rd	—	female	True
5	3rd	18	female	False
6	3rd	—	male	False
7	3rd	22	female	True
8	2nd	48	female	True

rows 1–8 of **22**

The MapSlice ResourceFunction can make the code somewhat more readable because it produces a sequence of parts rather than a List of parts.

Use MapSlice to create integer row keys (headers) in a Dataset:

In[ ]:= **Query [[▪] MapSlice + [#2 → # &] / * Association] [lifeboatDS]**

Out[ ]=

	class	age	sex	survived
1	3rd	16	female	True
2	1st	65	male	False
3	3rd	2	female	False
4	3rd	—	female	True
5	3rd	18	female	False
6	3rd	—	male	False
7	3rd	22	female	True
8	2nd	48	female	True

rows 1–8 of **22**

A third way of producing integer keys would be to get the lifeboat data out of the Dataset using Normal. Then use AssociationThread to add an integer key to each of the rows and put the resulting data back inside the Dataset.

Alternatively, AssociationThread the row keys with the rows:

In[ ]:= **Dataset [AssociationThread [(Length / * Range) [lifeboatDS] , Normal [lifeboatDS]]]**

Out[ ]=

	class	age	sex	survived
1	3rd	16	female	True
2	1st	65	male	False
3	3rd	2	female	False
4	3rd	—	female	True
5	3rd	18	female	False
6	3rd	—	male	False
7	3rd	22	female	True
8	2nd	48	female	True

rows 1–8 of **22**

Instead of using the composition (Length / * Range), I could use the ResourceFunction CorrespondingIntegers, which produces a List, $\{1, …, n\}$, where n is the length of the expression it confronts.

Use the ResourceFunction CorrespondingIntegers to index the Dataset:

In[∘]:= **Dataset [**
    AssociationThread [⟦▪⟧ CorrespondingIntegers ⊹ [lifeboatDS] , Normal [lifeboatDS]]]

Out[∘]=

	class	age	sex	survived
1	3rd	16	female	True
2	1st	65	male	False
3	3rd	2	female	False
4	3rd	—	female	True
5	3rd	18	female	False
6	3rd	—	male	False
7	3rd	22	female	True
8	2nd	48	female	True

rows 1–8 of 22

Computed Headers

I can also make the row headers a function of the data and its position in the Dataset. Here's an example taken from a Dataset on Major League Soccer (MLS).

Get the MLS Dataset out of the book's repository:

In[∘]:= **mlsDS = ResourceData [ro, "MLS List of Associations Dataset"]**

Out[∘]=

Club	LastName	FirstName	Position	BaseSalary	GuaranteedCompensati
CHI	Armas	Chris	M	$225 000.00	$225 000.00
CHI	Banner	Michael	M	$12 900.00	$12 900.00
CHI	Barrett	Chad	F	$41 212.50	$48 712.50
CHI	Blanco	Cuauhtemoc	F	2.49232×10^6	2.66678×10^6
CHI	Brown	C.J.	D	$106 391.00	$106 391.00
CHI	Busch	Jon	GK	$58 008.00	$58 008.00
CHI	Carr	Calen	F	$38 000.00	$50 500.00
CHI	Conde	Wilman	D	$144 000.00	$151 500.00

rows 1–8 of 4937

My first guess for an indexing function is the last name, the team, and the year. (You'll see that this doesn't work perfectly, but the failure is instructive.)

Creating an Association based on nonunique keys is usually a bad idea:

In[ ]:= **Query [Association, { ⌗LastName , ⌗Club , ⌗Year } → ⌗ &] [mlsDS] / /**
[▣] FormatDataset ⊹ [HeaderSize → 6]

Out[ ]=

			Club	LastName	FirstName	Position	BaseSala
Armas	CHI	2007	CHI	Armas	Chris	M	$225 000.(
Banner	CHI	2007	CHI	Banner	Michael	M	$12 900.0(
Barrett	CHI	2007	CHI	Barrett	Chad	F	$41 212.5(
Blanco	CHI	2007	CHI	Blanco	Cuauhtemoc	F	$2.49232
Brown	CHI	2007	CHI	Brown	C.J.	D	$106 391.(
Busch	CHI	2007	CHI	Busch	Jon	GK	$58 008.0(
Carr	CHI	2007	CHI	Carr	Calen	F	$38 000.0(
Conde	CHI	2007	CHI	Conde	Wilman	D	$144 000.(

rows 1–8 of **4916**

If you look carefully, you'll see that there are 5527 rows of the indexed Dataset
whereas there were 5553 to begin with. What's happened is that there may be two
people with the same last name on a team in a given year. Because the data has now
been transformed at its outer layer, an Association, it's dropped entries with duplicate
keys. Here's a better indexing function in which I include first names.

Use a combination of keys whose values are collectively unique to index a Dataset; use the
FormatDataset ResourceFunction so that the new row headers are displayed properly:

In[ ]:= **indexedMLS =**
Query [Association, { ⌗LastName , ⌗FirstName , ⌗Club , ⌗Year } → ⌗ &] [mlsDS] / /
[▣] FormatDataset ⊹ [HeaderSize → 6]

Out[ ]=

				Club	LastName	FirstN
Armas	Chris	CHI	2007	CHI	Armas	Chris
Banner	Michael	CHI	2007	CHI	Banner	Micha
Barrett	Chad	CHI	2007	CHI	Barrett	Chad
Blanco	Cuauhtemoc	CHI	2007	CHI	Blanco	Cuauh
Brown	C.J.	CHI	2007	CHI	Brown	C.J.
Busch	Jon	CHI	2007	CHI	Busch	Jon
Carr	Calen	CHI	2007	CHI	Carr	Calen
Conde	Wilman	CHI	2007	CHI	Conde	Wilma

rows 1–8 of **4937**

There's also a ResourceFunction called ValueMap designed to do exactly what I just displayed. You will notice that the argument inside the ValueMap function is exactly the same as the second argument I gave Query in the preceding example.

Use ValueMap to produce Keys for a Dataset:

In[•]:= **Query [[•] ValueMap [{ #LastName, #FirstName, #Club, #Year } &]] [mlsDS] //**
[•] FormatDataset [HeaderSize → 6]

Out[•]=

				Club	LastName	FirstN
Armas	Chris	CHI	2007	CHI	Armas	Chris
Banner	Michael	CHI	2007	CHI	Banner	Micha
Barrett	Chad	CHI	2007	CHI	Barrett	Chad
Blanco	Cuauhtemoc	CHI	2007	CHI	Blanco	Cuauh
Brown	C.J.	CHI	2007	CHI	Brown	C.J.
Busch	Jon	CHI	2007	CHI	Busch	Jon
Carr	Calen	CHI	2007	CHI	Carr	Calen
Conde	Wilman	CHI	2007	CHI	Conde	Wilma

rows 1–8 of **4937**

Regardless of which method you use to create the keys, it's now often faster to look up players. Compare these timings from first looking up a player with a conventional Query and then looking up the same player after indexing.

Looking up data in indexed Datasets is often faster:

In[•]:= **{ (EchoTiming) [Query [**
Key@ { "Bradley", "Michael", "TOR", DateObject [{ 2016 }] }] [indexedMLS]],
(EchoTiming) [Query [SelectFirst [{ #LastName, #FirstName, #Club, #Year } ===
{ "Bradley", "Michael", "TOR", DateObject [{ 2016 }] } &]] [mlsDS]] }

💡 0.0008

💡 0.034074

Out[•]=

Club	TOR
LastName	Bradley
FirstName	Michael
Position	M
BaseSalary	$6. \times 10^6$
GuaranteedCompensation	6.5×10^6
Year	2016

Club	TOR
LastName	Bradley
FirstName	Michael
Position	M
BaseSalary	$6. \times 10^6$
GuaranteedCompensation	6.5×10^6
Year	2016

Headers from External Data

If the row headers are taken from some external data, the process is similar. There are at least four alternative methods shown in the code that follows. I can either: (1) use MapIndexed and a Part function; (2) use MapIndexed and Extract rather than Part to take account of the index; (3) use the MapSlice ResourceFunction; or (4) take the external data and use it as the first argument to AssociationThread.

Use MapIndexed or AssociationThread to use precomputed data as row headers for indexing:

```
In[•]:= names = {"miss olivia heikkila", "mr noah eike", "miss lucy mogstad",
          "mr patrick hughes", "mr miguel gordon", "mrs scarlett jensen",
          "mr fletcher white", "mr dennis bishop", "mrs ferdinanda almeida",
          "mrs florence walker", "mr mae deschamps", "ms teresa santiago",
          "mr arthur simmons", "mr noah robinson", "mr rafael lozano",
          "ms lise lecomte", "mrs hannah bell", "mr nicolas knight", "mr alfonso fuentes",
          "miss juanita remijnse", "mr felix morris", "monsieur kaspar lefebvre"};
```

Create a Dataset with headers in four different ways, use SameQ to show that the methods yield the same result, and use Echo to display one of the identical results:

```
In[•]:= SameQ[ Echo[ Query[ MapIndexed[ Association[ Part[ names, #2[[1]] ] → #1 ] &] /*
              Apply[ Association ] ] [ lifeboatDS ] ],
          Query[ MapIndexed[ Association[ Extract[ names, #2 ] → #1 ] &] /*
              Apply[ Association ] ] [ lifeboatDS ],
          Query[ [▪] MapSlice + [ Association[ Part[ names, #2 ] → #1 ] &] /*
              Apply[ Association ] ] [ lifeboatDS ],
          Dataset[ AssociationThread[ names, Normal[ lifeboatDS ] ] ]
      ]
```

	class	age	sex	survived
miss olivia heikkila	3rd	16	female	True
mr noah eike	1st	65	male	False
miss lucy mogstad	3rd	2	female	False
mr patrick hughes	3rd	—	female	True
mr miguel gordon	3rd	18	female	False
mrs scarlett jensen	3rd	—	male	False
mr fletcher white	3rd	22	female	True
mr dennis bishop	2nd	48	female	True

rows 1-8 of 22

Out[•]= True

I could also use a ResourceFunction called ValueMapIndexed tailor made for this problem. It creates an Association from a List of values (ℓ). The values of the new Association are the same list of values (ℓ). The keys of the new Association are formed by MapIndexing a function over ℓ. There's also an operator form, used here, created by giving ValueMapIndexed the function it will ultimately apply when it encounters a List.

Use ValueMapIndexed to take a list of names and make them appropriate keys to the lifeboatDS Dataset:

In[•]:= **lifeboatDSWithNames =**
        Query [⊡ ValueMapIndexed ⊹ [Extract [names, #2] &]] [lifeboatDS]

Out[•]=

	class	age	sex	survived
miss olivia heikkila	3rd	16	female	True
mr noah eike	1st	65	male	False
miss lucy mogstad	3rd	2	female	False
mr patrick hughes	3rd	—	female	True
mr miguel gordon	3rd	18	female	False
mrs scarlett jensen	3rd	—	male	False
mr fletcher white	3rd	22	female	True
mr dennis bishop	2nd	48	female	True

rows 1–8 of 22

I can now retrieve data on various individuals simply by making the desired keys the first argument to Query.

Use the indices to retrieve data swiftly from a Dataset:

In[•]:= **Query [{ "miss olivia heikkila", "miss lucy mogstad", "mr miguel gordon",**
        "mr dennis bishop", "mrs hannah bell" }] [lifeboatDSWithNames]

Out[•]=

	class	age	sex	survived
miss olivia heikkila	3rd	16	female	True
miss lucy mogstad	3rd	2	female	False
mr miguel gordon	3rd	18	female	False
mr dennis bishop	2nd	48	female	True
mrs hannah bell	3rd	—	female	True

Delete Row Headers

This is easy. To delete row headers, just apply Values to the Dataset (or Association).

Use Values at the top level of a Dataset to get rid of row headers:

In[•]:= **Values [lifeboatDS]**

Out[•]=

3rd	16	female	True
1st	65	male	False
3rd	2	female	False
3rd	—	female	True
3rd	18	female	False
3rd	—	male	False
3rd	22	female	True
2nd	48	female	True

⤒ ∧ rows 1–8 of **22** ∨ ⤓

Turn Row Headers into Columns

It is sometimes useful for the row headers of a Dataset (the keys to the underlying Association) also to be columns (key-value pairs) in the Dataset. This structure lets one engage in various Dataset joins using a function such as JoinAcross. The best function to accomplish this goal is KeyValueMap, which, as discussed in a previous chapter, runs over key-value pairs and treats the key as the first argument and the value as the second argument. Accordingly, I use KeyValueMap here over the rows of the Dataset and append a new key-value pair in which the new key is "name" and the value is the original key. Notice that by doing it this way, I (deliberately) destroy the row keys.

Use KeyValueMap to convert row headers into a column (or columns) with values:

In[•]:= **Query [KeyValueMap [Association ["name" → ⌗1 , ⌗2] &]] [lifeboatDSWithNames]**

Out[•]=

name	class	age	sex	survived
miss olivia heikkila	3rd	16	female	True
mr noah eike	1st	65	male	False
miss lucy mogstad	3rd	2	female	False
mr patrick hughes	3rd	—	female	True
mr miguel gordon	3rd	18	female	False
mrs scarlett jensen	3rd	—	male	False
mr fletcher white	3rd	22	female	True
mr dennis bishop	2nd	48	female	True

⤒ ∧ rows 1–8 of **22** ∨ ⤓

You can create more than one column from the key. Here's an example.

Create more than one column from the row headers:

In[∘]:= **Query [KeyValueMap [**
Join [AssociationThread [{ "title", "name" } , StringSplit [#1, " ", 2]] , #2] &]] [
lifeboatDSWithNames]

Out[∘]=

title	name	class	age	sex	survived
miss	olivia heikkila	3rd	16	female	True
mr	noah eike	1st	65	male	False
miss	lucy mogstad	3rd	2	female	False
mr	patrick hughes	3rd	—	female	True
mr	miguel gordon	3rd	18	female	False
mrs	scarlett jensen	3rd	—	male	False
mr	fletcher white	3rd	22	female	True
mr	dennis bishop	2nd	48	female	True

⏫ ∧ rows 1–8 of 22 ∨ ⏬

If instead I want to preserve the row keys *and* add a column, I just change the function in KeyValueMap a little bit and RightComposition an Association function.

Create a column from the row headers but keep the row headers:

In[∘]:= **Query [(KeyValueMap [# → Association ["name" → #1, #2] &]) /* Association] [**
lifeboatDSWithNames]

Out[∘]=

	name	class	age	sex	survived
miss olivia heikkila	miss olivia heikkila	3rd	16	female	True
mr noah eike	mr noah eike	1st	65	male	False
miss lucy mogstad	miss lucy mogstad	3rd	2	female	False
mr patrick hughes	mr patrick hughes	3rd	—	female	True
mr miguel gordon	mr miguel gordon	3rd	18	female	False
mrs scarlett jensen	mrs scarlett jensen	3rd	—	male	False
mr fletcher white	mr fletcher white	3rd	22	female	True
mr dennis bishop	mr dennis bishop	2nd	48	female	True

⏫ ∧ rows 1–8 of 22 ∨ ⏬

Give a Column Orientation to a Dataset

Other computer languages and platforms, such as R, tend to create their Datasets as the equivalent of Associations between column names and columns. This "column-oriented" method is in contrast to the default Wolfram Language way of emphasizing rows of data, but it is easy enough in the Wolfram Language to shift from a row orientation to a column orientation, and, as will be discussed, it is frequently useful to do so.

The Transpose Method

There are several methods to switch between row orientation and column orientation. The first is the Transpose method. The code is incredibly simple. Here it is used on lifeboatDST. I show it in Normal form to make the structure more apparent.

Transpose converts a Dataset that is a row-oriented List of Associations into a column-oriented Association in which the Values are Lists:

In[•]:= **(lifeboatDST = Transpose [lifeboatDS]) / / Normal**

Out[•]= <| class → { 3rd, 1st, 3rd, 3rd, 3rd, 3rd, 3rd, 2nd,
        3rd, 2nd, 3rd, 3rd, 1st, 3rd, 1st, 2nd, 3rd, 3rd, 2nd, 3rd, 2nd, 2nd },
     age → { 16, 65, 2, Missing [ ], 18, Missing [ ], 22, 48, 14, 44, 33, 39, 19,
        29, 46, Missing [ ], Missing [ ], 22, 22, 56, Missing [ ], 50 },
     sex → { female, male, female, female, female, male, female, female, male, female,
        male, male, female, male, male, male, female, male, male, male, male, female },
     survived → { True, False, False, True, False, False, True, True, False, False, False,
        False, True, True, False, False, True, False, True, False, False, True } |>

If the Dataset has no column headers, one just gets a list of columns.

Transpose converts a Dataset that is a row-oriented List of Lists into a column-oriented List of Lists:

In[•]:= **(Transpose [Query [All, Values] [lifeboatDS]]) / / Normal**

Out[•]= { { 3rd, 1st, 3rd, 3rd, 3rd, 3rd, 3rd, 2nd, 3rd, 2nd, 3rd, 3rd, 1st, 3rd, 1st, 2nd,
        3rd, 3rd, 2nd, 3rd, 2nd, 2nd }, { 16, 65, 2, Missing [ ], 18, Missing [ ], 22, 48,
        14, 44, 33, 39, 19, 29, 46, Missing [ ], Missing [ ], 22, 22, 56, Missing [ ], 50 },
     { female, male, female, female, female, male, female, female, male, female, male,
        male, female, male, male, male, female, male, male, male, male, female },
     { True, False, False, True, False, False, True, True, False, False, False,
        False, True, True, False, False, True, False, True, False, False, True } }

One can Transpose the top levels of Datasets with more deeply nested data. Here, I obtain the planets Dataset and Transpose it. The result is an Association between characteristics of the planets (mass, radius, moons) and values for that data.

You can Transpose deeply nested Datasets at the top level:

In[ ]:=   **planets = ResourceData [ro, "Planets Deeply Nested Structure Dataset"]**

Out[ ]=

	Mass	Radius		Mass
Mercury	3.30104×10^{23} kg	2439.7 km		
Venus	4.86732×10^{24} kg	6051.9 km		
Earth	5.9721986×10^{24} kg	6367.4447 km	Moon	7.345
Mars	6.41693×10^{23} kg	3386. km	Phobos	1.072
			Deimos	$1.5 \times$
Jupiter	1.89813×10^{27} kg	69 173. km	Metis	$1. \times 1$
			Adrastea	$7. \times 1$
			Amalthea	2.07
			Thebe	$1.5 \times$
			63 total ›	

rows 1–5 of 8

In[ ]:=   **planetsT = Transpose [planets]**

Out[ ]=

	Mercury	Venus	Earth
Mass	3.30104×10^{23} kg	4.86732×10^{24} kg	5.9721986×10^{24} kg
Radius	2439.7 km	6051.9 km	6367.4447 km
Moons	‹| |›	‹| |›	‹| Moon → ‹| Mass → 7.3459×10

In a hierarchical Dataset such as planets, Transpose by default operates on the first two levels. Notice here, for example, that the data on each moon is presented as a row.

Extract parts of a Transposed Dataset:

In[ ]:=   **Query ["Moons", "Mars"] [planetsT]**

Out[ ]=

	Mass	Radius
Phobos	1.072×10^{16} kg	11.1 km
Deimos	1.5×10^{15} kg	6.2 km

Transpose has its limits, however, when used with Datasets. Although, as shown next, Transpose can rearrange deeply nested List-based and certain other conventional Wolfram Language data structures, these more elaborate operations do not (yet) work on more deeply nested Datasets.

Transpose (successfully) a 4 × 3 × 2 array into a 3 × 2 × 4 array:

```
In[ ]:= Module [ { array = Outer [ List, { 1, 2, 3, 4 }, { "A", "B", "C" } ] , tarray },
        tarray = Transpose [ array, { 3, 1, 2 } ] ;
        Echo [ Labeled [ MatrixForm @ array,
           StringTemplate [ "Dimensions are: `1`" ] [ Dimensions [ array ] ] ] ] ;
        Labeled [ MatrixForm @ tarray,
           StringTemplate [ "After Transpose, Dimensions are: `1`" ] [ Dimensions [ tarray ] ] ]
       ]
```

$$
\gg \quad \begin{pmatrix} \binom{1}{A} & \binom{1}{B} & \binom{1}{C} \\ \binom{2}{A} & \binom{2}{B} & \binom{2}{C} \\ \binom{3}{A} & \binom{3}{B} & \binom{3}{C} \\ \binom{4}{A} & \binom{4}{B} & \binom{4}{C} \end{pmatrix}
$$

Dimensions are: {4, 3, 2}

$$
Out[ ]= \quad \begin{pmatrix} \begin{pmatrix} 1 \\ 2 \\ 3 \\ 4 \end{pmatrix} & \begin{pmatrix} A \\ A \\ A \\ A \end{pmatrix} \\ \begin{pmatrix} 1 \\ 2 \\ 3 \\ 4 \end{pmatrix} & \begin{pmatrix} B \\ B \\ B \\ B \end{pmatrix} \\ \begin{pmatrix} 1 \\ 2 \\ 3 \\ 4 \end{pmatrix} & \begin{pmatrix} C \\ C \\ C \\ C \end{pmatrix} \end{pmatrix}
$$

After Transpose, Dimensions are: {3, 2, 4}

Try, unsuccessfully to use the same Transpose on a Dataset:

```
In[ ]:= Transpose [ planets, { 3, 1, 2 } ]
```

Out[ ]= Failure[⚠ Message: Dataset objects do not support arbitrary transpose operations.
                   Tag: Dataset]

If the Dataset is highly regular, however, the AssociationTranspose ResourceFunction can perform arbitrary transpose operations.

Here's a Dataset that has dimensions 3 × 4 × 2:

```
In[•]:=  ( SeedRandom [ 20 230 110 ] ;
          asc = [•] AssociationKeyDeflatten + @
              AssociationThread [ Tuples [ { { "♂", "♀", "⚥" }, CharacterRange [ "a", "d" ],
                  CharacterRange [ "α", "β" ] } ], RandomReal [ 1, 24 ] ];
          ( ds = Dataset [ asc ] ) / / Labeled [ ♯,
              StringTemplate [ "Dimensions of this Dataset are: `1`" ] [ Dimensions [ ♯ ] ] ] & )
```

		a		b		
		α	β	α	β	α
Out[•]=	♂	0.609165	0.767417	0.217978	0.00719154	0.323482
	♀	0.0240574	0.817491	0.316216	0.284887	0.823207
	⚥	0.138822	0.0610304	0.983682	0.318779	0.939545

Dimensions of this Dataset are: {3, 4, 2}

If I want the Dimensions of the Dataset to instead be $2 \times 3 \times 4$, I can get the contents of the Dataset with Normal, use an AssociationTranspose on it with $\{2, 3, 1\}$ as the second argument, and then re-convert the resulting expression into a Dataset.

Use AssociationTranspose to perform an arbitrary transposition on the Normal form of a Dataset and then convert the result back into a Dataset:

```
In[•]:=  Dataset [ [•] AssociationTranspose + [ Normal [ ds ], {2, 3, 1} ] ]
```

			♂		♀		⚥
	α	a	0.609165	a	0.0240574	a	0.138822
		b	0.217978	b	0.316216	b	0.983682
		c	0.323482	c	0.823207	c	0.939545
Out[•]=		d	0.295538	d	0.497086	d	0.512524
	β	a	0.767417	a	0.817491	a	0.0610304
		b	0.00719154	b	0.284887	b	0.318779
		c	0.223908	c	0.306863	c	0.250861
		d	0.17694	d	0.129254	d	0.234098

The Merge Method

A second method for switching to a column orientation is to rely on Merge [Identity] .

Use Merge with an Identity combiner to turn row-oriented Datasets that are Lists of Associations into column-oriented Datasets that are Associations of Lists:

In[•]:= **Normal [Query [Merge [Identity]] [lifeboatDS]]**

Out[•]= <| class → { 3rd, 1st, 3rd, 3rd, 3rd, 3rd, 3rd, 2nd,
          3rd, 2nd, 3rd, 3rd, 1st, 3rd, 1st, 2nd, 3rd, 3rd, 2nd, 3rd, 2nd, 2nd },
      age → { 16, 65, 2, Missing [ ] , 18, Missing [ ] , 22, 48, 14, 44, 33, 39, 19,
          29, 46, Missing [ ] , Missing [ ] , 22, 22, 56, Missing [ ] , 50 },
      sex → { female, male, female, female, female, male, female, female, male, female,
          male, male, female, male, male, male, female, male, male, male, male, female },
      survived → { True, False, False, True, False, False, True, True, False, False, False,
          False, True, True, False, False, True, False, True, False, False, True } |>

Reliance on Merge provides some additional capabilities. Here, I get the frequency distribution of each column. In the Wolfram Language front end, the output is dynamic and one can click on the rows or individual data items to drill down and get detailed information.

Use Merge with the Counts combiner to get the distribution of values for each column; compose the Counts with KeySorts to order the values:

In[•]:= **Query [Merge [Counts / * KeySort]] [lifeboatDS]**

Out[•]=

class	1st	3
	2nd	6
	3rd	13
age	2	1
	14	1
	16	1
	18	1
	19	1
	16 total ›	
sex	female	10
	male	12
survived	False	13
	True	9

A disadvantage of the Merge method is that it does not work when the rows are not Associations.

Merge fails when the rows are not Associations:

In[•]:= **Query [Merge [Identity] , Values] [lifeboatDS]**

Out[•]= Failure⎡ ⚠ Message: The argument 3rd is not a valid
                          list of Associations or rules or lists of rules.
                Tag: Merge   ⎤

Give a Row Orientation to a Dataset

Suppose one confronts a dataset that is in a column orientation. How does one convert it to a row orientation? Again, Transpose often works. Here, I re-Transpose the column-oriented variant of the lifeboat Dataset.

Two nested Transposes get the original Dataset back:

In[•]:= **Transpose [lifeboatDST]**

Out[•]=

class	age	sex	survived
3rd	16	female	True
1st	65	male	False
3rd	2	female	False
3rd	—	female	True
3rd	18	female	False
3rd	—	male	False
3rd	22	female	True
2nd	48	female	True

rows 1–8 of **22**

And this works if the Dataset is just a List of Lists rather than an Association of key-value pairs in which the values are Lists.

Transpose works on Datasets containing Lists of Lists:

In[ ]:=   **Transpose [Values [lifeboatDST]]**

Out[ ]=

3rd	16	female	True
1st	65	male	False
3rd	2	female	False
3rd	—	female	True
3rd	18	female	False
3rd	—	male	False
3rd	22	female	True
2nd	48	female	True

rows 1–8 of **22**

Transpose Datasets and the Double Transpose Trick

Previously in this chapter, I discussed functions that essentially Map over rows or undertake some variant of Mapping over the rows. These methods work satisfactorily if the Dataset is small. If the Dataset is large, however, the process of mapping over each row can be time consuming. An alternative method is to first Transpose the Dataset, perform the needed operation on what is now a row of data, and then re-Transpose the dataset back to the original form. I call this the "Double Transpose Trick." Mathematically, it is akin to a conjugation.

Change the Keys Using the Double Transpose Trick

To show the advantages, I first retrieve the entire Titanic Dataset from the repository for this book and then use Apply and Join to generate a Dataset that is one thousand times bigger than the Titanic Dataset.

To show this trick, I need a bigger boat:

In[ ]:= **oneThousandTitanics = Apply [Join, ConstantArray [titanicDS, 1000]]**

Out[ ]=

class	age	sex	survived
1st	29	female	True
1st	1	male	True
1st	2	female	False
1st	30	male	False
1st	25	female	False
1st	48	male	True
1st	63	female	True
1st	39	male	False

rows 1–8 of 1 309 000

Now, with the Double Transpose Trick, changing the names of the columns takes a few seconds on my machine. It takes about three times longer when I do not Transpose the data.

The Double Transpose Trick speeds up changing the names of columns:

In[ ]:= **columnNameChanger = Association ["cabin" → "class",**
"years" → "age", "gender" → "sex", "survival" → "survived"] ;

In[ ]:= **RepeatedTiming [**
Transpose [Query [columnNameChanger] [Transpose [oneThousandTitanics]]]]

Out[ ]= {5.8299,

cabin	years	gender	survival
1st	29	female	True
1st	1	male	True
1st	2	female	False
1st	30	male	False
1st	25	female	False
1st	48	male	True
1st	63	female	True
1st	39	male	False

rows 1–8 of 1 309 000

}

The computational work in this method comes mostly from Transposing the data. If the data is already in Transposed form and one wishes to keep it that way, changing the column names in this way takes well less than $\frac{1}{1000}$ of a second on my machine. Notice, by the way, that the output is elided because the Wolfram Language front end does not want to present a nightmarish list of one million values.

If the Transpose is already done and can be preserved, changing the names of columns is very fast:

In[•]:= **oneThousandTitanicsT = Transpose [oneThousandTitanics] ;**

In[•]:= **RepeatedTiming [Query [columnNameChanger] [oneThousandTitanicsT]]**

Out[•]= $\left\{ 0.000407661, \right.$

cabin	$\{ \ldots 1309000 \}$
years	$\{ \ldots 1309000 \}$
gender	$\{ \ldots 1309000 \}$
survival	$\{ \ldots 1309000 \}$

$\left. \right\}$

Here's a variant relying on the KeyReplace ResourceFunction applied to the Transposed Dataset. It's much slower than using the "official method" on the Transposed data but still has the virtue of a more lucid syntax.

Use the KeyReplace ResourceFunction on a Transposed Dataset to change column names:

In[•]:= **RepeatedTiming [**
     Query [[•] KeyReplace + [{ "class" → "cabin", "age" → "years", "sex" → "gender",
        "survived" → "survival" }]] [oneThousandTitanicsT]]

Out[•]= $\left\{ 4.59439, \right.$

cabin	$\{ \ldots 1309000 \}$
years	$\{ \ldots 1309000 \}$
gender	$\{ \ldots 1309000 \}$
survival	$\{ \ldots 1309000 \}$

$\left. \right\}$

The Double Transpose Trick with Listable Functions

Note that the Double Transpose Trick doesn't just work to fiddle with the keys. If one has a function that gains significant speed from listability or working on Lists, the Double Transpose Trick may likewise greatly speed up one's work. To see this, consider the following List containing one hundred random positions in the United States.

A display of random spots in the United States:

In[ ]:= **spots = (SeedRandom [20 220 720] ;**

    RandomGeoPosition [United States COUNTRY , 100] / / Thread) ;

GeoListPlot [spots]

Out[ ]=

Consider the following Dataset containing some other locations—they are from a Dataset I will use later in this chapter involving American Indian reservations. I will explain this kind of code in more detail later in the chapter.

Get reservation location data from the Wolfram Data Repository:

In[ ]:= **locationsDS = Query [1 ;; All ;; 40, KeyTake [{ "Name", "GeoLocation" }]] [**
    Query [1, ResourceData [#ResourceObject, "Dataset"] &] [
    ResourceSearch ["Indian Reservations"]]]

Out[ ]=

Name	GeoLocation
Coos, Lower Umpqua, and Siuslaw	42.81°N 124.4°W
Iowa (KS–NE)	39.97°N 95.38°W
Hoolehua–Palaau	21.17°N 157.1°W
Susanville	40.14°N 120.1°W
Nisqually	47.02°N 122.7°W
Tyonek	61.09°N 151.2°W
Lower Kalskag	61.52°N 160.4°W
Chefornak	60.15°N 164.3°W
rows 1–8 of 21	

Now what I want to do is compute, for each location in the Dataset, the spot in the original List to which they are closest. I could do this as follows.

Compute the closest spot to each reservation one reservation at a time and use RepeatedTiming to determine code efficiency:

```
In[•]:=  op1 = Query [ All,
              Association [ ♯, "NearestSpot" → GeoNearest [ spots, ♯GeoLocation ] [[1]] ] &];
          RepeatedTiming [ op1 [ locationsDS ] ]  //
             { ♯[[1]], FormatDataset [ HeaderSize → { Automatic, { 24, 12, 12 } } ] [ ♯[[2]] ] } &
```

Out[•]= { 0.033851,

Name	GeoLocation	NearestSpot
Coos, Lower Umpqua, and Siuslaw	42.81°N 124.4°W	44.27°N 121.7°W
Iowa (KS–NE)	39.97°N 95.38°W	40.78°N 94.6°W
Hoolehua–Palaau	21.17°N 157.1°W	36.6°N 120.3°W
Susanville	40.14°N 120.1°W	41.39°N 120.0°W
Nisqually	47.02°N 122.7°W	48.13°N 120.8°W
Tyonek	61.09°N 151.2°W	48.13°N 120.8°W
Lower Kalskag	61.52°N 160.4°W	48.13°N 120.8°W
Chefornak	60.15°N 164.3°W	48.13°N 120.8°W

rows 1–8 of 21   }

It works, but it takes longer than desired because the machine has to recompute the nearest function each time. But now let's Transpose the Dataset, apply GeoNearest to the entire list of locations in the Dataset and re-Transpose the Dataset back. The conjugation speeds up execution by roughly a factor of three.

Use the Double Transpose Trick to compute all the nearest spots all at once and much faster:

```
In[•]:=  op2 = Query [ (Association [ ♯,
              "NearestSpot" → Map [ First, GeoNearest [ spots, ♯GeoLocation ] ] ] &) ];
          RepeatedTiming [ Transpose [ op2 [ Transpose [ locationsDS ] ] ] ]
```

Out[•]= { 0.00760617,

Name	GeoLocation	NearestSpot
Coos, Lower Umpqua, and Siuslaw	42.81°N 124.4°W	44.27°N 121.7°W
Iowa (KS–NE)	39.97°N 95.38°W	40.78°N 94.6°W
Hoolehua–Palaau	21.17°N 157.1°W	36.6°N 120.3°W
Susanville	40.14°N 120.1°W	41.39°N 120.0°W
Nisqually	47.02°N 122.7°W	48.13°N 120.8°W
Tyonek	61.09°N 151.2°W	48.13°N 120.8°W
Lower Kalskag	61.52°N 160.4°W	48.13°N 120.8°W
Chefornak	60.15°N 164.3°W	48.13°N 120.8°W

rows 1–8 of 21   }

One caveat: as of Version 13, you can't Transpose a List of Associations using built-in functions, so if you have data in Normal form and you need to Transpose, consider either wrapping it in Dataset first or using the AssociationTranspose ResourceFunction as shown previously.

Defer Operation of a Descending Operator

Suppose I want a sorted List of the values in a particular column of a Dataset for a particular subset of rows. Sometimes, this is easy. On other occasions, however, it will require a more exact understanding of the order of operations in Query. To see the challenge, consider a Dataset like the Titanic Dataset but in which the columns are not in the same order as we have seen them.

Reverse the order of key-value pairs in the Titanic Dataset:

In[•]:= **titanicReversed =**
      Query [All, Reverse] [titanicDS] / / [▪] FormatDataset + [MaxItems → 10]

Out[•]=

survived	sex	age	class
True	female	29	1st
True	male	1	1st
False	female	2	1st
False	male	30	1st
False	female	25	1st
True	male	48	1st
True	female	63	1st
False	male	39	1st
True	female	53	1st
False	male	71	1st

rows 1–10 of **1309**

If I now run this query, the results are not what I expect. The value 17, for example, comes after 63 even though 17 is definitely less than 63. Moreover, the values for ages do not match the ages seen in the first ten rows of the preceding Dataset.

If you forget about order of operations, Sorts can yield unexpected results:

In[•]:= **Query [Select [⌗class === "1st" &] / ∗ Sort, ⌗age &] [titanicReversed]**

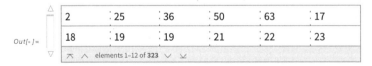

2	25	36	50	63	17
18	19	19	21	22	23

elements 1–12 of **323**

A look at the Normal form of the Query shows the problem. The sorting is done *before* the "age" is extracted. This precedence occurs because Sort (along with its predecessor Select) is a descending operator.

Here, I would actually like it to be ascending:

In[∘]:= **Query [Select [♯class === "1st" &] / ∗ Sort, ♯age &] / / Normal**

Out[∘]= Select [♯class === 1st &] / ∗ Sort / ∗ Map [♯age &]

I need the order to be the following:

In[∘]:= **Select [♯class === "1st" &] / ∗ Map [♯age &] / ∗ Sort;**

Here, I should probably just skip the Query business altogether and write the operator, just as I have previously, so that I have precise control over order of operations.

Explicitly create a RightComposition of functions in which one first Selects, then Maps "age", and then Sorts the ages:

In[∘]:= **(Select [♯class === "1st" &] / ∗ Map [♯age &] / ∗ Sort) [titanicReversed]**

Out[∘]=

1	2	4	6	11	13
14	15	16	16	16	17
△ ∧ elements 1–12 of **323** ∨ ∨					

If one feels one must use Query, however, the best bet is to create two queries and force Sort to be applied later in the process.

Using two Queries fixes the order of operations problem:

In[∘]:= **Query [Sort] [Query [Select [♯class === "1st" &] , ♯age &] [titanicReversed]]**

Out[∘]=

1	2	4	6	11	13
14	15	16	16	16	17
△ ∧ elements 1–12 of **323** ∨ ∨					

Alternatively, one could form a nested Query in which the last operator is Sort.

Wrapping Query operators in Query sometimes fixes order of operations problems:

In[∘]:= **Query [Query [Select [♯class === "1st" &] , ♯age &] / ∗ Sort] / / Normal**

Out[∘]= Select [♯class === 1st &] / ∗ Map [♯age &] / ∗ Sort

In[∘]:= **Query [Query [Select [♯class === "1st" &] , ♯age &] / ∗ Sort] [titanicReversed]**

Out[∘]=

1	2	4	6	11	13
14	15	16	16	16	17
△ ∧ elements 1–12 of **323** ∨ ∨					

In my experience, unexpected results from complex queries are frequently the result of order of operations issues. It's good practice to generate the Normal form of a Query that is creating problems. If the Normal form reveals that the operations are in an undesired sequence, one needs to: (1) use nested Queries to change the order; (2) use the Normal form as a basis for starting a program; (3) run multiple Queries instead of trying to get every operator into a single Query; or (4) dispense with Query and manually change the order of operations.

Exercises

6.1 Here's a Dataset. The column headers are "a", "b", and "c". Change them so that they are "Alpha", "b", and "Charlie".

```
abcDS = Dataset [ { <| "a" → 9, "b" → 8, "c" → 9 |>, <| "a" → 2, "b" → 7, "c" → 5 |>,
        <| "a" → 7, "b" → 7, "c" → 2 |>, <| "a" → 7, "b" → 3, "c" → 4 |> } ];
```

6.2 Use this code to retrieve the MLS Dataset from the ResourceObject for this book. Call it mlsDS. Now find out how many rows and columns it has.

```
mlsDS = ResourceData [ ro, "MLS List of Associations Dataset" ]
```

Club	LastName	FirstName	Position	BaseSalary	GuaranteedComp
CHI	Armas	Chris	M	$225 000.00	$225 000.00
CHI	Banner	Michael	M	$12 900.00	$12 900.00
CHI	Barrett	Chad	F	$41 212.50	$48 712.50
CHI	Blanco	Cuauhtemoc	F	$2.49232 × 10^6	$2.66678 × 10^6
CHI	Brown	C.J.	D	$106 391.00	$106 391.00
CHI	Busch	Jon	GK	$58 008.00	$58 008.00
CHI	Carr	Calen	F	$38 000.00	$50 500.00
CHI	Conde	Wilman	D	$144 000.00	$151 500.00

rows 1–8 of **4937**

6.3 Get rid of any rows in the MLS Dataset where the guaranteed compensation is Missing. Sort the remaining rows in the Dataset from highest guaranteed compensation to lowest. If there is a tie, sort it alphabetically by last name (A to Z), and if there is still a tie, sort it by year, earliest first. Hint 1: Sorting by the negative of a number is akin to a reverse sort. Hint 2: My code uses the MissingQ function and the Not function.

6.4 Here is some code that groups the data by team and year and computes the total salary. Run it. StringTemplate creates a TemplateObject expression that is similar to a function: when applied to arguments, it creates strings.

```
compensationByTeamYear =
  Query [ GroupBy [ StringTemplate [ "`1` - `2`" ] [ #Club, DateString [ #Year, "Year" ] ] &,
      Total, #GuaranteedCompensation &] [ mlsDS ]
```

Suppose I want to look at the previous data and compare just LA in 2010 with ORL in 2016 and TOR in 2016. My answer looks like this. Write the code to accomplish this.

LA–2010	$\$1.09786 \times 10^7$
ORL–2016	$\$1.15544 \times 10^7$
TOR–2016	$\$2.17985 \times 10^7$

6.5 A pure defender in the MLS data is designated by having a "D" in the position column. Find all the pure defenders with a guaranteed compensation of over \$1 million in any year. Produce a **Dataset** showing only their club, year, last name, first name, and guaranteed compensation (in that order). Sort the results by guaranteed compensation from high to low. Do as little computational work as possible, remembering that sorting on a lot of data takes a good deal of work. Here's my answer.

Club	Year	LastName	FirstName	GuaranteedCompensation
NY	2010	Marquez	Rafael	$\$5.544 \times 10^6$
NY	2012	Marquez	Rafael	$\$4.6 \times 10^6$
NY	2011	Marquez	Rafael	$\$4.6 \times 10^6$
LA	2015	Gonzalez	Omar	$\$1.45 \times 10^6$
POR	2016	Ridgewell	Liam	$\$1.25 \times 10^6$
LA	2014	Gonzalez	Omar	$\$1.25 \times 10^6$
POR	2014	Ridgewell	Liam	$\$1.2 \times 10^6$
POR	2015	Ridgewell	Liam	$\$1.15 \times 10^6$

6.6 Compute the ratio of guaranteed compensation to base salary for all players on the Houston Dynamo (HOU) in 2016. Sort the ratio from highest to lowest. Do not show the club or year in your output. My output looks like the following.

LastName	FirstName	Position	BaseSalary	GuaranteedCompensation	SalaryR
Steinberger	Zach	M	\$63 000.00	\$79 250.00	1.25794
Warner	Collen	M	\$149 934.00	\$177 434.00	1.18341
Torres	Erick	F	\$575 000.00	\$650 000.00	1.13043
Clark	Ricardo	M	\$319 200.00	\$356 700.00	1.11748
Garcia	Boniek	M	\$225 000.00	\$247 500.00	1.1
Beasley	DaMarcus	D	\$750 000.00	\$813 333.33	1.08444
Mansally	Kenny	D	\$77 500.00	\$84 000.00	1.08387
Rodriguez	Raul	D	\$350 000.00	\$379 333.33	1.08381

rows 1–8 of **27**

6.7 Here's some code that computes the total base salary for each team and year combination.

baseByTeamYear = Query [Select [StringQ [#Club] &] / *
     GroupBy [StringTemplate ["`1` − `2`"] [#Club , DateString [#Year , "Year"]] &],
  Total, #BaseSalary &] [mlsDS]

CHI–2007	$4.41252 × 10^6$
CHV–2007	$1.67827 × 10^6$
CLB–2007	$1.88955 × 10^6$
COL–2007	$2.18115 × 10^6$
DAL–2007	$2.79074 × 10^6$
DC–2007	$2.10132 × 10^6$
HOU–2007	$2.35005 × 10^6$
KC–2007	$2.44193 × 10^6$

rows 1–8 of **213**

Suppose that you were given this **baseByTeamYear** Dataset and were not given the raw MLS data. I want a Dataset that looks like this, with the team, year, and total base salaries in different columns. Hint 1: My answer uses **With**. Hint 2: My answer uses **StringSplit**. Hint 3: StringSplit ["HOU−2018","−"] yields { "HOU","2018" } .

Team	Year	Total Base Salary
CHI	2007	$4.41252 × 10^6$
CHV	2007	$1.67827 × 10^6$
CLB	2007	$1.88955 × 10^6$
COL	2007	$2.18115 × 10^6$
DAL	2007	$2.79074 × 10^6$
DC	2007	$2.10132 × 10^6$
HOU	2007	$2.35005 × 10^6$
KC	2007	$2.44193 × 10^6$

rows 1–8 of **213**

6.8 Take every five hundredth row of the MLS **Dataset** and put it into a column orientation. Then get just the resulting data without the **Dataset** wrapper.

Tech Notes

- One could also use the Double Transpose Trick described in this chapter to rename columns. This would avoid having to make one call of **KeyMap** per row. When the **Dataset** is small to begin with, however, the Double Transpose Trick may be slower. One can use two Transposes to rename just some of the columns.

In[*]:= **rename2Columns = KeyMap [# /. { "class" → "cabin", "sex" → "gender" } &] ;**

In[ ]:= **RepeatedTiming [Transpose [Query [rename2Columns] [Transpose [lifeboatDS]]]]**

Out[ ]= $\Big\{0.00171148,$

cabin	age	gender	survived
3rd	16,	female	True
1st	65	male	False
3rd	2	female	False
3rd	—	female	True
3rd	18	female	False
3rd	—	male	False
3rd	22	female	True
2nd	48	female	True

rows 1–8 of **22**

$\Big\}$

- I noted in the text that it can sometimes be a little faster to use MapAt to change existing columns in a Dataset rather than rely on Association dropping all but the last value for duplicate keys. One disadvantage, however, of using MapAt is that it's challenging to use it to change values based on multiple columns. Try, for example, to use MapAt to write a function that changes age upwards by one year for males and downwards by one year for females.

- One can also use Hash to index data. Hash is a function that takes any input and produces a unique string of a fixed length. Different input to Hash almost always produces different output, so by using MapIndexed to include a unique row number in the input to Hash, one is pretty much guaranteed unique keys for the resulting outer Association, avoiding undesired row deletion. Here, I create unique indices for the MLS players.

In[ ]:= **mlsHashed =**
Query [MapIndexed [(Hash [{ #1, #2 }, "CRC32", "HexString"] → #) &] / ∗
Association] [mlsDS]

Out[ ]=

	Club	LastName	FirstName	Position	BaseSalary	Guar
73d6079a	CHI	Armas	Chris	M	$225 000.00	$225
c418af50	CHI	Banner	Michael	M	$12 900.00	$12 9
a0f35203	CHI	Barrett	Chad	F	$41 212.50	$48
629cad47	CHI	Blanco	Cuauhtemoc	F	$2.49232 × 10^6	$2.6
845804e8	CHI	Brown	C.J.	D	$106 391.00	$106
45873b60	CHI	Busch	Jon	GK	$58 008.00	$58 0
b52c45d1	CHI	Carr	Calen	F	$38 000.00	$50 5
be9a6e62	CHI	Conde	Wilman	D	$144 000.00	$151

rows 1–8 of **4937**

If I now create a quick mapping between salient player data and Hash, I can look up information very swiftly.

```
In[•]:= lookupMLS =
        Dispatch [ Normal [ KeyValueMap [ { k , v } ↦ { v [ "LastName" ] , v [ "FirstName" ] ,
                    v [ "Club" ] , DateString [ v [ "Year" ] ] } → k , mlsHashed ]
            ]
        ]
```

Out[•]= Dispatch [⊞ ≫ Length: 5553]

```
In[•]:= EchoTiming [
        Query [ { "Bradley", "Michael", "TOR", "2016" } / . lookupMLS ] [ mlsHashed ] ]
```

⏱ 0.000675

Club	TOR
LastName	Bradley
FirstName	Michael
Position	M
BaseSalary	$6. \times 10^6$
GuaranteedCompensation	6.5×10^6
Year	2016

- Notice that in some of the code in the text dealing with aggregate measures, the columns with mean ages did not have headers; put another way, each row of the result was a List rather than an Association with keys. This is because using the anonymous function #age& rather than KeyTake ["age"] as the extractor stripped off the keys. One can continue to use the #age& anonymous function and restore the keys by making the "aggregator" function—the one that operates on the aggregates produced by the "extractor" function (#age&)—a function that itself produces an Association. Notice that since Mean is now wrapped inside an Association, missing values are no longer automatically deleted; one has to write code to explicitly delete them.

```
In[•]:= Query [ GroupBy [ #sex & ] ,
        <| "mean age" → Mean [ DeleteMissing [ #1 ] ] |> &, #age & ] [ lifeboatDS ]
```

	mean age
female	27.375
male	36.2222

- Alternatively, one could preserve the keys using **KeyTake** rather than an anonymous function as the "extractor" function and then combine the list of Associations result using the **Merge** [**Mean** [**Delete**. **Missing** [⌗]] & operator as the aggregator function. Notice that if one proceeds this way, one does not have control over the column header; because the **List** of Associations that were fed into the **Merge** operator all had "age" as their single key, the output of the **Merge** operator likewise must also have "age" as its single key.

In[◦]:= **Query [GroupBy [⌗sex &] ,**
    Merge [Mean [DeleteMissing [⌗]] &] , KeyTake ["age"]] [lifeboatDS]

Out[◦]=

	age
female	27.375
male	36.2222

7 | Advanced Recipes

This chapter uses a data resource from the Wolfram Data Repository (wolfr.am/WDR). To access the data, evaluate the following code.

Acquire the ResourceObject from the Wolfram Data Repository:

In[•]:= **ro = ResourceObject ["Sample Data for Query Book"]**

Out[•]= ResourceObject[⊞ 🏛 Name: Sample Data for Query Book »
Type: DataResource
Description: Data to support the Wolfram Media book Query: Getting Information from Data wit...]

You can also evaluate this piece of code, which will result in the default number of rows in Datasets being eight instead of the usual 20.

Use SetOptions to change the default value of rows displayed in a Dataset:

In[•]:= **SetOptions [Dataset, MaxItems → 8] ;**

Introduction

In this chapter, I provide more advanced recipes to tackle issues I have confronted in the real world of data analysis. The grouping of recipes into basic or more advanced is, I admit, somewhat arbitrary, but these recipes either involve more intricate programming or require at least some background in more complex mathematical topics, such as statistics or machine learning. I also try to show various "recipe substitutions," such as using various resource functions instead of built-in Wolfram Language code. As in the previous chapter involving more basic recipes, sometimes you may be able to use the code almost as is without significant alteration. Other times, you will need some understanding of the underlying concepts presented in this book. The later recipes often require more code or greater sophistication to implement.

The data for this chapter is again stored in the ResourceObject named ro that has already been retrieved.

I again make extensive use of the imaginary lifeboat from the Titanic.

Retrieve the lifeboat data from the Data Repository for this book:

In[*]:= **lifeboatDS = ResourceData [ro, "Lifeboat List of Associations Dataset"]**

Out[*]=

class	age	sex	survived
3rd	16	female	True
1st	65	male	False
3rd	2	female	False
3rd	—	female	True
3rd	18	female	False
3rd	—	male	False
3rd	22	female	True
2nd	48	female	True

rows 1–8 of **22**

I also load up the Titanic dataset since I will use it a lot as well.

Dare I say, raise the Titanic:

In[*]:= **titanicDS = ResourceData [ro, "Titanic List of Associations Dataset"]**

Out[*]=

class	age	sex	survived
1st	29	female	True
1st	1	male	True
1st	2	female	False
1st	30	male	False
1st	25	female	False
1st	48	male	True
1st	63	female	True
1st	39	male	False

rows 1–8 of **1309**

Recipe 1: Use Column Aggregates to Derive New Columns

Suppose I want a new column in the dataset that relies on some aggregation of values in a column (or multiple columns) of the dataset, like computing the percentile age of each passenger in the lifeboat. For example, I want to know that the sixth passenger on the lifeboat (who is 18) is older than only 24% of the lifeboat passengers. Computing the percentiles, however, requires an examination of the entire age column. As of Version 13.3, row computations based on column aggregations is not a trivial matter in the Wolfram Language.

Here's one way to do it. First, Transpose the data. Now use the built-in EmpiricalDistribution function to get the distribution of ages, protecting it from missing values with DeleteMissing. Now create a function f that takes an association and adds a key-value pair in which "AgePercentile" is the key and the percentile value of "age" is the value, again dealing carefully with missing values in the age column. Map that function f over the rows of passengers in the lifeboat by putting it in the second position to a second Query.

Use a Query on a transposed Dataset and then map a function derived from that Query over the original data to compute columns based on column aggregates. Precise timing will vary based on the speed of your machine:

```
In[ ]:= Module [ { dist, f },
          dist = Query [ ⌗age & / * DeleteMissing / * EmpiricalDistribution ] [
             Transpose [ titanicDS ] ] ;
          f = Association [ ⌗, "AgePercentile" →
                If [ NumericQ [ ⌗age ] , Round [ CDF [ dist, ⌗age ] , 0.01 ] , ⌗age ] ] &;
          Query [ All, f ] [ lifeboatDS ]
       ] / / RepeatedTiming
```

Out[ ]= {0.0049274,

class	age	sex	survived	AgePercentile
3rd	16	female	True	0.13
1st	65	male	False	0.99
3rd	2	female	False	0.03
3rd	—	female	True	—
3rd	18	female	False	0.18
3rd	—	male	False	—
3rd	22	female	True	0.32
2nd	48	female	True	0.89

rows 1–8 of 22

}

One doesn't have to use Transpose if one doesn't want to. Here's the same concept implemented again using two Queries but this time obtaining the EmpiricalDistribution by using the operator form of Extract to extract the age column. This method is slightly faster on this problem. The Transpose method is likely to scale better, however.

Use the operator form of Extract with position argument {All,"age"} to extract the age column and use that to compute a column aggregate:

```
In[ ]:= Module [ {dist =
            Query [ (Extract [ {All, "age"} ] / * DeleteMissing / * EmpiricalDistribution ) ] [
              lifeboatDS ],
          f},
        f = Association [ ♯, "AgePercentile" →
              If [ NumericQ [ ♯age ] , Round [ CDF [ dist, ♯age ] , 0.01 ] , ♯age ] ] &;
        Query [ All, f ] [ lifeboatDS ]
        ] / / RepeatedTiming
```

Out[ ]= {0.00253804,

class	age	sex	survived	AgePercentile
3rd	16	female	True	0.18
1st	65	male	False	1.0
3rd	2	female	False	0.06
3rd	—	female	True	—
3rd	18	female	False	0.24
3rd	—	male	False	—
3rd	22	female	True	0.47
2nd	48	female	True	0.82

rows 1–8 of 22 }

If one prefers to represent a column as a sequence of position specifications rather than a particular position, one can use the Slice ResourceFunction rather than the Extract operator.

Use the Slice operator with position arguments All and "age" to extract the age column and use that to compute a column aggregate:

```
In[ ]:= Module [ {dist =
            Query [ ( [▪] Slice + [ All, "age" ] / * DeleteMissing / * EmpiricalDistribution ) ] [
              lifeboatDS ],
          f},
        f = Association [ ♯, "AgePercentile" →
              If [ NumericQ [ ♯age ] , Round [ CDF [ dist, ♯age ] , 0.01 ] , ♯age ] ] &;
        Query [ All, f ] [ lifeboatDS ]
        ] / / RepeatedTiming
```

class	age	sex	survived	AgePercentile
3rd	16	female	True	0.18
1st	65	male	False	1.0
3rd	2	female	False	0.06
3rd	—	female	True	—
3rd	18	female	False	0.24
3rd	—	male	False	—
3rd	22	female	True	0.47
2nd	48	female	True	0.82

Out[•]= {0.00273755, ... }

rows 1–8 of **22**

Recipe 2: Aggregate Single Measures by Group

Often one wants to take a Dataset, break it up into groups, and then calculate a single aggregate measure for each group. (In the spreadsheet world, this operation is sometimes called a "pivot table.") In the abstract, the form of the code will generally involve an initial grouping based on some "grouper" function, an "extractor" function that will extract information from each row in each grouping, and an "aggregator" function (alternatively called a "reducer") that will operate over the collection of information thus extracted from each grouping. Thus, without Query but with the use of operator forms, the process might look something like the following code. I've colored the code so that, roughly speaking, green is grouping, red is extracting, and blue is aggregating.

The equivalent of MapReduceOperator using function composition but not Query:

```
In[•]:=  GroupBy[grouper] /* Map[Map[extractor] /* aggregator];
```

Or, if one wanted to use the MapLevel ResourceFunction, one could write it this way:

```
In[•]:=  GroupBy[grouper] /* [•] MapLevel [extractor, {2}] /* Map[aggregator];
```

And, if one wanted to use Query, one could write it as follows:

```
In[•]:=  Query[GroupBy[grouper], aggregator, extractor];
```

To take a concrete example, let's compute for each sex the mean age of the passengers on the lifeboat. I group by sex, extract the age, and reduce by Mean. Here's how one might attempt it without the use of Query.

Use a MapReduce on the lifeboat without Query:

In[•]:= (GroupBy [⊞sex &] / ∗ Map [Map [⊞age &] / ∗ Mean / ∗ N]) [lifeboatDS]

Out[•]=

female	0.1 (219. + 2. Missing[])
male	0.0833333 (326. + 3. Missing[])

Notice that this method does not produce the likely desired result because there are certain passengers for whom the age information is missing. I could refine the code to instead read as follows.

Protect the reducer Mean function from missing values:

In[•]:= (GroupBy [⊞sex &] / ∗ Map [Map [⊞age &] / ∗ DeleteMissing / ∗ Mean / ∗ N]) [
   lifeboatDS]

Out[•]=

female	27.375
male	36.2222

I could also try writing it this way to take advantage of the MapLevel ResourceFunction:

In[•]:= (GroupBy [⊞sex &] / ∗ [•] MapLevel + [⊞age &, {2}] / ∗
   Map [DeleteMissing / ∗ Mean / ∗ N]) [lifeboatDS]

Out[•]=

female	27.375
male	36.2222

But this is a bit ugly. Alternatively, we could use Query, which has some built-in intelligence to deal with missing values. When Mean is an unwrapped operator inside Query, the default behavior is for missing values to be deleted before the mean is taken. Thus, I can write out the algorithm as follows.

Use Query's built-in handling of missing values to perform an effective MapReduceOperator:

In[•]:= Query [GroupBy [⊞sex &] , Mean / ∗ N, ⊞age &] [lifeboatDS]

Out[•]=

female	27.375
male	36.2222

Notice that in the previous code, I relied on the default treatment provided by Query for missing values. Here, it all worked out. But in some instances, at least as of Mathematica 13.1, the default treatment will produce incorrect results without any warning. Compare the following two very similar Queries. The results are different and only the one on the left is actually correct. The answer on the right is incorrect!

Default Missing handling by Query can sometimes lead to problems:

In[•]:= { Query [GroupBy [♯sex &] , Mean, ♯age &] [lifeboatDS] ,
Query [GroupBy [♯sex &] , Mean, KeyTake ["age"]] [lifeboatDS] }

Out[•]= {

female	27.375
male	36.2222

,

	age
female	21.9
male	27.1667

}

By setting the MissingBehavior option to None, the problem becomes apparent.

Set MissingBehavior→None to see the cause of the problem:

In[•]:= Query [GroupBy [♯sex &] , Mean / * N,
KeyTake ["age"] , MissingBehavior → None] [lifeboatDS]

Out[•]=

	age
female	0.1 (219. + 2. Missing[])
male	0.0833333 (326. + 3. Missing[])

I can fix the problem by (1) before GroupBy, making sure that there are no missing "age" values to begin with or (2) after GroupBy, Selecting only those associations produced by KeyTake for which "age" has a numeric value. I show the success of both of these techniques here.

Two different ways to restore the correct answer by protecting Mean from Missing values:

In[•]:= { Query [Select [(MissingQ / * Not) [♯age] &] / * GroupBy [♯sex &] ,
Mean / * N, KeyTake ["age"] , MissingBehavior → None] [lifeboatDS] ,
Query [GroupBy [♯sex &] , Select [(MissingQ / * Not) [♯age] &] / * Mean / * N,
KeyTake ["age"] , MissingBehavior → None] [lifeboatDS] }

Out[•]= {

	age
female	27.375
male	36.2222

,

	age
female	27.375
male	36.2222

}

I can also use the MapReduceOperator ResourceFunction here but I again need to be careful. I use a grouper (sex ♯ &), an extractor (♯ age &) and a reducer (DeleteMiss·. ing / * Mean / * N).

Use MapReduceOperator to cleanly derive the Mean age by gender, protecting explicitly against Missings:

In[•]:=   [▪] **MapReduceOperator** ⊕ **[(♯sex &) → (♯age &) ,**
         DeleteMissing /* Mean /* N] [lifeboatDS]

Out[•]=

female	27.375
male	36.2222

Notice though that wrapping the MapReduceOperator in Query will not save me from an incorrect answer if I am not careful. I must still protect my Mean in the reducer composition from Missing values.

MapReduceOperator is vulnerable to problems with Missing values:

In[•]:=   **Query [** [▪] **MapReduceOperator** ⊕ **[(♯sex &) → (♯age &) , Mean /* N]] [lifeboatDS]**
         (*yields wrong answer*)

Out[•]=

female	21.9
male	27.1667

Recipe 3: Make the Keys in Each Row of Data Identical

Suppose that as it happened, there were no men in third class on the Titanic. I create that artificial scenario in the following code.

Get rid of third-class men from the Dataset (sorry, Jack Dawson):

In[•]:=   **noThirdsMen =**
         Query [Select [Not [♯class === "3rd" && ♯sex === "male"] &]] [titanicDS]

Out[•]=

class	age	sex	survived
1st	29	female	True
1st	1	male	True
1st	2	female	False
1st	30	male	False
1st	25	female	False
1st	48	male	True
1st	63	female	True
1st	39	male	False

rows 1–8 of **816**

I now envision a common form of basic data analysis: group the data by class and get a Counts of the gender. Here's what I hope to get: the second level of the data structure is presented horizontally with a zero in the cell for third-class men.

A horizontally structured display showing no third-class men:

	female	male
1st	144	179
2nd	106	171
3rd	216	0

But, as it turns out, here's what I get if I do a straightforward Query.

Use Query with three arguments to first group the data, then get the sex of each person within each group, and then count the number of persons of each sex within each group:

In[ ]:= **Query [GroupBy [⌗class &] , Counts, ⌗sex &] [noThirdsMen]**

Out[ ]=

1st	female	144
	male	179
2nd	male	171
	female	106
3rd	female	216

I have two problems. The first is that the orientation of the level of what should be "rows" is vertical rather than the desired horizontal. The second is that there is no zero value for males in third class. Use of the operator form of the ItemCounts Resource·. Function is perhaps the simplest fix for this issue. The idea is simply to list the possibilities for which one wants a count value, even if that value is zero. This small change in code will also automatically result in the rows in fact taking on the desired horizontal orientation. An additional virtue of ItemCounts is that category order will be consistent, which, as discussed in the previous chapter, will make the Dimensions of the result conform to what is more likely one's expectation.

Temporarily store the output from a Query using With, Echo its dimensions, and return the output of the Query:

In[ ]:= **With [{ result =**
       Query [GroupBy [#class &] , [▣] ItemCounts + [{ "female", "male" }] , #sex &] [
          noThirdsMen] } , Echo [Dimensions [result]] ;
       result]

» {3, 2}

Out[ ]=

	female	male
1st	144	179
2nd	106	171
3rd	216	0

The result can, of course, be formatted using the FormatDataset ResourceFunction:

In[ ]:= **Query [GroupBy [#class &] , [▣] ItemCounts + [{ "female", "male" }] , #sex &] [**
       noThirdsMen] / / [▣] FormatDataset + [
       ItemStyle → { None, { Red, Blue } } , Background → Lighter @ Yellow]

Out[ ]=

	female	male
1st	144	179
2nd	106	171
3rd	216	0

If one doesn't like ResourceFunctions or doesn't remember ItemCounts, one can create a default Association and then Join that with the results from a Query that just uses Counts. This method works because, if there are multiple elements with the same key, all but the last of these elements are dropped.

Create a function that Joins the output from Counts with an Association containing default values of 0 for each possible category:

In[ ]:=
Query [GroupBy [#class &] , Counts /*
       (Join [Association ["female" → 0, "male" → 0] , #] &) , #sex &] [noThirdsMen]

Out[ ]=

	female	male
1st	144	179
2nd	106	171
3rd	216	0

One can also do the same thing with a different ResourceFunction: JoinRest.This function creates an operator that joins its immediate argument with whatever it then confronts. It works here because in joined associations with duplicate keys, the last value confronted prevails.

Use JoinRest to create default values for various keys in an Association:

In[•]:= [•] **JoinRest** ✦ **[<|"a" → 0, "b" → 0|>] [<|"a" → 6|>]**

Out[•]= **<| a → 6, b → 0 |>**

Use JoinRest to get explicit zero count values and create a horizontally oriented display:

In[•]:= **Query [GroupBy [♯class &] , Counts / ✶**
  [•] **JoinRest** ✦ **[Association ["female" → 0, "male" → 0]] , ♯sex &] [noThirdsMen]**

	female	male
1st	144	179
2nd	106	171
3rd	216	0

Out[•]=

Recipe 4: Create Multiple Aggregate Measures of Grouped Data

The methods shown in the previous section hint at how one can perform a more complex Query involving grouped data. Say one wants a presentation showing, for each sex grouping, the number of passengers, the number of passengers in first class, and the mean age. Here's an image of what I want.

	count	1st	mean age
female	10	1	27.375
male	12	2	36.2222

To do this, let's work backwards in imagining the pipeline of necessary code. First, let's imagine that I already have an Association containing two keys: one for the ages of the passengers and one for their cabin classes. Here's a function I could write that would take that Association and produce one with the number of passengers, the number of passengers in first class, and the mean age. I call the function statisticalMeasures. I use ↦ notation to denote a function instead of ♯ notation because, sometimes, when there are a lot of nested functions defined using ♯, the parser can get confused about the intent.

Create a function that takes an Association and determines three statistical measures based on differing keys:

```
In[ ]:= statisticalMeasures =
          ( a ⟼ Association [ "count" → Length [ a [ "age" ] ] , "1st" → Count [ a [ "class" ] ,
             "1st" ] , "mean age" → Mean [ DeleteMissing [ a [ "age" ] ] ] ] );
```

That's the final piece of the pipeline of code I need to get the desired output. I also need code, though, that gets the lifeboat data into the requisite form: an Association containing two key-value pairs, one whose values contain a list of ages and one whose values contain a list of cabin classes.

I'm going to first deliberately do this incorrectly so you can better understand how the code ultimately succeeds. I apply Normal to the Dataset simply so you can more clearly see what would be inside it.

The wrong way to get the data ready for the production of multiple statistics:

```
In[ ]:= Normal [ Query [ GroupBy [ ♯sex & ] , All, KeyTake [ { "age", "class" } ] ] [ lifeboatDS ] ]
```

```
Out[ ]= <| female → { <| age → 16, class → 3rd |>, <| age → 2, class → 3rd |>,
           <| age → Missing [ ] , class → 3rd |>, <| age → 18, class → 3rd |>,
           <| age → 22, class → 3rd |>, <| age → 48, class → 2nd |>,
           <| age → 44, class → 2nd |>, <| age → 19, class → 1st |>,
           <| age → Missing [ ] , class → 3rd |>, <| age → 50, class → 2nd |> },
         male → { <| age → 65, class → 1st |>, <| age → Missing [ ] , class → 3rd |>,
           <| age → 14, class → 3rd |>, <| age → 33, class → 3rd |>,
           <| age → 39, class → 3rd |>, <| age → 29, class → 3rd |>,
           <| age → 46, class → 1st |>, <| age → Missing [ ] , class → 2nd |>,
           <| age → 22, class → 3rd |>, <| age → 22, class → 2nd |>,
           <| age → 56, class → 3rd |>, <| age → Missing [ ] , class → 2nd |> } |>
```

Notice that for each gender key, I get a List of Associations, which is not the form of data I want. Instead, I want an Association whose values are Lists. The Merge [Identity] function fixes the problem. It takes those lists of Associations and creates a single Association containing two keys: one for the ages of the passengers and one for their cabin classes. I again apply Normal to the Dataset simply so you can more clearly see what would be inside it.

Use Merge to get the data in shape for the production of multiple statistical measures:

```
In[ ]:= Normal [ Query [ GroupBy [ ♯sex & ] ,
          Merge [ Identity ] , KeyTake [ { "age", "class" } ] ] [ lifeboatDS ] ]
```

```
Out[ ]= <| female → <| age → { 16, 2, Missing [ ] , 18, 22, 48, 44, 19, Missing [ ] , 50 },
           class → { 3rd, 3rd, 3rd, 3rd, 3rd, 2nd, 2nd, 1st, 3rd, 2nd } |>,
         male → <| age → { 65, Missing [ ] , 14, 33, 39, 29, 46, Missing [ ] , 22, 22, 56, Missing [ ] },
           class → { 1st, 3rd, 3rd, 3rd, 3rd, 3rd, 1st, 2nd, 3rd, 2nd, 3rd, 2nd } |> |>
```

I can now put the two pieces of the pipeline together and get the desired result.

Use the RightComposition (/ *) of a Merge and the statistical measures function to create a Dataset that computes multiple measures for various groups:

In[ ]:= **Query [GroupBy [#sex &] , Merge [Identity] / * statisticalMeasures,**
KeyTake [{ "age", "class" }]] [lifeboatDS]

Out[ ]=

	count	1st	mean age
female	10	1	27.375
male	12	2	36.2222

Applying Normal to the Query shows the order of operations:

In[ ]:= **Normal [Query [GroupBy [#sex &] ,**
Merge [Identity] / * statisticalMeasures, KeyTake [{ "age", "class" }]]]

Out[ ]= GroupBy [#sex &] / * Map [Map [KeyTake [{ age, class }]]] / *
Merge [Identity] / * Function [a, Association [count → Length [a [age]],
1st → Count [a [class], 1st], mean age → Mean [DeleteMissing [a [age]]]]]]]

Use the MapLevel ResourceFunction to avoid nested Map functions in the composition of operators:

In[ ]:= **(GroupBy [#sex &] / * [■] MapLevel ⬦ [KeyTake [{ "age", "class" }], {2}] / ***
Map [Merge [Identity] / * statisticalMeasures]) [lifeboatDS]

Out[ ]=

	count	1st	mean age
female	10	1	27.375
male	12	2	36.2222

Another alternative is to avoid the whole Query business and just use GroupBy. I've color coded its grouping, extracting, and aggregation components.

Make the second argument of GroupBy a Rule going from a grouping function on the left-hand side to an extracting function on the right-hand side:

In[ ]:= **GroupBy [lifeboatDS, (#sex &) → KeyTake [{ "age", "class" }] ,**
Merge [Identity] / * statisticalMeasures]

Out[ ]=

	count	1st	mean age
female	10	1	27.375
male	12	2	36.2222

Notice that if I do not care about a lot of needless data flowing into the Merge operator, I can simplify this Query further by deleting the KeyTake extractor function. I let all the data flow into the Merge, and then in statisticalMeasures, I just use the components of the data that I actually need.

Use GroupBy to group the data by the sex of the passenger, then Merge the data and apply the statisticalMeasures function to the merged data:

In[ ]:= **Query [GroupBy [⨤sex &] , Merge [Identity] / ∗ statisticalMeasures] [lifeboatDS]**

Out[ ]=

	count	1st	mean age
female	10	1	27.375
male	12	2	36.2222

Recipe 5: "Cross Tabulate" Data

Suppose I want to break down the lifeboat data by sex and class and find out how many passengers are in each category. Here is code to accomplish the equivalent of this form of pivot table. Notice the code is a bit tricky with a nested Map.

KeySort is added at the end to force a horizontal rather than vertical presentation of the inner associations:

In[ ]:= **(GroupBy [⨤sex &] / ∗ Map [GroupBy [⨤class &] / ∗ Map [Length] / ∗ KeySort]) [lifeboatDS]**

Out[ ]=

	1st	2nd	3rd
female	1	3	6
male	2	3	7

I could also use a feature of GroupBy wherein one groups using two functions wrapped in a List. This accomplishes a recursive grouping.

Use RightComposition on a sequence of operators to cross tabulate gender by cabin class:

In[ ]:= **(GroupBy [{ ⨤sex &, ⨤class & }] / ∗ Map [Map [Length] / ∗ KeySort]) [lifeboatDS]**

Out[ ]=

	1st	2nd	3rd
female	1	3	6
male	2	3	7

Again, if I took advantage of MapLevel, I could write it this way:

In[ ]:= **(GroupBy [{ ⌗sex &, ⌗class &}] /***
         [•] MapLevel + **[Length, {2}] / * Map [KeySort]) [lifeboatDS]**

Out[ ]=

	1st	2nd	3rd
female	1	3	6
male	2	3	7

Query makes the code somewhat simpler. I will call this result **crosstab** for later reference.

Use Query with GroupBy as the first and second arguments to break down data recursively:

In[ ]:= **crosstab =**
         Query [GroupBy [⌗sex &] , GroupBy [⌗class &] / * KeySort, Length] [lifeboatDS]

Out[ ]=

	1st	2nd	3rd
female	1	3	6
male	2	3	7

Again, I could use a single GroupBy with recursive grouping by wrapping the two grouping slot functions sex⌗ & and ⌗class & in a List.

Use a single GroupBy with a List of functions to group recursively within a Query:

In[ ]:= **Query [GroupBy [{ ⌗sex &, ⌗class &}] / * KeySort, KeySort, Length] [lifeboatDS]**

Out[ ]=

	1st	2nd	3rd
female	1	3	6
male	2	3	7

Again, one doesn't have to use Query; here's how to do the same thing using GroupBy and then postfix the result with a KeySort mapped to both level 0 (the top of the expression) and level 1. The use of level 0 is perhaps a little obscure, but it does work.

Use GroupBy to group the passengers recursively by sex and class, get the length of each subgroup, and then KeySort the results at the top level and the first level:

In[ ]:= **GroupBy [lifeboatDS, { ⌗sex &, ⌗class &}, Length] / / (Map [KeySort, ⌗, {0, 1}] &)**

Out[ ]=

	1st	2nd	3rd
female	1	3	6
male	2	3	7

The previous tabulation is presented in "wide" form with row and column headers. Suppose I wanted, however, to have a narrow presentation with only row headers. I could then simply group by both sex and class simultaneously. Notice that grouping by {# sex, # class} & is very different than grouping by {# sex &, # class &}. The former creates a single List of sex and class and groups by that. The latter first groups by using sex # & only and then breaks ties among the members of each of those groupings using # class &.

Those familiar with the tidyverse and dplyr in the R programming language will note the parallels to the use of wide versus long form in creating pivot tables.

Use a function that creates a List of column values to group the data:

In[•]:= **Query [GroupBy [{#sex , #class } &] , Length] [lifeboatDS] / /**
   [•] FormatDataset + [HeaderDisplayFunction → (# &)]

Out[•]=

female	3rd	6
male	1st	2
male	3rd	7
female	2nd	3
female	1st	1
male	2nd	3

In the previous code, the key is presented in two columns because it is a List. To avoid this presentation, I can use StringTemplate to make the key into a single string from the values of the underlying Associations.

Use StringTemplate as part of the grouping function to create attractive row headers:

In[•]:= **Query [GroupBy [StringTemplate ["`sex` – `class`"]] , Length] [lifeboatDS]**

Out[•]=

female–3rd	6
male–1st	2
male–3rd	7
female–2nd	3
female–1st	1
male–2nd	3

Recipe 6: Get Row and/or Column Aggregates of Data

Often one wants various aggregate measures of the rows and/or columns of a Dataset. The following code shows how to create row totals. I first create a general-purpose function called totaler that takes an association and appends a key-value pair that computes the total of the values in the association. (It doesn't have to be total, of course; it could be mean, median or whatever other aggregate measure is desired). I then use Query to map that function over the rows in the crosstab dataset.

Compute and display row totals in a dataset:

In[ ]:= **totaler = Association [♯, "Total" → Total [♯]] &;**

In[ ]:= **withRowTotals = Query [All, totaler] [crosstab]**

Out[ ]=

	1st	2nd	3rd	Total
female	1	3	6	10
male	2	3	7	12

If one prefers to work outside the Query framework, one can always use Map directly.

Map the totaler function at the first level of the Dataset:

In[ ]:= **Map [totaler] [crosstab]**

Out[ ]=

	1st	2nd	3rd	Total
female	1	3	6	10
male	2	3	7	12

By using Transpose, I can add column totals to our presentation.

Use Transpose to compute and display column aggregates:

In[ ]:= **Query [All, totaler] [Transpose [withRowTotals]]**

Out[ ]=

	female	male	Total
1st	1	2	3
2nd	3	3	6
3rd	6	7	13
Total	10	12	22

If I want the data back in its original orientation in which sexes were on the rows and cabin classes were on the columns, I just Transpose again. This is the Double Transpose Trick discussed in Chapter 6.

The Double Transpose Trick works (in versions of Mathematica before 13, one may need to run the ResetDataset ResourceFunction on the result to get it to format properly).

Add column totals by transposing the Dataset, mapping totaler over the rows (formerly columns) and retransposing:

In[*]:= **Transpose [Query [All, totaler] [Transpose [withRowTotals]]]**

Out[*]=

	1st	2nd	3rd	Total
female	1	3	6	10
male	2	3	7	12
Total	3	6	13	22

Those who dislike the Query framework can try this alternative (which works in versions of Mathematica before 13 without any need to run the ResetDataset ResourceFunction on the result).

Run the same code as before but execute it directly as an operating pipeline without Query:

In[*]:= **(Map [totaler] / * Transpose / * Map [totaler] / * Transpose) [crosstab]**

Out[*]=

	1st	2nd	3rd	Total
female	1	3	6	10
male	2	3	7	12
Total	3	6	13	22

Recipe 7: Prepare Data for Statistical Analysis Functions

I can do statistics with Query and a Dataset. Suppose, for example, that I want to develop a logistic regression that predicts survival on the lifeboat based on age, cabin class, and sex. I first need to delete any rows that have missing values since LogitModelFit does not accommodate them. Second, because LogitModelFit expects the responses (a.k.a. "dependent variable", a.k.a. "target") to be probability values between 0 and 1, I also need to convert the True/False values for the survival column. I use Boole to turn False into 0 and True into 1. Notice also that I get rid of the keys only after I've done the MapAt. That way, I don't have to remember that "survived" is the fourth column in the Dataset; I can just use the name "survived" to designate the part of each row that I want to transform.

Use the statistical analysis function LogitModelFit as an element in the first argument to Query:

In[•]:= **lmf1 = Query [DeleteMissing [⌗ , 1, 2] & / * (LogitModelFit [⌗ , 3 items +] &) ,**
MapAt [Boole, { "survived" }] / * Values] [lifeboatDS]

Out[•]= FittedModel$\left[\dfrac{1}{1 + e^{\ll 19 \gg + \ll 7 \gg}} \right]$

In[•]:= **lmf1 ["ParameterTable"]**

Out[•]=

	Estimate	Standard Error	z-Statistic	P-Value
1	−0.491826	1.57555	−0.312161	0.754918
class [1st]	0.925322	1.81712	0.509225	0.610594
class [2nd]	2.36838	1.74516	1.35711	0.174745
age	−0.0391711	0.0477965	−0.819541	0.412478
sex [female]	1.10734	1.26881	0.872738	0.382806

With Version 12 and later, there's another option for dealing with missing values: synthesize replacements in an intelligent way. Here's some simple code that does the job. It looks just like the previous code except that SynthesizeMissingValues has replaced DeleteMissing.

Compose SynthesizeMissingValues and LogitModelFit as an alternative way to develop a statistical model:

In[•]:= **lmf2 = Query [SynthesizeMissingValues / * (LogitModelFit [⌗ , 3 items +] &) ,**
MapAt [Boole, { "survived" }] / * Values] [lifeboatDS]

Out[•]= FittedModel$\left[\dfrac{1}{1 + e^{\ll 19 \gg + \ll 7 \gg}} \right]$

Of course, one can use all the features of the SynthesizeMissingValues function. Here, I use the "KernelDensityEstimation" method.

Customize the method of SynthesizeMissingValues:

In[•]:= **lmf3 =**
Query [(SynthesizeMissingValues [⌗ , Method → "KernelDensityEstimation"] &) / *
(LogitModelFit [⌗ , 3 items +] &) ,
MapAt [Boole, { "survived" }] / * Values] [lifeboatDS]

Out[•]= FittedModel$\left[\dfrac{1}{1 + e^{\ll 19 \gg + \ll 7 \gg}} \right]$

Although this is not a book about statistics, it's impossible for me not to take the opportunity to compare the models produced by these three variants of logistic regression. Notice that the positive effect of gender on survival has a p-value of more than 0.05 absent synthesis of missing values. This fact might make some statisticians deny that gender played a role in Titanic survival. Particularly when sample sizes are small, treatment of missing values matters!

The results of LogitModelFit can differ significantly depending on how one handles missing values:

In[•]:= **MapThread [Framed [Labeled [▦]] &,**
 { Through [{ lmf1, lmf2, lmf3 } ["ParameterTable"]],
 { "No synthesis of missing values", "Default synthesis of missing values",
 "KDE synthesis of missing values" } }] / / (Column / ∗ Framed)

Out[•]=

	Estimate	Standard Error	z-Statistic	P-Value
1	−0.491826	1.57555	−0.312161	0.754918
class [1st]	0.925322	1.81712	0.509225	0.610594
class [2nd]	2.36838	1.74516	1.35711	0.174745
age	−0.0391711	0.0477965	−0.819541	0.412478
sex [female]	1.10734	1.26881	0.872738	0.382806

No synthesis of missing values

	Estimate	Standard Error	z-Statistic	P-Value
1	−1.15319	1.53107	−0.75319	0.451336
class [1st]	0.425976	1.86041	0.228969	0.818893
class [2nd]	0.951785	1.42692	0.667021	0.504759
age	−0.0229459	0.0464668	−0.493813	0.621438
sex [female]	2.30465	1.08528	2.12355	0.0337078

Default synthesis of missing values

	Estimate	Standard Error	z-Statistic	P-Value
1	−1.66551	1.36947	−1.21618	0.223918
class [1st]	0.162477	1.72453	0.0942157	0.924938
class [2nd]	0.603081	1.28119	0.47072	0.637841
age	−0.00435834	0.0385127	−0.113166	0.909899
sex [female]	2.44493	1.06545	2.29474	0.0217482

KDE synthesis of missing values

Recipe 8: Prepare Data for Machine Learning Functions

This recipe shows how to use the Classify function to determine who lives or dies on the Titanic. Classify is a form of automated machine learning (AutoML) in which the machine picks the classification algorithm to be used as well as the optimal training parameters.

I start by adhering to an important tradition in machine learning. I break up the data so that a random fraction of it (here, 23) is used for training and the remainder (here, 13) is used for testing.

There are several ways to do this. One is to create indices in the Dataset and then use RandomSample to randomly assign $\frac{2}{3}$ of the rows corresponding to those indices to a training set and the remainder to a test set. As shown next, the CorrespondingIntegers ResourceFunction and the TakeDrop function combine to implement this idea.

Get training and test indices of the data to be used in machine learning:

In[•]:= (SeedRandom [1] ;
         { trainingIndices, testingIndices } =
           With [{ trainingSize = Round [2 * Length [titanicDS] / 3] },
              TakeDrop [RandomSample [⊡ CorrespondingIntegers ⊹ [titanicDS]],
                trainingSize]]) // ⊡ Terse ⊹ [5]

Out[•]//Short= { { 29, 17, 1022, 138, 1203, 1085, 806, 1121, 318, 1217, 989, 1259, 1112, 95, 914, 107, 262,
         966, 890, 1222, 835, 1172, 237, 279, 1197, 168, 1163, 300, 851, 512, 1098, 886,
         55, 466, 247, 200, 511, 1132, ≪797≫, 620, 346, 964, 232, 891, 1195, 52, 565, 148,
         1194, 451, 985, 558, 703, 390, 452, 1230, 1245, 336, 166, 831, 354, 957, 216, 934,
         991, 1300, 1166, 1286, 694, 410, 869, 486, 609, 1240, 761, 362, 667 }, ≪1≫ }

I can now run Classify. To do so I put the data in one of several forms the Wolfram
Language's supervised machine learning functions can accept. One of those forms is a
List in which each element is a Rule. The left-hand side of each rule is a set of predictor values (features) in the form of a List or an Association (with the same number and
order of keys) and the right-hand side is the response value (target).

Turn off reporting functions; execution of this code will speed up presentation of the results:

In[•]:= SetOptions [Classify, TrainingProgressReporting → None] ;

Create rules running from input features to target to prepare the training data for the Classify
machine learning function:

In[•]:= cl = Query [trainingIndices / * Classify,
         KeyDrop [⌗ , "survived"] → ⌗survived &] [titanicDS]

Out[•]= ClassifierFunction [⊞ ⊠ | Input type: {Nominal, Numerical, Nominal }
                           Classes: False, True]

Use Switch to convert True and False values for the survived column to "survived" and "died":

In[•]:= titanicDS1 = Query [All,
         MapAt [Switch [⌗ , True, "survived", False, "died"] &, "survived"]] [titanicDS]

Out[•]=

class	age	sex	survived
1st	29	female	survived
1st	1	male	survived
1st	2	female	died
1st	30	male	died
1st	25	female	died
1st	48	male	survived
1st	63	female	survived
1st	39	male	died

rows 1–8 of **1309**

I could also use the ResourceFunction TableToTrainingSet to get each row of the data in the correct form. The second argument to TableToTrainingSet designates the column of the data that will serve as the target. Here, it is the survived column.

Use the TableToTrainingSet ResourceFunction with "survived" as the target to put the data in the right form for Classify:

In[∘]:= **clTTTS =**
  Query [trainingIndices / * ([▪] TableToTrainingSet + [#, "survived"] &) / * Classify] [titanicDS]

Out[∘]= ClassifierFunction[[⊞] [diagram] Input type: {Nominal, Numerical, Nominal }
                                                    Classes: False, True   ]

I can now see how the classifier performs on data it has not seen before. I grab the testing data, convert it to the correct form using TableToTrainingSet (which, despite its name, doesn't care if the data is for training or testing), and then deploy ClassifierMea⁝. surements using the previously built ClassifierFunction and the testing data. I add Quiet to the input to prevent an irksome error message that sometimes appears.

Use the test data and the classifier to build a ClassifierMeasurementsObject from which one can obtain classifier performance statistics:

In[∘]:= **cmo =**
  Quiet@Query [testingIndices / * ([▪] TableToTrainingSet + [#, "survived"] &) / *
    (ClassifierMeasurements [cl, #] &)] [titanicDS]

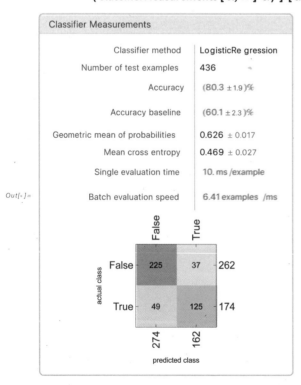

Classifier Measurements	
Classifier method	LogisticRe gression
Number of test examples	436
Accuracy	$(80.3 \pm 1.9)\%$
Accuracy baseline	$(60.1 \pm 2.3)\%$
Geometric mean of probabilities	0.626 ± 0.017
Mean cross entropy	0.469 ± 0.027
Single evaluation time	10. ms /example
Batch evaluation speed	6.41 examples /ms

I can now compute various properties of our classifier's performance on the previously unseen test data. The Cohen's kappa statistic, by the way, measures how well our classifier does relative to class-frequency-weighted random guessing. A statistic of 0.5 or higher is generally pretty good.

The AutoML Classify function did pretty well:

In[∘]:= **cmo [{ "Accuracy", "CohenKappa", "ConfusionMatrixPlot" }]**

Out[∘]:= $\left\{0.802752, 0.583933,\right.$ 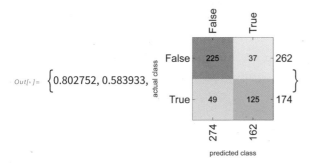 $\left.\right\}$

Alternative Machine Learning Forms

The Wolfram Language machine learning functions accept data in various forms; sometimes one form works better than another. Here is an example in which the data takes the form of a Rule in which the left-hand side is the values of the features used for classification and the right-hand side is the targets. I unwrap each of the resulting Datasets by Mapping Normal, and I then postfix Terse to keep the output short.

Write a function that uses two queries to transform the Dataset into a Rule in which the left-hand side is a List of Lists containing the features and the right-hand side is a List of targets:

In[∘]:= **mlDataAsRule [ds_Dataset , targetColumn_] :=**
   Map [Normal, Query [All, KeyDrop [targetColumn] / * Values] [ds] →
      Query [All, KeyTake [targetColumn] / * Values / * First] [ds]]

Apply that function to the training data in the Titanic Dataset:

In[∘]:= **(classifierInput2 = mlDataAsRule [titanicDS [trainingIndices] , "survived"]) / /**
   Map [[∘] Terse + [3]]

Out[∘]:= { { 1st, 35, female } , { 1st, 24, male } , { 3rd, 28, male } ,
      { 1st, 19, female } , { 3rd, Missing [ ] , male } , ≪864≫, { 3rd, 34, male } ,
      { 3rd, 30, male } , { 2nd, 22, female } , { 3rd, 45, female } } →
   { True, False, False, True, False, False, True, True, True, True, False, True,
      False, True, True, False, True, ≪839≫, True, False, False, False, False,
      False, False, False, True, False, False, False, False, False, True, True, False }

I can check that this works.

Classify succeeds on this form of input:

In[ ]:= **Classify [classifierInput2]**

Out[ ]= ClassifierFunction⎡ ➕ ⬛ Input type: {Nominal, Numerical, Nominal } ⎤
⎣ Classes: False, True ⎦

Neural networks, however, sometimes prefer an Association between columns and values. This is easy to do. Functions like NetTrain cannot presently deal readily with missing values, so I get rid of them. Then I Transpose the data and remove the resulting expression from its Dataset wrapper by applying Normal. Finally, to make the output easier to read, I Map the Terse ResourceFunction over each of the values in the resulting Association.

Use Transpose to transform the Dataset into a single column-oriented Dataset sometimes preferred for neural network training:

In[ ]:= **(trainingData =**
 Normal@Transpose [Query [trainingIndices / * (DeleteMissing [# , 1, 2] &)] [
 titanicDS]]) / / Map [[▪] Terse ▪ [5]]

Out[ ]= <| class → { 1st, 1st, 3rd, 1st, 3rd, 3rd, 1st, 3rd,
 3rd, 1st, ≪681≫, 3rd, 3rd, 2nd, 3rd, 2nd, 3rd, 3rd, 3rd, 2nd, 3rd },
 age → { 35, 24, 28, 19, 42, 25, 21, 29, 1, 4, 21, 35, 24, 26, 32, 15, 22, 32, 29, 35, 40,
 ≪659≫, 27, 16, 51, 38, 14, 20, 58, 26, 29, 27, 25, 33, 21, 36, 43, 36, 30, 34, 30, 22, 45 },
 sex → { female, male, male, female, male, male, male, female, ≪685≫,
 male, male, male, male, male, male, female, female },
 survived → { True, False, False, True, False, True, True, True, False, True, True,
 ≪679≫, False, False, True, False, False, False, False, False, True, True, False } |>

Now, here's the code I need to generate and train the neural network. It's from the tutorial on neural networks in the official Wolfram Language documentation. You don't need to understand it; you should just verify that our data transformation has succeeded.

I first set up the encoders and training architectures needed for training.

Create the encoders, classEncoder and genderEncoder, and the neural network architecture needed to train a survival model for the Titanic:

In[ ]:= **classEncoder = NetEncoder [{ "Class", { "1st", "2nd", "3rd" }, "UnitVector" }];**
 genderEncoder = NetEncoder [{ "Class", { "male", "female" }, "UnitVector" }];

In[•]:= (net = NetGraph [{ CatenateLayer [ ] , LinearLayer [ ] , LogisticSigmoid } ,
          { { NetPort ["class"] , NetPort ["age"] , NetPort ["sex"] } → 1 ,
          1 → 2 → 3 → NetPort ["survived"] } , "class" → classEncoder ,
          "age" → "Scalar" , "sex" → genderEncoder , "survived" → "Boolean"]) / /
       ((Information [♯ , "SummaryGraphic"] &) / ∗ Framed)

Out[•]=

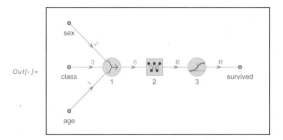

Now I train. It just takes about five hundred rounds for everything to stabilize.

Train a simple neural network to predict survival on the Titanic:

In[•]:= results = NetTrain [net, trainingData, All, MaxTrainingRounds → 500]
       trained = results ["TrainedNet"]

Out[•]= NetTrainResultsObject[
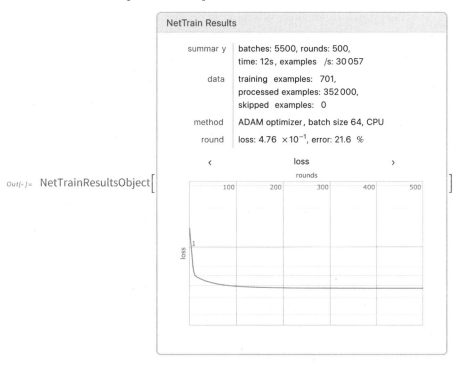
]

Out[•]= NetGraph[
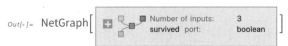
]

Success!

We then see what this trained neural network predicts for any particular group of people.

Use **trained** on two people by creating an **Association** in which the keys are the features used by the neural nets and the values are listed for each person:

In[•]:= **trained [**
   <| "age" → { 37, 64 } , "sex" → { "female", "male" } , "class" → { "2nd", "1st" } |>]

Out[•]= { True, False }

In[•]:= **trained [<| "age" → { 37, 64 } , "sex" → { "female", "male" } ,**
   "class" → { "2nd", "1st" } |> , "Probabilities"]

Out[•]= { 0.618457, 0.222115 }

I can use **NetMeasurements** to assess the performance of the trained neural net on the test data. The first argument is a neural network, the second argument is the test data in the same form as the training data, and the third argument is a list of measurements.

Use **Transpose** to put the data in the same form used in training the neural network:

In[•]:= **(testData =**
   Normal@Transpose [Query [testingIndices / * (DeleteMissing [#, 1, 2] &)] [
   titanicDS]]) / / Map [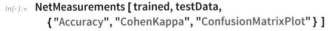 **Terse [2]]**

Out[•]= <| class → { 1st, 3rd, 3rd, 1st, 3rd, 2nd, 2nd, 2nd,
   3rd, 3rd, «325», 2nd, 3rd, 2nd, 3rd, 2nd, 1st, 2nd, 1st, 1st, 2nd },
   age → { 16, 40, 32, 61, 9, 18, 42, 21, 5, 19, 1, 27, 40, 41, 31, 26, 32, 21, 33, 14, 18,
   «303», 36, 80, 27, 18, 31, 21, 28, 17, 42, 47, 52, 23, 27, 28, 21, 30, 19, 42, 29, 21, 54 },
   sex → { female, male, male, male, male, male, male, male, «329»,
   male, male, male, female, female, male, male, male },
   survived → { True, False, True, False, False, False, False, False, True, False, True,
   «323», True, False, True, False, False, False, True, True, False, False, False } |>

Use **NetMeasurements** to see how the trained network performs on **testData**; the third argument sets forth a **List** of desired performance statistics:

In[•]:= **NetMeasurements [trained, testData,**
   { "Accuracy", "CohenKappa", "ConfusionMatrixPlot" }]

Out[•]= { 0.817391, 0.617133, 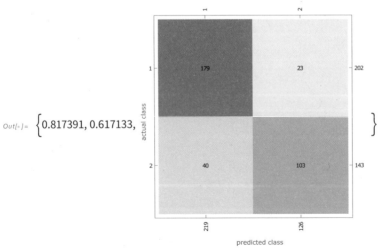 }

With just a little bit of extra coding I can also borrow all the functionality from ClassifierMeasurements. All I have to do is wrap our trained classifier in Classify (which creates a ClassifierFunction) and designate data paired with the "survived" key as providing the correct classification.

Use Classify to convert a properly structured and trained neural network to a ClassifierFunction:

In[ ]:= **trainedAsClassifier = Classify [trained]**

Out[ ]= ClassifierFunction[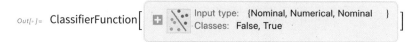]

In[ ]:= **cmoFromNet = ClassifierMeasurements [trainedAsClassifier, testData → "survived"]**

Out[ ]=

Classifier Measurements

Classifier method	Net
Number of test examples	345
Accuracy	$(81.7 \pm 2.1)\%$
Accuracy baseline	$(58.6 \pm 2.7)\%$
Geometric mean of probabilities	0.600 ± 0.010
Mean cross entropy	0.511 ± 0.017
Single evaluation time	4.72 ms /example
Batch evaluation speed	30.4 examples /ms

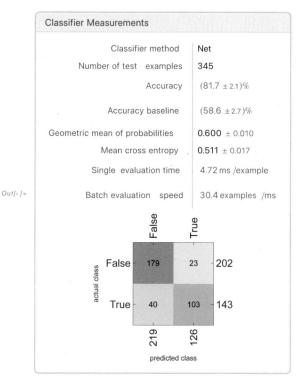

I can then derive the same statistics about our classifier as if I had developed it using the AutoML capabilities provided by Classify itself.

Take a ClassifierMeasurementsObject and feed it a List of performance measures:

In[ ]:= **cmoFromNet [{ "Accuracy", "CohenKappa", "ConfusionMatrixPlot" }]**

Out[ ]= $\left\{ 0.817391, 0.617133, \right.$ 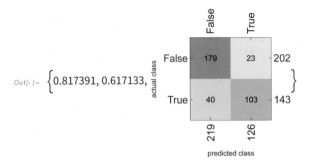 $\left. \right\}$

Recipe 9: Combine Graphics with Query

I can also generate useful visualizations using the programming techniques described in this book. Suppose I want to make a "violin plot" (or DistributionChart, as it is known in the Wolfram Language) of the ages of the passengers on the lifeboat broken down by their cabin class. The recipe is a little different than that described for getting aggregate measures by group. Instead of the aggregation function being some sort of statistical computation, it is a visualization.

Use a visualization function in conjunction with GroupBy to compare characteristics of groups of data:

In[ ]:= **Query [GroupBy [#class &] , DistributionChart, #age &] [lifeboatDS]**

Out[ ]=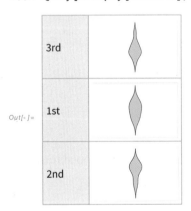

Recall from the discussion in Chapter 5 that if one wants a more fully decorated plot, one can use ItemDisplayFunction → (# &). Doing so will preserve whatever custom display options one added to the code that generates the plot. Here I add a plot label and axes that are displayed inside the Dataset.

Use options to create decorated DistributionCharts; apply FormatDataset with an ItemDisplayFunction to prevent simplified presentation of the graphics:

In[ ]:= **Query [GroupBy [♯class &],**
    DistributionChart [♯, PlotLabel → "age distribution", Axes → True] &, ♯age &] [
    lifeboatDS] // ▣ FormatDataset ₊ [ItemDisplayFunction → (♯ &)]

Out[ ]=

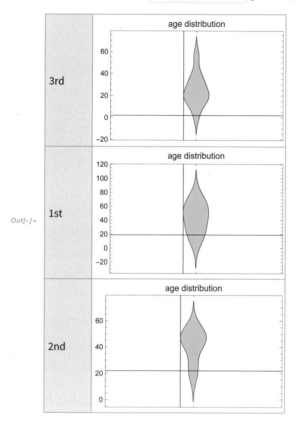

Or, if one wants to avoid the Query framework, one can just use GroupBy directly. I won't show it here, but one can use the same programming techniques as before to create and preserve graphic decorations.

Make the second argument of GroupBy a Rule going from a grouping function on the left-hand side to an extracting function on the right-hand side then aggregate the extracted data using a third argument:

In[∘]:= **GroupBy [lifeboatDS, (⌗class &) → (⌗age &) , DistributionChart]**

Out[∘]=

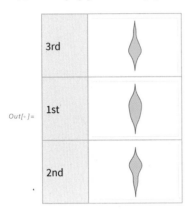

I can use MapReduceOperator to do the same thing. I wrap my operator in Query out of habit, but here there is no real need to do so.

Use the MapReduceOperator paradigm with a visualization "aggregator" function to see different features of groups of data:

In[∘]:= **Query [([▪] MapReduceOperator ↓) [(⌗class &) → (⌗age &) , DistributionChart]] [lifeboatDS]**

Out[∘]=

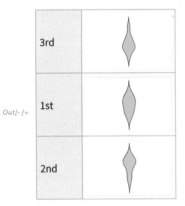

Notice that if one leaves the depictions wrapped in Dataset, the graphics are fairly basic even if one deliberately adds complications (although PlotLabel → "Age Distribution by Cabin Class" does work).

I just generated three graphics, one for each cabin class. One might also want, however, a single graphic that displays the distribution of ages for all three passenger classes. Here's the recipe. Note that this function will be at the end of our processing pipeline.

First create a function named legendedMultipleChartFunction that takes an association in which the keys are cabin classes and the values are ages:

```
In[ ]:= legendedMultipleChartFunction = DistributionChart [ ⌗ ,
            ChartLegends → Automatic, PlotLabel → "Age Distribution by Cabin Class",
            ChartStyle → Map [ GrayLevel, { 0, 0.3, 0.6 } ] ] &;
```

I then use a more complex GroupBy operator in which I group by class but only produce the ages, then sort the classes to coerce them to go in order from first to second to third, and then take the resulting association and apply legendedMultipleChartFunction to it. There's no need to wrap this up in Query because everything operates at the top level.

Use RightComposition (/ *) to group with a visualization function to see a composite visualization of the data:

```
In[ ]:= ( GroupBy [ (⌗class &) → (⌗age &) ] / * KeyTake [ { "1st", "2nd", "3rd" } ] / *
            legendedMultipleChartFunction ) [ lifeboatDS ]
```

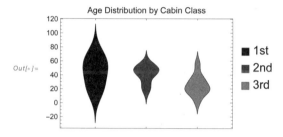

Here's another example. Let's take the entire Titanic Dataset and plot the probability of survival as a function of "sex". I'll use the ResourceFunction Proportions in order to do this. Here's how it works.

Proportions returns the proportion of times that each distinct element appears in a list:

```
In[ ]:= [▪] Proportions + [ { "c", "a", "b", "a", "a", "b", "b", "c", "c", "b" } ]
```

$$Out[ ]= \left\langle \left| c \to \frac{3}{10}, a \to \frac{3}{10}, b \to \frac{2}{5} \right| \right\rangle$$

I'm also going to make use of a custom plotting function: myBarChart. It's a type of BarChart. I'm naming it and putting it in a separate cell for pedagogic purposes; in the real world, I'd probably declare it as a local variable using With or simply make it an anonymous function.

I will use myBarChart later in my Query:

```
In[ ]:= myBarChart = ( BarChart [ ⌗ , PlotLabel → "Probability of Survival on the Titanic",
            ChartStyle → { Red, Blue }, ChartLegends → Automatic ] & ) ;
```

Notice that I wrap the values in the "survived" column in a string to make them easier to work with as Association keys. Also notice the use of RightComposition in the combiner function. First I get the proportions, then, with the # True & anonymous function, I get the number of survivors. I then stick it all in one legended plot.

Use the MapReduceOperator paradigm and the Proportions ResourceFunction chained with an anonymous function to get a single graphic showing the probability of survival broken down by sex:

In[•]:= **Query [** [•] **MapReduceOperator** ₊ **[(#sex &)** → **(ToString [#survived] &) ,**
  [•] **Proportions** ₊ **/ * (#True &)] / * myBarChart] [titanicDS]**

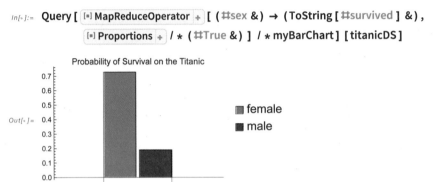

I can take this code and go further. Now I want to break down survival by both cabin class *and* gender. Essentially, all I do is push the arguments to Query from the prior code down one level and insert a GroupBy [# class &] . I also insert KeySort before BarChart so that the ordering of "male" and "female" data is consistent. I postfix Normal to the output because the resulting Dataset object unfortunately balks at displaying the Graphics object and instead uses an elided form.

Insert GroupBy as the first argument in a Query that breaks down survival first by class and then produces a visualization of survival by sex:

In[•]:= **Query [GroupBy [#class &] ,**
  [•] **MapReduceOperator** ₊ **[(#sex &)** → **(ToString [#survived] &) ,**
   [•] **Proportions** ₊ **/ * (#True &)] / ***
  KeySort / * myBarChart] [titanicDS] / / Normal

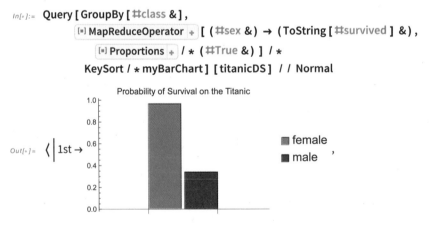

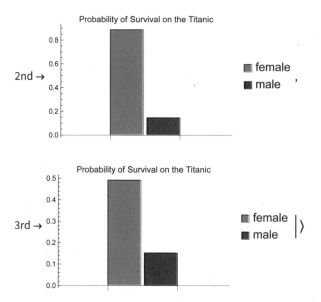

I can also create a single plot comparing survival by cabin class and gender. Just to show how it's done, I use ChartLabels instead of ChartLegends and use an indexed ColorData function to color the bars.

Use GroupBy to place data in a form for a BarChart comparing survival by cabin class and sex:

```
In[*]:=   ( GroupBy [ titanicDS, ♯class &, GroupBy [ ♯ , (♯sex &) → (♯survived &),
             [*] Proportions + / * (♯ [ True ] &) ] &] ) / / KeySort / /
          ( BarChart [ ♯ , PlotLabel → "Probability of Survival on the Titanic",
             ChartStyle → ColorData [ 63 ] , ChartLabels → Automatic ] & )
```

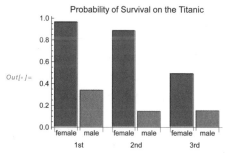

Recipe 10: Retrieve Information from the Wolfram Data Repository

Suppose, for example, I want to do some geospatial analysis of American Indian reservations in the United States. I might see if there is any information in the Wolfram Data Repository. To do this, I use ResourceSearch. I want to be careful with my arguments. If I use just "Indian," I might get stuff relating to the nation of India. If I use "Large Indian Reservations," that might be too specific and lead the search engine to miss information on American Indian reservations generally.

Use ResourceSearch to obtain a dataset about information from the Wolfram Data Repository regarding "Indian Reservations":

In[ ]:=   **reservationResources = ResourceSearch ["Indian Reservations"]**

Name	ResourceType	ResourceObject	Description
Indian Reservations	DataResource	ResourceObject["Indian Reservations"]	This dataset represe

Out[ ]=

By default, ResourceSearch returns a Dataset, which is great because we now know how to use them. As of September 2022, the Dataset reservationResources has just one element. I can now find out what properties the associated ResourceObject possesses.

Use Query to obtain information on the ResourceObjects found by the search:

In[ ]:=   **reservationsProperties =**
         Normal [Query [1, ⌗ResourceObject ["Properties"] &] [reservationResources]]

Out[ ]=   { AllVersions, AutoUpdate, Categories, ContentElementLocations, ContentElements,
         ContentSize, ContentTypes, ContributedBy, ContributorInformation,
         DatedElementVersions, DefaultContentElement, Description, Details,
         Documentation, DocumentationLink, DOI, DownloadedVersion, ExampleNotebook,
         ExampleNotebookObject, Format, InformationElements, Keywords,
         LatestUpdate, Name, Originator, Properties, PublisherID, PublisherUUID,
         RelatedSymbols, ReleaseDate, RepositoryLocation, ResourceLocations,
         ResourceType, SeeAlso, ShortName, SourceMetadata, Title, UUID, Version,
         VersionInformation, VersionsAvailable, WolframLanguageVersionRequired }

I now know I can directly ask for the "ContentElements".

Use Query to obtain the "ContentElements" of a particular ResourceObject found earlier:

In[ ]:=   **reservationsContentElements = Normal [**
            Query [1, ⌗ResourceObject ["ContentElements"] &] [reservationResources]]

Out[ ]=   { ColumnDescriptions, ColumnNames, Dataset }

I see that one of the "ContentElements" is Dataset. I'll grab it using the ResourceData.

Extract the "Dataset" content element from the ResourceObject with information on American Indian reservations:

In[ ]:= **reservationsDS =**
Query [1, ResourceData [#ResourceObject , "Dataset"] &] [reservationResources]

Out[ ]=

Name	AreaDescription	ComponentType
Coos, Lower Umpqua, and Siuslaw	Reservation	Reservation or Statistical Entity
Shoalwater Bay	Indian Reservation	Reservation or Statistical Entity
Redwood Valley	Rancheria	Reservation or Statistical Entity
Sherwood Valley	Rancheria	Reservation or Statistical Entity
Laytonville	Rancheria	Reservation or Statistical Entity
Manchester–Point Arena	Rancheria	Reservation or Statistical Entity
Robinson	Rancheria	Reservation or Statistical Entity
Big Lagoon	Rancheria	Reservation or Statistical Entity

rows 1–8 of 827   columns 1–10 of 11

I can also take a sample entry to see all the columns of information:

In[ ]:= **reservationsDS [1]**

Out[ ]=

Name	Coos, Lower Umpqua, and Siuslaw
AreaDescription	Reservation
ComponentType	Reservation or Statistical Entity
RecognitionFlag	Federally
FunctionalStatus	IR/ORTL
Land	$82\,966\ m^2$
Water	$2912\ m^2$
Length	$0.022285\ m$
Area	$9.\times 10^{-6}\ m^2$
GeoLocation	42.81°N 124.4°W
Polygon	$\{\cdots_4\}$

Now I'm free to do whatever I want with the data. I choose to generate a map showing me driving directions from a location in Denver, Colorado, to the center of the nearest reservation.

Use GeoNearest and TravelDirections inside Query to route me from Denver to the nearest American Indian reservation:

In[•]:= **denver = GeoPosition [{ 39.7618, −104.881 }] ;**
Query [(GeoNearest [♯ , denver] &) / ∗ First / ∗
(TravelDirections [{ denver, ♯ }] &) / ∗ (GeoGraphics [{ Red, Thick,
♯ ["TravelPath"] }] &) , ♯GeoLocation &] [Normal@reservationsDS]

Out[•]=

Or I could make a map of American Indian reservations occupying more than 2500 square miles that are within a designated geographic region.

Pipeline Select, visualization functions, and functions that construct geographic primitives to map and label large American Indian reservations within a geographic region:

```
In[•]:= Module [ { reservations, geoDisplay, bigReservations, geoPrimitivesFunction },
    reservations = indiansDataResources [ "ResourceObject" ] ;
    geoDisplay = (Framed [ GeoGraphics [ { Purple, ♯ }, ImageSize → 500,
            GeoRange → { { 32.5, 37.5 }, { −101, −94 } }, ImageSize → 400 ] ] &) ;
    bigReservations = ( ♯Land > Quantity [ 2500, "Miles"² ] &) ;
    geoPrimitivesFunction =
        { ♯Polygon, Text [ Style [ ♯Name, 10, FontColor → Blue ], ♯GeoLocation ] } &;
    Query [ Select [ bigReservations ] /* geoDisplay, geoPrimitivesFunction ] [
        reservationsDS ]
]
```

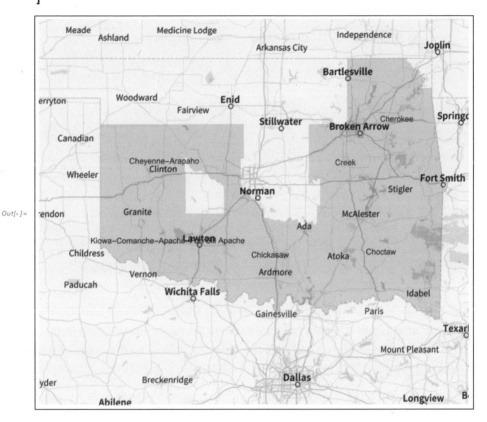

Recipe 11: Flatten Hierarchy in a Dataset or Convert One Dataset into Multiple Related Datasets

The planets Dataset provided with the Wolfram Language is a deeply nested data structure. That is, it's content is an Association whose rows are Associations, some of whose values are themselves Associations.

Load in a hierarchical Dataset on the planets and their moons:

In[ ]:= **planets = ResourceData [ro, "Planets Deeply Nested Structure Dataset"]**

Out[ ]=

		Mass	Radius	Moons		
					Mass	Radius
	Mercury	3.30104×10^{23} kg	2439.7 km			
	Venus	4.86732×10^{24} kg	6051.9 km			
	Earth	5.9721986×10^{24} kg	6367.4447 km	Moon	7.3459×10^{22} kg	1737.5 km
	Mars	6.41693×10^{23} kg	3386. km	Phobos	1.072×10^{16} kg	11.1 km
				Deimos	1.5×10^{15} kg	6.2 km
	Jupiter	1.89813×10^{27} kg	69173. km	Metis	$1. \times 10^{17}$ kg	21.5 km
				Adrastea	$7. \times 10^{15}$ kg	8.2 km
				63 total ›		
	Saturn	5.68319×10^{26} kg	57316. km	Tarqeq	—	3.5 km
				Pan	4.9×10^{15} kg	12.8 km
				61 total ›		
	Uranus	8.68103×10^{25} kg	25266. km	Cordelia	4.5×10^{16} kg	20.1 km
				Ophelia	5.4×10^{16} kg	21.4 km
				27 total ›		
	Neptune	1.02410×10^{26} kg	24553. km	Naiad	1.9×10^{17} kg	33. km
				Thalassa	3.7×10^{17} kg	41. km
				13 total ›		

What we might prefer, however, are two Datasets, the first of which has data on the planets and the second of which has data on the moons but that also tells us the planet that each moon orbits. Here's one way to create this "relational database." I won't pretend that it's easy. Perhaps a reader of this book will come up with a better method!

First, let's get rid of the moon information and then use the technique previously described to turn the keys for each row into the value for a column named "PlanetName".

Transform the planets Dataset into one in which the planet names are columns and there is no moon information:

In[◦]:= **planetTable = Query [KeyValueMap [Association ["PlanetName" → #1 , #2] &] , KeyDrop ["Moons"]] [planets]**

Out[◦]=

PlanetName	Mass	Radius
Mercury	3.30104×10^{23} kg	2439.7 km
Venus	4.86732×10^{24} kg	6051.9 km
Earth	5.9721986×10^{24} kg	6367.4447 km
Mars	6.41693×10^{23} kg	3386. km
Jupiter	1.89813×10^{27} kg	69 173. km
Saturn	5.68319×10^{26} kg	57 316. km
Uranus	8.68103×10^{25} kg	25 266. km
Neptune	1.02410×10^{26} kg	24 553. km

Now that I have a Dataset containing just planet information, I want to get a Dataset containing just moon information with a link to the associated planet. Here's a picture of what I am hoping to produce.

PlanetName	Moon	Mass	Radius
Earth	Moon	7.3459×10^{22} kg	1737.5 km
Mars	Phobos	1.072×10^{16} kg	11.1 km
Mars	Deimos	1.5×10^{15} kg	6.2 km
Jupiter	Metis	$1. \times 10^{17}$ kg	21.5 km
Jupiter	Adrastea	$7. \times 10^{15}$ kg	8.2 km
Jupiter	Amalthea	2.07×10^{18} kg	83.45 km
Jupiter	Thebe	1.5×10^{18} kg	49.3 km
Jupiter	Io	8.9298×10^{22} kg	1821.6 km

rows 1–8 of **167**

I want the name of the moon to be a value in a column, not a key, but I also want the planet name to be a column and not a key. So here's what needs to happen. First, I need a function that extracts the moons. Then, just as I showed previously, I need to transform each key that identifies the moons into the value of a column named "Moon".

Use KeyValueMap to perform this transformation, just as discussed in an earlier recipe:

In[◦]:= **insertMoonNameColumn =
"Moons" /* KeyValueMap [{ k , v } ⟼ Association ["Moon" → k , v]];**

To turn the planet name into a column entry for each moon, I have to use much the same technique, but because many planets have a List of moons and not just a single moon, the function KeyValueMap is itself mapped over the moons. Finally, I need to Flatten the result because, otherwise, I would end up with a List of Lists of Associations as the data rather than the desired List of Associations.

Use RightComposition and Flatten to achieve the List of Associations:

In[•]:=   **insertPlanetNameColumn = KeyValueMap [**
          { k , v } ⟼ Map [Association ["PlanetName" → k , #] & , v]] / ∗ Flatten;

Now let's put the Query together; look at it in Normal form and make sure the order of operations is correct:

In[•]:=   **Query [insertPlanetNameColumn, insertMoonNameColumn]   / / Normal**

Out[•]=   Map [GeneralUtilities ` Slice [Moons] / ∗
          KeyValueMap [Function [{ k, v }, Association [Moon → k, v]]]] / ∗
          KeyValueMap [Function [{ k, v }, (Association [PlanetName → k, #1] &) / @v]] / ∗ Flatten

Looks good! First grab the moons, then stick the moon name in, then Map the planet name insertion operation over all of the moons, and finally Flatten it all down. No more complicated than making a soufflé.

Create a Dataset that relates a planet to moons and provides data on each moon:

In[•]:=   **moonTable = Query [insertPlanetNameColumn, insertMoonNameColumn] [planets]**

Out[•]=

PlanetName	Moon	Mass	Radius
Earth	Moon	7.3459×10^{22} kg	1737.5 km
Mars	Phobos	1.072×10^{16} kg	11.1 km
Mars	Deimos	1.5×10^{15} kg	6.2 km
Jupiter	Metis	$1. \times 10^{17}$ kg	21.5 km
Jupiter	Adrastea	$7. \times 10^{15}$ kg	8.2 km
Jupiter	Amalthea	2.07×10^{18} kg	83.45 km
Jupiter	Thebe	1.5×10^{18} kg	49.3 km
Jupiter	Io	8.9298×10^{22} kg	1821.6 km

rows 1–8 of **167**

I'm now in a position to create a single flat Dataset object. I just JoinAcross the planetTable and the moonTable using the "PlanetName" column to perform the link. But, before I do so, I need to rename the "Mass" and "Radius" columns in one of the Datasets to avoid duplicates. I'll use the KeyReplace ResourceFunction to do so.

Join the planet and moon datasets together and use KeyReplace to prevent unwanted Association override:

```
In[•]:=  moonDB = Dataset [ JoinAcross [ Normal @ planetTable,
            Normal @ Query [ All, [▪] KeyReplace ⊹ [ { "Mass" → "MoonMass",
              "Radius" → "MoonRadius" } ] ] [ moonTable ], "PlanetName" ] ]
```

Out[•]=

PlanetName	Mass	Radius	Moon	MoonMass	MoonRadius
Earth	5.9721986×10^{24} kg	6367.4447 km	Moon	7.3459×10^{22} kg	1737.5 km
Mars	6.41693×10^{23} kg	3386. km	Phobos	1.072×10^{16} kg	11.1 km
Mars	6.41693×10^{23} kg	3386. km	Deimos	1.5×10^{15} kg	6.2 km
Jupiter	1.89813×10^{27} kg	69173. km	Metis	$1. \times 10^{17}$ kg	21.5 km
Jupiter	1.89813×10^{27} kg	69173. km	Adrastea	$7. \times 10^{15}$ kg	8.2 km
Jupiter	1.89813×10^{27} kg	69173. km	Amalthea	2.07×10^{18} kg	83.45 km
Jupiter	1.89813×10^{27} kg	69173. km	Thebe	1.5×10^{18} kg	49.3 km
Jupiter	1.89813×10^{27} kg	69173. km	Io	8.9298×10^{22} kg	1821.6 km

⊼ ⋀ rows 1–8 of **167** ⋁ ⋊

I can now do fun things like sort the moons according to their (approximate) density and find which planets that they orbit. Notice that I've wrapped Query around the first argument to subordinate its precedence in the pipeline of operators created by Query. I can't sort the density column until I've created it. An alternative to a nested Query would be to have two separate Queries, the first computing the density and the second sorting by density.

Find the densest moons in the solar system:

$$In[•]:= \text{sphericalDensity} [\text{mass}\_, \text{radius}\_] := \frac{mass}{\frac{4}{3} \pi \, radius^3}$$

In[ ]:= **Query [Query [ReverseSortBy [#Density &]] ,**
(Association [KeyDrop [#, { "Mass", "Radius" }] ,
"Density" → sphericalDensity [#MoonMass, #MoonRadius]] &)] [moonDB]

Out[ ]=

PlanetName	Moon	MoonMass	MoonRadius	Density
Jupiter	Sponde	$1. \times 10^{13}$ kg	1.0 km	$4. \times 10^{12}$ kg/km^3
Jupiter	Pasithee	$1. \times 10^{13}$ kg	1.0 km	$4. \times 10^{12}$ kg/km^3
Jupiter	Orthosie	$1. \times 10^{13}$ kg	1.0 km	$4. \times 10^{12}$ kg/km^3
Jupiter	Kale	$1. \times 10^{13}$ kg	1.0 km	$4. \times 10^{12}$ kg/km^3
Jupiter	Euporie	$1. \times 10^{13}$ kg	1.0 km	$4. \times 10^{12}$ kg/km^3
Jupiter	Io	8.9298×10^{22} kg	1821.6 km	3.527×10^{12} kg/km^3
Earth	Moon	7.3459×10^{22} kg	1737.5 km	3.343×10^{12} kg/km^3
Jupiter	Adrastea	$7. \times 10^{15}$ kg	8.2 km	$3. \times 10^{12}$ kg/km^3

rows 1–8 of **167**

It looks like Jupiter has the densest moons although our own moon is fairly dense, too.

Recipe 12: Create Overlapping Sets of Data

I've shown in this book how to use GroupBy to separate data into non-overlapping subsets and then apply various functions to each of the groupings. But what if one wants overlapping subsets? Suppose, for example, returning to the Titanic Dataset, I want to know the survival rate by cabin class for males overall, males age 20 or over, and males age 40 or over. I could, of course, run three different Queries.

Use Table and multiple Queries to obtain information on overlapping rows in a Dataset:

In[ ]:= **Row [Table [Framed [Labeled [**
Query [Select [#sex === "male" && #age ≥ i &] /* GroupBy [#class &] ,
(Join [Association ["True" → 0, "False" → 0] , Counts [#]] &) /* KeySort,
ToString [#survived] &] [titanicDS] ,
StringTemplate ["males age `1` and over"] [i]]] , { i, { 0, 20, 40 } }]]

Out[ ]=

	False	True			False	True			False	True
1st	98	53		1st	94	47		1st	60	22
2nd	135	23		2nd	120	11		2nd	35	2
3rd	290	59		3rd	221	43		3rd	40	2
	males age 0 and over				males age 20 and over				males age 40 and over	

Here's another way. I could first get the positions of these three age groups in the Dataset in three Queries.

Create a list of positions in a Dataset, each of which will satisfy a particular criterion:

```
In[•]:= ( positions = Table [ Normal [ Query [
                Position [ a_Association /; a ["sex"] === "male" && a ["age"] > i] / *
                Map [ First ] ] [ titanicDS ] ], {i, 0, 40, 20 } ] ) / / Shallow
```

```
Out[•]//Shallow=  { {2, 4, 6, 8, 10, 11, 15, 17, 20, 21, ≪648≫ },
                {4, 6, 8, 10, 11, 15, 17, 20, 21, 23, ≪509≫ }, {6, 10, 11, 15, 31, 35, 39, 40, 46, 48, ≪139≫ } }
```

I could then use these indices in a Query that uses RightComposition with the positions creating a mapping (over each of the groupings created by Position) of the MapReduceOperator ResourceFunction. I will fully admit it's a bit byzantine, but it shows what can be done with some creativity and a good understanding of the operator pipeline produced by Query.

Create a single Dataset showing statistics on male survival broken down by overlapping age categories and cabin class; use the "Detailed" DatasetTheme for better visualization:

```
In[•]:= maleSurvivalByOverlappingAges =
        With [ { f1 = [•] MapReduceOperator + [ ( ♯class &) → ( ToString [ ♯survived ] &) ,
                Counts / * KeySort ],
            f2 = AssociationThread [ { "All", "Over 20", "Over 40" }, ♯ ] &},
            Query [ positions / * Map [ f1 ] / * f2 ] [ titanicDS ]
        ] / / [•] FormatDataset + [ DatasetTheme → { "Detailed" } ]
```

Out[•]=

	1st		2nd		3rd	
	False	True	False	True	False	True
All	98	53	135	23	290	59
Over 20	94	47	120	10	209	39
Over 40	58	21	32	2	34	2

Exercises

7.1 Take the Major League Soccer (MLS) data and compute for players on the 2017 Vancouver Whitecaps (VAN) what fraction of the total guaranteed compensation each player received. Present the information by adding a column labeled "Share" to the **Dataset** and then reverse sorting the resulting **Dataset** on that value. Round the value in that new column to the nearest 0.001. I don't want to see the columns "Club" and "Year" because these are constants for the selected players. Play with timings and try to program it in the most efficient and lucid way. Here's a picture of my result.

LastName	FirstName	Position	BaseSalary	GuaranteedCompensation	Share
Montero	Fredy	F	1.4×10^6	1.8×10^6	0.223
Laba	Matias	M	$725\,000.00	$885\,500.00	0.11
Shea	Brek	M–D	$625\,000.00	$670\,000.00	0.083
Reyna	Yordy	M–F	$440\,000.04	$533\,700.04	0.066
Techera	Cristian	M	$352\,000.00	$377\,000.00	0.047
Ousted	David	GK	$360\,000.00	$378\,933.33	0.047
Waston	Kendall	D	$350\,000.00	$368\,125.00	0.046
Tchani	Tony	M	$275\,000.00	$308\,333.33	0.038

rows 1–8 of **32**

7.2 Consider the MLS data for the years 2013 through 2017. Group that data by year and then by club and determine the median guaranteed compensation. Your result should look like this picture.

	2013	2014	2015	2016	2017
VAN	$83\,000.00	$99\,500.00	$112\,000.00	$121\,917.25	$135\,625.00
DAL	$85\,875.00	$97\,875.00	$130\,000.00	$130\,633.00	$152\,500.00
TOR	$71\,000.00	$92\,000.00	$125\,000.00	$119\,125.00	$133\,450.00
NE	$95\,354.17	$122\,375.00	$106\,458.34	$116\,666.67	$148\,333.33
NY	$79\,999.92	$115\,000.00	$92\,606.19	—	—
SJ	$94\,625.00	$130\,285.00	$100\,000.00	$114\,166.67	$175\,992.00
PHI	$82\,695.75	$102\,163.67	$121\,000.00	$138\,000.00	$135\,500.00
CHI	$119\,950.00	$82\,664.99	$102\,916.67	$112\,708.33	$135\,000.00

rows 1–8 of **27**

Hint 1: To get the rows that have a year after, say, 2015, I would write Select [# Year > Date Object [{ 2015 }] &] . Hint 2: To convert DateObject [{ 2015 }] to a string, I would write DateString [DateObject [{ 2015 }] , "Year"] . Hint 3: My code uses the ResourceFunction JoinRest. Hint 4: My code also uses AssociationThread and Range.

7.3 Retrieve the "Year" (as a number), the "Club", the "Position", and the numeric value of "GuaranteedCompensation" from all rows of the mlsDS Dataset. Take the result and keep only those rows in which none of the items have missing values. Then do a multivariate linear regression on the remaining data that best fits guaranteed compensation to "Year", "Club", and "Position". Treat "Club" and "Position" as nominal variables. Compute the adjusted R^2 of your result. You should get a value under 0.1 as your result. Hint 1: You will likely need to use Query twice in your code. Hint 2: DateValue [DateObject [{ 2014 }] , "Year"] returns the value 2014. Hint 3: QuantityMagnitude [192, "USDollars"] returns the value 192. Hint 4: If you have not performed linear regressions a lot in the Wolfram Language, look up the NominalVariables option in the documentation and find out how to extract properties such as "RSquared".

7.4 Get the Dataset from a resource in the Wolfram Data Repository on tornadoes in the United States. You should end up with something like this.

Location	Number	Date	StateNumber	Magnitude	Injurie
Missouri, United States	1	Sat 31 Dec 1949 03:11:00	1	F3	3
Missouri, United States	1	Sat 31 Dec 1949 03:11:00	1	F3	3
Illinois, United States	1	Sat 31 Dec 1949 03:11:10	1	F3	0
Illinois, United States	2	Sat 31 Dec 1949 03:11:55	2	F3	3
Ohio, United States	3	Sat 31 Dec 1949 03:16:00	1	F1	1
Arkansas, United States	4	Sat 31 Dec 1949 13:05:25	1	F3	1
Missouri, United States	5	Sat 31 Dec 1949 01:19:30	2	F2	5
Illinois, United States	6	Sat 31 Dec 1949 01:21:00	3	F2	0

rows 1–8 of **61 217**   columns 1–10 of **12**

7.5 You will notice that some of the tornado magnitudes are designated with an F number while others are designated with an EF number. The EF designation is more modern. Make a BarChart showing, for tornadoes with an EF magnitude, the mean number of injuries from tornadoes broken down by the magnitude of the tornado. Here's what my chart looks like. Hint 1: I use StringTake in my answer. Hint 2: I also use the function called twisterChart in the following code.

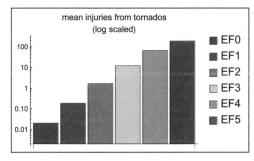

```
twisterChart [ a_Association ] :=
    Framed [ BarChart [ Values [ a ] , ChartLegends → Keys [ a ] ,
        ChartStyle → "DarkRainbow", ScalingFunctions → "Log10",
        PlotLabel → "mean injuries from tornados\n ( log scaled ) " ] ] ;
```

7.6 Create a graphic showing the trajectories for all tornadoes in the **Dataset** that killed at least five people. Do not consider tornadoes on which you do not have start and end information. I show a picture of my result here. Hint 1: My **Query** uses **GeoPath**. Hint 2: My **Query** uses **GeoGraphics**.

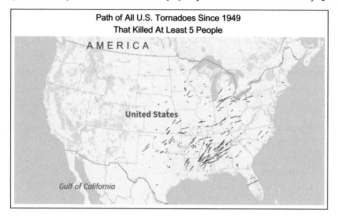

7.7 One last tornado exercise. Assume a tornado follows the shortest path between its start and end. Group the tornadoes with an EF magnitude according to their magnitude and produce histograms showing, for each grouping, the distribution of miles traveled. Hint 1: Make sure to use **UnitConvert** to convert all your distances to miles. Hint 2: Create a common horizontal scale by using something like **Histogram [♯, PlotRange → { {0, 150}, Automatic }]** & as your visualization function. Hint 3: I used **MapReduceOperator** to get the job done. Hint 4: You will need to put the result in **Normal** form. Hint 5: You should get rid of tornadoes where you don't know the start or end location. My answer looks something like this.

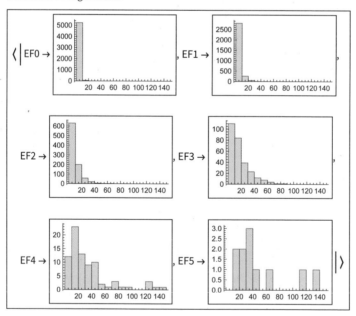

Tech Notes

- Prior to Version 13.3, the Wolfram Language's various statistics functions, such as **LinearModelFit**, required a data format that the later-built machine learning functions, such as **Classify** and **Predict**, did not accept. **LinearModelFit** and its cousins wanted the data in the form of an array in which the last column represented the dependent variable. By contrast, **Classify**, **Predict** and other supervised learning functions would not generally accept the data in that format. They accepted data in the form of $\{example_1 \rightarrow class_1, example_2 \rightarrow class_2, ...\}$ or $\{in_1, in_2, ...\} \rightarrow \{out_1, out_2, ...\}$. Version 13.3 created greater unification by augmenting the data formats that statistics functions like **LinearModelFit** will accept.

Here's an example. Suppose one has the following tiny dataset.

Create a dataset with four columns.

```
In[*]:= tiny = Dataset [ { Association [ "w" → 2, "x" → 3, "y" → 4, "z" → 5 ],
         Association [ "w" → 5, "x" → 2, "y" → 8, "z" → 7 ],
         Association [ "w" → 0, "x" → 1, "y" → 2, "z" → 4 ],
         Association [ "w" → -1, "x" → 3, "y" → 0, "z" → 2 ] } ]
```

Out[*]=

w	x	y	z
2	3	4	5
5	2	8	7
0	1	2	4
-1	3	0	2

In the past, if I wanted to first run a **LinearRegression** on z using x and y and then use **Predict** on the same data, I would need two different data manipulations.

Create two functions that represent the relationship between the features (independent variables) and target (dependent variable) in different ways.

```
In[*]:= arrayFunction = { #x, #y, #z } &;
         featuresToTargetFunction =  { #x, #y } → #z &;
```

Put the data in the form of an array in which the last column is the dependent variable and run a linear regression on it.

```
In[*]:= Query [ LinearModelFit [ #, {x, y}, {x, y} ] &, arrayFunction ] [ tiny ]
```

Out[*]= FittedModel[2.93617 - 0.223404 x + 0.590426 y]

Put the data in the form of a List of rules in which each left-hand side is a list of features and each right-hand side is a target; run a supervised machine learning algorithm on it.

```
In[*]:= Query [ Predict, featuresToTargetFunction ] [ tiny ]
```

Out[*]= PredictorFunction[[+] Input type: {Numerical, Numerical }
                                Method: LinearRegression]

As of Version 13.3, I can interchange statistics functions and machine learning functions and use the same data format.

Use the machine learning representation of data, even with statistics functions.

In[∘]:= **Map [f ⟼ Query [f , featuresToTargetFunction] [tiny] , { LinearModelFit, Predict }]**

Out[∘]= { LinearModelFit [{ {3, 4} → 5, {2, 8} → 7, {1, 2} → 4, {3, 0} → 2 }],

PredictorFunction [⊞ ☇ | Input type: {Numerical, Numerical }
Method: LinearRegression] }

- At various points in this chapter, I used **SeedRandom** before generating random values. In the real world of data analysis, I wouldn't do this as, in some sense, it lets me "rig" the results. I do so here only so that the book has replicable results, which is valuable for pedagogic purposes.

- Notice that in some of the code in the text dealing with aggregate measures, the columns with mean ages did not have headers; put another way, each row of the result was a List rather than an association with keys. This is because using the anonymous function ♯age& rather than KeyTake ["age"] as the extractor stripped off the keys. One can continue to use the ♯age& anonymous function and restore the keys by making the aggregator function—the one that operates on the aggregates produced by the extractor function (♯age&)—a function that itself produces an **Association**. Notice, however, that since **Mean** is now wrapped inside the **Association** that serves as the aggregator, missing values are no longer automatically deleted; one has to write code to explicitly delete them.

In[∘]:= **Query [GroupBy [♯sex &] ,**
  <| "mean age" → Mean [DeleteMissing [♯1]] |> &, ♯age &] [lifeboatDS]

Out[∘]=

	mean age
female	27.375
male	36.2222

- Alternatively, one could preserve the keys using **KeyTake** rather than an anonymous function as the extractor function, and then combine the List of Associations result using the Merge [Mean [Delete˙. Missing [♯]] &] operator as the aggregator function. Notice that if one proceeds this way, one does not have control over the column header. Because the Associations in the List that was fed into the Merge operator all had "age" as their single key, the output of the Merge operator likewise must also have "age" as its single key.

In[∘]:= **Query [GroupBy [♯sex &] ,**
  Merge [Mean [DeleteMissing [♯]] &] , KeyTake ["age"]] [lifeboatDS]

Out[∘]=

	age
female	27.375
male	36.2222

More to Explore

Though the users of this text are far more advanced, some good catch-up resources exist in sections 30–34 and 40 of *An Elementary Introduction to the Wolfram Language* (wolfr.am/eiwl)

The neural network tutorial referenced earlier in this chapter is found here (wolfr.am/NeuralNetworksGuide)

8 | Import and Export

This chapter uses a data resource from the Wolfram Data Repository (wolfr.am/WDR). To access the data, evaluate the following code.

Acquire the **ResourceObject** from the Wolfram Data Repository:

In[•]:= **ro = ResourceObject ["Sample Data for Query Book"]**

Out[•]= ResourceObject[⊞ 🏛 Name: Sample Data for Query Book »
Type: DataResource
Description: Data to support the Wolfram Media book Query:
Getting Information from Data wit...]

Use **SetOptions** to change the default value of rows displayed in a **Dataset**:

In[•]:= **SetOptions [Dataset, MaxItems → 8] ;**

Introduction

Thus far in this book, I've gotten the data out of the Wolfram Data Repository or the example data distributed with the Wolfram Language. This is great when such data is precisely what you hope to work on, but in the real world, such convenience is seldom the case. Generally, you want to work on "wild data" that either lives on your file system or somewhere on the internet. Accessing this information is of such obvious importance that you might question the deferral of this topic until this late in the book. You can read this book in any order you choose, of course, but I have chosen to place it later because it helps to have a working knowledge of the transformation techniques described in the preceding chapters before attempting to tackle wild data.

The main goal of this chapter is to expose the most important export and import formats you are likely to see as a data scientist. This skill will let you collaborate with colleagues who may be using different systems and will let you piggyback on others' efforts to collect and clean data. Now, as of Version 13.3, there are 242 file formats that the Wolfram Language knows how to capture, so I obviously can't cover all of them. Instead, after a brief introduction to the concept of format and "Elements",

I focus on the six formats I suspect most data scientists using the Wolfram Language will encounter, WXF, Text, CSV, Excel (XLS, XLSX), JSON and ZIP. I conclude the chapter with a brief look at how to get data out of a Google Sheet by asking it to create the equivalent of an Excel spreadsheet or CSV file. The skills learned in importing and exporting information from and to these formats should transfer to other formats you may want to use.

I use internal data in this chapter because there's a tricky issue of showing wild data in a static book. The internet is an ever changing place, and were I to provide you with a URL, the content might not be there when you read this book. I also don't want to clutter up this book with file names that are specific to my computer. I will therefore periodically use ExportString to show you exactly what happens when I export this data to a file. When I do so, I will then sometimes use ImportString to get the information back into the Wolfram Language kernel in a form requested. Other times, I will export from the kernel to a temporary file created by using the Wolfram Language function CreateFile. When I do so, I will bring it back into the kernel with the Import function. By doing it this way I can: (1) make very clear exactly what is going on (there are a number of subtleties); (2) avoid the need to rely on internet resources that may change over time and make the lessons learned here non-replicable; and (3) avoid dependency on the precise content of my own local storage system (and preserve a little privacy).

The "Format" and "Elements" Concept

Before addressing specific formats in which you can import or export data, it's also important to explain a vital concept: "Elements". When you import or export in the Wolfram Language, you usually have choices about what precisely is to be imported or exported, the "Format" in which it is to be imported or exported, and the "Elements" that are to be imported or exported. Let's take an example.

Suppose I want to export this expression:

In[•]:= **testExpression = { { 1, 2, 3 }, { 4, 5, 6 } };**

If I ExportString it with the "CSV" format, I get this:

In[•]:= **(exportedTestExpresssion = ExportString [testExpression, "CSV"]) / /**
    [•] ShowQuotes +

Out[•]= **"1,2,3\n4,5,6\n"**

A few code notes before proceeding. As its name suggests, ExportString creates a string. Its first argument is the Wolfram Language expression one seeks to convert to a string. The second argument is the format in which the string is to be constructed. The ResourceFunction ShowQuotes is a bit like InputForm in that it shows quotation marks around strings.

I can change the export format and see the results of ExportString change dramatically. If, for example, I ExportString the same expression with the popular JSON format, I get the following.

Export an expression to JSON with ExportString and use ShowQuotes:

In[•]:= **ExportString [testExpression, "JSON"] / / [•] ShowQuotes +**

Out[•]= " [\n\t [\n\t\t1,\n\t\t2,\n\t\t3\n\t] ,\n\t [\n\t\t4,\n\t\t5,\n\t\t6\n\t] \n] "

The results are very different, so the format of the export matters.

The same dependence on format exists for Import operations too. The following code shows, for example, that when I import the identical string first as "Text" and then as "CSV", the kernel holds, respectively, a single string or a List of Lists.

Create a file that holds a List of Lists (testExpression) exported in "CSV" format; if you want a purely temporary file, use CreateFile [ ] instead of an actual file name:

In[•]:= **testCSVFile = Export ["testcsvfile.csv", testExpression, "CSV"]**

Out[•]= testcsvfile.csv

Import a file exported as CSV using two different formats:

In[•]:= **{ Import [testCSVFile, "Text"] / / [•] ShowQuotes + ,**
      Import [testCSVFile, "CSV"] / / [•] ShowQuotes + }

Out[•]= { "1,2,3\n4,5,6", { { 1, 2, 3 }, { 4, 5, 6 } } }

This result should not shock persons with a good understanding of computer science. The same pattern of bits existing on my hard drive $(\{0, 1, 0, 0, 1, 0, 0, 0\})$ could be interpreted as either the integer 72 or as the letter H. It all depends on how I direct my computer to understand the matter.

The meaning of a string depends on how it is interpreted:

In[•]:= **{ ImportString ["H", "UnsignedInteger8"] , ImportString ["H", "Character8"] }**

Out[•]= { { 72 }, { H } }

Each combination of operation (Export, ExportString, Import, and ImportString) and format generally has its own "Elements" that provide additional control over these operations. To discover the "Elements" relative to an operation and a format, one adjusts the final argument to the operation. Instead of just writing the format, one creates a List in which the format is the first part and the word "Elements" is the second part. Here's an example where I try to find what "Elements" are available if I try to Import a file as CSV.

Discover the "Elements" available for Import when using a CSV format:

In[ ]:=   **Import [testCSVFile, { "CSV", "Elements" }]**

Out[ ]=   { Data, Dataset, Dimensions, Grid, MaxColumnCount, RawData, RowCount, Summary }

I now see that there are many things I can try to get out. Here, for example, I determine the number of rows in this file when imported as CSV.

Use the "RowCount" element to find out how many rows are in a CSV file:

In[ ]:=   **Import [testCSVFile, { "CSV", "RowCount" }]**

Out[ ]=   **2**

Here I import data using the "Text" format but as "Words". Now, instead of one single string, I get two strings, each corresponding to what the importer believes is the equivalent of a word.

Use the "Words" element to find out how many "words" the kernel interprets to be in a "Text" file:

In[ ]:=   **Import [testCSVFile, { "Text", "Words" }] / /** [▪] **ShowQuotes** +

Out[ ]=   { "1,2,3", "4,5,6" }

Each combination of transaction and format also has its default specification so that when I write Import [testStream, "CSV"], what I really mean is Import [testStream, { "CSV", "Data" }]. Mastery over format and element specifications can be crucial to effectively sending data to others or receiving data from them in the desired form.

Using the WXF Format

If you know that your data is going to be used by people using the Wolfram Language, the most straightforward export format is WXF, Wolfram exchange format. You can export virtually any Wolfram Language expression this way. To export to a file, use Export followed by the name of the file you want to hold the data, followed by the expression you want to export, followed by the format string "WXF". One virtue of this method is that the reimportation should work precisely the same regardless of what operating system is being used; this is not always the case with certain other formats. I'll show that method here, using ExportString rather than Export for the reasons described in the introductory material and postfixing the result with the ResourceFunction ShowQuotes so you can see what the string really looks like.

Use ResourceData with "Dinghy List of Associations" to extract the relevant data from the ResourceObject ro:

In[•]:= **dinghy = ResourceData [ro, "Dinghy List of Associations"]**

Out[•]= { <| class → 3rd, age → 16, sex → female, survived → True |>,
      <| class → 1st, age → 65, sex → male, survived → False |>,
      <| class → 3rd, age → 2, sex → female, survived → False |>,
      <| class → 3rd, age → Missing [ ] , sex → female, survived → True |>,
      <| class → 3rd, age → 18, sex → female, survived → False |> }

Export a List of Associations as a "WXF" file:

In[•]:= **(wxfString = ExportString [dinghy, "WXF"]) / / [•] ShowQuotes +**

Out[•]= "8:f sListA –SclassS3rd–SageC –SsexSfemale–SsurvivedsTrueA –SclassS1st–S
      ageCA–SsexSmale–SsurvivedsFalseA –SclassS3rd–SageC –SsexSfemale–S
      survivedsFalseA –SclassS3rd–SagefsMissing–SsexSfemale–SsurvivedsTrueA –S
      classS3rd–SageC –SsexSfemale–SsurvivedsFalse"

There can be a significant difference in file sizes, particularly with data, such as titanic, that has a lot of repeated keys and values. I can, therefore, add an option "PerformanceGoal" → "Size" that, in my experience, can yield significant compression advantages.

The "PerformanceGoal" option to WXF exports can significantly affect file size; again, if you want purely temporary files, use CreateFile [ ] instead of actual file names:

In[•]:= **dinghyExports = { Export ["file1.wxf", dinghy, "WXF"] ,**
      Export ["file2.wxf", dinghy, "WXF", "PerformanceGoal" → "Size"] }

Out[•]= { file1.wxf, file2.wxf }

In[•]:= **Map [FileSize, dinghyExports]**

Out[•]= { 290. B , 118. B }

Just so you feel confident that this all works, I'll reimport the files I have just exported and make sure they are exactly the same as the original dinghy.

The compression achieved by "PerformanceGoal"→"Size" is non-lossy:

In[•]:= **SameQ [Import [dinghyExports〚1〛, "WXF"] , Import [dinghyExports〚2〛, "WXF"] , dinghy]**

Out[•]= True

Using the Text Export Format

It is common for users to want to represent information as a string of characters. To do this, one would use the "Text" export format. Here, for example, I use ExportString with some text, postfixing as before with ShowQuotes.

Export dialogue from *Hamlet* as text:

In[ ]:= **(textString = ExportString ["To be or not to be", "Text"]) / /** [▪] **ShowQuotes** +

Out[ ]= "To be or not to be"

I can import it right back.

Import exported dialogue from *Hamlet*:

In[ ]:= **ImportString [textString, "Text"] / /** [▪] **ShowQuotes** +

Out[ ]= "To be or not to be"

I can export things as text that are not strings in the Wolfram Language.

You can export almost anything as "Text" with Export or ExportString:

In[ ]:= **ExportString [Sqrt [π] , "Text"]**

Out[ ]= Sqrt [Pi]

Importing as "Text" can be useful to see what is going on inside some other representation of data, such as HTML. Suppose, for example, that htmlString represented the contents of some website.

Assign verbatim HTML to a variable:

In[ ]:= **htmlString = "< ! DOCTYPE html>**
      <html>
      <body>

      <h1>My First Heading< / h1>

      <p>My first paragraph.< / p>

      < / body>
      < / html>";

I could export it to a file quite literally using the "Text" format and then import it as HTML using the Import command and the "HTML" format specifier. I'd get a reasonable looking output, but I wouldn't learn much about the internals of the HTML encoding.

Export a string of characters as "Text", even though it might well be a representation of an HTML file:

In[◦]:= **htmlFile = Export ["file.txt", htmlString, "Text"]**

Out[◦]= file.txt

Import an HTML file as HTML:

In[◦]:= **Import [htmlFile, "HTML"]**

Out[◦]= My First Heading
My first paragraph.

If, however, I imported the same information as "Text", I could see exactly what was going on. Sometimes, it's useful to import a file in a format that had not been intended by its creator.

Import an HTML file as "Text":

In[◦]:= **Import [htmlFile, "Text"]**

Out[◦]= < ! DOCTYPE html>
<html>
<body>

<h1>My First Heading< / h1>

<p>My first paragraph.< / p>

< / body>
< / html>

Other times, however, importing a file as "Text" that had been intended for other purposes is not the best idea. Here, for example, I choose to import a simulated file as "Text" that was likely created as a CSV file.

Create some text (csvTextString) that is formatted in the same way as CSV and **Import** it as "Text":

In[◦]:= **csvTextString =**
"\"class\", \"age\", \"sex\", \"survived\"\n\"3rd\", 16, \"female\", \"True\"\n\"1st\",
65, \"male\", \"False\"\n\"3rd\", 2, \"male\", \"False\"\n\"3rd\",
\"Missing [ ] \", \"female\", \"True\"\n\"3rd\", 18, \"female\", \"False\"\n";

In[◦]:= **ImportString [csvTextString, "Text"]**

Out[◦]= "class", "age", "sex", "survived"
"3rd", 16, "female", "True"
"1st", 65, "male", "False"
"3rd", 2, "male", "False"
"3rd", "Missing [ ] ", "female", "True"
"3rd", 18, "female", "False"

Because the information is still text, the structure of the information contained therein is obscure. This material is representing an array with five rows and four values with a header row. That's not only hard to see in the text representation, it's hard to get information out. If, for example, I wanted the value of the third row and second column, I might end up doing something ugly like first splitting the string by new line characters and then splitting each resulting line with commas. Moreover, I'd have to remember to take the header line into account when doing the final Part operation.

Extract information out of a CSV file imported as "Text":

```
In[•]:= Part [ Map [ StringSplit [ #, "," ] &, StringSplit [ csvTextString, "\n" ] ], 1 + 3, 2 ]

Out[•]= 2
```

To get information that consists of rows with elements separated by commas into the kernel in a more structured way, I need to import in a different way; perhaps, as shown in the next section, in CSV format.

Using the CSV Export Format

Perhaps the most common data format used today is CSV (comma-separated values). It's been around since the 1970s. Basically, it's a human-readable string in which elements are separated by commas and "rows" are separated by new line characters. It's not well suited to exporting general Wolfram Language expressions. It's best used for tabular data, such as arrays with numbers or strings in them, and although it can represent ragged arrays in which different lines have different numbers of elements, I would not recommend using it for that purpose.

Here's an example of a CSV export of a List of Lists. Again, so you can see it, I'll use the ExportString function on an expression created from the dinghy data structure. If you wanted to export to an actual file, you'd just preface the arguments given here with the name of the file. I'll again postfix with the ShowQuotes ResourceFunction so you can see what's inside.

Export a List of Lists as a CSV-format string:

```
In[•]:= ( dinghyValuesWithHeader = Prepend [ Query [ All, Values ] [ dinghy ],
              Normal [ Keys [ dinghy〚1〛 ] ] ] ) / / [•] ShowQuotes +

Out[•]= { { "class", "age", "sex", "survived" }, { "3rd", 16, "female", True },
          { "1st", 65, "male", False }, { "3rd", 2, "female", False },
          { "3rd", Missing [ ], "female", True }, { "3rd", 18, "female", False } }
```

Export a List of Lists as "CSV" and use ShowQuotes to show how elements end up being placed inside quotation marks:

In[•]:=   (csvString = ExportString [dinghyValuesWithHeader, "CSV"]) / / ⌊▪⌋ ShowQuotes +

Out[•]=   "\"class\", \"age\", \"sex\", \"survived\"\n\"3rd\", 16, \"female\", \"True\"\n\"1st\",
65, \"male\", \"False\"\n\"3rd\", 2, \"female\", \"False\"\n\"3rd\",
\"Missing [ ] \", \"female\", \"True\"\n\"3rd\", 18, \"female\", \"False\"\n"

Notice a few things. First, there are new line characters denoted by \n every time one starts a new row of the underlying expression. Second, expressions like True that are not Wolfram Language strings are represented as strings once exported. Third, the inner quotes are shown with a \". Also, it's perfectly fine to export via CSV data that has "types" that computer systems tend to treat differently, such as an integer, a string, a real number, or even a Wolfram Language expression. Although the Wolfram Language doesn't generally use the concept of a "Record" or a "Struct" or similar ideas used in other computer languages, the CSV format is able to accept these heterogeneous data containers.

Not only can each row in a CSV format have different types, but the columns can have different types as well. The second column of the expression just exported, for example, contains strings and a missing value.

Now let's turn to importing information contained in a CSV format. I first write csvString to a file.

Export a List of Lists as CSV:

In[•]:=   csvFile = Export ["dinghyfile.csv", dinghyValuesWithHeader, "CSV"]

Out[•]=   dinghyfile.csv

In[•]:=   FilePrint@csvFile

"class", "age", "sex", "survived"
"3rd", 16, "female", "True"
"1st", 65, "male", "False"
"3rd", 2, "female", "False"
"3rd", "Missing [ ] ", "female", "True"
"3rd", 18, "female", "False"

Here I try to get back csvString, telling the kernel that the information is formatted as "CSV". The result is mostly what I wanted, a List of Lists; the ExportString and Import·. String have made a round trip, returning mostly what I started with. The round trip is not perfect, however. Because Missing [ ] ends up being exported as "Missing [ ] ", it ends up being "Missing [ ] " rather than Missing [ ] when reimported. A failure to be aware of, this point can lead to trouble when the imported data structure is used. If preservation of data type is crucial, exporting in WXF format is better.

Import CSV-formatted information as "CSV":

In[ ]:= **csvImport = Import [csvFile, "CSV"]**

Out[ ]= { { class, age, sex, survived }, { 3rd, 16, female, True }, { 1st, 65, male, False },
{ 3rd, 2, female, False }, { 3rd, Missing [ ], female, True }, { 3rd, 18, female, False } }

Use **ShowQuotes** to show whether expressions are strings or not:

In[ ]:= **csvImport / /** [▪] **ShowQuotes** +

Out[ ]= { { "class", "age", "sex", "survived" }, { "3rd", 16, "female", "True" },
{ "1st", 65, "male", "False" }, { "3rd", 2, "female", "False" },
{ "3rd", "Missing [ ] ", "female", "True" }, { "3rd", 18, "female", "False" } }

Now it's easy to get back the third row and second column (assuming I remember about the header row).

It's often easier to extract information when you **Import** in the "native format" of the file:

In[ ]:= **csvImport⟦1 + 3, 2⟧**

Out[ ]= 2

There's a lot more that can be done when importing material from the CSV format. To begin with, sometimes CSV files are huge (think gigabytes), so one might want to get information on them before using up internet bandwidth. Alternatively, one can ask that the information be imported in a different form. Both of these tasks can be done by using a more complex second argument to **Import**. Here, for example, I engage in discovery, asking what forms of information about the CSV file are available. As noted in the introductory materials, one can use this { " *format* ", "Elements" } argument on other data formats too.

Find out what "Elements" are available to import from a CSV file:

In[ ]:= **csvImportElements = Import [csvFile, { "CSV", "Elements" }]**

Out[ ]= { Data, Dataset, Dimensions, Grid, MaxColumnCount, RawData, RowCount, Summary }

I use **AssociationMap** over all but the "Dataset", "RawData", and "Grid" elements to show what each of these elements looks like. I exclude those three elements at this time because, if the data were in fact to be gigabyte sized, attempting to import them might prove challenging.

Use AssociationMap to find out almost all elements available via Import for a CSV file:

In[ ]:= **AssociationMap [Import [csvFile, { "CSV", ⌗ }] &,**
DeleteCases [csvImportElements, "Dataset" | "RawData" | "Grid"]]

Out[ ]= ⟨ | Data → { {class, age, sex, survived}, {3rd, 16, female, True}, {1st, 65, male, False},

{3rd, 2, female, False}, {3rd, Missing [ ], female, True}, {3rd, 18, female, False} },
Dimensions → {6, 4}, MaxColumnCount → 4, RowCount → 6,

	Format	CSV
	RowCount	6
Summary →	MaxColumnCount	4
	FileName	dinghyfile.csv
	FileSize	165. B

| ⟩

Once you have successfully imported information that was in a CSV format, you have to figure out what to do with it. I've covered most of this earlier in the book, but some timely repetition and clarification might be appropriate. Here, for example, I transform the Wolfram Language expression obtained from an ImportString as CSV into a List of Associations on the assumption that the first row of the data represents a row header and the remainder consists of information. The idea is to get a common List of keys for each row of what will ultimately turn into a List of Associations. To do this, I use Map and AssociationThread to create key-value pairs in which the keys are consistent and the values are the elements of each of the remaining rows of the imported data.

Convert the CSV import into a List of Associations:

In[ ]:= **listOfAssociationsCSV = With [{ innerKeys = First [csvImport] },**
Map [AssociationThread [innerKeys, ⌗] &, Rest [csvImport]]
]

Out[ ]= { ⟨| class → 3rd, age → 16, sex → female, survived → True |⟩,
⟨| class → 1st, age → 65, sex → male, survived → False |⟩,
⟨| class → 3rd, age → 2, sex → female, survived → False |⟩,
⟨| class → 3rd, age → Missing [ ], sex → female, survived → True |⟩,
⟨| class → 3rd, age → 18, sex → female, survived → False |⟩ }

There's now also the really simple DatasetWithHeaders ResourceFunction that automates this process.

Use **DatasetWithHeaders** to take tabular data in which the first row is the column names and turn it into a **Dataset**:

In[ ]:=   [▪] **DatasetWithHeaders** + **[csvImport]**

Out[ ]=

class	age	sex	survived
3rd	16	female	True
1st	65	male	False
3rd	2	female	False
3rd	Missing[]	female	True
3rd	18	female	False

If I wanted row headers (outer keys), I could use one of the basic recipes from Chapter 7 and proceed as follows.

Convert the CSV import into an **Association** of Associations:

In[ ]:=   **associationOfAssociationsCSV =**
      [▪] **ValueMapIndexed** + **[ToString [#2 ⟦1⟧] &] [listOfAssociationsCSV]**

Out[ ]=   ⟨| 1 → ⟨| class → 3rd, age → 16, sex → female, survived → True |⟩,
      2 → ⟨| class → 1st, age → 65, sex → male, survived → False |⟩,
      3 → ⟨| class → 3rd, age → 2, sex → female, survived → False |⟩,
      4 → ⟨| class → 3rd, age → Missing [ ] , sex → female, survived → True |⟩,
      5 → ⟨| class → 3rd, age → 18, sex → female, survived → False |⟩ |⟩

Notice that I can wrap **Dataset** around either of these results.

Convert prior CSV imports into Datasets:

In[ ]:=   **Map [Dataset, { listOfAssociationsCSV, associationOfAssociationsCSV }]**

Out[ ]=

class	age	sex	survived
3rd	16	female	True
1st	65	male	False
3rd	2	female	False
3rd	Missing[]	female	True
3rd	18	female	False

	class	age	sex	survived
1	3rd	16	female	True
2	1st	65	male	False
3	3rd	2	female	False
4	3rd	Missing[]	female	True
5	3rd	18	female	False

There's yet another way to directly create a **Dataset** out of a CSV file: ask for it by modifying the second argument to "CSV". I'm going to do it imperfectly first so you understand the fix I make the second time.

Import the **Dataset** element of a CSV file:

In[•]:= **ImportString [csvString, { "CSV", "Dataset" }]**

Out[•]=

class	age	sex	survived
3rd	16	female	True
1st	65	male	False
3rd	2	female	False
3rd	Missing[]	female	True
3rd	18	female	False

Yes, I've returned a **Dataset** object, but it is treating the headers as just another row of information. That's not what I intended. To fix this, I use the **HeaderLines** option.

Import the **Dataset** element of a CSV file with a header line:

In[•]:= **datasetCSV = Import [csvFile, { "CSV", "Dataset" } , HeaderLines → 1]**

Out[•]=

class	age	sex	survived
3rd	16	female	True
1st	65	male	False
3rd	2	female	False
3rd	Missing[]	female	True
3rd	18	female	False

The ImportCSVToDataset ResourceFunction works very similarly to the code just described:

In[•]:= 　[▪] **ImportCSVToDataset** ＋ [**csvFile**]

Out[•]=

class	age	sex	survived
3rd	16	female	True
1st	65	male	False
3rd	2	female	False
3rd	Missing[]	female	True
3rd	18	female	False

Importing and Fixing Ragged Data

All of that went just fine, but people are often sloppy in generating CSV files. Here's a string representation of one, for example, where one of the rows has an extra element.

Export a ragged List of Lists as a CSV file:

In[•]:= **raggedCSVFile = Export ["raggedfile.csv",**
{ { "class", "age", "sex", "survived" }, { "3rd", 16, "female", True },
{ "1st", 65, "male", False }, { "3rd", 2, "male", False, "extra" },
{ "3rd", 47, "female", True }, { "3rd", 18, "female", False } }, "CSV"]

Out[•]= raggedfile.csv

I can Import it back without apparent difficulty.

Import a CSV file containing a ragged List of Lists:

In[•]:= **csvImportRagged = Import [raggedCSVFile, "CSV"]**

Out[•]= { { class, age, sex, survived }, { 3rd, 16, female, True }, { 1st, 65, male, False },
{ 3rd, 2, male, False, extra }, { 3rd, 47, female, True }, { 3rd, 18, female, False } }

It works, but if I now try to turn this into a List of Associations using the same code as before, I get an error.

A typical method of turning a List of Lists into a List of Associations does not succeed here:

In[•]:= **listOfAssociationsCSV2 = With [{ innerKeys = First [csvImportRagged] },**
Map [AssociationThread [innerKeys, #] &, Rest [csvImportRagged]]
]

··· AssociationThread: {class, age, sex, survived} and {3rd, 2, male, False, extra} must have the same length.

Out[•]= { <| class → 3rd, age → 16, sex → female, survived → True |>,
<| class → 1st, age → 65, sex → male, survived → False |>,
AssociationThread [{ class, age, sex, survived }, { 3rd, 2, male, False, extra }],
<| class → 3rd, age → 47, sex → female, survived → True |>,
<| class → 3rd, age → 18, sex → female, survived → False |> }

If I try to bypass this problem by importing the file as a Dataset, I don't get an error message, but I do get a problematic response.

Import a ragged CSV file as a Dataset:

In[ ]:= **Import [raggedCSVFile, { "CSV", "Dataset" }]**

Out[ ]=

{class, age, sex, survived}
{3rd, 16, female, True}
{1st, 65, male, False}
{3rd, 2, male, False, extra}
{3rd, 47, female, True}
{3rd, 18, female, False}

Fortunately, this issue happens often enough that there's a built-in fix: the "FillRows" option. It creates an inner key of an empty string to regularize the dimensions of the Dataset and permits a more attractive presentation.

Use the "FillRows" option to regularize the dimensions of the CSV file being imported:

In[ ]:= **repairedCSVImport =**
Import [raggedCSVFile, { "CSV", "Dataset" } , "FillRows" → True, HeaderLines → 1]

Out[ ]=

class	age	sex	survived	
3rd	16	female	True	
1st	65	male	False	
3rd	2	male	False	extra
3rd	47	female	True	
3rd	18	female	False	

Now we have something respectable. I can use Query to transform the result into something palatable. I might, for example, want to drop the final column.

Drop the last column of a CSV file imported as a Dataset:

In[•]:= **With [{ lastKey = Last [Keys [repairedCSVImport〚1〛]] } ,**
    Query [All, KeyDrop [lastKey]] [repairedCSVImport]]

Out[•]=

class	age	sex	survived
3rd	16	female	True
1st	65	male	False
3rd	2	male	False
3rd	47	female	True
3rd	18	female	False

Or I might want to assume that the empty values in the last column should be represented by Missing [ ], which will appear as "—" in the table.

Represent empty fields as Missing [ ] in a CSV file imported as a Dataset:

In[•]:= **With [{ lastKey = Last [Keys [repairedCSVImport〚1〛]] } ,**
    Query [All, MapAt [# / . "" :→ Missing [ ] &, { lastKey }]] [repairedCSVImport]
    ]

Out[•]=

class	age	sex	survived	
3rd	16	female	True	—
1st	65	male	False	—
3rd	2	male	False	extra
3rd	47	female	True	—
3rd	18	female	False	—

One final issue with CSV: interpretation. If you look carefully at the "Elements" one could import out of a CSV file, you will notice that both "Data" and "RawData" are present. By default, when one imports without an element specification, one gets "Data". In this format, the CSV importer is making some guesses as to what representation of the data is preferred once it leaves its life as a string and enters life as a Wolfram Language expression. Thus, when I imported the dinghy information, it assumed that the string "16" actually meant the number 16. I've found that, usually, the importer gets it right, but if you want the importer not to engage in interpretation, use "RawData" instead. I show this in the next example by using a List as the second argument to the ImportString function and letting "RawData" be the second element. You can see that the "numbers" in the original data are represented as strings.

Import a CSV file as "RawData" to avoid the interpretation of strings that are numbers as numbers:

In[•]:= **Import [csvFile, {"CSV", "RawData"}] / /** [▪] **ShowQuotes** +

Out[•]= { {"class", "age", "sex", "survived"}, {"3rd", "16", "female", "True"},
   {"1st", "65", "male", "False"}, {"3rd", "2", "female", "False"},
   {"3rd", "Missing [ ] ", "female", "True"}, {"3rd", "18", "female", "False"} }

There are certain other guesses the CSV importer may make when importing from a file or string. If you don't want those guesses to be made, "RawData" is your friend.

Using the Excel (XLS, XLSX) Format

A lot of data in the world is contained in Microsoft Excel spreadsheets. Fortunately, the Wolfram Language is great at importing these and the code is similar to that used for importing CSV format files. The main difference is that Excel spreadsheets can have multiple sheets. Here, I Export the same data structure I used for CSV export but this time convert it to the XLSX format used in modern times by Excel. I could also Export to XLS, the earlier format used and that may possibly be needed by some legacy systems.

Export a List of Lists to XLSX (the Microsoft Excel format):

In[•]:= **xlsxFile = Export ["file.xlsx", dinghyValuesWithHeader, "XLSX"]**

Out[•]= file.xlsx

Notice what happens when I read it back, however.

XLSX files are Lists of Lists of Lists when imported:

In[•]:= **Import [xlsxFile, "XLSX"]**

Out[•]= { { { class, age, sex, survived}, {3rd, 16., female, True}, {1st, 65., male, False},
   {3rd, 2., female, False}, {3rd, , female, True}, {3rd, 18., female, False} } }

Instead of it being the original List of Lists, it's nested one more level deep: a List of Lists of Lists. That's because the importer assumes the material could just be the first sheet of a potentially multisheet Excel file. Here's an Export that takes advantage of this multisheet capability of Excel. I Export the dinghy information as the first sheet and the cabin information as the second sheet, giving names to each sheet.

Export a List of Lists of Lists as a multisheet Excel file:

In[•]:= **cabinValues = { {"1st", 300, True, {1, 2} }, {"2nd", 200, True, {3, 4} },**
   {"3rd", 100, False, {4, 5, 6} }, {"crew", 80, False, {6, 7} } };

In[•]:= **(xlsxFile2 = Export ["file2.xlsx",**
   { "dinghy" → dinghyValuesWithHeader, "cabins" → cabinValues }, "XLSX"])

Out[•]= file2.xlsx

I can reimport all of the simulated file. Now the fact that the output is a List of Lists of Lists should make more sense. The first part of the imported data is the dinghy information; the second part is the cabin information.

Import a multisheet Excel file to get a List of Lists of Lists:

In[•]:= **Import [xlsxFile2, "XLSX"]**

Out[•]= { { {class, age, sex, survived}, {3rd, 16., female, True}, {1st, 65., male, False},
   {3rd, 2., female, False}, {3rd, Missing [ ], female, True}, {3rd, 18., female, False} },
   { {1st, 300., True, {1, 2} }, {2nd, 200., True, {3, 4} },
   {3rd, 100., False, {4, 5, 6} }, {crew, 80., False, {6, 7} } } }

I can also choose to discover what information I can get about an Excel file. Much of it is the same as for CSV, but there is more information, such as the "Formulas" and "Sheets", that is included.

XLSX files have "Elements" including "Formulas" and "Sheets":

In[•]:= **Import [xlsxFile2, { "XLSX", "Elements" }]**

Out[•]= { Data, Dataset, Dimensions, FormattedData,
   Formulas, Images, SheetCount, Sheets, Summary}

Thus, I can do something like this.

Get the name of the sheets in an Excel file:

In[•]:= **Import [xlsxFile2, { "XLSX", "Sheets" }]**

Out[•]= { dinghy, cabins }

Then I could choose just to import the dinghy sheet by making the last argument a List in which "XLSX" is the first element (specifying format), "Sheets" is the second element (specifying the element to be Imported), and "dinghy" is the third argument, specifying which particular sheet I want to Import.

Import just certain sheets from an Excel file:

In[•]:= **Import [xlsxFile2, { "XLSX", "Sheets", "dinghy" }]**

Out[•]= { {class, age, sex, survived}, {3rd, 16., female, True}, {1st, 65., male, False},
   {3rd, 2., female, False}, {3rd, Missing [ ], female, True}, {3rd, 18., female, False} }

I could also ask for just the data without the header line by adding an option.

Tell the XLSX importer that the data has a header line:

In[•]:= **Import [xlsxFile2, { "XLSX", "Sheets", "dinghy" }, HeaderLines → 1]**

Out[•]= { {3rd, 16., female, True}, {1st, 65., male, False}, {3rd, 2., female, False},
   {3rd, Missing [ ], female, True}, {3rd, 18., female, False} }

Once I have the XLSX material imported, I can turn it into data structures the same way as shown with CSV files.

Turn imports of multiple sheets from an Excel file into a deeply nested data structure:

In[•]:= **Association [**
    "dinghy" → Import [xlsxFile2, { "XLSX", "Dataset", "dinghy" }, HeaderLines → 1],
    "cabin" → Import [xlsxFile2, { "XLSX", "Dataset", "cabins" }, HeaderLines → 0]]

Out[•]= ⟨| dinghy →

class	age	sex	survived
3rd	16.0	female	True
1st	65.0	male	False
3rd	2.0	female	False
3rd	Missing[]	female	True
3rd	18.0	female	False

,

cabin →

1st	300.0	True	{1, 2}
2nd	200.0	True	{3, 4}
3rd	100.0	False	{4, 5, 6}
crew	80.0	False	{6, 7}

|⟩

Using the JSON Format

The JSON (JavaScript Object Notation) format has become very popular in recent years for structuring hierarchical data. Here I export the dinghy information, converting Missings to "" because JSON does not like general Wolfram Language expressions but wants more basic data types like strings or integers or reals or lists of these items.

Export a List of Associations as JSON:

In[•]:= **dinghy2 = dinghy /. Missing [_ _ _] :→ "";**

In[◦]:= (jsonExport = ExportString [dinghy2, "JSON"]) / / Framed

Out[◦]=

```
[
    {
        "class":"3rd",
        "age":16,
        "sex":"female",
        "survived":true
    },
    {
        "class":"1st",
        "age":65,
        "sex":"male",
        "survived":false
    },
    {
        "class":"3rd",
        "age":2,
        "sex":"female",
        "survived":false
    },
    {
        "class":"3rd",
        "age":"",
        "sex":"female",
        "survived":true
    },
    {
        "class":"3rd",
        "age":18,
        "sex":"female",
        "survived":false
    }
]
```

Notice how it looks an awful lot like the Wolfram Language; the only significant changes are that the outer List is denoted with square brackets, the inner Association is denoted with curly braces, the arrows are just colons, and the Wolfram Language Booleans have been put in lowercase.

Let's write the expression to a file.

Export a List of Associations as a JSON file:

In[◦]:= jsonFile = Export ["file.json", dinghy2, "JSON"]

Out[◦]= file.json

I can import JSON files and get back something similar to, but not identical to, the original exported material. Notice that the inner Associations have turned into Lists.

Import a data structure exported to JSON as a List of Associations, returned as a List of Lists:

In[∘]:= (jsonImport = Import [jsonFile, "JSON"]) / / [▣] ShowQuotes +

Out[∘]= { {"class" → "3rd", "age" → 16, "sex" → "female", "survived" → True },
     {"class" → "1st", "age" → 65, "sex" → "male", "survived" → False },
     {"class" → "3rd", "age" → 2, "sex" → "female", "survived" → False },
     {"class" → "3rd", "age" → "", "sex" → "female", "survived" → True },
     {"class" → "3rd", "age" → 18, "sex" → "female", "survived" → False } }

We can use the FileFormatProperties function (added in Version 13) to discover other import formats that might return the original expression perfectly.

FileFormatProperties returns a property for a given format, such as "JSON":

In[∘]:= jsonProperties = FileFormatProperties ["JSON", "ImportElements"]

Out[∘]= { Data, Dataset, Summary }

The "Dataset" format sounds very promising because Dataset is what one well might use to hold a list of Associations.

Import a JSON file as a Dataset:

In[∘]:= jsonImport = Import [jsonFile, "Dataset"]

Out[∘]=

class	age	sex	survived
3rd	16	female	True
1st	65	male	False
3rd	2	female	False
3rd		female	True
3rd	18	female	False

You should have learned enough by this point in the book that you know how to make the structure change necessary.

Use Normal to convert this Dataset to a List of Associations:

In[∘]:= Normal [jsonImport]

Out[∘]= { <| class → 3rd, age → 16, sex → female, survived → True |>,
     <| class → 1st, age → 65, sex → male, survived → False |>,
     <| class → 3rd, age → 2, sex → female, survived → False |>,
     <| class → 3rd, age → , sex → female, survived → True |>,
     <| class → 3rd, age → 18, sex → female, survived → False |> }

Now let's try something new. Let's export just the Values from dinghy2. I get something that looks an awful lot like a List of Lists. I'm adding the "Compact" → True optional argument to save space on the page.

Setting the "Compact"→True option compresses the presentation of JSON data:

In[•]:= **ExportString [Query [All, Values] [dinghy2], "JSON", "Compact" → True]**

Out[•]= [["3rd", 16, "female", true], ["1st", 65, "male", false], ["3rd", 2,
"female", false], ["3rd", "", "female", true], ["3rd", 18, "female", false]]

JSON can also handle the export of Associations of Associations so long as the keys
are strings. Again, there's an easy translation between JSON and the Wolfram
Language: Lists are [ ], Associations are { }, and arrows are :.

The JSON exporter can handle Associations of Associations:

In[•]:= **ExportString [[•] ValueMapIndexed + [ToString [♯2〚1〛]] &] [dinghy2],
"JSON", "Compact" → True]**

Out[•]= { "1": { "class":"3rd","age":16,"sex":"female","survived":true }, "2": { "class":"1st","age":65,"
sex":"male","survived":false }, "3": { "class":"3rd","age":2,"sex":"female","survived":false
}, "4": { "class":"3rd","age":"","sex":"female","survived":true }, "5": { "class":"3rd","age":
18,"sex":"female","survived":false } }

Also, notice that although JSON cannot handle general Wolfram Language expressions, it can handle Lists just fine, even when they are deep in a data structure.

The JSON exporter can handle deeply nested data structures involving Lists and Associations:

In[•]:= **SeedRandom [20230113];**
**ExportString [Query [All, Append [♯, "randomlist" → RandomInteger [{ 0, 9 }, 3]] &] [
dinghy2], "JSON", "Compact" → True]**

Out[•]= [{ "class":"3rd","age":16,"sex":"female","survived":true,"randomlist": [6,7,2] }, { "class":"1
st","age":65,"sex":"male","survived":false,"randomlist": [6,8,8] }, { "class":"3rd","age":2
,"sex":"female","survived":false,"randomlist": [6,6,1] }, { "class":"3rd","age":"","sex":"
female","survived":true,"randomlist": [2,6,5] }, { "class":"3rd","age":18,"sex":"female","
survived":false,"randomlist": [5,4,1] }]

Using the ZIP Format

Files are often large. Storing them is expensive and transmitting them takes time, so it's
often a good idea to compress them or to compress groups of them. Many compression
formats have evolved over the years, but ZIP is probably still the most popular. Here I
generate a simulated ZIP "archive" in which the first "file" contains a CSV formatting
of the dinghy passengers and the second file contains a JSON formatting of the cabin
information. I deliberately "mislabel" the CSV file with a .txt suffix to show that one
can force whatever format one chooses on files stored within the archive regardless of
the name given to them.

Export two Lists of Lists to a ZIP archive with CSV and JSON formats, respectively, and with nonstandard file extensions:

```
In[ ]:=  zipFile = Export [ "file.zip", { { "passengers.txt", "CSV" } → dinghy2,
           { "cabins.json", "JSON" } → cabinValues }, "ZIP" ]
```

```
Out[ ]=  file.zip
```

If I now run Import on the result, I do not get back the contents of the information put into the ZIP. Instead, I get a list of the filenames inside the ZIP.

Import a ZIP file and get the name of the files contained within:

```
In[ ]:=  Import [ zipFile, "ZIP" ]
```

```
Out[ ]=  { passengers.txt, cabins.json }
```

If I want a particular file within the archive, I ask for it by name and specify the format in which I want it returned. Here I ask for the "passengers.txt" file returned as if it were a CSV file.

Import a particular file inside a ZIP archive with a file format that is nonstandard for the extension used in the file name:

```
In[ ]:=  ( reimportPassengers = Import [ zipFile, { "passengers.txt", "CSV" } ] )  / /
           [▪] ShowQuotes  +
```

```
Out[ ]=  { { "< | \"class\" –> \"3rd\", \"age\" –> 16, \"sex\" –> \"female\", \"survived\" –> True | >" },
           { "< | \"class\" –> \"1st\", \"age\" –> 65, \"sex\" –> \"male\", \"survived\" –> False | >" },
           { "< | \"class\" –> \"3rd\", \"age\" –> 2, \"sex\" –> \"female\", \"survived\" –> False | >" },
           { "< | \"class\" –> \"3rd\", \"age\" –> \"\", \"sex\" –> \"female\", \"survived\" –> True | >" },
           { "< | \"class\" –> \"3rd\", \"age\" –> 18, \"sex\" –> \"female\", \"survived\" –> False | >" } }
```

Notice two issues. The first is that, because the exported data was an Association, the export to CSV converted that Association into a string. CSV does not really understand Wolfram Language expressions that well. So, when I reimport it, I get back strings instead of what I likely want, which are Associations. We can fix that problem by mapping ToExpression over the data. ToExpression gives the expression obtained by interpreting strings or boxes as Wolfram Language input.

Use ToExpression to convert string representations of Associations to the intended Wolfram Language expressions:

```
In[ ]:=  Map [ ToExpression, reimportPassengers ]  / /  [▪] ShowQuotes  +
```

```
Out[ ]=  { { <| "class" → "3rd", "age" → 16, "sex" → "female", "survived" → True |> },
           { <| "class" → "1st", "age" → 65, "sex" → "male", "survived" → False |> },
           { <| "class" → "3rd", "age" → 2, "sex" → "female", "survived" → False |> },
           { <| "class" → "3rd", "age" → "", "sex" → "female", "survived" → True |> },
           { <| "class" → "3rd", "age" → 18, "sex" → "female", "survived" → False |> } }
```

The second issue is to note what would have happened if I had omitted the CSV format specification and simply used the file name of "passengers.txt" as the second argument to the Import function. The importer would then have assumed based on the .txt file extension that I wanted the data parsed as text. Here is what I would have gotten. Probably not at all what I wanted.

Failure to include a third argument to Import can lead to unintended consequences:

In[•]:= **Import [zipFile, "passengers.txt"]**

Out[•]= "< | ""class"" -> ""3rd"", ""age"" -> 16, ""sex"" -> ""female"", ""survived"" -> True | >"
"< | ""class"" -> ""1st"", ""age"" -> 65, ""sex"" -> ""male"", ""survived"" -> False | >"
"< | ""class"" -> ""3rd"", ""age"" -> 2, ""sex"" -> ""female"", ""survived"" -> False | >"
"< | ""class"" -> ""3rd"", ""age"" -> """", ""sex"" -> ""female"", ""survived"" -> True | >"
"< | ""class"" -> ""3rd"", ""age"" -> 18, ""sex"" -> ""female"", ""survived"" -> False | >"

Here I ask for the "cabins.json" file within the archive returned. Even though I don't specify that the data should be parsed as if it were in JSON format, the importer correctly guesses that such is the case due to the .json extension in the file name.

Import a file bearing a .json extension within a ZIP archive and see the importer correctly guess that I want the material parsed as JSON:

In[•]:= **Import [zipFile, "cabins.json"]**

Out[•]= { { 1st, 300, True, { 1, 2 } }, { 2nd, 200, True, { 3, 4 } },
{ 3rd, 100, False, { 4, 5, 6 } }, { crew, 80, False, { 6, 7 } } }

I could also ask for it as text. I'm only going to get the first two hundred characters to save space.

Import a JSON file from a ZIP archive as "Text":

In[•]:= **Import [zipFile, { "cabins.json", "Text" }] / /**
((StringTake [⌗, 200] &) / * ▣ ShowQuotes +)

Out[•]= " [\n\t [\n\t\t\"1st\",\n\t\t300,\n\t\ttrue,\n\t\t [\n\t\t\t1,\n\t\t\t2\n\t\t] \n\t] ,\n\t [\n\t\t\t\"2
nd\",\n\t\t200,\n\t\ttrue,\n\t\t [\n\t\t\t3,\n\t\t\t4\n\t\t] \n\t] ,\n\t [\n\t\t\t\"3rd\",\n\t\
t100,\n\t\tfalse,\n\t\t [\n\t\t\t4,\n\t\t\t5,\n\t\t\t6\n\t\t] \n\t] ,\n\t [\n\t\t\t\"crew\",\n\t\
t80,\n\t\tfalse,\n\t\t [\n\t\t\t6,\n\t\t\t"

Using the Google Sheets Format

There's no Import format exactly meant for Google Sheets, spreadsheets located on Google Drive. Still, it is not hard to retrieve them. Here's an image of one I've made available to the public. It's very simple and describes key events in an important American legal case, Marbury v. Madison. There are two "sheets," one called "Chronology" and the other called "People."

One way to go about retrieving the information is to use Google Sheets to download the spreadsheet as an Excel file and then simply use the material in this chapter on importing from Excel. That works splendidly, but it does take the extra step of requesting a download, which is fine if one has to do it once but less fun if one has to do it on a number of spreadsheets or if one has to do it repeatedly as the content of the spreadsheet changes.

To obtain the contents programmatically, one can essentially do the same thing, but instead of mousing over and clicking **Download ▶ Microsoft Excel (.xlsx)** within the Google Sheets interface, one sends a customized URL string to Google. I obtain the spreadsheet's "sharing" URL from within Google Sheets. (I'm not aware of how one can automate this process.)

Assign the URL of a Google spreadsheet to a Wolfram Language variable:

In[ ]:= **sharingURL = "https: / / docs.google.com / spreadsheets / d / 1
        VnBo43s6VnlRzv1g8XkTeLkECFyeAPLlkZFX4psV4AE / edit?usp=sharing";**

Now use StringReplace to replace the material after the final / with "export?format=xlsx".

Change the URL to tell the Google Sheet to export itself as XLSX:

In[ ]:= **url = StringReplace [sharingURL, "edit?usp=sharing" → "export?format=xlsx"]**

Out[ ]= https: / / docs.google.com / spreadsheets / d / 1
        VnBo43s6VnlRzv1g8XkTeLkECFyeAPLlkZFX4psV4AE / export?format=xlsx

Now I can import it as an **XLSX** object. Note that we get both sheets of the spreadsheet.

Import both sheets of a Google spreadsheet as XLSX:

In[•]:= **googleToXLSX = Import [url, "XLSX"]**

Out[•]= { { {Event, Date}, {Congress enacts Judiciary Act of 1789, 9 / 24 / 1789}, ·
  {John Marshall named Secretary of State, 6 / 6 / 1800},
  {John Marshall confirmed as Chief Justice, 2 / 4 / 1801},
  {Congress enacts Midnight Judges bill (Judiciary Act of 1801) , 2 / 13 / 1801},
  {House elects Jefferson President, 2 / 17 / 1801},
  {Adams submits Marbury + 41 others to Senate as JPs, 3 / 2 / 1801},
  {Senate confirms Marbury + 41 others as JPs, 3 / 3 / 1801},
  {James Marshall goes to Alexandria to deliver JP Commissions, 3 / 3 / 1801},
  {Thomas Jefferson takes office as President, 3 / 4 / 1801},
  {James Madison appointed Secretary of State, 3 / 5 / 1801},
  {Thomas Jefferson tells Madison not to deliver commissions, 4 / 1 / 1801},
  {Marbury warns Jefferson he seeks mandamus in Supreme Court, 12 / 16 / 1801},
  {Supreme Court holds hearing, 12 / 17 / 1801},
  {Supreme Court rules Madison has to show cause, 12 / 18 / 1801},
  {Congress abolishes 1802 Supreme Court term, 4 / 1 / 1802},
  {Marbury petitions Senate for journal showing confirmation, 1 / 28 / 1803},
  {Senate refuses 15 – 13 to provide copy, 1 / 31 / 1803},
  {Supreme Court (John Marshall) issues Marbury v. Madison, 2 / 24 / 1803} },
 { {FirstName, LastName}, {John, Marshall}, {James, Marshall},
  {Thomas, Jefferson}, {William, Marbury}, {James, Madison}, {John, Adams} } }

I can then use the techniques described in this book to get the data into a more computable form. Suppose, for example, that I want a List of Associations for the first sheet. I can write the following code.

Convert a sheet of a Google spreadsheet imported as XLSX into a List of Associations:

In[•]:= **marburyEvents = With [{ header1 = First [First [googleToXLSX]] },**
  Map [AssociationThread [header1, ⌗] &, Rest [googleToXLSX⟦1⟧]]]

{ <| Event → Congress enacts Judiciary Act of 1789, Date → 9 / 24 / 1789 |>,
 <| Event → John Marshall named Secretary of State, Date → 6 / 6 / 1800 |>,
 <| Event → John Marshall confirmed as Chief Justice, Date → 2 / 4 / 1801 |>,
 <| Event → Congress enacts Midnight Judges bill (Judiciary Act of 1801) ,
  Date → 2 / 13 / 1801 |>,
 <| Event → House elects Jefferson President, Date → 2 / 17 / 1801 |>,
 <| Event → Adams submits Marbury + 41 others to Senate as JPs, Date → 3 / 2 / 1801 |>,
 <| Event → Senate confirms Marbury + 41 others as JPs, Date → 3 / 3 / 1801 |>,
 <| Event → James Marshall goes to Alexandria to deliver JP Commissions,
  Date → 3 / 3 / 1801 |>,
 <| Event → Thomas Jefferson takes office as President, Date → 3 / 4 / 1801 |>,
 <| Event → James Madison appointed Secretary of State, Date → 3 / 5 / 1801 |>,
 <| Event → Thomas Jefferson tells Madison not to deliver commissions,
  Date → 4 / 1 / 1801 |>,
 <| Event → Marbury warns Jefferson he seeks mandamus in Supreme Court,
  Date → 12 / 16 / 1801 |>,
 <| Event → Supreme Court holds hearing, Date → 12 / 17 / 1801 |>,
 <| Event → Supreme Court rules Madison has to show cause, Date → 12 / 18 / 1801 |>,
 <| Event → Congress abolishes 1802 Supreme Court term, Date → 4 / 1 / 1802 |>,

    ⟨| Event → Marbury petitions Senate for journal showing confirmation,
        Date → 1 / 28 / 1803 |⟩,
    ⟨| Event → Senate refuses 15–13 to provide copy, Date → 1 / 31 / 1803 |⟩,
    ⟨| Event → Supreme Court (John Marshall) issues Marbury v. Madison,
        Date → 2 / 24 / 1803 |⟩ }

And if I wanted an Association of Lists for the second sheet, I could write the following code.

Convert a sheet of a Google spreadsheet imported as XLSX into an Association of Lists:

In[ ]:= **Query [Association, First [⊞] → Rest [⊞] &] [Transpose [googleToXLSX⟦2⟧]]**

Out[ ]= ⟨| FirstName → { John, James, Thomas, William, James, John },
      LastName → { Marshall, Marshall, Jefferson, Marbury, Madison, Adams } |⟩

If, by the way, you just want the first sheet of a Google Sheets document, it's even easier. Replace the end of the sharing URL with "export?format=csv".

Create a string that will tell a Google spreadsheet to export its first sheet as CSV:

In[ ]:= **urlCSV = StringReplace [sharingURL, "edit?usp=sharing" → "export?format=csv"]**

Out[ ]= https: / / docs.google.com / spreadsheets / d / 1
      VnBo43s6VnIRzv1g8XkTeLkECFyeAPLIkZFX4psV4AE / export?format=csv

Now you can import it as a Dataset in just one line of code that looks exactly like what you would do if the file were a CSV one.

Import the first sheet of a Google spreadsheet as a Dataset with proper column names; use the FormatDataset ResourceFunction to help the result fit on a printed page:

In[ ]:= **marburyDataset = Import [urlCSV, "Dataset", HeaderLines → 1] / /**
      [▪] FormatDataset **+** **[ItemSize → 24, ItemStyle → 9]**

Out[ ]=

Event	Date
Congress enacts Judiciary Act of 1789	9/24/1789
John Marshall named Secretary of State	6/6/1800
John Marshall confirmed as Chief Justice	2/4/1801
Congress enacts Midnight Judges bill (Judiciary Act of 1801)	2/13/1801
House elects Jefferson President	2/17/1801
Adams submits Marbury + 41 others to Senate as JPs	3/2/1801
Senate confirms Marbury + 41 others as JPs	3/3/1801
James Marshall goes to Alexandria to deliver JP Commissions	3/3/1801

rows 1–8 of **18**

From this, I can use the techniques from the earlier chapters to produce a timeline of the case. I've moved from a Google spreadsheet to a Wolfram Language graphic.

Import the data from a Google spreadsheet and create a timeline of Marbury v. Madison based on the result:

```
In[•]:= With [
         { plot = ( ( TimelinePlot [ ♯ , PlotTheme → "Web", PlotRange → { DateObject [ { 1800, 6,
                       1 } ] , DateObject [ { 1803, 12, 1 } ] } , ImageSize → 570,
                    PlotLabel → "Chronology of Marbury v. Madison"] &) / * Framed ) ,

           eventForm =
             Labeled [ Interpreter [ "Date" ] [ ♯Date ] , Pane [ ♯Event , 1.6 * 72 ] ] &},
           Query [ plot, eventForm ] [ marburyDataset ] ]
```

Out[•]=

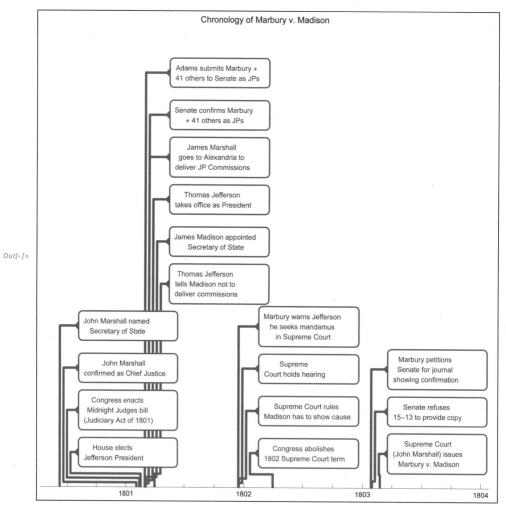

File Formats Listed

WXF	Wolfram Exchange Format (WXF) byte arrays can be created with BinarySerialize and read with BinaryDeserialize
text	regular text support for a variety of Western character encodings and the Unicode standard
CSV	comma–separated values (CSV) format is the most basic and common spreadsheet format
XLS, XLSX	Microsoft Excel's format, fully compatible with the 2007 standard
JSON	derived from JavaScript Object Notation and based on a subset of the JavaScript programming language
ZIP	popular data compression and archival format, fully supported in the Wolfram Language
Google Sheets	unlike CSV and XLS, the Wolfram Language does not support but one can easily extract them

Exercises

Some of these exercises are taken from data at the University of California at Irvine's Machine Learning Repository. This repository has been around for some time and I hope that its data and URLs will be consistent over the lifespan of this book.

8.1 Go to the example data and retrieve the Gettysburg Address like this.

gettysburg = ExampleData [{ "Text", "GettysburgAddress"}] ;

Now export it as text to a location on your computer. Alternatively, simulate the export using ExportString or use CreateFile as I did in the main text to create a temporary file. If you create a temporary file, make sure to get its name so you can import it back.

8.2 Now reimport the file or string you just created but as a **List** of words. Hint: "Elements". You might want to just postfix a **Take** of the first 20 words or so to get the point and save space.

8.3 Set forth below is a URL. It references some data, but we don't really know what format the data is in. Import the data as text and see if you can make a guess as to what format might be appropriate to capture the meaning of the data.

iris = "http: / / archive.ics.uci.edu / ml / machine–learning–databases / iris / iris.data";

8.4 See if it makes sense to import the data at the URL as a CSV file. Use the **ResourceFunction ShowQuotes** to see precisely what you retrieved. Do you agree that CSV looks like a sensible import format?

8.5 Reexport the iris data you imported as a JSON string. Make the output compact.

8.6 Evaluate the following code. It provides the URL of an Excel file relating to cryotherapy. How many sheets are in the Excel spreadsheet?

cryoCSV =
    "https: / / archive.ics.uci.edu / ml / machine–learning–databases / 00429 / Cryotherapy.xlsx";

8.7 You should find that one of the sheets (perhaps the only sheet) is called "CrayoDataset". Import it as a Dataset so the first line of the data contains headers.

8.8 Here's a URL to a zip archive: http://archive.ics.uci.edu/ml/machine-learning-databases/00454/dataset.zip. Assign it to the variable victorian.

8.9 It's a ZIP file. Find out what files are contained in it.

8.10 You should see a file name that ends in readme.txt. Import that file as text. Because the archive is large (even though this file is small), this may take a minute or so to run.

8.11 There's another file in the archive that ends with data–train.csv. Find out what "Elements" are available for Import from that file.

8.12 See if you can figure out how to get the Dimensions of the file without having to actually Import the data.

8.13 The code below assigns the web address of data on wine to the variable wineURL. Import the data at this address as text. Call your result wineText.

wineURL =
    "http: / / archive.ics.uci.edu / ml / machine–learning–databases / wine–quality / winequality–white.csv";

8.14 What I hope you see is that it is a "semicolon-separated value file" that is like a CSV file but each row has its 12 values separated by semicolons. Unfortunately, this choice of a semicolon as a separator is going to make it impossible to import it properly using the CSV importer (in Version 13.2) and get out a data structure, each row of which has 12 values. To get around this, import it instead as text with the "Lines" element. Call your result wineLines.

8.15 Now read up on the StringSplit function in the Wolfram Language documentation and turn your import into a List of Lists with dimensions 4899 × 12 and call it wineListOfLists.

8.16 Here's a challenge: Take a look at the first line of the answer from the preceding exercise either in InputForm or using the ResourceFunction ShowQuotes. What you should see is that each element of the resulting List has embedded quotation marks in it. This is not what we want! Try to write a function that fixes the problem and imports the data in a way that eliminates the embedded quotation marks.

The following exercises with the wine data are a review of material taught in the previous chapters of this book. They are likely to prove challenging.

8.17 Turn your List of Lists into a List of Associations, each of whose keys are the first row of the data but with no embedded quotation marks. Call your result wineListOfAssociations. Hint: Perhaps you should use deleteEmbeddedQuotations. For extra credit, use the ResourceFunction ToCamelCase so that there are no spaces in the key names.

8.18 As a final step, see if the "numbers" in the data have been imported as numbers or as strings. If they are strings, write code to turn them into numbers. Turn your result into a Dataset called wineDataset. Hint 1: ToExpression. Hint 2: The third argument to Query.

8.19 Compute the variance of the quality column. Present your answer as a number and call it qualityVariance.

8.20 Run the following code to create training and testing components to your Dataset. See if you can understand what the code is doing.

```
( SeedRandom [ 1 ] ;
    wineDatasets = Query [ RandomSample /* ( AssociationThread [ { "training", "testing" },
        TakeDrop [ ♯, Round [ 0.7 * Length [ ♯ ] ] ] ] & ) ] [ wineDataset ] ) ;
```

8.21 Now use what you learned in the first part of this book to write a Query that will yield a PredictorFunction based on the training data. Note that your results may differ slightly depending on the method selected by the automated machine learning algorithm. Call the result **pre**. Hint 1: Values. Hint 2: Most @♯ → Last @♯ &.

8.22 Use the result from the previous question to produce a PredictorMeasurementsObject called **pmo** that sees how well the predictor you made is able to predict the quality of wines in the testing data created earlier.

8.23 "ComparisonPlot" is a property of a PredictorMeasurementsObject. Make a "ComparisonPlot" from **pmo** showing the predicted quality of the wine on the *x* axis and the actual quality of the wine on the *y* axis.

8.24 Would you say the quality of the wine is easy to predict accurately from the data or does good wine, perhaps, have a certain *je ne sais quoi*? Test your belief by computing the "RSquared" property of the PredictorMeasurementsObject.

Tech Notes

- You can try to Import from a file or Export to a file without specifying a format. When you do so, the kernel will attempt to guess the format based on the name of the file. Thus, if your file is **myfile.csv**, the kernel will assume you want to import (or export) as "CSV". I don't recommend you do this, though. It's worth spending some time thinking about the best format and telling the kernel what to do.

- If you Export Lists of strings as "Text", the strings are concatenated and separated by a new line character.

In[ ]:= **ExportString [{** "Is this a dagger which I see before me,
The handle toward my hand?", "Come, let me clutch thee.
I have thee not, and yet I see thee still." **}, "Text"]** // [▪] **ShowQuotes** ＋

Out[ ]= "Is this a dagger which I see before me,\nThe handle toward my hand?\nCome, let me clutch thee.\nI have thee not, and yet I see thee still."

- If you try to export a non-string to "Text", ExportString runs ToString to convert the expression to a string and exports the result.

In[ ]:= **ExportString [{** "To be or not to be", Solve [a x + b == 0, x] **}, "Text"]** //
[▪] **ShowQuotes** ＋

Out[ ]= "To be or not to be\n{ { x -> - (b / a) } }"

- The HeaderLines option can also cope with CSV files where the first "column" is what the Wolfram Language would think of as a row header (or outer key). Here I construct such a data structure.

In[ ]:= **indexedDinghy =**
  Query [All, Values] [MapThread [Association ["index" → ToString [#1] , #2] &,
    { [•] CorrespondingIntegers + [dinghy] , dinghy }]]

Out[ ]= { { 1, 3rd, 16, female, True } , { 2, 1st, 65, male, False } , { 3, 3rd, 2, female, False } ,
  { 4, 3rd, Missing [ ] , female, True } , { 5, 3rd, 18, female, False } }

- Now I add the column headers on to the data structure, ExportString it as CSV, and reimport it as { "CSV","Dataset" } , but tell ImportString that the first column and the first row are headers.

In[ ]:= **ImportString [ExportString [**
    Prepend [indexedDinghy, { "index", "class", "age", "sex", "survived" }] , "CSV"] ,
    { "CSV", "Dataset" } , HeaderLines → { 1, 1 }]

	class	age	sex	survived
1	3rd	16	female	True
2	1st	65	male	False
3	3rd	2	female	False
4	3rd	Missing[]	female	True
5	3rd	18	female	False

Out[ ]=

- If I use "Formulas" as the second argument to the Import of an Excel spreadsheet, I get a list of all the formulas used in the document. This can be useful in auditing a complex Excel spreadsheet. Here's the kind of data structure you can get this way. The image below compares the result of importing XLSX (and taking the first part) and importing the formulas (and taking the first part). I've wrapped Grid around each result to make the structure more clear.

Column A	Column B	Column C
9.	4.	4.
4.	−1.	3.
7.	2.	5.

A2−5	SUM (B$2:B2)
A3−5	SUM (B$2:B3)
A4−5	SUM (B$2:B4)

- JSON has limitations in dealing with data containing symbolic heads such as Quantity. When the ages of the passengers are converted into a "Years" Quantity, the export to JSON results in the age turning into a string.

In[ ]:= **dinghy2WithQuantities = Query [All, MapAt [Quantity [# , "Years"] &, 2]] [dinghy2]**

Out[ ]= { ⟨| class → 3rd, age → 16 yr , sex → female, survived → True |⟩ ,
  ⟨| class → 1st, age → 65 yr , sex → male, survived → False |⟩ ,
  ⟨| class → 3rd, age → 2 yr , sex → female, survived → False |⟩ ,
  ⟨| class → 3rd, age → yr , sex → female, survived → True |⟩ ,
  ⟨| class → 3rd, age → 18 yr , sex → female, survived → False |⟩ }

In[ ]:= **ExportString [dinghy2WithQuantities, "JSON"]**

  ⊙ Export : Expression Quantity cannot be exported as JSON.

Out[ ]= **$Failed**

- If I want to send general-purpose Wolfram Language expressions in JSON, I can use a cousin format called "ExpressionJSON".

In[ ]:= **jsonExpressionExport = ExportString [dinghy, "ExpressionJSON", "Compact" → True]**

Out[ ]= ["List", ["Association", ["Rule", "'class'", "'3rd'"] , ["Rule", "'age'", 16] , ["Rule", "'sex'",
      "'female'"] , ["Rule", "'survived'", true]] , ["Association", ["Rule", "'class'",
      "'1st'"] , ["Rule", "'age'",65] , ["Rule", "'sex'", "'male'"] , ["Rule", "'survived'",
      false]] , ["Association", ["Rule", "'class'", "'3rd'"] , ["Rule", "'age'", 2] , ["Rule",
      "'sex'", "'female'"] , ["Rule", "'survived'", false]] , ["Association", ["Rule",
      "'class'", "'3rd'"] , ["Rule", "'age'", ["Missing"]] , ["Rule", "'sex'", "'female'"] ,
      ["Rule", "'survived'", true]] , ["Association", ["Rule", "'class'", "'3rd'"] ,
      ["Rule", "'age'", 18] , ["Rule", "'sex'", "'female'"] , ["Rule", "'survived'", false]]]

- I can now reimport it and get exactly what I sent out.

In[ ]:= **ImportString [jsonExpressionExport, "ExpressionJSON"]**

Out[ ]= { <| class → 3rd, age → 16, sex → female, survived → True |> ,
      <| class → 1st, age → 65, sex → male, survived → False |> ,
      <| class → 3rd, age → 2, sex → female, survived → False |> ,
      <| class → 3rd, age → Missing [ ] , sex → female, survived → True |> ,
      <| class → 3rd, age → 18, sex → female, survived → False |> }

- You can think of "ExpressionJSON" as an alternative to WXF as a way of sending human-readable Wolfram Language data structures to other users. There are also a number of other variants of JSON covered in the Wolfram Language & System Documentation Center.

More to Explore

To learn more about Import and Export of the hundreds of formats known to the Wolfram Language, see the guide page on basic formats (wolfr.am/BasicFormats) **and all formats** (wolfr.am/ListingFormats)

Answers to Exercises

2 | Data Structures and Functions

2.1 Here is a list of expressions: $\{-46, 7, p[4], p[3,4], p[2, q[5,6]], 4+7\ i, \frac{9}{10}\}$. Which of them can you successfully use **Part** on and which generate an error message?

$$\left\{(-46)\ [\![1]\!], 7, 4, 3, 2, (4+7\ i)\ [\![1]\!], \frac{9}{10}\ [\![1]\!]\right\}$$

⋯ Part : Part specification $(-46)[\![1]\!]$ is longer than depth of object.

⋯ Part : Part specification $(4+7\ i)[\![1]\!]$ is longer than depth of object.

⋯ Part : Part specification $\frac{9}{10}\ [\![1]\!]$ is longer than depth of object.

⋯ General : Further output of Part::partd will be suppressed during this calculation.

2.2 Write a function that takes a **List**, such as $\{3, 5\}$, and computes the absolute value of the difference between the two numbers. Here the right answer would be 2. Hint 1: The function for computing absolute value is **Abs**. Hint 2: Your function should use **Part**.

Function [x, Abs [x⟦1⟧ – x⟦2⟧]]

2.3 Use **Total** and **Map** to compute the sum of the absolute value of the differences between the following pairs of numbers $\{\{3, 5\}, \{8, 9\}, \{6, 6\}, \{-2, 11\}\}$. You should get 16.

Total [Map [Function [x, Abs [x⟦1⟧ – x⟦2⟧]], { {3, 5}, {8, 9}, {6, 6}, {-2, 11} }]]

16

2.4 The Manhattan distance between two points is the sum of the absolute value of the differences in the x coordinates and y coordinates. So, if one point is at $\{2, 9\}$ and the other point is at $\{5, 1\}$, the absolute value of the differences are 3 and 8 and the Manhattan distance is 11. Find me the Manhattan distance between the points given below. Hint: You should probably use **Thread** or **Transpose**. (There is a built-in **ManhattanDistance** function; it would be clever to use it, but you would lose the educational benefits of the exercise.)

point1 = {4, 12};
point2 = {3, 5};
Total [Map [Total] [Transpose [{ point1, –point2 }]]]

8

Total [Transpose [{ point1, –point2 }], 2]

8

2.5 Augment the matrix of information contained in **mls2** by inserting a first column that numbers the players from 1 to 4899.

MapIndexed [Prepend [⌗ , ⌗2 ⟦1⟧] &, mls2]

{{1, CHI, Armas, Chris, M, $225 000.00 , $225 000.00 , Year: 2007 },
{2, CHI, Banner, Michael, M, $12 900.00 , $12 900.00 , Year: 2007 },
{3, CHI, Barrett, Chad, F, $41 212.50 , $48 712.50 , Year: 2007 }, ⟨⟨ 5527 ⟩⟩ ,
{5531, VAN, Waston, Kendall, D, $350 000.00 , $368 125.00 , Year: 2017 },
{5532, VAN, Williams, Sheanon, D, $175 000.00 , $184 000.00 , Year: 2017 }}

Full expression not available   (original memory size: 3.5 MB   )

2.6 Find the base salary of the last player in the **mls2** data.

mls2⟦−1, 5⟧

$175 000.00

2.7 Find the median base salary of all the players in the **mls2** data.

Median [Part [mls2, All, 5]]

$78 652.00

2.8 Find the **Mean** difference between the guaranteed compensation and base salary for all players in the mls2 data. Then do the same computation but **Select** only players whose last names are not equal to Beckham. The **Unequal** operator in the Wolfram Language is !=.

Mean [Map [⌗ ⟦6⟧ − ⌗ ⟦5⟧ &, mls2]]

$20 710.48

Mean [Map [⌗ ⟦6⟧ − ⌗ ⟦5⟧ &, Select [⌗ ⟦2⟧ ≠ "Beckham" &] [mls2]]]

$19 647.19

2.9 Here's some code that would let you find rows of the MLS dataset that are from 2009:

Select [⌗ [[7]] == Year: 2009 &] [mls2] . Find me the player on the Houston Dynamo team with the highest guaranteed compensation in 2009. Hint: Your answer output should be { Ricardo, Clark }.

Part [
    ReverseSortBy [Select [⌗ ⟦1⟧ == "HOU" && ⌗ ⟦7⟧ == Year: 2009 &] [mls2] , ⌗ ⟦6⟧ &], 1, {3, 2}]

{ Ricardo, Clark }

2.10 What team-year combination had the highest number of players with base salaries over $250,000? Hint: To write $250,000 use Quantity [250000, "USDollars"] .

Part [ReverseSortBy [GatherBy [Select [mls2, ⌗ ⟦5⟧ > Quantity [250 000, "USDollars"] &] ,
        { ⌗ ⟦1⟧, ⌗ ⟦7⟧ } &] , Length] ⟦1⟧, 1, {1, 7}]

{ DAL, Year: 2017 }

3 | Association

3.1 Get the first three rows of dinghy.

dinghy〚Range [3] 〛

{ <| class → 3rd, age → 16, sex → female, survived → True |>,
     <| class → 1st, age → 65, sex → male, survived → False |>,
     <| class → 3rd, age → 2, sex → female, survived → False |> }

3.2 Get the sex and survived columns of dinghy.

dinghy〚All, { "sex", "survived" } 〛

{ <| sex → female, survived → True |>,
     <| sex → male, survived → False |>, <| sex → female, survived → False |>,
     <| sex → female, survived → True |>, <| sex → female, survived → False |> }

3.3 Get the age and cellphone number of the third and fourth passengers in dinghy. Since the third passenger did not, in fact, have a cellphone, return a Missing value for that piece of data. Use operator forms of functions where possible.

Lookup [{ "age", "cellphone" }] [dinghy〚 { 3, 4 } 〛]

{ { 2, Missing [KeyAbsent, cellphone] }, { Missing [ ], Missing [KeyAbsent, cellphone] } }

3.4 Figure out how to make this.

{ <| "id"→1, "class"→"3rd", "age"→16, "sex"→"female", "survived"→True |>, <| "id"→2, "class"→"1st", "age"→65, "sex"→"male", "survived"→False |>, <| "id"→3, "class"→"3rd", "age"→2, "sex"→"female", "survived"→False |>, <| "id"→4, "class"→"3rd", "age"→Missing [ ], "sex"→"female", "survived"→ True |>, <| "id"→5, "class"→"3rd", "age"→18, "sex"→"female", "survived"→False |> }

MapIndexed [Prepend [#1, "id" → First @ #2] &, dinghy]

3.5 Now figure out how to make this.

<| "Frederica"→<| "class"→"3rd", "age"→16, "sex"→"female", "survived"→True |>, "George"→<| "class", "1st", "age"→65, "sex"→"male", "survived"→False |>, "Harold"→<| "class"→"3rd", "age"→2, "sex"→"female", "survived"→False |>, "Ida"→<| "class"→"3rd", "age"→Missing [ ], "sex"→"female", "survived"→True |>, "Jeanette"→<| "class"→"3rd", "age"→18, "sex"→"female", "survived"→False |> |>

AssociationThread [{ "Frederica", "George", "Harold", "Ida", "Jeanette" }, dinghy]

3.6 Compute the median age of the passengers on the Titanic broken down by cabin class. You are going to get error messages if you don't figure out how to deal with data for which the age is missing.

(Select [Not [MissingQ [#age]] &] /∗
        GroupBy [#class &] /∗ Map [Map [#age &] /∗ Median]) [titanic]

<| 1st → 39, 2nd → 29, 3rd → 24 |>

3.7 Find the distribution of guaranteed compensation in 2015 for MLS players based on their listed position. Create a histogram for each position that has at least 25 players. Hint 1: Remember to wrap your years in **DateObject** because that's the way they are denoted in the data. Hint 2: Please remember to put parentheses around your **Slot** functions. Use this **Histogram** function and sample output to guide you.

histo = Histogram [#, Automatic, Automatic, PlotRange → { { 0, 1 000 000 }, Automatic }] &;

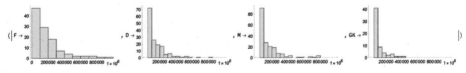

(Select [#Year === DateObject [{2015}] &] /∗
        (assoc ⟼ GroupBy [assoc, (#Position &) → (#GuaranteedCompensation &)]) /∗
        Select [Length [#] ≥ 25 &] /∗ Map [histo]) [mlsA]

4 | Query

4.1 Get the first and fourth passenger from dinghy.

Query [{ 1, 4 }] [dinghy]

{ <| class → 3rd, age → 16, sex → female, survived → True |> ,
  <| class → 3rd, age → Missing [ ] , sex → female, survived → True |> }

4.2 Did the third passenger on the dinghy survive?

Query [3, ⌗survived &] [dinghy]

False

4.3 Recall the planets data (ResourceData [ro, "Planets Deeply Nested Structure"]). What is the median mass of the moons of Jupiter?

planets = ResourceData [ro, "Planets Deeply Nested Structure"] ;

Query ["Jupiter", "Moons", Median, "Mass"] [planets]

3.2×10^{14} kg

4.4 Provide a breakdown of the survival of Titanic passengers (the whole ship, not just the small sample) by the sex of the passenger.

Query [GroupBy [⌗sex &] , Counts, ⌗survived &] [titanic]

<| female → <| True → 339, False → 127 |> , male → <| True → 161, False → 682 |> |>

4.5 Find the male passengers on the Titanic over age 40. Break down whether they survived based on their cabin class. Hint 1: You may want to read the documentation on the **And** function. Present the results so that the **False** response always appears before the **True** response. For extra credit, sort the classes according to the fraction that died. Hint 2: You might want to reread the material in the preceding chapter on Boolean keys and read up on the **ToString** function. Hint 3: Think hard about order of operations in your **Sort** and whether one or two Queries might be better here.

$$\textbf{Query [SortBy [} \frac{\text{⌗False}}{\text{⌗True + ⌗False}} \textbf{ &]] [}$$
  Query [Select [⌗age > 40 && ⌗sex === "male" &] /* GroupBy [⌗class &] ,
    Counts /* KeySort, ToString @⌗survived &] [titanic]]

<| 1st → <| False → 58, True → 21 |> ,
  2nd → <| False → 32, True → 2 |> , 3rd → <| False → 34, True → 2 |> |>

4.6 Do all exercises 3.1 through 3.3 from the preceding chapter using **Query**.

(*3.1*)

Query [1 ;; 3] [dinghy]

{ <| class → 3rd, age → 16, sex → female, survived → True |> ,
  <| class → 1st, age → 65, sex → male, survived → False |> ,
  <| class → 3rd, age → 2, sex → female, survived → False |> }

(*3.2*)

Query [All, { "sex", "survived" }] [dinghy]

{ <| sex → female, survived → True |> ,
  <| sex → male, survived → False |> , <| sex → female, survived → False |> ,
  <| sex → female, survived → True |> , <| sex → female, survived → False |> }

(*3.3*)
Query [3 ;; 4, Lookup [{ "age", "cellphone" }]] [dinghy]
{ { 2, Missing [KeyAbsent, cellphone] }, { Missing [ ], Missing [KeyAbsent, cellphone] } }

4.7 Use Query to compute the median age of the passengers on the Titanic broken down by cabin class.

Query [GroupBy [⌗class &], Median, ⌗age &] [titanic]

<| 1st → 39, 2nd → 29, 3rd → 24 |>

4.8 Use MeanAround instead of Mean to break down the approximate mean age of Titanic passengers by sex. Hint: Does MeanAround deal with Missings the same way as Mean? If not, how might a function with DeleteMissing be inserted into the pipeline to fix matters. Note: MeanAround was introduced in Version 12; you can't do this with earlier versions.

Query [GroupBy [⌗class &], (DeleteMissing [⌗, 1] &) / * MeanAround, ⌗age &] [titanic]

<| 1st → 39.2 ± 0.9, 2nd → 29.5 ± 0.8, 3rd → 24.8 ± 0.5 |>

5 | The Dataset

5.1 Convert a List of the integers from 2 to 11 into a dataset. Assign your result to the variable r10.

r10 = Dataset [Range [2, 11]]

2	3	4	5	6	7	8	9	10	11

5.2 See what r10 looks like in Normal form.

Normal [r10]

{ 2, 3, 4, 5, 6, 7, 8, 9, 10, 11 }

5.3 Find out what types the Dataset uses to describe the elements of r10. You may wish to run Needs ["TypeSystem`"] first.

Needs ["TypeSystem`"];
Dataset`GetType [r10]
Vector [Atom [Integer], 10]

5.4 Use Query to create a new Dataset whose values are the even elements of r10. (If the orientation is now different than for r10, it is because the data has fewer elements.)

Query [Select [EvenQ [⌗] &]] [r10]

2
4
6
8
10

5.5 Use the syntactic sugar (implicit **Query** method) described in this chapter to write the same "query" as in the prior problem (selecting only the even elements of r10) but without explicitly using the Query function.

r10 [Select [EvenQ [#] &]]

2
4
6
8
10

5.6 Run the code lifeboat=ResourceData [ro, "Lifeboat List of Associations"] . Create a **Dataset** named lifeboatW out of the resulting List of Associations that uses the "Web" theme.

lifeboat = ResourceData [ro, "Lifeboat List of Associations"] ;

lifeboatW = Dataset [lifeboat, DatasetTheme → "Web"]

class	age	sex	survived
3rd	16	female	True
1st	65	male	False
3rd	2	female	False
3rd	—	female	True
3rd	18	female	False
3rd	—	male	False
3rd	22	female	True
2nd	48	female	True

rows 1–8 of 22

5.7 Try and recreate the "Web" theme shown before using various presentation options. You do not have to get the colors exactly correct. Also, you may need to use **DatasetTheme** in order to get the column dividers.

Dataset [lifeboat, DatasetTheme → { "ColumnDividers", Darker [Red] },
HeaderStyle → Darker [Pink] , HeaderBackground → Lighter [Pink] ,
DatasetTheme → "Web", Background → { { { White, Lighter [Gray, 0.8] } } }]

class	age	sex	survived
3rd	16	female	True
1st	65	male	False
3rd	2	female	False
3rd	—	female	True
3rd	18	female	False
3rd	—	male	False
3rd	22	female	True
2nd	48	female	True

rows 1–8 of 22

5.8 Write a Query that retrieves only the survivors in lifeboatW and then drops the "survived" column. See if you can preserve the formatting of lifeboatW. Hint: Using the DatasetQuery ResourceFunction might make this easier.

[▪] **DatasetQuery** ➕ [Select [⌗survived == True &] , KeyDrop ["survived"]] [lifeboatW]

class	age	sex
3rd	16	female
3rd	—	female
3rd	22	female
2nd	48	female
1st	19	female
3rd	29	male
3rd	—	female
2nd	22	male

rows 1–8 of 9

5.9 Write a Query that retrieves passengers age 50 or older in lifeboatW and then drops the "age" column. Preserve the formatting of lifeboatW except change the HeaderBackground to Yellow.

[▪] **DatasetQuery** ➕ [Select [⌗age ≥ 50 &] , KeyDrop ["age"] ,
   "Inheritance" → Association ["Additions" → { HeaderBackground → Yellow }]] [lifeboatW]

class	sex	survived
1st	male	False
3rd	male	False
2nd	female	True

5.10 In the famous 1997 movie *Titanic*, a main character (portrayed by actress Kate Winslet) is Rose, a 17-year-old girl who travels in first class. Take ExampleData [{ "Dataset", "Titanic" }] and then use either Query or the implicit Query method to find the passengers on the Titanic who meet this description. Assign your result to the variable roses. You should find two possible passengers.

titanic = ExampleData [{ "Dataset", "Titanic" }] ;

roses = Query [Select [⌗age == 17 && ⌗sex === "female" && ⌗class === "1st" &]] [titanic]

class	age	sex	survived
1st	17	female	True
1st	17	female	True

5.11 Get the Major League Soccer (MLS) dataset out of the **ResourceObject** for this book with the code mls=ResourceData [ro, "MLS List of Associations Dataset"] .

mls = ResourceData [ro, "MLS List of Associations Dataset"]

Club	LastName	FirstName	Position	BaseSalary	GuaranteedCompensation	Year
CHI	Armas	Chris	M	$225 000.00	$225 000.00	2007
CHI	Banner	Michael	M	$12 900.00	$12 900.00	2007
CHI	Barrett	Chad	F	$41 212.50	$48 712.50	2007
CHI	Blanco	Cuauhtemoc	F	$2.49232 × 10^6	$2.66678 × 10^6	2007
CHI	Brown	C.J.	D	$106 391.00	$106 391.00	2007
CHI	Busch	Jon	GK	$58 008.00	$58 008.00	2007
CHI	Carr	Calen	F	$38 000.00	$50 500.00	2007
CHI	Conde	Wilman	D	$144 000.00	$151 500.00	2007

rows 1–8 of **5553**

5.12 Get the median guaranteed compensation for players in 2016 broken down by position and sorted from high to low. Hint: The date is stored as a **DateObject**.

mls [Select [#Year === DateObject [{ 2016 }] &] / * GroupBy [#Position &],
Median, #GuaranteedCompensation &] / / ReverseSort

M/F	$281 250.00
F–M	$280 114.07
F	$167 500.00
M	$130 750.00
D/M	$121 250.00
F/M	$121 091.50
D	$115 837.33
M–D	$114 166.67

rows 1–8 of **12**

5.13 Display the MLS data so that any dollar figures are rounded to the nearest ten thousand. (You will want to use an IPD function to do so.) Put the last name of the player in 24 point type and the first name of the player in 8-point type. Create alternating row backgrounds of white and very light blue. Instead of displaying the first 20 items and then requiring a new "page" to be chosen, display only the first eight items before a new "page" must be chosen. Hint: The BaseSalary and GuaranteedCompensation are stored as **Quantity** objects. Here's how one could round $34,343 to the nearest $10,000: Round [Quantity [34343, "USDollars"] , Quantity [10000, "USDollars"] .

r10000 [item_, _, _] :=
Switch [item, Quantity [_, "USDollars"] , Round [item, Quantity [10 000, "USDollars"]] , _, item]

`[×]` **FormatDataset** `+` **[MaxItems → 8, ItemDisplayFunction → (r10000 [#1 , #2 , #3] &) ,**
Background → { { {White, Lighter [Blue, 0.9] } } },
ItemStyle → { { _, "LastName" } → 24, { _, "FirstName" } → 8 }] [mls]

Club	LastName	FirstName	Position	BaseSalary	GuaranteedCompensation	Year
CHI	**Armas**	Chris	M	$220 000	$220 000	Year: 2007
CHI	**Banner**	Michael	M	$10 000	$10 000	Year: 2007
CHI	**Barrett**	Chad	F	$40 000	$50 000	Year: 2007
CHI	**Blanco**	Cuauhtemoc	F	$2 490 000	$2 670 000	Year: 2007
CHI	**Brown**	C.J.	D	$110 000	$110 000	Year: 2007
CHI	**Busch**	Jon .	GK	$60 000	$60 000	Year: 2007
CHI	**Carr**	Calen	F	$40 000	$50 000	Year: 2007
CHI	**Conde**	Wilman	D	$140 000	$150 000	Year: 2007

rows 1–8 of **5553**

5.14 Did you notice that the labeling of positions is inconsistent? Sometimes, for example, a player is
listed as playing "M / F", which I am confident means midfielder-forward, and other times, they are
listed as playing "M–F", which I am confident means the same thing. It appears that sometimes a "/"
is used to designate alternative positions and sometimes a "-" is used for the same purpose. Improve
the dataset so that the encoding of the position column is consistent. Use an implicit Query to do
this. Call your result mls2. Hint 1: The "Position" column may contain Missings or things that aren't
strings. How are you going to handle that? Hint 2: My code uses MapAt.

mls2 = Query [
 MapAt [If [StringQ [#] , StringReplace [#, " / " → "–"] , #] & , {All, "Position" }]] [mls]

Club	LastName	FirstName	Position	BaseSalary	GuaranteedCompensation	Year
CHI	Armas	Chris	M	$225 000.00	$225 000.00	2007
CHI	Banner	Michael	M	$12 900.00	$12 900.00	2007
CHI	Barrett	Chad	F	$41 212.50	$48 712.50	2007
CHI	Blanco	Cuauhtemoc	F	$2.49232 × 10^6	$2.66678 × 10^6	2007
CHI	Brown	C.J.	D	$106 391.00	$106 391.00	2007
CHI	Busch	Jon	GK	$58 008.00	$58 008.00	2007
CHI	Carr	Calen	F	$38 000.00	$50 500.00	2007
CHI	Conde	Wilman	D	$144 000.00	$151 500.00	2007

rows 1–8 of **5553**

5.15 Reformat your answer (mls2) so that only six rows display at a time, the headers are red, the column backgrounds alternate in color between orange and pink, and the columns are divided by thick yellow lines.

[≡] **FormatDataset** [+] [MaxItems → 6,
  Background → { None, { { Orange, Pink } } }, HeaderBackground → Red,
  DatasetTheme → { "ColumnDividers", { AbsoluteThickness [4] , Yellow } }] [mls2]

Club	LastName	FirstName	Position	BaseSalary	GuaranteedCompensation	Year
CHI	Armas	Chris	M	$225 000.00	$225 000.00	2007
CHI	Banner	Michael	M	$12 900.00	$12 900.00	2007
CHI	Barrett	Chad	F	$41 212.50	$48 712.50	2007
CHI	Blanco	Cuauhtemoc	F	$2.49232 × 10^6	$2.66678 × 10^6	2007
CHI	Brown	C.J.	D	$106 391.00	$106 391.00	2007
CHI	Busch	Jon	GK	$58 008.00	$58 008.00	2007

rows 1–6 of **5553**

5.16 Now determine the median salary in 2017 by position using the improved MLS data (mls2). Format your answer so that the rows alternate in color between Gray and Lighter@Gray. Some soccer experts might agree with me that goalkeepers are underpaid relative to their value in the game. Hint: Remember that dates are stored as DateObjects so that what may appear as 2017 is actually DateObject [{ 2017 }].

[≡] **DatasetQuery** [+] [Select [#Year === DateObject [{ 2017 }] &] / * GroupBy [#Position &] ,
  Median, #GuaranteedCompensation &, "Inheritance" → Association ["Additions" →
    { DatasetTheme → { "AlternatingRowBackgrounds", { Gray, Lighter @ Gray } } }]] [mls2]

M	$167 750.00
D	$123 700.00
F	$173 000.00
GK	$90 200.00
M–F	$161 689.50
F–M	$140 004.00
D–M	$125 002.00
M–D	$99 062.50

6 | Basic Recipes

6.1 Here's a **Dataset**. The column headers are "a", "b", and "c". Change them so that they are "Alpha", "b", and "Charlie".

abcDS = Dataset [{ <| "a" → 9, "b" → 8, "c" → 9 |>, <| "a" → 2, "b" → 7, "c" → 5 |>,
    <| "a" → 7, "b" → 7, "c" → 2 |>, <| "a" → 7, "b" → 3, "c" → 4 |> }];
Query [All, [≡] **KeyReplace** [+] [{ "a" → "Alpha", "c" → "Charlie" }]] [abcDS]

Alpha	b	Charlie
9	8	9
2	7	5
7	7	2
7	3	4

6.2 Use this code to retrieve the MLS **Dataset** from the **ResourceObject** for this book. Call it **mlsDS**. Now find out how many rows and columns it has.

mlsDS = ResourceData [ro, "MLS List of Associations Dataset"]

	Club	LastName	FirstName	Position	BaseSalary	GuaranteedCompensation	Year
	CHI	Armas	Chris	M	$225 000.00	$225 000.00	2007
	CHI	Banner	Michael	M	$12 900.00	$12 900.00	2007
	CHI	Barrett	Chad	F	$41 212.50	$48 712.50	2007
	CHI	Blanco	Cuauhtemoc	F	$2.49232 × 10^6	$2.66678 × 10^6	2007
	CHI	Brown	C.J.	D	$106 391.00	$106 391.00	2007
	CHI	Busch	Jon	GK	$58 008.00	$58 008.00	2007
	CHI	Carr	Calen	F	$38 000.00	$50 500.00	2007
	CHI	Conde	Wilman	D	$144 000.00	$151 500.00	2007

rows 1–8 of **5553**

Dimensions [mlsDS]

{ 5553, 7 }

6.3 Get rid of any rows in the MLS **Dataset** where the guaranteed compensation is **Missing**. Sort the remaining rows in the **Dataset** from highest guaranteed compensation to lowest. If there is a tie, sort it alphabetically by last name (A to Z), and if there is still a tie, sort it by year, earliest first. Hint 1: Sorting by the negative of a number is akin to a reverse sort. Hint 2: My code uses the **MissingQ** function and the **Not** function.

Query [Select [Not [MissingQ [⌗GuaranteedCompensation]] &] / ∗
     SortBy [{ –⌗GuaranteedCompensation &, ⌗LastName &, ⌗Year &}]] [mlsDS]

	Club	LastName	FirstName	Position	BaseSalary	GuaranteedCompensation	Year
	ORL	Kaka	—	M	$6.66 × 10^6	$7.1675 × 10^6	2014
	ORL	Kaka	—	M	$6.66 × 10^6	$7.1675 × 10^6	2015
	ORL	Kaka	—	M	$6.66 × 10^6	$7.1675 × 10^6	2016
	ORL	Kaka	—	M	$6.66 × 10^6	$7.1675 × 10^6	2017
	TOR	Giovinco	Sebastian	F	$5.6 × 10^6	$7.11556 × 10^6	2016
	TOR	Giovinco	Sebastian	F	$5.6 × 10^6	$7.11556 × 10^6	2017
	TOR	Giovinco	Sebastian	M	$5.6 × 10^6	$7.11556 × 10^6	2015
	SEA	Dempsey	Clint	F	$4.913 × 10^6	$6.69519 × 10^6	2014

rows 1–8 of **5552**

6.4 Here is some code that groups the data by team and year and computes the total salary. Run it. StringTemplate creates a TemplateObject expression that is similar to a function: when applied to arguments, it creates strings.

```
compensationByTeamYear =
  Query [ GroupBy [ StringTemplate [ "`1` – `2`" ] [ ⧣Club , DateString [ ⧣Year, "Year" ] ] &] ,
      Total, ⧣GuaranteedCompensation &] [ mlsDS ]
```

CHI–2007	4.7163×10^6
CHV–2007	1.78965×10^6
CLB–2007	2.10823×10^6
COL–2007	2.2813×10^6
DAL–2007	3.07276×10^6
DC–2007	2.27639×10^6
HOU–2007	2.43415×10^6
KC–2007	2.63755×10^6

rows 1–8 of **219**

Suppose I want to look at the previous data and compare just LA in 2010 with ORL in 2016 and TOR in 2016. My answer looks like this. Write the code to accomplish this.

```
KeyTake [ compensationByTeamYear, {"LA–2010", "ORL–2016", "TOR–2016"} ]
```

LA–2010	1.09786×10^7
ORL–2016	1.15544×10^7
TOR–2016	2.17985×10^7

6.5 A pure defender in the MLS data is designated by having a "D" in the position column. Find all the pure defenders with a guaranteed compensation of over $1 million in any year. Produce a Dataset showing only their club, year, last name, first name, and guaranteed compensation (in that order). Sort the results by guaranteed compensation from high to low. Do as little computational work as possible, remembering that sorting on a lot of data takes a good deal of work. Here's my answer.

```
Query [ Select [ ⧣Position === "D" &&
            ⧣GuaranteedCompensation > Quantity [ 1 000 000, "USDollars" ] &] / *
      Query [ ReverseSortBy [ ⧣GuaranteedCompensation &] ] ,
      KeyTake [ {"Club", "Year", "LastName", "FirstName", "GuaranteedCompensation"} ] ] [ mlsDS ]
```

Club	Year	LastName	FirstName	GuaranteedCompensation
NY	2010	Marquez	Rafael	5.544×10^6
NY	2012	Marquez	Rafael	4.6×10^6
NY	2011	Marquez	Rafael	4.6×10^6
LA	2015	Gonzalez	Omar	1.45×10^6
POR	2016	Ridgewell	Liam	1.25×10^6
LA	2014	Gonzalez	Omar	1.25×10^6
POR	2014	Ridgewell	Liam	1.2×10^6
POR	2015	Ridgewell	Liam	1.15×10^6

6.6 Compute the ratio of guaranteed compensation to base salary for all players on the Houston Dynamo (HOU) in 2016. Sort the ratio from highest to lowest. Do not show the club or year in your output. My output looks like the following.

```
Query [ Select [ ♯Club === "HOU" && ♯Year === DateObject [ {2016} ] &] / *
     Query [ ReverseSortBy [ ♯SalaryRatio &] ], Association [ KeyDrop [ ♯, {"Club", "Year"} ],
        "SalaryRatio" → ♯GuaranteedCompensation / ♯BaseSalary ] &] [ mlsDS ]
```

LastName	FirstName	Position	BaseSalary	GuaranteedCompensation	SalaryRatio
Steinberger	Zach	M	$63 000.00	$79 250.00	1.25794
Warner	Collen	M	$149 934.00	$177 434.00	1.18341
Torres	Erick	F	$575 000.00	$650 000.00	1.13043
Clark	Ricardo	M	$319 200.00	$356 700.00	1.11748
Garcia	Boniek	M	$225 000.00	$247 500.00	1.1
Beasley	DaMarcus	D	$750 000.00	$813 333.33	1.08444
Mansally	Kenny	D	$77 500.00	$84 000.00	1.08387
Rodriguez	Raul	D	$350 000.00	$379 333.33	1.08381

rows 1–8 of **27**

6.7 Here's some code that computes the total base salary for each team and year combination.

```
baseByTeamYear = Query [ Select [ StringQ [ ♯Club ] &] / *
     GroupBy [ StringTemplate [ "`1`–`2`" ] [ ♯Club , DateString [ ♯Year, "Year" ] ] &],
        Total, ♯BaseSalary &] [ mlsDS ]
```

CHI–2007	4.41252×10^6
CHV–2007	1.67827×10^6
CLB–2007	1.88955×10^6
COL–2007	2.18115×10^6
DAL–2007	2.79074×10^6
DC–2007	2.10132×10^6
HOU–2007	2.35005×10^6
KC–2007	2.44193×10^6

rows 1–8 of **213**

Suppose that you were given this **baseByTeamYear** Dataset and were not given the raw MLS data. I want a **Dataset** that looks like this, with the team, year, and total base salaries in different columns. Hint 1: My answer uses **With**. Hint 2: My answer uses **StringSplit**. Hint 3: StringSplit ["HOU–2018","–"] yields { "HOU","2018" } .

KeyValueMap [With [{ ss = StringSplit [#1 , "–"] } , Association ["Team" → ss[[1]],
"Year" → ss[[2]], "Total Base Salary" → #2]] &, baseByTeamYear]

Team	Year	Total Base Salary
CHI	2007	4.41252×10^6
CHV	2007	1.67827×10^6
CLB	2007	1.88955×10^6
COL	2007	2.18115×10^6
DAL	2007	2.79074×10^6
DC	2007	2.10132×10^6
HOU	2007	2.35005×10^6
KC	2007	2.44193×10^6

rows 1–8 of **213**

6.8 Take every five hundredth row of the MLS **Dataset** and put it into a column orientation. Then get just the resulting data without the **Dataset** wrapper.

Transpose [Query [1 ;; –1 ;; 500] [mlsDS]] / / Normal

⟨| Club → { CHI, SJ, SEA, DAL, RSL, CHI, KC, TOR, TOR, DC, CLB, TOR } ,
LastName → { Armas, Glinton, Ljungberg, Rodriguez, Russell, Puppo,
Medranda, Junior, Giovinco, Hamid, Duka, Cheyrou } , FirstName →
{ Chris, Gavin, Fredrik, Milton, Robbie, Federico, Jimmy, Gilberto, Sebastian, Bill, Dilly, Benoit } ,
Position → { M, F, M, F, D–M, F, M, F, M, GK, M, M } ,

BaseSalary → { $225 000.00 , $60 000.00 , 1.3×10^6 , $84 000.00 , $128 250.00 , $100 000.00 ,
$35 125.00 , 1.145×10^6 , 5.6×10^6 , $325 000.00 , $175 000.00 , $65 004.00 } ,

GuaranteedCompensation → { $225 000.00 , $60 000.00 , 1.314×10^6 ,
$114 000.00 , $134 001.43 , $100 000.00 , $35 125.00 , 1.205×10^6 ,
7.11556×10^6 , $370 500.00 , $175 000.00 , $65 004.00 } ,

Year → { Year: 2007 , Year: 2008 , Year: 2009 , Year: 2010 , Year: 2011 , Year: 2012 ,
Year: 2013 , Year: 2014 , Year: 2015 , Year: 2016 , Year: 2017 , Year: 2017 } |⟩

7 | Advanced Recipes

7.1 Take the Major League Soccer (MLS) data and compute for players on the 2017 Vancouver Whitecaps (VAN) what fraction of the total guaranteed compensation each player received. Present the information by adding a column labeled **"Share"** to the **Dataset** and then reverse sorting the resulting **Dataset** on that value. Round the value in that new column to the nearest 0.001. I don't want to see the columns **"Club"** and **"Year"** because these are constants for the selected players. Play with timings and try to program it in the most efficient and lucid way. Here's a picture of my result.

ro = ResourceObject ["Sample Data for Query Book"] ;
(∗not needed if already run∗)
SetOptions [Dataset, MaxItems → 8] ;
mlsDS = ResourceData [ro, "MLS List of Associations Dataset"] ;

```
Module [ { van2017 = Query [
        Select [ ⌗Year === DateObject [ { 2017 } ] && ⌗Club === "VAN" & ] ] [ mlsDS ] , total } ,
    total = Query [ Total, ⌗GuaranteedCompensation & ] [ van2017 ] ;
    Query [ ReverseSortBy [ ⌗Share & ] ] [
      Query [ All, Association [ KeyDrop [ ⌗, { "Club", "Year" } ] , "Share" →
            Round [ ⌗GuaranteedCompensation / total, 0.001 ] ] & ] [ van2017 ] ]
]
```

LastName	FirstName	Position	BaseSalary	GuaranteedCompensation	Share
Montero	Fredy	F	1.4×10^6	1.8×10^6	0.223
Laba	Matias	M	$725 000.00	$885 500.00	0.11
Shea	Brek	M–D	$625 000.00	$670 000.00	0.083
Reyna	Yordy	M–F	$440 000.04	$533 700.04	0.066
Techera	Cristian	M	$352 000.00	$377 000.00	0.047
Ousted	David	GK	$360 000.00	$378 933.33	0.047
Waston	Kendall	D	$350 000.00	$368 125.00	0.046
Tchani	Tony	M	$275 000.00	$308 333.33	0.038

rows 1–8 of **32**

7.2 Consider the MLS data for the years 2013 through 2017. Group that data by year and then by club and determine the median guaranteed compensation. Your result should look like this picture.

Hint 1: To get the rows that have a year after, say, 2015, I would write Select [⌗ Year > DateObject ˙.
[{ 2015 }] &] . Hint 2: To convert DateObject [{ 2015 }] to a string, I would write DateString [Date ˙.
Object [{ 2015 }] , "Year"] . Hint 3: My code uses the ResourceFunction JoinRest. Hint 4: My code also
uses AssociationThread and Range.

```
Query [ Select [ ⌗Year > DateObject [ { 2012 } ] & ] / * GroupBy [ ⌗Club & ] ,
    GroupBy [ DateString [ ⌗Year, "Year" ] & ] / *
      [▪] JoinRest ✛ [ AssociationThread [ ToString / @ Range [ 2013, 2017 ] , Missing [ ] ] ] ,
    Median, ⌗GuaranteedCompensation & ] [ mlsDS ]
```

	2013	2014	2015	2016	2017
VAN	$83 000.00	$99 500.00	$112 000.00	$121 917.25	$135 625.00
DAL	$85 875.00	$97 875.00	$130 000.00	$130 633.00	$152 500.00
TOR	$71 000.00	$92 000.00	$125 000.00	$119 125.00	$133 450.00
NE	$95 354.17	$122 375.00	$106 458.34	$116 666.67	$148 333.33
NY	$79 999.92	$115 000.00	$92 606.19	—	—
SJ	$94 625.00	$130 285.00	$100 000.00	$114 166.67	$175 992.00
PHI	$82 695.75	$102 163.67	$121 000.00	$138 000.00	$135 500.00
CHI	$119 950.00	$82 664.99	$102 916.67	$112 708.33	$135 000.00

rows 1–8 of **27**

7.3 Retrieve the "Year" (as a number), the "Club", the "Position", and the numeric value of
"GuaranteedCompensation" from all rows of the **mlsDS Dataset**. Take the result and keep only
those rows in which none of the items have missing values. Then do a multivariate linear
regression on the remaining data that best fits guaranteed compensation to "Year", "Club", and
"Position". Treat "Club" and "Position" as nominal variables. Compute the adjusted R^2 of your

result. You should get a value under 0.1 as your result. Hint 1: You will likely need to use Query twice in your code. Hint 2: DateValue [DateObject [{2014}] , "Year"] returns the value 2014. Hint 3: QuantityMagnitude [192, "USDollars"] returns the value 192. Hint 4: If you have not performed linear regressions a lot in the Wolfram Language, look up the NominalVariables option in the documentation and find out how to extract properties such as "RSquared".

```
Query [ Select [ FreeQ [ _Missing ] ] / *
       ( LinearModelFit [ #, {1, y, c, p}, {y, c, p}, NominalVariables → {c, p} ] &) ] [
   Query [ All, {DateValue [ #Year, "Year"] , #Club, #Position,
          QuantityMagnitude [ #GuaranteedCompensation ] } &] [ mlsDS ] ] [ "RSquared" ]
0.0674337
```

7.4 Get the Dataset from a resource in the Wolfram Data Repository on tornadoes in the United States. You should end up with something like this.

```
tornadoes = ResourceObject [ "Tornadoes in the U.S., 1950 – 2015"] ;

tornadoesDS = ResourceData [ tornadoes, "Dataset"]
```

Location	Number	Date	StateNumber	Magnitude	Injurie
Missouri, United States	1	Sat 31 Dec 1949 03:11:00	1	F3	3
Missouri, United States	1	Sat 31 Dec 1949 03:11:00	1	F3	3
Illinois, United States	1	Sat 31 Dec 1949 03:11:10	1	F3	0
Illinois, United States	2	Sat 31 Dec 1949 03:11:55	2	F3	3
Ohio, United States	3	Sat 31 Dec 1949 03:16:00	1	F1	1
Arkansas, United States	4	Sat 31 Dec 1949 13:05:25	1	F3	1
Missouri, United States	5	Sat 31 Dec 1949 01:19:30	2	F2	5
Illinois, United States	6	Sat 31 Dec 1949 01:21:00	3	F2	0

rows 1–8 of **61 217**   columns 1–10 of **12**

7.5 You will notice that some of the tornado magnitudes are designated with an F number while others are designated with an EF number. The EF designation is more modern. Make a BarChart showing, for tornadoes with an EF magnitude, the mean number of injuries from tornadoes broken down by the magnitude of the tornado. Here's what my chart looks like. Hint 1: I use StringTake in my answer. Hint 2: I also use the function called twisterChart in the following code.

```
twisterChart [ a_Association ] :=
   Framed [ BarChart [ Values [ a ] , ChartLegends → Keys [ a ] , ChartStyle → "DarkRainbow",
         ScalingFunctions → "Log10", PlotLabel → "mean injuries from tornados\n ( log scaled ) "] ];
Query [ twisterChart ] [
   Query [ Select [ StringTake [ #Magnitude, 2] === "EF" &] / * GroupBy [ #Magnitude &] / *
         Query [ Sort ] , Mean / * N, #Injuries &] [ tornadoesDS ]
]
```

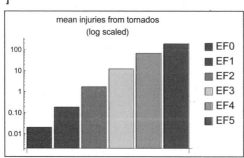

7.6 Create a graphic showing the trajectories for all tornadoes in the Dataset that killed at least five people. Do not consider tornadoes on which you do not have start and end information. I show a picture of my result here. Hint 1: My Query uses GeoPath. Hint 2: My Query uses GeoGraphics.

Query [Select [QuantityMagnitude [⌗Fatalities] ≥ 5 &&
         Not [MissingQ [⌗Start] | | MissingQ [⌗End]] &] / ∗ (Framed [GeoGraphics [⌗,
         PlotLabel → "Path of All U.S. Tornadoes Since 1949\nThat Killed At Least 5 People",
         ImageSize → 400] &) , GeoPath [{ ⌗Start , ⌗End }] &] [tornadoesDS]

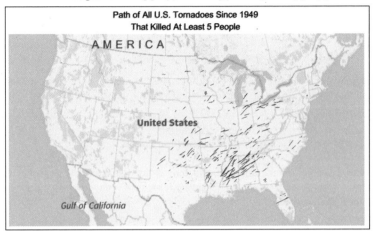

7.7 One last tornado exercise. Assume a tornado follows the shortest path between its start and end. Group the tornadoes with an EF magnitude according to their magnitude and produce histograms showing, for each grouping, the distribution of miles traveled. Hint 1: Make sure to use UnitConvert to convert all your distances to miles. Hint 2: Create a common horizontal scale by using something like Histogram [⌗, PlotRange → { { 0, 150 } , Automatic }] & as your visualization function. Hint 3: I used MapReduceOperator to get the job done. Hint 4: You will need to put the result in Normal form. Hint 5: You should get rid of tornadoes where you don't know the start or end location. My answer looks something like this.

Framed [Query [Select [StringTake [⌗Magnitude , 2] === "EF" &&
         Not [MissingQ [⌗Start] | | MissingQ [⌗End]] &] / ∗ [•] MapReduceOperator + [
         (⌗Magnitude &) → (UnitConvert [GeoDistance [{ ⌗Start , ⌗End }] , "Miles"] &) ,
         Framed [Histogram [⌗, { 10 } , PlotRange → { { 0, 150 } , Automatic } ,
         ImageSize → 150]] &] / ∗ KeySort] [tornadoesDS]   / / Normal
]

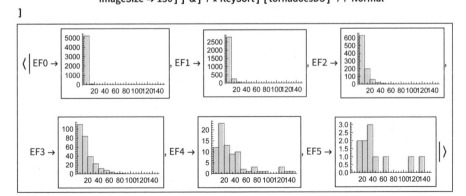

8 | Import and Export

8.1 Go to the example data and retrieve the Gettysburg Address like this.

gettysburg = ExampleData [{ "Text", "GettysburgAddress" }] ;

Now export it as text to a location on your computer. Alternatively, simulate the export using ExportString or use CreateFile as I did in the main text to create a temporary file. If you create a temporary file, make sure to get its name so you can import it back.

gettysburg = Export ["gettysburg.txt", gettysburg, "Text"]

gettysburg.txt

8.2 Now reimport the file or string you just created but as a **List** of words. Hint: "**Elements**". You might want to just postfix a Take of the first 20 words or so to get the point and save space.

Import [gettysburg, "Words"] / / Take [♯, 20] &

{ Four, score, and, seven, years, ago,, our, fathers, brought,
forth, upon, this, continent, a, new, nation:, conceived, in, liberty,, and }

8.3 Set forth below is a URL. It references some data, but we don't really know what format the data is in. Import the data as text and see if you can make a guess as to what format might be appropriate to capture the meaning of the data.

iris = "http: / / archive.ics.uci.edu / ml / machine−learning−databases / iris / iris.data";

Import [iris, "Text"]

8.4 See if it makes sense to import the data at the URL as a CSV file. Use the ResourceFunction ShowQuotes to see precisely what you retrieved. Do you agree that CSV looks like a sensible import format?

(irisCSV = Import [iris, "CSV"]) / / ([=] ShowQuotes [+] / ∗ [=] Terse [+] [ ])

{ { 5.1, 3.5, 1.4, 0.2, "Iris−setosa" }, ≪149≫, { } }

8.5 Reexport the iris data you imported as a JSON string. Make the output compact.

ExportString [irisCSV, "JSON", "Compact" → True] / / [=] Terse [+] [10]

[[5.1,3.5,1.4,0.2,"Iris−setosa"] , [4.9,3.0,1.4,0.2,"Iris−setosa"] , [4.7,3.2,1.3,0.2,"Iris−setosa"] , [4.6,3.1,
1.5,0.2,"Iris−setosa"] , [5.0,3.6,1.4,0.2,"Iris−setosa"] , [5.4,3.9,1.7,0.4,"Iris−setosa"] , [4.6,3.4,1.4,
0.3,"Iris−setosa"] , [5.0,3.4,1.5,0.2,"Iris−setosa"] , [4.4,2.9,1.4,0.2,"Iris−setosa"] , [4.9,3.1,1.5,0.1,
"Iris−setosa"] , [5.4,3.7, ...
−virginica"] , [6.9,3.1,5.1,2.3,"Iris−virginica"] , [5.8,2.7,5.1,1.9,"Iris−virginica"] , [6.8,3.2,5.9,2.3,"Iris−
virginica"] , [6.7,3.3,5.7,2.5,"Iris−virginica"] , [6.7,3.0,5.2,2.3,"Iris−virginica"] , [6.3,2.5,5.0,1.9,"
Iris−virginica"] , [6.5,3.0,5.2,2.0,"Iris−virginica"] , [6.2,3.4,5.4,2.3,"Iris−virginica"] , [5.9,3.0,5.1,
1.8,"Iris−virginica"] , [ ]]

8.6 Evaluate the following code. It provides the URL of an Excel file relating to cryotherapy. How many sheets are in the Excel spreadsheet?

cryoCSV =
"https: / / archive.ics.uci.edu / ml / machine−learning−databases / 00429 / Cryotherapy.xlsx";
Import [cryoCSV, "Sheets"]

{ CrayoDataset }

8.7 You should find that one of the sheets (perhaps the only sheet) is called **"CrayoDataset"**. Import it as a Dataset so the first line of the data contains headers.

Import [cryoCSV, { "Dataset", "CrayoDataset" } , HeaderLines → 1]

sex	age	Time	Number_of_Warts	Type	Area	Result_of_Treatment
1.0	35.0	12.0	5.0	1.0	100.0	0.0
1.0	29.0	7.0	5.0	1.0	96.0	1.0
1.0	50.0	8.0	1.0	3.0	132.0	0.0
1.0	32.0	11.75	7.0	3.0	750.0	0.0
1.0	67.0	9.25	1.0	1.0	42.0	0.0
1.0	41.0	8.0	2.0	2.0	20.0	1.0
1.0	36.0	11.0	2.0	1.0	8.0	0.0
1.0	59.0	3.5	3.0	3.0	20.0	0.0
1.0	20.0	4.5	12.0	1.0	6.0	1.0
2.0	34.0	11.25	3.0	3.0	150.0	0.0
2.0	21.0	10.75	5.0	1.0	35.0	0.0
2.0	15.0	6.0	2.0	1.0	30.0	1.0
2.0	15.0	2.0	3.0	1.0	4.0	1.0
2.0	15.0	3.75	2.0	3.0	70.0	1.0
2.0	17.0	11.0	2.0	1.0	10.0	0.0
2.0	17.0	5.25	3.0	1.0	63.0	1.0
2.0	23.0	11.75	12.0	3.0	72.0	0.0
2.0	27.0	8.75	2.0	1.0	6.0	0.0
2.0	15.0	4.25	1.0	1.0	6.0	1.0
2.0	18.0	5.75	1.0	1.0	80.0	1.0

rows 1–20 of **90**

8.8 Here's a URL to a zip archive: http://archive.ics.uci.edu/ml/machine-learning-databases/00454/dataset.zip. Assign it to the variable victorian.

victorian = "http: / / archive.ics.uci.edu / ml / machine−learning−databases / 00454 / dataset.zip";

8.9 It's a ZIP file. Find out what files are contained in it.

Import [victorian, "ZIP"]

{ dataset / Gungor_2018_VictorianAuthorAttribution_data.csv,
    dataset / Gungor_2018_VictorianAuthorAttribution_data−train.csv,
    dataset / Gungor_2018_VictorianAuthorAttribution_readme.txt}

8.10 You should see a file name that ends in **readme.txt**. Import that file as text. Because the archive is large (even though this file is small), this may take a minute or so to run.

(Import [victorian, { "dataset / Gungor_2018_VictorianAuthorAttribution_readme.txt",
         "Text" }]) / / [≡] Terse �਼ [10]

≪6709≫

8.11 There's another file in the archive that ends with **data−train.csv**. Find out what "Elements" are available for Import from that file.

victorianElements = Import [victorian,
        { "dataset / Gungor_2018_VictorianAuthorAttribution_data−train.csv", "Elements" }]
{ Data, Dataset, Dimensions, Grid, MaxColumnCount, RawData, RowCount, Summary }

8.12 See if you can figure out how to get the Dimensions of the file without having to actually Import the data.

```
Import [ victorian,
   {"dataset / Gungor_2018_VictorianAuthorAttribution_data−train.csv", "Dimensions"} ]
{53 679, 2}
```

8.13 The code below assigns the web address of data on wine to the variable **wineURL**. Import the data at this address as text. Call your result **wineText**.

```
wineURL =
    "http: / / archive.ics.uci.edu / ml / machine−learning−databases / wine−quality / winequality−
       white.csv";
( wineText = Import [ wineURL, "Text" ] )  / / Short
```

"fixed acidity";"volatile acidity";"citr … 8;0.8;0.02;22;98;0.98941;3.26;0.32;11.8;6

8.14 What I hope you see is that it is a "semicolon-separated value file" that is like a CSV file but each row has its 12 values separated by semicolons. Unfortunately, this choice of a semicolon as a separator is going to make it impossible to import it properly using the CSV importer (in Version 13.2) and get out a data structure, each row of which has 12 values. To get around this, import it instead as text with the "Lines" element. Call your result **wineLines**.

```
( wineLines = Import [ wineURL, {"Text", "Lines"} ] )  / /  [▪] Terse  ✦  [ ]
```

{ "fixed acidity";"volatile acidity";"ci … ";"pH";"sulphates";"alcohol";"quality", «4897», … }

8.15 Now read up on the **StringSplit** function in the Wolfram Language documentation and turn your import into a List of Lists with dimensions 4899×12 and call it **wineListOfLists**.

```
( wineListOfLists = Query [ All, StringSplit [ ♯, ";" ] & ] [ wineLines ] )  / /  [▪] Terse  ✦  [ 10 ]
```

{ { "fixed acidity", "volatile acidity", "citric acid", "residual sugar", "chlorides",
     "free sulfur dioxide", "total sulfur dioxide", "density", "pH", "sulphates", "alcohol", "quality" },
   {7, 0.27, 0.36, 20.7, 0.045, 45, 170, 1.001, 3, 0.45, 8.8, 6},
   {6.3, 0.3, 0.34, 1.6, 0.049, 14, 132, 0.994, 3.3, 0.49, 9.5, 6}, «4893»,
   {6.5, 0.24, 0.19, 1.2, 0.041, 30, 111, 0.99254, 2.99, 0.46, 9.4, 6},
   {5.5, 0.29, 0.3, 1.1, 0.022, 20, 110, 0.98869, 3.34, 0.38, 12.8, 7},
   {6, 0.21, 0.38, 0.8, 0.02, 22, 98, 0.98941, 3.26, 0.32, 11.8, 6} }

8.16 Here's a challenge: Take a look at the first line of the answer from the preceding exercise either in InputForm or using the ResourceFunction ShowQuotes. What you should see is that each element of the resulting List has embedded quotation marks in it. This is not what we want! Try to write a function that fixes the problem and imports the data in a way that eliminates the embedded quotation marks.

```
deleteEmbeddedQuotations [ s_String ] := StringDelete [ s, "\"" ]

Import [ wineURL, "Table", "FieldSeparators" → ";" ]  / /  Take [ ♯, 5 ] &  / /  [▪] ShowQuotes  ✦
```

{ { "fixed acidity", "volatile acidity", "citric acid", "residual sugar", "chlorides",
     "free sulfur dioxide", "total sulfur dioxide", "density", "pH", "sulphates", "alcohol", "quality" },
   {7, 0.27, 0.36, 20.7, 0.045, 45, 170, 1.001, 3, 0.45, 8.8, 6},
   {6.3, 0.3, 0.34, 1.6, 0.049, 14, 132, 0.994, 3.3, 0.49, 9.5, 6},
   {8.1, 0.28, 0.4, 6.9, 0.05, 30, 97, 0.9951, 3.26, 0.44, 10.1, 6},
   {7.2, 0.23, 0.32, 8.5, 0.058, 47, 186, 0.9956, 3.19, 0.4, 9.9, 6} }

8.17 Turn your List of Lists into a List of Associations, each of whose keys are the first row of the data but with no embedded quotation marks. Call your result wineListOfAssociations. Hint: Perhaps you should use deleteEmbeddedQuotations. For extra credit, use the ResourceFunction ToCamelCase so that there are no spaces in the key names.

(wineListOfAssociations =
    Map [AssociationThread [Map [(deleteEmbeddedQuotations / * [■] ToCamelCase +) ,
        First [wineListOfLists]] , ⇅] &, Rest [wineListOfLists]]) // [■] Terse + [10]

{ <| fixedAcidity → 7, volatileAcidity → 0.27, citricAcid → 0.36, residualSugar → 20.7,
    chlorides → 0.045, freeSulfurDioxide → 45, totalSulfurDioxide → 170,
    density → 1.001, pH → 3, sulphates → 0.45, alcohol → 8.8, quality → 6|>,
    <|≪1≫|>, ≪4894≫, <|≪1≫|>, <| fixedAcidity → 6, volatileAcidity → 0.21,
    citricAcid → 0.38, ≪6≫, sulphates → 0.32, alcohol → 11.8, quality → 6|> }

8.18 As a final step, see if the "numbers" in the data have been imported as numbers or as strings. If they are strings, write code to turn them into numbers. Turn your result into a Dataset called wineDataset. Hint 1: ToExpression. Hint 2: The third argument to Query.

wineDataset = Dataset [Query [All, All, ToExpression] [wineListOfAssociations]]

fixedAcidity	volatileAcidity	citricAcid	residualSugar	chlorides	freeSulfurDioxide	tota
7	0.27	0.36	20.7	0.045	45	170
6.3	0.3	0.34	1.6	0.049	14	132
8.1	0.28	0.4	6.9	0.05	30	97
7.2	0.23	0.32	8.5	0.058	47	186
7.2	0.23	0.32	8.5	0.058	47	186
8.1	0.28	0.4	6.9	0.05	30	97
6.2	0.32	0.16	7	0.045	30	136
7	0.27	0.36	20.7	0.045	45	170
6.3	0.3	0.34	1.6	0.049	14	132
8.1	0.22	0.43	1.5	0.044	28	129
8.1	0.27	0.41	1.45	0.033	11	63
8.6	0.23	0.4	4.2	0.035	17	109
7.9	0.18	0.37	1.2	0.04	16	75
6.6	0.16	0.4	1.5	0.044	48	143
8.3	0.42	0.62	19.25	0.04	41	172
6.6	0.17	0.38	1.5	0.032	28	112
6.3	0.48	0.04	1.1	0.046	30	99
6.2	0.66	0.48	1.2	0.029	29	75
7.4	0.34	0.42	1.1	0.033	17	171
6.5	0.31	0.14	7.5	0.044	34	133

rows 1–20 of **4898**   columns 1–10 of **12**

8.19 Compute the variance of the quality column. Present your answer as a number and call it qualityVariance.

qualityVariance = Query [Variance / * N, ⇌quality &] [wineDataset]

0.784356

8.20 Run the following code to create training and testing components to your Dataset. See if you can understand what the code is doing.

```
( SeedRandom [ 1 ] ;
    wineDatasets = Query [ RandomSample / * (AssociationThread [ { "training", "testing" },
        TakeDrop [ ♯ , Round [ 0.7 * Length [ ♯ ] ] ] ] &) ] [ wineDataset ] );
```

8.21 Now use what you learned in the first part of this book to write a Query that will yield a PredictorFunction based on the training data. Note that your results may differ slightly depending on the method selected by the automated machine learning algorithm. Call the result pre. Hint 1: Values. Hint 2: Most @♯ → Last @♯ &.

pre = Query ["training", Values / * Predict, (Most @♯ → Last @♯ &)] [wineDatasets]

PredictorFunction[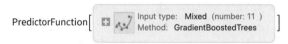]

8.22 Use the result from the previous question to produce a PredictorMeasurementsObject called pmo that sees how well the predictor you made is able to predict the quality of wines in the testing data created earlier.

pmo = Query ["testing", Values / * (PredictorMeasurements [pre, ♯] &) ,
    (Most @♯ → Last @♯ &)] [wineDatasets]

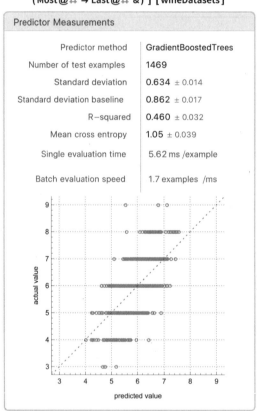

8.23 "ComparisonPlot" is a property of a PredictorMeasurementsObject. Make a "ComparisonPlot" from **pmo** showing the predicted quality of the wine on the *x* axis and the actual quality of the wine on the *y* axis.

pmo ["ComparisonPlot"]

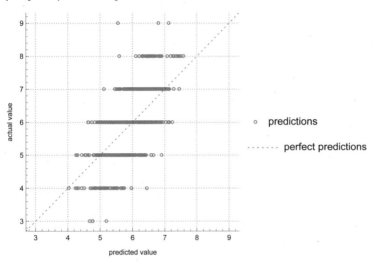

8.24 Would you say the quality of the wine is easy to predict accurately from the data or does good wine, perhaps, have a certain *je ne sais quoi?* Test your belief by computing the "RSquared" property of the PredictorMeasurementsObject.

pmo ["RSquared"]

0.459786

Index